Praise for *We're Still Here Ya Bastards*

"Gratz provides a moving chronicle of the efforts of real people to rebuild their battered city in the face of bad engineering, cynical politicians, incompetent bureaucrats and greedy developers. It frames the challenges urban revitalization, inequality and gentrification in a smart and nuanced way. This book is an absolute must read for anyone who cares about the future of our communities and nation."—Richard Florida, author of *The Rise of the Creative Class* and professor at NYU

"Roberta Gratz knows as much about the way cities work as anyone alive. In *We're Still Here Ya Bastards* she turns her sharp, experienced eye on New Orleans, post-Katrina, and delivers a lucid assessment of the city's stunning progress as well as its chronic, sometimes toxic, problems. Drawing on a broad variety of voices, this is a valuable addition to the growing body of literature about this most complex and beautiful city."—Tom Piazza, author of *Why New Orleans Matters* and *City of Refuge*

"No major American event of this century has generated so much myth as the 2005 flooding of New Orleans. Roberta Gratz tackles these assumed truths with two essential tools: the tenacity of an old-style journalist and the devotion of a Jane Jacobs–style urbanist. She chronicles the city's improbable and unpredicted recovery, without the dubious help of big plans, a recovery that, like her reporting, was and is literally ground-up. Most important to me, she writes not only with understanding, but with deep affection for this incomparable city."—Harry Shearer

"Do we need another Katrina book? No. Not just any book. We need this one. Whether the subject is education, healthcare, urban development or environmental preservation, Roberta Gratz has masterfully assembled a chorus of New Orleans voices to tell the story of their city. This book is a clarion call to the nation and the world."—Lolis Eric Elie, story editor, HBO's *Treme*

"After the Katrina and BP oil-spill disasters, officials in New Orleans only made matters worse through incompetence and self-dealing. It took the unelected citizenry to rise up and put things right. It's a hell of a story, painstakingly reported and recounted here in stirring detail."—John Berendt, author of *Midnight in the Garden of Good and Evil*

"What happens when one of the United States's urban treasures is damaged, seemingly beyond repair? How does the nation respond—and what does the response tell us of the state of the union? *We're Still Here Ya Bastards* brings to life the immediacy of the struggles to rebuild New Orleans in the aftermath of Hurricane Katrina. If you have wondered what has happened in the decade since television cameras recorded the drowning of a great American city—from the Ninth Ward to Lakeview, from the French Quarter and Treme through Uptown and Mid-City—Roberta Gratz's page-turning account is for you. As a native New Orleanian, I am grateful to her for uncovering these critical histories."—Leslie Harris, Associate Professor of History and African American Studies, Emory University

"A great American story: how people who love New Orleans keep saving it, and big money and bad government keep screwing it over."—Roy Blount Jr., author of *Feet on the Street: Rambles Around New Orleans*

"New Orleanians don't often light out for the territories. So there was no question of their returning from mandatory exile to this semi-ruined city and rebuilding from the ground up. As Roberta Gratz shows in this brilliant book, it was their grassroots activism, reinforced by cadres of voluntourists who came for a week then decided to stay put, that has been bringing this storied town back from disaster."—Lawrence N. Powell, author of *The Accidental City: Improvising New Orleans*

"Roberta Gratz is America's most innovative urban chronicler of our time. If you really want to know the true story of New Orleans after Katrina, you must read her thorough account of one of America's devastating natural disasters."—Laurie Beckelman, cultural consultant and former Chair of the New York City Landmarks Preservation Commission

"Disaster, even terrible disaster, can also be an opportunity. A decade after Hurricane Katrina, Roberta Gratz offers a sharp take on what a recovering New Orleans got right—and wrong. Her assessment is sure to provoke debate. But no one who cares about 'The City that Care Forgot' can ignore this detailed and deeply humane report."—Jed Horne, author of *Desire Street* and *Breach of Faith*

"Roberta Gratz's collage of post-Katrina New Orleans sparkles with stunning and sometimes controversial insights. Written with grace and deep feeling, she takes Jane Jacobs' heritage into new territory and confirms the author's status as our leading urbanist." —S. Frederick Starr, Chairman of the Central Asia-Caucasus Institute at the School of Advanced International Studies, Johns Hopkins University

"*We're Still Here Ya Bastards* is a colorful, authoritative account of how the unsung people of New Orleans–instead of inept Federal agencies, crooked local 'leaders' and soulless developers–refused to let a great American city die."—Curtis Carter Wilkie, co-author of *City Adrift: New Orleans Before and After Katrina*

"In this powerful book, Roberta Brandes Gratz turns her deep understanding of the work of Jane Jacobs into an astonishing account of how imaginative community activists like Jacobs emerge and grow in the wake of a disaster like Katrina. In virtually every domain of urban life—in housing, health care, education, economic development, and environmental protection—she discovers New Orleanians whose diagnosis of the problems and alternatives to the solutions are vastly more creative and effective than all the politicians, bureaucrats, and professionals who have dominated our television screens. That we have heard little or nothing about these people says much about our distrust of democracy. A masterpiece of reportage and analysis!"—Richard Rabinowitz, Phd, President, American History Workshop

"Ten years after the flooding of New Orleans, the city is still recovering. A street-level portrait of the people who came back to rebuild their homes, *We're Still Here Ya Bastards* illustrates how the tight-knit communities of the Crescent City are reclaiming their city—in spite of the so-called experts, predatory free-marketeers, and government bureaucrats."—Josh Neufeld, author of *A.D.: New Orleans After the Deluge*

We're Still Here Ya Bastards

Also by Roberta Brandes Gratz

A Frog, A Wooden House, A Stream and A Trail: 10 Years of Community Change in Central Europe (2001, Rockefeller Brothers Fund)

The Living City: How America's Cities Are Being Revitalized by Thinking Small in a Big Way

Cities Back from the Edge: New Life for Downtown

The Battle for Gotham: New York in the Shadow of Robert Moses and Jane Jacobs

We're Still Here Ya Bastards

How the People of New Orleans Rebuilt Their City

Roberta Brandes Gratz

NATION
BOOKS
New York

Books published by Nation Books are available at special discounts for
bulk purchases in the United States by corporations, institutions, and other
organizations. For more information, please contact the Special Markets
Department at the Perseus Books Group, 2300 Chestnut Street, Suite 200,
Philadelphia, PA 19103, or call (800) 810-4145, extension 5000, or e-mail
special.markets@perseusbooks.com.

Support for this book was provided by:

Furthermore:
a program of the J.M.Kaplan Fund

Cover design and title inspired by a photograph by Sandra Morris of a bike shop still
open after the hurricane.

Designed by Jack Lenzo

Library of Congress Cataloging-in-Publication Data
Gratz, Roberta Brandes.
  We're still here ya bastards : how the people of New Orleans rebuilt their city / Roberta
Brandes Gratz.
    pages cm
  Includes bibliographical references and index.
  ISBN 978-1-56858-744-8 (hardback) -- ISBN 978-1-56858-500-0 (e-book) 1. Com-
munity development--Louisiana--New Orleans. 2. Urban renewal--Louisiana--New
Orleans--Citizen participation. 3. City planning--Louisiana--New Orleans--Citizen
participation. 4. Hurricane Katrina, 2005--Social aspects. 5. New Orleans (La.)--
History--21st century. I. Title.
  HN80.N45G73 2015
  307.1'2160976335--dc23
                              2014047653

10 9 8 7 6 5 4 3 2 1

For the people of New Orleans.

Contents

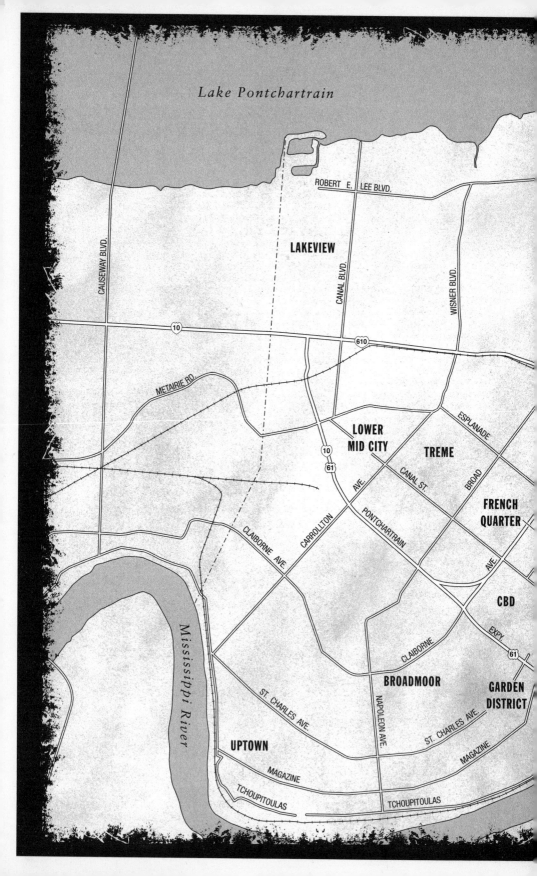

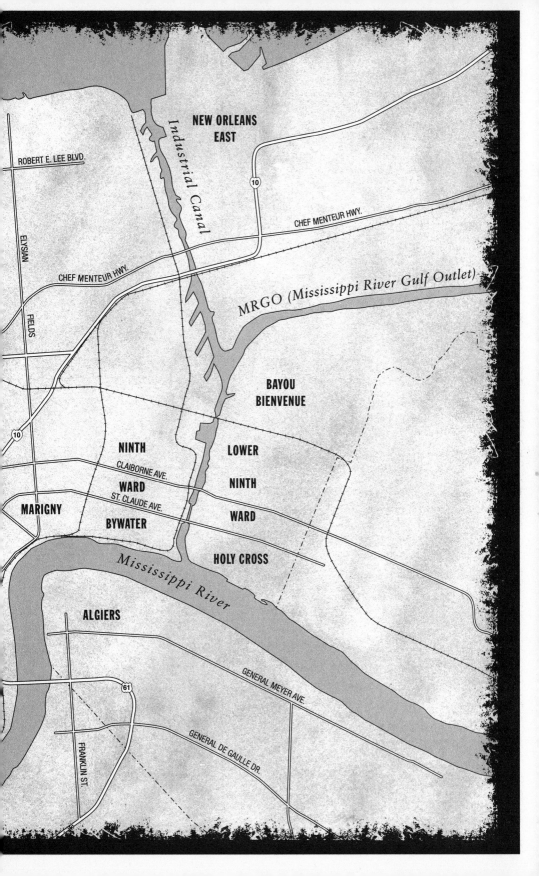

New Orleans developed into something greater than a mere entrepôt for a continent. It became a state of mind, built on the edge of disaster, where the lineages of three continents and countless races and ethnicities were forced to crowd together on slopes of the natural levee and somehow learn to improvise a coexistence whose legacy may be America's only original contribution to world culture.

—Lawrence N. Powell, *The Accidental City: Improvising New Orleans*[1]

New Orleans looked wonderful, as it always does. It is certainly one of the most beautiful cities in the world, although how the people who live there manage to make it so remains a mystery to me.

—John Kennedy Toole, author of *A Confederacy of Dunces,* in a letter to friend Joel L. Fletcher[2]

Preface

On August 29, 2005, an ill wind swept across New Orleans. Her name was Katrina. Like countless others around the world, I was transfixed in front of the television, watching in horror as Hurricane Katrina swept across the Gulf Coast with a force beyond words.[1] First, I watched the gale-force winds uproot trees and suck up roofs, sending them flying around like toys. The swirls and waves of water were equally frightening. Over the course of the weekend, I could hardly stop watching, scarcely understanding the level of human suffering and physical destruction that was unfolding before my eyes.

I cringed at the sight of people stranded on rooftops, children airlifted by helicopter, families huddled in makeshift boats, and elderly and infirm persons resting on floating platforms ingeniously assembled by family members or friends who pulled them through the water as they walked alongside. I marveled at brave citizen-rescuers reaching out to people they probably didn't know. And I hugged my golden retriever, Sasha, as I watched beloved animals stranded and alone.

I had visited New Orleans a few times over the years and included a small bit about the place in each of my three books.[2] I was clearly a fan. I was not one of the millions who celebrated its music, food, or rich diverse culture, although I appreciated all those things. Instead, I valued New Orleans for its *urbanism*—its tightly placed streets, exuberant culture, rich architecture, and unique density. Throughout the 1950s and '60s, many American cities had swept clean their historic core of mixed-scale buildings on pedestrian-oriented streets, dating from layers of past and present eras in pursuit of the elusive promise of Urban Renewal.

During World War II, cities across the country experienced the deterioration that came with national investment geared toward war. After the war, the idea prevailed that the future lay only in the suburbs. To abet that future—to provide inexpensive housing for returning vets and to shift the war economy to a domestic one—federal investment went primarily to the development of the suburbs and suburban transportation. The national policy to rebuild cities, Urban Renewal, meant demolishing old neighborhoods to build new high-rise towers in the park or to make way for highways to carry urban dwellers to the new suburbs. In the 1950s, functional, redeemable neighborhoods populated with rooted urban residents fell under the bulldozer. Surviving communities struggled not to succumb. The deterioration spread as demolition fatally tore thread after thread of the intricate urban fabric. Population loss accelerated. In the mid-1960s, as a young newspaper reporter, I witnessed this government-sponsored devastation, writing about New York City neighborhoods experiencing destruction.[3] I observed people fighting to save their homes and neighborhoods. The only successful efforts were those where demolition was resisted—where people rebuilt their homes, favored new construction that fit in with the existing neighborhood, and fought to save parks, neighborhood landmarks, and business areas—and enlightened city officials partnered with local efforts to create a positive impact.

New Orleans had done its share of thoughtless destruction but, miraculously, it remained a real city, thanks to successful citizen resistance to ill-conceived ideas of progress. There was still a real fabric of streets, distinct neighborhoods, corner stores, and pockets of local businesses as well as a substantial downtown anchored by the French Quarter—at one time, the largest historic district in the country.[4]

In my first book, *The Living City,* I wrote about how urban regeneration works—incrementally, organically, from the bottom up—not by means of big, publicly funded developer projects or big visitor attractions. I cited the French Quarter to demonstrate how a historic district, if large enough, could accommodate both the most extreme honky-tonk street and the most stylish residential life within blocks of each other while keeping them separate.[5] In *Cities Back from the Edge,* I discussed many examples of cities that were regenerating slowly, off any official radar, throughout the 1980s. I spotlighted the Garden District of New Orleans, which by the 1970s had deteriorated. A public transit line—in this case, the fabled St. Charles Streetcar—helped sustain that sizable but frayed district during the hardest times and then facilitated its regeneration.[6] The streetcar helped preserve the "mixed-use" nature of that corridor as well. Those cities that retained their public transit demonstrated the kind of gradual, organic, citizen-led regeneration that I observed and celebrated in both of these books. In *The Battle for Gotham,* I explored the conflicting urban philosophies of Robert Moses and Jane Jacobs and cited the successful fight to stop a Moses-conceived highway through the French Quarter. I also noted that one neighborhood in the Lower Garden District around Coliseum Square was reviving after the highway ramp that originally destroyed it came down.[7]

But the New Orleans I was watching on television in 2005 was not the city with which I was familiar. Like so many visitors, I hadn't ventured far beyond the celebrated, popular areas. As an observer of cities, I should have known better. But what I did know for sure was what I had observed and written about for years: if energized and not thwarted, resident populations and local businesses are better at rebuilding their cities and neighborhoods than government officials and credentialed experts, or oversized government funding programs and the redevelopment network that feeds off them. Local wisdom trumps distant assumed expertise every time.

As I watched, I wondered: What would be the post-Katrina narrative of this storied city? Would New Orleanians dig their heels in and show a "can-do spirit" despite the extraordinary adversity and endless impediments confronting them? Would this disaster provide an excuse to do the wrong things by the perpetrators of the cataclysmic mistakes that had undermined many of our great cities? Would a feeding frenzy ensue whereby the politically well-connected managed to secure the post-disaster contracts? I knew that this was a narrative I wanted to follow closely and write about as events unfolded. I wanted to help in some small way to advance positive change. But where to start?

Through the Association of Community Organizations for Reform Now (ACORN),[8] a national grassroots member organization headquartered in New Orleans, I met Durwin Hill, a resident of the Lower Ninth Ward. Like all residents of the Lower Nine and other flooded neighborhoods, he was initially not allowed to go back to his home—not even to open the windows, air out the house, and assess the damage. It would be four months after the storm until Lower Nine residents were given the green light to return, the last community permitted to do so. The official explanation was the lack of electricity, safe drinking water, and street lights in the Lower Nine, as well as the degree of damage. But these were hollow excuses used in order to impose restrictions on a low-income neighborhood that, as would soon become clear, city officials and business leaders did not want to see repopulated. Other similarly devastated neighborhoods were open to residents sooner.

With press credentials secured from *The Nation* magazine, I went down to New Orleans in October 2005 and was allowed into the Lower Ninth Ward to accompany Durwin as he viewed his home for the first time after Katrina. At the guarded checkpoint, Durwin's wife was denied entry with us: I was allowed to bring only one resident, so she waited in the car. Durwin, a solidly built

New Orleans native, was a skilled carpenter and house renovator. He pulled loose the plywood with which he had carefully covered his front door and windows before evacuating, only to discover that the eight feet of water that immersed his simple brick house on concrete slab had ruined everything in sight, including the two attached rear apartments occupied by his sons. Inside, the atmosphere was fetid and impenetrable. Furniture blocked doorways. Soggy sofas were upended. Family pictures and decorative objects were scattered about. Saturated carpeting felt squishy underfoot. Nothing was where it had been, and a quick glance confirmed that nothing was salvageable.

"It was in worse shape when I bought it," he said with an upbeat spirit that stunned me. "I fixed it once and I'll do it again." Like thousands of other homeowners, Durwin would gut the property down to the studs, hauling rotted wall boards, carpeting, and furniture out to the sidewalk. Mold, of varying colors, needed to be bleached off everything. And then, only then, could the rebuilding begin. The total destruction I witnessed would surely have defeated me if I were in that situation. It took me awhile to absorb the spirit I was witnessing.

I stood with Durwin outside in the cracked mud lawn where a huge tree had fallen, just missing his house but landing on his wife's car. Painfully, he surveyed the neighborhood around him as if he was assessing the cherished objects in his living room. He pointed first to a policeman's "shotgun" house, recently fixed up catty-corner to his own. The classic shotgun is a long narrow house in which, according to legend, one could shoot a gun straight through from the front door to the back door without hitting a wall. Durwin noted the corner bar/restaurant, an authentic neighborhood gathering place where he and his friends exchanged news and discussed the problems of the world. The simple white stucco façade with green scripted letters announced that this was "Chic's Place." He then pointed to a narrow shotgun that had been empty for a year because "the old lady died and her nephew who inherited it left it just as she and her mother had furnished it way back." He expressed disappointment that "the nice young white couple next door" who had moved here from Texas to teach in the nearby school left after they were laid off because of pre-Katrina budget cuts. He described taking meals to one neighbor and attending the wedding of another and recounted memories of his own school days. Each school he attended was just a short walk away.

Another resident walked by with her cousin. They had sneaked in past the guards and were checking out assorted family homes. Her mother, thirteen aunts and uncles, and nineteen of their children owned homes at one time or another on three contiguous blocks nearby. "You couldn't get into trouble in this neighborhood without someone telling your mom," she said, laughing despite the wreckage she was looking at. "In front of whoever's house you were at, lunch time is where you ate." I've heard many such descriptions of New Orleanian life in the years since. "If you ask me about someone," yet another resident told me, "I may not know him but I'll know his people."

As I listened to these stories, I recognized the residents' strength of character and will. I was observing a picture of New Orleans that did not come across on television or in the general press. I was fascinated, moved, and inspired. I had been writing about cities for many years, and I had seen over and over again that the key to urban regeneration was the resilience of local people—not the self-important city officials and developers who erroneously pursued big projects, pushed their own agendas, and failed to deliver on their promises. While big plans rarely live up to their expectations, small actions always exceed theirs.

In New Orleans, in the immediate aftermath of the storms, I saw years of stories I had written coming together into one big one—as the South Bronx and Savannah, Georgia, had been for me in the 1970s. I watched the earliest beginnings of the South Bronx and Savannah resurgence and wrote about them in *The Living*

City. Based on that history and all I had observed and written about since, I knew what the experts would say after Katrina and, based on what I was already seeing, I knew New Orleans would defy them.

I began to visit New Orleans regularly after the storms, writing occasional stories[9] and getting to know the city. During each visit, I drove around the city, walked through neighborhoods talking to survivors, and looked for small signs of recovery. I saw the floodwater lines on every house and learned how to read the ubiquitous Xs—known as "Katrina tattoos"—that denoted whether people and dogs had been rescued or found dead. I saw packs of abandoned and hungry-looking dogs and sepia-colored lawns, and wondered why there were so many abandoned cars if people reportedly didn't have them to evacuate in. Nighttime was particularly eerie. So few houses were lit up. During the day, people able to return to their neighborhoods were already working on cleaning out the ruined contents of their homes. Some were rebuilding during the day but going elsewhere to spend the night. More came on weekends, driving long distances from wherever they were temporarily staying.

Thousands of refrigerators clogged the sidewalks. Many had writing on them. One read "The Twin Towers/Our 9/11"; another, "Do Not Open. Tom Benson Inside." Benson, the owner of the Saints, spoke of moving the football team to another city after Katrina. The graffiti on buildings powerfully displayed the anger and anguish of a distressed population with no means of formal communication: "U loot, we shoot," "F*** FEMA," "We're Still Here Ya Bastards," "FEMA—Fix Everything My Ass," "Bagdad."

Humor occasionally entered the grim picture. "Don't try" warned looters on the side of a rug shop, followed by "I am sleeping inside with a big dog, an ugly woman, two shotguns, and a claw hammer." A week later, an update was added: "Still here. Woman left. Cooking a pot of dog gumbo." Then a further revision at the end of the month: "Welcome back, y'all. Grin and bear it."[10] Historian Lawrence Powell, not long after the hurricane, commented on the city's ability to find humor in the worst of conditions:

> Already mounds of trash are piling up on neutral grounds, as median strips are called . . . bearing handmade signs: "Toxic Art, This Exhibition Will Kill You!" The windshields of cars ashed over in Nagasaki brown are painted with "For Sale, Like New!" Or, at one badly submerged car lot: all cars "89% off, some even free." We're creative in our profanity, too. The latest local brush-off is: "Go FEMA yourself!"[11]

A few restaurants and cafés were open, though some were doing business on the sidewalk because their interiors were ruined or the electricity was off. Anything open drew people in to share stories, inquire about neighbors and friends, and get information.[12] FEMA trailers were visible in the front yards of very few homes. Indeed, the story behind these trailers was scandalous beyond anything reported in the press. One gentleman lucky enough to have one placed in his driveway wasn't allowed to use it until the water was connected. A plumber friend of his was willing to do the job for free, but instead he had to wait endlessly for a FEMA contractor to do it. He would not get a key until that was done. If he entered before that, he would be trespassing. This was the first of many signs of a predatory, disaster economy in action, as we will see throughout this book.

Another homeowner I talked to was waiting for a FEMA contractor electrician to do a job that he was professionally trained to do himself. He had been waiting weeks while cleaning out and repairing his own two-story bungalow-style house that had flooded only on the ground floor. He said his house would be livable before the trailer was accessible. Yet another homeowner received a trailer by Thanksgiving, but it was not until after

Easter that he could get the city to inspect the electrical hookup so he could occupy it. Other property owners had secured blue tarps from FEMA to cover their houses until the roofs could be repaired. The blue tarp became the new city symbol.

In 2007, I bought a modest double shotgun house in the Bywater neighborhood, an interesting area filled with colorful shotguns and two-story galleried houses of all stages of restoration and decay. Once a blue-collar community, the Bywater was slowly becoming a destination for artists, musicians, and young people seeking homes with character. Many houses were vacant and home values were still reasonable. An economically and racially diverse population was in residence. Gentrification was under way but at least, it seemed, slow and gradual. Bordering the Mississippi, the Bywater sustained no serious flooding.

In the years since, New Orleans has become my second home. I have written a number of stories, always eager to learn more and observe the ups and downs of the inevitable recovery in progress. I knew it would happen, and although many things surprised me, my expectations were met more often than not. What I found, what I observed over the past decade, is what this book is about.

Cities are never lacking in wise, energetic, passionate, and dedicated citizens who know best how to rebuild their communities. New Orleans has more than its share of such citizens. They are the ones most responsible for their city's recovery. They do not get enough credit. As my friend Karen Gadbois said at a conference of community rebuilders in 2006: "There is no other Cavalry coming. We are the ones we've been waiting for. We are the Cavalry."

Introduction

The Live Oaks

Nothing defines New Orleans better than the Live Oak trees that line its streets, grace its parks, provide shade and shelter during the relentlessly hot summers, and buffer storm winds. The leafy long branches of the curbside trees spread horizontally so far across the street toward each other that they form lush canopies of green, adding an elegant aura to even the most downtrodden rows of houses. The green lasts all winter. In the spring, new leaves emerge as old ones fall; thus the term *Live,* which distinguishes them from other oaks that remain leafless and dormant in winter. As they grow, twisting and turning in the winds, the Live Oaks gain their strength by anticipating the way the winds blow and adapting to the fierce changes in weather.

In City Park, home to more than three thousand Live Oaks,[1] not one of the two thousand trees lost during or after the storm was a historic Live Oak, reported Chief Development Officer John Hopper: "[These trees] are uniquely suited to our weather and better able to withstand flooding and wind than many other species."[2]

"The environment of oak trees is something that separates New Orleans from Atlanta or Houston," observed S. Frederick Starr, noted author of many books on New Orleans. "Most of old New Orleans streets had balconies that covered the sidewalks and the oaks were an extension of the canopy. They made the city's weather bearable."[3]

The strength and endurance of the Live Oaks do indeed have a particular significance, notes science writer Janine Benyus, author of *Biomimicry: Innovation Inspired by Nature*. They are, perhaps, a metaphor for the city itself and the strength of its people. Live Oaks grow in clusters, Benyus points out, and their spreading roots form a deep network connecting one tree to the next.[4] That network holds the extended tree family together. The trees survive so well because they are indigenous to the region. In New Orleans, where they are frequently subjected to fierce coastal storms, they have endured because their twisting branches spread outward as well as upward, leaving ample room for the wind to pass through them. The leaves of the Live Oaks curl up in a storm to let the wind pass by. Their roots spread wide but stay firmly connected to the thick, gnarled parental trunk, lending strength and balance to the branches above.

The city of New Orleans is much like its great Live Oak trees—strong, disaster resistant, and amazingly resilient. Deep-rooted family networks provide a human infrastructure that gives strength to residents and allows them to support each other, while overcoming the failings of governments and financial hardships. Time reveals the city's strengths just as it has proven the strength and endurance of the Live Oaks, many of which are hundreds of years old. The loss of limbs and leaves from many of the Live Oaks during Hurricane Katrina and Hurricane Rita (which, as noted, followed one month later) left the city feeling denuded, with too much sun burning through where shade had once prevailed. But the trees are growing back, leaf by leaf and limb by limb.

Before Katrina, as Fred Starr pointed out in a conversation with me, "New Orleans already had the poorest tree cover of any major city, based on aerial photographs." For decades, he added, the city has failed at replanting many Live Oaks while the power company, Entergy, unceasingly obliterates many trees. Even worse is what Fred calls "the palm tree phenomenon, a total waste," whereby the city is planting palm trees—even though they are not native, they fall during storms, and they are expensive because they must be planted full-grown. Individuals and organizations such as Parkway Partners sponsor tree replanting but are unable to keep up. This points up an important theme in the recent history of New Orleans: local leaders working to fill the gap left by government.

In no other American city have familial networks remained as strongly rooted to particular neighborhoods, making the history of New Orleans unique. Like the Live Oaks with their strong interconnected root systems, the city's white, African-American, and Creole of Color families have gained strength from their habitation in well-defined neighborhoods over many generations. Many New Orleanians live in mortgage-free houses that their grandfathers or fathers built. They don't leave them easily. To be sure, other American cities also had deeply entrenched demographic patterns before post–World War II redevelopment policies and relocation choices dispersed families geographically. In New Orleans, however, these patterns proved more resistant to disruption than elsewhere. As documented throughout this book, the resilient nature of New Orleanians is one reason why the recovery of the city, primarily through the rebuilding and revitalization efforts of local residents and community leaders, has been so successful throughout the past decade.

But more than just resilience explains the recovery of New Orleans since the devastation of Katrina—which was a "man-made" disaster, not a "natural" one. As New Orleans writer Randy Fertel told me: "Those are fighting words here if you talk about Katrina as a natural disaster; it wasn't a natural disaster but a federal flood caused by the Corps screw-up." On August 31, 2010, a few days after the fifth anniversary of Katrina, author Tom Piazza wrote in his *Huffington Post* blog:

At first it looked as if New Orleans had been smacked by a hurricane, which, of course, it had. It would take awhile longer for people to understand that the images that halted the coffee cup en route to the mouth . . . were the result not of a natural disaster, bad as the hurricane was, but of a catastrophic planning and engineering failure on the part of the Army Corps of Engineers. Many still don't realize it. Of course, many also think that Iraq planned the 9/11 attacks.[5]

• • •

The overwhelming failure of the federal government and its myriad private contractors during and after Hurricane Katrina is inexplicable. What compounds the tragedy and prevents the public from understanding what really happened was the success of the Army Corps of Engineers and the Bush White House's perpetration of so many false reports and explanations. As musician, author, radio host, and film and TV personality Harry Shearer asked in a conversation: "How is it the Corps of Engineers screws up time and again and no one gets fired? Nothing happens."[6] Some myth-busting about Katrina and the immediate aftermath is in order.

Myth: Katrina was a "natural disaster."
Fact: Katrina has been recognized as the most catastrophic failure in the history of American engineering.

Myth: The levees were "overtopped" by the intensity of the high water.
Fact: The levees collapsed in fifty-three places due to engineering design errors and "were responsible for 87 percent of the flooding, by volume."[7]

Myth: Katrina was a Category 4–5 hurricane.

Fact: It was a Category 3 when it reached New Orleans and
had been anticipated by hurricane simulations a few
years before.

Several books since have vividly detailed the storm but probably the best of them are Jed Horne's *Breach of Faith* and Ivor
van Heerden and Mike Bryan's *The Storm*.[8] Horne does a masterful job of setting the record straight on a number of issues:
C. Ray Nagin (the mayor of New Orleans from 2002 to 2012)
and his emotional outbursts coupled with the delay in his calling
for a mandatory evacuation;[9] despite her poor TV performance,[10]
Kathleen Blanco (the governor of Louisiana from 2004 to 2008)
declaring a state of emergency three days before Katrina struck
(one day before Mississippi), ordering the evacuation of the New
Orleans Metropolitan area on Saturday afternoon, placing the
National Guard and state agencies on alert and then struggling to
get White House attention; and FEMA head Michael D. Brown's
total incompetence, his attempt to blame everything on "a 'dysfunctional' relationship between unnamed Louisiana politicians
[Blanco and Nagin]," and his belated admission that FEMA had
sponsored a disaster drill a year earlier during which the entire
Katrina scenario—levee inadequacies, widespread flooding, and a
high death rate—had been simulated in an exercise called "Hurricane Pam."[11] Months after Katrina, it was revealed that President
Bush had been officially informed of this simulation on the afternoon of the storm. That meeting was taped.[12]

Other failures at all levels of government in the immediate
days after Katrina are well documented by Horne and others:
the lack of a city evacuation plan, the Red Cross's no-show, the
city's turndown of offers of evacuation assistance from the four
national railroads that pass through New Orleans, FEMA's delay
in requesting assistance and, worse, its outright rejection of free

help from corporations, foreign governments, doctors, firefighters from all over the United States, and even regular FEMA contractors (Brown insisted on first setting up a chain of command, making sure that volunteers "checked in" with FEMA and obtained official badges). The hidden agenda, as we will see, was to give lucrative contracts to the right people.

Who can forget that, finally, three days after Katrina, President Bush cut short his Texas vacation and had Air Force One "fly low" over the drowned city to get a glance of the disaster on his way back to DC. This in contrast to President Lyndon B. Johnson who, forty years earlier, showed up just one day after Hurricane Betsy, said he was there to help, marshaled all kinds of assistance, and then ordered the Army Corps of Engineers to build stronger levees.

But most fascinating of all, as highlighted by both Horne and van Heerden, was the successful strategy, presumably contrived by the "master of spin," Karl Rove, to make Governor Blanco look indecisive after President Bush offered to "federalize" the Louisiana National Guard—a proposal she considered for three days and then declined since it offered no value. The president's declaration of a national emergency on the Saturday of the storm actually meant that the federal government was already officially in charge pursuant to the Stafford Act of October 2000.[13] Thus, federalizing further was an unnecessary ploy to shift the focus of failure to Blanco. Mississippi's Republican governor Haley Barbour was not given the same meaningless opportunity, nor did he ask for it.[14] It was a useless gesture but a good public relations gimmick worthy of Rove. The ploy was officially denied, of course, but then Brown is reported to have told a group of graduate students in New York that someone in the White House came up with this strategy "because Blanco was a female Democrat, but stay out of Mississippi, where Governor Haley Barbour was a male Republican."[15] At that time, Blanco was the only Democratic governor in the South. Both governors and states were treated quite differently, as van Heerden points out:

In January 2007, Governor Blanco confirmed other reports that Louisiana, burdened with 80 percent of the storm damage from Katrina and Rita, received only 55 percent of federal relief funds. FEMA had given Mississippi, with 31,000 families living in trailers, $280 million for Katrina Cottages, while Louisiana's 64,000 families living in trailers merited only $74 million.[16]

In fact, if Governor Blanco had agreed to let the effort be federalized, she would not have been able to activate the National Guard to address Louisiana's needs on the ground. The Posse Comitatus Act of 1878, passed after Reconstruction and updated in 1981, purposely prevented the federal government from using the Armed Forces to enforce state or local laws. The National Guard was exempt from the prohibition and thus able to enforce laws in its own state. The Coast Guard was exempt because of its maritime police power. As it turned out, Governor Blanco did indeed use the National Guard to police New Orleans after the storms.

The post-Katrina intergovernmental intrigue and corruption outlined by Horne and van Heerden read like a grade-B mystery novel. Few players come out looking good, with some notable exceptions: the Louisiana Department of Wildlife and Fisheries deploying its flotilla of boats, the Coast Guard pulling people off rooftops in helicopters, and most important, the random citizens in real or makeshift boats picking up anyone they could find in distress. They didn't wait for Brown's authorization. The TV images of those helicopters pulling people off rooftops were the most dramatic ones of all. Fortunately, none of the real rescuers sought FEMA's permission—which probably would have been denied, in any case.

Peter Dreier, chair of the Urban & Environmental Policy Department at Occidental College, noted: "[W]hile government emergency planners scrambled to get relief to stricken communities, the *USS Bataan*—an 844-foot ship with 1,200 sailors, helicopters, doctors, hospital beds for 600 patients, six operating rooms, food and water—was cruising in the Gulf of Mexico, awaiting relief orders."[17]

And then there were all those politically well-connected contractors who would get choice assignments, fulfilling them with infinitely less efficiency than experienced locals and at great expense, as will be outlined later. The Katrina recovery demolishes the oft-repeated myth that private industry can do things better than government. When they did it better, the price was (and is) unconscionably high.

From a distance, the aftermath of the storm was as dramatic as it was incomprehensible. For those on the outside, the pain can never fully be comprehended. As Horne noted:

> For those not caught in the maelstrom, it could be difficult to grasp just how uniquely appalling the first week was in New Orleans. No American city of comparable size had seen anything remotely like it since the San Francisco earthquake of 1906. The terror attacks on NY had been confined to Lower Manhattan. A day after Katrina, four-fifths of New Orleans was underwater, four times [Hurricane] Betsy's floodplain [1965], an area seven times as big as all of Manhattan. And the wretched masses huddled at the Superdome and the convention center were only the visible part of a ghost city of homeless New Orleanians—perhaps a quarter of a million in number—now scattered across the nation.[18]

The strongest thread in the whole disaster-and-recovery story was the old-fashioned volunteerism evident at every stage—the barn-raising instinct that is so much a part of the American soul, the instinct to help spontaneously and without compensation. This took on an added dimension in the New Orleans story because strangers overcame historic prejudices of race, class, and gender and simply did what needed to be done. The number of volunteers probably exceeds any other effort historically, and people are still coming to help even now. Horne describes this volunteer effort vividly:

> Fortunately, as FEMA brass dithered and dined well, an armada of small craft had begun fanning out over the flooded city. . . . An informal flotilla estimated at 300 craft would work Katrina's aftermath in New Orleans. . . . No one told the self-appointed captains to mass on the edges of the flooded city and launch their boats. No one had to. In a culture built on fishing and intimately familiar with hurricanes, no one needed to say a word. There was a sense of duty in responding to a flood.[19]

Just imagine: All those outdoorsmen and -women of every possible background and occupation dropped everything and figured out how to get their small boats to the places they were needed on the Monday after Katrina, whereas the federal government took until Wednesday to organize the feeblest of rescue efforts and the Red Cross refused to come into the city at all. Wednesday was when Defense Secretary Rumsfeld set up a Katrina Task Force to start the ball rolling. On the same day, FEMA suspended boat operations based on the false notion that the city was too dangerous to enter. That night, for the same erroneous reason, Mayor Nagin ordered city police to stop search efforts and focus on law enforcement instead. How many more would have died without those citizen-heroes is too hard to imagine.

• • •

New Orleanians started saving themselves and their city during Katrina and before any level of government officially lent a hand—and they haven't stopped since. These "civic leaders," in fact, are what this book is really about. To this day, they are overcoming government policies and prejudices at all levels, forcing government agencies to do the right thing, organizing new community-based groups, challenging questionable public and private efforts (some successfully, others not), forging new paths to recovery, and illustrating once again that bottom-up, resident-led efforts are the most effective and enduring way to regenerate cities. Their recovery story comprises not just the small victories that added up to big, productive change but also the big failures that made their lives so difficult, and still do. This book is about both the victories and the failures.

This book does not dwell on the many evacuees who did not return. There were those who were unable to get sufficient insurance and enough federal Road Home[20] money to rebuild because the value of their home was based on its pre-Katrina assessment (good for owners with supplemental savings) rather than on its rebuilding cost (bad for those without additional funds). Many injustices derive from this first one. *No one* could have rebuilt for the amount that his or her home was valued before Katrina. There were those who found jobs elsewhere, paying better than the minimum-wage jobs that New Orleans ever offered. There were those who found neighborhoods and schools elsewhere that were safer and more functional for their children. There were the elderly and infirm who died under the stress of the experience, or who feared returning without access to their church or to the healthcare previously available at Charity Hospital. There were the 5,100 or more public housing tenants[21] whose solidly built projects from the 1930s and '40s were undamaged or minimally damaged but demolished nevertheless. There were those with special-needs children not accommodated by the restructured charter school system. And, finally, there were those who resettled near relatives and found a stable life and new social networks.

Many reasons explain why some residents didn't come back. But the more interesting story is about the people who did and their extraordinary individual and collective efforts to rebuild. The official insensitivity, the bureaucratic impediments, the government paralysis, and the blatant inequities could easily have defeated the faint of heart. But not the people who populate this book.

Their story could begin anywhere. I choose to start it in the Lower Ninth Ward, which was little known before Katrina, and much misunderstood, but fascinating in its own right. The story of the Lower Ninth Ward, three long miles from the French Quarter in the city's most downriver corner, is just part of the larger narrative, but it is a good place to begin. Katrina put the Lower Nine in the spotlight, "rocketing it from local obscurity to worldwide infamy as the most beleaguered urban neighborhood in the world's wealthiest nation."[22]

Chapter 1

The Lower Ninth Ward

Out on Deslonde Street,
Life rolled by like a great slow-moving wheel
I knew every pebble, every Live Oak tree
Everything I could see and feel
Life across the canal was heaven for folks from the country,
Lots were jungly, big enough for chickens
Pigs, goats and horses, big enough for wishing
Neighbors knew each other so well
We'd talk on the porch without speaking,
Take care of our families, make church when you can,
Cash our paychecks on the weekend
We were fine, fine in the Lower Nine
Let 'dem Creoles in the city dress up and parade in the street,
We were fine, fine in the Lower Nine
It's a ten acre world and it's enough world for me
When the banana boat would roll in
The whole block smelled so sweet
Banana bread pudding, banana cream pie
Fried bananas at breakfast, bananas 'til you cry
Sittin' around the kitchen table
It's all shoulders and elbows and kicks
Okra, corn and tomatoes and biscuits this high,

And "Gimme that, fool, get your own damn grits!"
We were fine, fine in the Lower Nine
Oyster shells crushing under bare feet
We were fine, fine in the Lower Nine
Wasting away a summer day wit' my best buddy, Pete
Cousins, they'd show up from Thibodaux
Looking for a better life in the city
Talking in plantation accents 'bout that alligator
Long as Cadillacs and not as near pretty
Everybody shouting and laughing
'Til mama shuts 'em up by snapping
When I die, do not bring me back to that place
We were fine, fine in the Lower Nine
Hey! Good morning Mr. Butler, Miss Pie
How 'bout 'dis heat?
Oh, we were fine, fine in the Lower Nine,
Here in our Blue Heaven down on Deslonde Street
Here in our Blue Heaven down on Deslonde Street
Here in our Blue Heaven down on Deslonde Street

—Paul Sanchez and Colman DeKay,
"Fine in the Lower Nine"[1]

No New Orleans neighborhood was more devastated by the hurricanes of 2005 than the Lower Ninth Ward.[2] None was more wiped clean of homes or had so many houses transported off their foundation, relocated blocks away. The northwestern flank of the district was damaged worst of all; it was here that the levee failed and a two-hundred-foot barge came through, landing on top of a yellow school bus and creating a surge of brutal force. Driveways and foundations were all that remained of many houses. Sporadic three-tiered concrete entrance steps and staircases to nowhere gave eerie testimony to what had been. Random segments of wrought-iron fence remained standing. People were stranded on rooftops. Gasoline and sewage fouled the water, and a toxic gumbo covered the neighborhood for weeks.[3] Anyone who drove around the Lower Nine right after Katrina could be forgiven for thinking that the situation was hopeless. The visuals were stunning and the TV crews could not get enough of the scorched-earth environment.

Before the storms, the Lower Nine was the poster child for the city's most challenging ills, or so most reporters thought. Central- and mid-city neighborhoods could have better served that purpose, but they didn't offer the same visual tableau. "Poverty-stricken," "crime-ridden," and "way below sea level" were the totally erroneous impressions that most audiences were given. "An unsalvageable wasteland." TV reports set the tone for the world after the storms, obscuring the true picture of a relatively stable, socially and economically significant multigenerational community of low- and modest-income people. In other words, a working-class community with a roughly 60 percent homeowner-ship rate,[4] the highest rate in the city.[5] The Lower Nine had poorly staffed and underfunded schools, no free-standing library, only two fire stations and no police precinct, meager bus service, no health facilities nor any supermarket, and surely no banks. Not that all other neighborhoods had what was missing here, but in its totality, the Lower Nine probably had the least. Given its separation from the rest of the city by the Industrial Canal and the draw-bridges over it, the Lower Nine felt the absence of basic services more acutely. The sense of psychological and physical separation was intense.

It is important to note that, while the Industrial Canal is what separates the Lower Nine from the rest of the city, walling off low-income neighborhoods was a common pattern in American cities. Too often, Urban Renewal wiped out such neighborhoods, or highways isolated what remnants were spared. Highly functional downtown business and residential districts owned by and serving black urban America were once commonplace. Remnants are now hard to find. Claiborne Avenue, before the I-10 destroyed it, was just such a place—a magnificent one at that, lined with a double allée of Live Oaks that covered two miles of neutral ground. Urban Renewal, in fact, destroyed black urban America. Every city once had stable residential neighborhoods and a black commercial district where residents could own businesses, buy insurance, bank, and shop—all the things denied them by white institutions. Those locations were the first to be targeted by Urban Renewal and highway building, the easiest politically to destroy. Just go to the Martin Luther King Boulevard in any city and you will likely find a public housing project, a highway, or, even worse, an emptiness that testifies to promises broken. Being separated by water makes the Lower Nine unusual, if not unique, but only in terms of the source of separation, not the separation itself.

The storms exposed certain long-standing conditions in the economically and socially divided city of New Orleans. These dysfunctional inequities are present in many American cities. In New Orleans, they are simply exaggerated—and then exaggerated even more in the Lower Nine. The Lower Nine had its fair share of blight, abandoned properties, and drug dealing even before the storms. But it was by no means an impoverished wasteland.

Media attention was directed to the Industrial Canal, but the significant harm caused by the Mississippi River Gulf Outlet (MR-GO), dug as a shipping channel, should not be minimized. Katrina's first surge sent massive amounts of water through MR-GO and into the Industrial Canal, flooding St. Bernard Parish, adjacent to the Lower Nine, with ten feet of water.[6] The impact did not immediately reach the Lower Nine coming in from St. Bernard Parish, and when it did, it was not severe. In fact, the water started receding quickly. The catastrophic breach of the Industrial Canal levee came twenty-four hours *after* the first surge from St. Bernard entered the Lower Nine. The time delay is significant, since many residents of the Lower Nine thought the worst was over. That might have remained the case had the levee not failed.

For years, the Corps assured the people of New Orleans that they were safe. It was not true.[7] "The overtopping would have been minor without the breach," according to Ivor van Heerden, a world-renowned hurricane specialist and the deputy director of the Louisiana State University (LSU) Hurricane Center during the time of the storm. It was the levee failure where the barge came through, *not* the hurricane per se, that drowned the Lower Nine. The barge broke loose in the MR-GO during Katrina, entered the Industrial Canal, and then burst through the breach. Van Heerden's post-Katrina investigation into the levee failures found that several of the fifty-three breaches around the city were probably due to both poor engineering and shoddy construction of the levees by the Army Corps of Engineers.

On the land side of the levee breach, nothing was left that could testify that this predominantly black community had a strength and deep roots that would be the envy of low-income communities in many cities. Richard Campanella, a geographer at the Tulane School of Architecture, noted:

> By no means was the Lower Ninth Ward the poorest or lowest-lying neighborhood of the entire city. It actually boasted a higher home-ownership rate than the city as a whole, and its lowest-lying areas (four feet below sea level) lay three to four feet *above* the lowest zones of Lakeview and Gentilly, and eight feet higher than the lowest spots in New Orleans East. . . . Isolated from public view, dismissed by the historical and architectural community, and plagued by the same social ills found throughout inner-city America, the rear sections [north] of the Lower Ninth Ward seemed like a world unto itself—cherished by residents, avoided by everyone else.[8]

The Lower Ninth Ward is divided into two distinct areas: the older, southern half along the Mississippi River, known as Holy Cross, and the northern half where the barge broke through, essentially north of Claiborne Avenue, and referred to only as the Lower Ninth Ward. The two areas are quite different.

Holy Cross was named after a distinguished Catholic school that trained many blacks and whites who went into the priesthood.[9] The school was built in 1895 near the river's wharves. The area, a locally designated historic district, was originally a series of plantations fronting on the river and stretching north in long fan-shaped formations. These narrow strips gave everyone equitable access to both the river shipping area and the fertile land stretching back behind the natural levees to marshes, unsuitable for farming. Here, close to the river, the ground is higher than in the area north of Claiborne. German and Irish immigrants as well as African-Americans settled in Holy Cross. By 1900, a number of Holy Cross small farms were providing produce, poultry, and dairy products to New Orleans markets.

North of Claiborne was the last of the two-square-mile district to have been developed. After World War II, the new riverfront industries drew new people, black and white, to be freight handlers, mechanics, and banana boat workers and to fill other blue-collar jobs. Basic city services were extended as industry expanded. Suburban-style houses and traditional "shotguns" were built for first-time home buyers; these structures were in close proximity to one another and comfortably dense. Many residents built their own homes. Simplicity dominated. They built for their needs, not for style.

Today, the community is a mixture of finely crafted shotgun houses and bungalows, mixed in with nondescript brick homes and the occasional larger Victorian house. Many of the brick ranch-style homes started out as wood-framed structures. In the 1950s, brick was considered stylish and practical as well as sturdy; wood, by contrast, takes a beating in the hot sun and needs more maintenance. Thus, many homeowners bricked over the wood and, in the process, improved their houses' insulation, strength, and appearance. Many bricklayers lived in this neighborhood and worked on their own homes, in addition to others.

The classic shotgun style dominates. Long and narrow, with its front oriented to the street, the shotgun can be either bare-bones architecture or highly ornamented. Either way, it provides an excellent example of how to make the most of limited space: no hallways, no wasted room. Shotguns are built with the natural environment in mind; they are all about ventilation, passive cooling, large windows, and shutters to let air in and keep the hot sun out—a truly place-specific design.

Two of the city's most spectacular historic houses are in Holy Cross: the turn-of-the-century, three-story captain's houses right at the Mississippi River behind the natural levee. They are an anomaly in the city. Heavily ornamented with brackets, spindles, and all manner of gingerbread, these splendid survivors are guaranteed to surprise and delight any visitor. Shockingly, they were included on the city's early list of demolition targets put together for FEMA by the Shaw Group, the private contractor hired to survey house conditions after the storm. Soon after Katrina, when so-called inspectors were assigned by Shaw to survey the damage condition of all houses in New Orleans, it was revealed that these individuals were nothing more than a ragtag group of seemingly random people—a hairdresser, pizza delivery man, and pet groomer were among them—with no professional construction or engineering expertise. Individual property owners and various groups had to fight against their demolition lists. Astonishingly, those lists are still in use today.[10]

While exploring the history of the Lower Nine, the image of the Live Oak comes to mind. A rich community grew here—rich in roots, family history, connections, networks, proximity to relatives and lifelong friends. "Everyone knows everyone," many residents told me. In order to understand *neighborhood* and *community*—not as developers purport to build them, or planners to map them, or architects to design them, or politicians to campaign in them—one need only meet the residents of the Lower Ninth Ward and travel its web of streets. These qualities are in fact shared by a stunning number of New Orleans neighborhoods, but they weren't spotlighted by the mainstream media during Katrina.

This was not the "poverty-stricken" Lower Ninth Ward depicted by public officials and TV commentators. Modest income, yes. Minimum-wage jobs, yes. But even the latter descriptions are too simplified. Chefs from the French Quarter, teachers, carpenters, mechanics, seamstresses, shopkeepers, dockworkers, restaurant and hotel workers, Harrah's casino employees, and civil servants—these are just some of the professionals who made up this working-class neighborhood. The Lower Nine is the area where many New Orleans musicians learned their art from an early age, and where music remains as much a part of daily sustenance as the legendary cuisine. Fats Domino came from the Lower Ninth Ward and returned after the hurricanes to his renovated modest yellow-and-black house. Trumpeter Kermit Ruffin and many other jazz notables got their start here as well. Significantly, 40–45 percent of the pre-Katrina population in the Lower Nine were retired seniors, accounting statistically for the large below-poverty-line number often cited by the press.[11]

After Katrina, not all of the Lower Nine looked as deserted and dismal as the vicinity of the levee breach. Further east and away from the breach but still north of Claiborne, occasional houses survived, flooded but still in their rightful place. A mix of surviving modest clapboard shotguns and newer brick ranch-style houses provided a hint of what had filled the neighborhood before the storm.

• • •

Josephine Short Butler, a slight, soft-spoken woman of eighty-nine with close-cropped hair, was one of the first residents to move back into a rebuilt house in the Lower Nine. When I asked her in 2011 if she was concerned about returning to a deserted neighborhood, Josephine chuckled, leaned forward, and said: "Honey, when we moved here in 1948, there was nobody. It was farmland." Mud and oyster shells served as street pavement, and everything from the church to the closest bus stop was at least a forty-five-minute walk away. Returning after Katrina was a little like the old days, she added with a smile. She never doubted for a minute that she would be back and that others would follow. At the time of our conversation in 2011, neighbors were already beginning to return to this thinly populated area.

Josephine's daughter, Chirrie Butler Harris, came too, moving in to live with her mother as she had before the storm. Next door was Josephine's close friend and neighbor of twenty-five years, Gwendolyn Guice. It was a package deal, two houses built with the help of LSU architects and ACORN Housing[12] and against official city policy that wanted no rebuilding in this neighborhood. Students helped design and build the houses, volunteers from Covenant House—a crisis center for homeless youth—also helped, and a church provided the landscaping. Financing came from a California bank. Loans were repaid with insurance and Road Home funds. Both solid pine houses sit elevated, five feet off the ground, on the same quarter-acre lot that the destroyed homes were on. Part of the rebuilding package, too, was help with the renovation of the brick ranch-style homes of Josephine's two granddaughters, Tanya and Tracy Harris, around the corner.

I had met Tracy Harris during my first visit after Katrina in 2005. Later, we continued to communicate via e-mail. The frustration and anguish she was experiencing reflected those of her neighbors. On November 2, she wrote:

> Now, almost nine weeks since Katrina, residents in Lakeview are able to go in to clean up, assess damage and meet at their locations with adjusters to settle claims but the Lower Nine residents are barricaded out of their community and met by

M-16 toting National Guardsmen, who tell them and their
adjusters that they must go on a bus tour, with no getting off
by threat of imprisonment? Insurance adjusters are not able
to assess property damage for this single section of the city.
How are residents able to rebuild in this manner? How can a
fair, accurate or proper inspection be completed by way of a
drive-by photo session?

By October 5 of that year, most Orleanians were allowed
back into their neighborhoods, but not those in the Lower Nine,
allegedly due to lack of utilities and running water. By mid-
October, the Army Corps of Engineers had pumped the last
water out of the whole city. It was not so much the flooding that
decimated the houses but the mold and rot. Within three weeks
of the storms, most of the Lower Nine was dry. It took another
three weeks to completely remove the remaining water. But residents were not allowed to move back or even clean out until January, four months after Katrina, the last neighborhood allowed
to open. By then, mold and rot had done the job. Holy Cross was
dry within days of the flood but suffered the same fate as the rest
of the Lower Nine. No wonder the world thought this was the
end of the Lower Ninth Ward. The destruction from the storm
was beyond calculation. Many wondered how or even whether the
legendary city itself could recover. Few thought the Lower Nine
would—except the people who lived there.

If there was one thing most of the estimated pre-Katrina
19,500[13] Lower Nine residents had in common, it was a commitment to place and a determination to return. People have been
coming back slowly, despite impediments at every level of government. One drive-through is not sufficient: only visit after visit do
the small signs of new life become visible.

North of Claiborne, Josephine's neighborhood, has been
steeped in mythology from its earliest development. Far removed
from the city's core, it has long been both out of sight and out of

mind. "It was not a place that many black people knew about," explained Tanya Harris. "It was remote and somewhat mysterious." There was just one bus per day from downtown. The two drawbridges contributed a feeling of separateness, even isolation. "A different feeling from the rest of the city," one longtime resident told me. "It was full of large lots, where you could raise your kids and grow a garden."

The Lower Nine appealed to those families who had come from the strawberry, sugar cane, and cotton regions of the South looking not only for better job opportunities but for a chance to own land, build a house, and become independent from the uncertainty of crop yields. This included Josephine's family, the Butler/Harris clan. Many transplants, like Cherry Butler—Josephine's husband—stayed in rooming houses in Central City or Uptown when they first arrived in the 1940s. They moved to the Lower Nine to buy land and build a house. The building was a collective family effort. They built in close proximity to each other, which accounts for the large number of family clusters. The first generation of the family to come, like many African-American transplants, did so not just for the promise of better job opportunities but also to live in a less treacherously segregated city.

Freedom in New Orleans was a world of difference compared to other areas of the South. Discrimination here was severe, to be sure, but less harsh than in either Central Louisiana or Mississippi, where life as a sharecropper was one step above slavery and full of unpredictable and dangerous risks.

Cherry Butler was the first in his extended family to own land and build a house, initially for his mother and then for himself and Josephine. The landscape was reminiscent of the rural Louisiana country life that Cherry had left behind—a combination of woods and openness that allowed him to raise pigs, chickens, horses, and dogs while still working a regular job. The crushed oyster shell streets were soft on bare feet. Life was simple and revolved around work, family, porch visits, and church. Neighbors watched out for neighbors. The Lower Nine continued to grow throughout the 1950s as job opportunities on the river and in factories increased.

"Everyone had a second job," said Tanya. "Supplementing one's income was critical." Eventually, the open land gave Cherry the opportunity to raise beagles, train them for hunting, and then sell them. He also planted a sizable garden. A bountiful harvest followed—collard greens, okra, turnips, tomatoes, broccoli, green beans, chickens, rabbits, and more. "He grew things meant for everybody, neighbors, relatives, whoever needed anything," Tanya told me. "People would come by, wave their bag, and head to the garden to take what they needed."

Architect Andrés Duany called this pattern of building for your own family "self-building." With the professionalism of the building process, he observed, came the requirements—actually, hurdles that included drawings, permitting, contractors, and inspections. Under the self-building system, family members built for each other with, as Duany noted, "small builders paid in cash or by barter. Most of these simple, pleasant houses were paid off. They had to be because they do not meet any sort of code and are therefore not mortgageable by standards."[14] By keeping construction costs low and not taking on debt to build, residents had the free time to focus on sociability, creative cooking, playing or listening to music, and telling stories. Duany called for this "lifestyle choice" to be protected:

> Somehow there must be a process whereupon people can build simple, functional houses for themselves, either by themselves or by barter with professionals. There must be free house designs that can be built in stages and do not require an architect, complicated permits, or inspections; there must be common-sense technical standards. Without this there will be the pall of debt for everyone. . . .
>
> For three centuries Americans built for themselves. They built well enough, so long as it was theirs. Individual

responsibility could be trusted. We must return to this as an option. Of course, this is not for everybody. There are plenty of people in New Orleans who follow the conventional American eight-hour workday. But the culture of this city does not flow from them; they may provide the backbone of New Orleans but not its heart.[15]

Throughout the twentieth century, the Lower Nine remained distinct from the rest of the city. It was a different culture: residents were slow to give up their "country" ways. This was an area not frequently visited by people on the downtown side of the canal, except through invitations from family members. This remains true today. So the Lower Nine's separateness and somewhat mysterious aura endured. Hurricane Katrina caused the myths to mushroom. The most exaggerated of these emerged while water still covered the area in 2005. The phenomenon of people stranded on rooftops was simplistically attributed to poverty and the lack of car ownership by the mainstream media. "Ridiculous," observes Tanya. "If you drive around the community and see every house with a driveway that costs between $2,000 to $4,000 to create, you would understand, of course, that many people had cars. But people waited too long to leave. There was real apathy about hurricanes. People evacuated for prior hurricanes, went to Florida for three days, spent $500 they didn't have, lost income from work they couldn't afford, and came home to find nothing wrong with their house. No. Many people just didn't believe it would be bad."

Tanya and her family left, as did many. The stranded ones hadn't gone before the levee broke. When that cascade of water came, it was too late, even for those with cars. Distrust of the power structure was common in the Lower Nine and not without reason, as will be illustrated throughout this book. Thus, official warnings were met with skepticism.

Leaving for *any* reason would have been difficult for many in this community. People felt very protective of the property they owned. They belonged to those houses as much as the houses belonged to them. As with many Americans, it was their only investment, a standard way to build equity. When everything they own is tied up in real estate and the community, residents tend not to evacuate easily and leave that property unprotected.

The pre-Katrina population of the neighborhood defies categorization. Consider, for example, the demographics of Tracy's block, which she described in an e-mail:

> House 1 and 2 are rentals
> House 3, owner occupied by a hospital security officer and her husband, a truck driver
> House 4, owner occupied by a daycare facility owner and her husband, a city maintenance supervisor
> House 5, owner occupied by a special education teacher with a master's degree
> House 6, owner occupied by a New Orleans Water Board employee with her husband, a limo driver
> House 7, owner occupied by me, a gift shop/coffee shop owner and my husband, certified in Culinary Arts, who works for Chef Emeril Lagasse as a Sous Chef
> House 8, owner occupied by my sister, Tanya
> House 9, owner occupied by a retired, disabled college music professor whose brother is Larry Lundy, the owner of all the Southeastern Louisiana Pizza Hut restaurants
> House 10, owner occupied by a mail carrier and his wife, an accountant

The next block, she said, was equally varied: nurses, mechanics, retirees, truck drivers, police officers, firefighters, teachers, and so on. And, she pointed out, the 40 percent retired population matches the percentage that CNN was saying during storm coverage is "unemployed, not seeking employment, and has no desire to seek employment." She noted that her grandmother lives mortgage-free on her late husband's International Longshoremen's Association (ILA) Local pension, Social Security, and Medicare, totaling $1,000 per month. She added:

> Technically, she is indeed below the poverty line in America. Really, she only spends $250 a month on food, utilities, cable, and meds. That means she is saving 75 percent of her monthly income. I don't know about you, Ms. Gratz, but I don't get to keep 75 percent of my monthly income. She is representative of what the retired population in the Lower Nine is all about. Retired teachers, retired mail carriers, retired longshoremen, retired nurses, and retired service industry workers all completely content to enjoy their remaining lives as they so choose.

Measuring society by statistics obscures life as it is lived. Thus, while the statistics reported on TV or in newspapers post-Katrina may have been accurate, the inferences drawn from them could be complete lies. (As British prime minister Disraeli quipped: "There are three kinds of lies: lies, damned lies, and statistics.")[16] In many instances, the discrepancy between Lower Nine city planners' perceptions and local realities did not change their planning strategies. Poverty needs to be understood in all its nuances, not just as a percentage of the populace. "We never got a sense we were living in poverty," Tanya said when talking about her frustration over hearing all the experts debate what should happen to the "impoverished" Lower Nine. "We had lawyers, civil servants, and other professionals living here," she pointed out.

The call for "economic integration," so prevalent after Katrina, seemed to be code words for redeveloping targeted neighborhoods and the public housing projects. "We already had economically and racially mixed neighborhoods," Tanya added with an edge in her voice. "Some of us can afford to leave for higher-income districts but choose to stay because we are so connected to our community. If we didn't have confidence in the neighborhood's rebirth, we'd leave. We all have family living here, too." Tanya and other Orleanians proudly cite the integrated nature of many neighborhoods. "You can go two or three blocks away from the upscale homes on Saint Charles Avenue, owned mostly by rich white people," Tanya observes, "and you'll find low-income families of different races living nearby and side-by-side." This diversity is proudly noted by white residents of the city as well. "Three blocks from Saint Charles Avenue is the hood," an Uptown resident observed.

This characteristic, historians note, is a legacy of slavery, whereby slaves, servants, and free people of color lived in the smaller houses near the mansions where they worked. Some even owned their own homes. Michael Eric Dyson describes "bustling ethnic and racial interactions—driven in part by the unique 'backyard' patterns, where blacks and whites lived near each other, a practice that had its roots in slavery."[17] From its earliest beginnings, New Orleans had a diverse population of French, Native American, African, and Spanish families. "American's first genuinely multi-cultural metropolis," Richard Campanella called it.[18] Partly because Louisiana surrendered early in the Civil War and sustained little damage, many of New Orleans's patterns of life, already set, endured. The population mixture of the Lower Ninth Ward is clearly one such pattern.

• • •

Residents of the Lower Nine were rescuing themselves and each other from the minute the levee breached. They didn't stop when the water was gone. For example, since no school here was designated to reopen, members of the community cleaned out and reopened Martin Luther King School on their own. Structurally sound houses were "red tagged," targeted for demolition (green meant habitable, yellow questionable) without even proper notice given to the owners. This was a citywide problem, but residents here saw it as more evidence of city leadership not wanting them back. "Because we were always isolated as a community," noted writer, activist, and educator Kalamu Ya Salaam, who was raised in Holy Cross, "we had a strong sense of making things happen for ourselves and for helping one another. It was automatic. My father would stop and give rides to people, white or black. He didn't have to know them. It was just part of who we were." Kalamu is a tall, strong-looking man with a speckled gray beard and high forehead. We talked over cups of coffee at Rose Nicaud Café in the Marigny, a stone's throw from the French Quarter. This legendary coffee shop is named after a slave woman who in the early 1800s was the first known coffee vender in New Orleans and started the first public coffeehouse in the French Market.

Kalamu's father served as a medic in World War II and the Korean War but was refused a job at the VA Hospital in New Orleans as a lab technician after he returned to the States. He spent years writing letters to various officials and was eventually hired but never promoted. "My father was a country boy who taught us to grow food so we would never be hungry," said Kalamu, whose name means "pen of peace" in Swahili. "We kept the block clean, not just the house, and many family members lived nearby." "This is the largest nativist city in the US," he added, observing that it is difficult for outsiders to understand the depth of family roots here. In fact, Louisiana is one of the top three states from which people do not leave.[19]

Holy Cross and the whole Lower Nine, Kalamu pointed out, were always self-sufficient in ways that avoided dependency on the larger city. Like many neighborhoods, he said, "we had pharmacies, theaters, doctor's offices, lots of churches, all kinds of stores." This pattern, of course, was true of other neighborhoods in New Orleans and those across the country where segregation limited access to white-owned stores, entertainment venues, and services. But the Lower Nine's self-sufficiency was particularly significant, considering its physical separation.

Neglect by the city government was notorious; the Lower Nine was always the last to receive city services, if they were received at all, Kalamu said. Denial by government of community services and infrastructure, utilities, transit, police officers, fire fighters, and similar necessities is no different from the redlining of that same neighborhood by banks and insurance companies: both result in the undermining of home values and quality of life, making stability difficult.

Kalamu pointed to post-Katrina federal and local funding that was meant for this community but eventually shifted and was spent elsewhere in the city. In January 2013, for example, City Hall announced the completion of twenty-five capital projects worth $60 million and the beginning of another twenty-seven projects with a total value of $87 million. Of those completed projects, $2,581,198 was spent in the Lower Nine and $12,460,039 in Algiers on the West Bank across from the French Quarter.[20] Algiers did not flood during Katrina but nevertheless gained a beautiful new library and a new school through the efforts of former city councilwoman Jackie Clarkson. The Lower Nine didn't get a high school until 2014. "We're always last on the list whenever the feds send money to New Orleans, and by the time our chance comes, the money is gone, spent elsewhere," said Reverend Gilbert Scie of the Greater Little Zion MB Church in Holy Cross.

Yet, through all its hard luck, the Lower Nine maintained the largest homeownership rate in the city—owing, most likely, to the large number of family-built homes still lived in by descendants. If, as often stated, homeownership is a sign of stability, the time is long overdue to officially revalue the Lower Ninth Ward.

When it became clear that committed Lower Nine residents were determined to rebuild regardless of the judgment and warnings of experts and at a pace their financial capacity would allow, government finally responded. In 2012, a defunct sports field at the northern edge was rebuilt by the city and a basketball court with night lights, tennis courts, and ball fields were built with combined funds from a Community Block Grant, disaster relief, and FEMA. In 2013, eight years after Katrina, a new fire station was built (combining the two that were there before the storm) as was a replacement for the Sanchez Community Center and pool. Some streets had been repaved, particularly the ones intended for trucks leading to the Mississippi River wharfs.

These changes have occurred slowly, in pockets. I loved taking visitors to a four-block stretch at the eastern edge, bordering Jackson Barracks. House after red brick ranch-style house with lovely planted yards and cars in the driveways made it hard to believe that the disaster had happened. Scattered elsewhere were pockets of two, three, four rebuilt houses, leading me to conclude that family networks had rebuilt together—just as Josephine Butler wasn't coming back without her neighbor and friend next door and her granddaughters on the next block. Even a few speculator-built shotgun houses appeared, many of them rental properties. Plenty of overgrown brush and land returning to the wild were visible as well, giving the area an almost rural look.

To an outsider, conditions may still look bleak at best and hopeless at worst in the Lower Ninth Ward. But even the first-time visitor can't help but recognize the home-building energy and gradual renewal unfolding in this community. Fifty blocks from downtown and a total mindset away, the Lower Nine—even with new tax-paying households, solar roofs, and kids playing—to the uninitiated can still undoubtedly appear to be on the edge of hopelessness. That is a mistaken conclusion. Only by observing the Lower Nine over many years—nine, in my case—and seeing new structures during every visit, with construction always happening somewhere in the neighborhood, only then does one appreciate the gradual but steady progress of a community that continuously defies expectations.

Chapter 2

The View from Above

A cynical view supported by the facts. They don't want people coming back, period.

—Lolis Eric Elie, former *Times-Picayune* columnist

Katrina laid bare who has the benefits, who is exploited, who is used and who is ignored.

—Monique Harden, environmental justice attorney

The power elites of New Orleans would use Katrina to advance a broad new agenda aimed at creating a stronger (and whiter) power structure and growing a population with a smaller proportion of African-Americans, especially poor ones. The Lower Ninth Ward was only one piece of the new agenda; the larger city was the real target. As one New Orleanian put it: "If you are not paranoid in New Orleans, you aren't paying attention."

In a chilling way, James Reiss would articulate the agenda to come. Reiss, a wealthy businessman, is a former chairman of the Regional Transit Authority; his power and influence in the city are formidable. A descendant of an old-line Uptown family, he resides in an exclusive gated community, the only one in the city that is actually locked. Reiss returned after Katrina by helicopter; he flew in an Uzi-toting Israeli security company to guard his house and neighborhood, landing across St. Charles Avenue in Audubon Park.

Reiss told the *Wall Street Journal* in September of 2005: "Those who want to see this city rebuilt want to see it done in a completely different way: demographically, geographically and politically." He also suggested—or threatened—that he and his friends "would leave the city unless New Orleans improved its services and reduced the number of poor people. . . . I'm not just speaking for myself here. The way we've been living is not going to happen again, or we're out."[1] Joseph Canizaro, one of the city's wealthiest developers and the one who would be given a leadership role in the recovery by Mayor Nagin, summed it up clearly: "We have a clean sheet to start again. And with that clean sheet we have some very big opportunities."[2]

Opportunities for whom?

Then there was the comment made to me at an Uptown garden party a year later: "New Orleans is not recovering; we're going in a new direction." Alphonse Jackson, the secretary of Housing and Urban Development, underscored that new direction when he told the *Houston Chronicle* that New Orleans was "not going to be as black as it was for a long time, if ever again."[3] Lawrence Powell, shortly after the storms, posed the real question: "Can a *diverse* New Orleans be rebuilt without reproducing the awful inequities of the pre-disaster past?"[4]

It was clear who was going to set the new exclusionist agenda for the city. Since 67 percent of the city was black before Katrina, the target was obvious. The new agenda for a whiter, richer city would be a bombshell for all of New Orleans, but especially for the mostly black, working poor. "Wherever we were stranded," wrote community organizer and ACORN founder Wade Rathke, "that news met us as a roundhouse to the chin, knocking all of us back on our heels and waking us up to the fact that the new reality was going to be a fight for our lives and our very right to come back."[5]

In 2005, First Lady Barbara Bush, after reportedly expressing some compassion for the refugees at the Astrodome, had no doubts: "What I'm hearing, which is sort of scary, is that they all want to stay in Texas. Everybody is so overwhelmed by the hospitality. And so many of the people in the arena here, you know, were underprivileged anyway, so this is working very well for them."[6] Others wondered if the "diaspora" was "beneficial" to the poor who were dispersed to presumably better job markets and school locations. The mainstream commentary after the storm all seemed to go in that direction.

The message of who was or was not welcome back was loud and clear.

The press reported that forty of the city's most well-connected leaders had met in Dallas (where Mayor Nagin had sought refuge for his family from the storm) right after Katrina to begin to plan for the recovery. No report of the committee's proceeding exists. Nagin, however, in his self-published book, *Katrina's Secrets: Storms After the Storm,* reported being "blindsided" by this meeting. He claimed, in his inimitably self-serving way, that he was "looking forward to some serious dialogue with our captains of industry on how we could rebuild our city better than before." Instead, he found himself invited to an "insensitive purge" in which the group offered "their vision of a *new* New Orleans where mint juleps would once again be the drink of choice in a bleached, adult Disney World–like city."[7]

After that meeting, the mayor founded the Bring New Orleans Back (BNOB) Committee,[8] a seventeen-member group headed by developer Joseph Canizaro, friend of and large donor to President George Bush.[9] The group included Reiss as well. Canizaro then established a land-use subcommittee and invited the Urban Land Institute (ULI) to come to New Orleans to help develop a rebuilding plan—as close to letting the fox in to guard the chickens as one could imagine. ULI is a very prestigious national developer organization. While its members are primarily developers, the nonprofit organization draws on the expertise of diverse professions. It conducts research and issues useful reports on such subjects as development trends, compact development, sustainability, and smart growth.

Members of the BNOB land-use subcommittee began talking about a "smaller, more progressive version of a unique American city," about replacing "blight with renovation" and rebuilding "a smarter, better engineered New Orleans," all requiring painful political decisions and a tough-as-nails resolve.

Martha Carr and Jeffrey Meitrodt wrote in the *Times-Picayune* on Christmas Day after the hurricanes:

> The toughest decision of all is already on the agenda: how to reduce the city's geographical footprint to a size that can be adequately covered by available police, sewer, water and other services. The fight pits advocates of careful planning against residents nostalgic to resettle every area of the city immediately. Whether politicians have the courage and skills to build consensus around a more compact city remains to be seen.[10]

"Nostalgic"? Is that what the residents were whose lives, families, memories, and core beings were embodied in the homes just recently destroyed? And "careful planning" as defined by whom? "Careful planning" is what is always done from the top down but never accomplishes as much as what bubbles up organically from the citizenry below. With "careful planning," cities are rebuilt and replaced; with the citizenry-led change, the same places are regenerated and reborn, combining new and old into vibrant authentic places. Change comes either way but the actual outcomes are decidedly different. Top-down planning often treats residents and businesses like objects on a chessboard, moving them hither and yon, all for perfectly "logical" planning reasons but with no sensitivity for peoples' lives, roots, family and social networks, desires, or connections to community institutions like churches or schools.

The days of Urban Renewal were a dramatic example of such insensitivity, and many communities still suffer the negative social and economic impacts of that era.

Dr. Mindy Fullilove, a public health psychiatrist, has written two excellent books on this subject, illustrating the catastrophic impact on peoples' lives of "chessboard" planning that doesn't give agency to citizens. These books, *Root Shock: How Tearing Up City Neighborhoods Hurts America and What We Can Do About It,*[11] and *Urban Alchemy: Restoring Joy in America's Fractured Cities,*[12] should be mandatory reading for anyone in the reimagining, reengineering, or city planning business. *Root shock* is a traumatic stress reaction to the loss of a person's entire emotional ecosystem. Fullilove learned about this phenomenon from studying people displaced by Urban Renewal in the 1950s and '60s in the Hill District of Pittsburgh, the Central Ward of Newark, and Roanoke, Virginia. "The longing for home can kill people," Mindy told me in conversation. "The psychiatric implications of displacement are more serious than is anywhere understood."

The elitist vision for New Orleans's future was quite a Christmas present for those still suffering in the aftermath of the storms. It was a sure indicator of what was to come from the most prestigious and powerful people of the city, for whom it is difficult to grasp that what is seemingly logical might not be right for the city. Planning rhetoric always appears so logical at first glance.

The BNOB Committee issued a report, "Action Plan for New Orleans," dated January 30, 2006.[13] The rationale of the report was "public safety." The city needed to shrink the footprint and eliminate some flooded areas where people were living. "The public discussion centered on whether some parts of the city should be abandoned or rebuilt. 'Footprint' and 'shrinkage' were the words of the hour."[14] It was simply too dangerous for residents to live in vulnerable areas, experts contended. But in what sense "vulnerable"? Fifty percent of the city from downtown to the lake is below sea level.[15] But, in a sense, half the country could be described as living in dangerous areas, vulnerable to mud slides, tornadoes, forest fires, and floods.

The ULI report painted a picture of the doom that would beset the city if some of the "tough choices" were not made. Of greatest concern was the prospect that individual property owners would rebuild as they saw fit, even in low-lying areas in potential danger of future floods. In fact, by November 2005, five weeks after Katrina, hundreds if not thousands of homes were already gutted and ready for rebuilding. Since half of the city's residents were expected never to return, the experts opined, the city landscape would have pockets of rebuilt homes and streets with only a few homes surrounded by blight.[16] This condition happens to exist in many urban neighborhoods around the country, but in the report it was made to sound like a new circumstance, negative and intractable.

One should take special note of the projection, based on speculation, that half of New Orleans's residents would never return to the city. In fact, 44 percent, 198,893, were back by July 2006 and 59 percent, 267,658, by July 2007. As of July 2011, 78 percent, 356,512, had returned. In 2012, the population of 369,250 represented 81 percent of its pre-storm population of 455,188.[17] In that year, New Orleans was the fastest-growing urban center in the country. No expert predicted this. By 2013, the population had reached 378,715. Projections of doom and gloom after the storms were seemingly pulled out of thin air, with terrible consequences: major city policies and private plans are often shaped by these speculative assumptions and projections. The mainstream forecast for New Orleans's population was as ludicrous in retrospect as the predictions of planning experts in the 1980s that New York City's diminishing population would shrink to 5 million. By then, in fact, New York was already starting its slow, incremental rebound. Thirty years later, not very long in the life of cities, New York City's population exceeds 8 million.

It was said by officials, planners, and developers that nothing should happen without a plan. In New Orleans, the concern after the storms was that people would haphazardly rebuild every-where, instead of rebuilding "responsibly." But "responsibly" defined by whom? Only areas that could muster "sufficient pop-ulation" should be rebuilt, it was suggested by experts. The city's footprint should be "shrunk" to match the needs and conditions of the diminished city. Defenders of the ULI report responded to public anger by explaining that neighborhoods would not be "eliminated," just "shrunk." In reality, elimination and shrinkage mean the same thing. Shrinkage leads to more shrinkage and so on. In addition, the rhetoric called for rebuilding "equitably" and "without delay" and for "strengthening and empowering neigh-borhoods." But how do you "empower" neighborhoods while cre-ating impediments to the return of the community?

On January 23, 2006, *Houston Chronicle* reporter Kim Cob wrote:

> The non-profit Urban Land Institute advised the city in Novem-ber to consider returning flood-prone areas such as the Lower Ninth Ward to wetlands. A city planning committee has rec-ommended that New Orleans shrink its "footprint" to adjust for a smaller population, using forced buyouts, if necessary, to eject homeowners from neighborhoods deemed not viable.[18]

This was, in sum, the seemingly logical concept of shrink-age—an idea still widely discussed by people within and outside of New Orleans. It baffles me. Consider all the environmentally inappropriate construction around this country: the beaches of Malibu, Miami, and North Carolina; the sliding ocean hillsides of Los Angeles; the millions of acres of wetlands disastrously filled in for development of expensive suburban divisions; the once-burned and subsequently rebuilt homes in vulnerable virgin forests in critical areas of Nevada, Arizona, New Mexico, Colorado, and Montana; even the homes rebuilt multiple times in Oklahoma's tornado alley. With all that has been developed or rebuilt despite the warnings of environmentalists, how is it that only the flooded New Orleans neighborhoods should be "shrunk" for environmental reasons? These were not vacant, abandoned neighborhoods. If people want to rebuild, aware of potential future danger, they have the right to take that risk.[19]

The ULI report raised fears that the city would be filled with empty spaces scattered among standing houses—the "jack-o-lantern" effect or "gap-tooth" syndrome. But then City Councilman Oliver Thomas noted: "Look, the jack-o-lantern effect is nothing new. There's always been a jack-o-lantern pattern. For 30 years, people have been living with abandoned houses down the block."[20] Tim Ryan, then chancellor of the University of New Orleans (UNO), was quoted in the *Times-Picayune* as indicating that he saw nothing wrong with the "jack-o-lantern" effect. Ryan advocated just what ULI and city leaders were afraid of: real "free market forces," which involve property owners making their own decision about whether or not to risk returning. This was an honest interpretation of "free market forces," not what free market advocates usually have in mind. The elites' version of a free market is one in which an official plan includes incentives for developers to respond to the market. Ryan said it best:

> We can plan until we're blue in the face, but it's going to be the market that determines what is going to happen. And if we don't recognize that, we're going to have a bunch of real pretty plans that will be very unsuccessful. . . . In the old days of city development, that is pretty much how it happened. You don't develop everything right away. You'd have this patchwork, where you've got two houses on a block and a lot of empty lots. It didn't seem to cause people a tremendous amount of concern back then.[21]

He could have been describing the early days of the Lower Nine, which Josephine Butler remembers as being "like the country."

New settlers followed the Butlers in due time, when the real market dictated. And that is what was already happening in many pockets of the city, as discussed.

Accompanying the ULI report for the BNOB land-use subcommittee were maps with green circles showing areas to be redeveloped into parks, mostly the hardest-hit Lower Ninth Ward, Lakeview, and Broadmoor. These circles became known as the "green dots." The maps were explosive, revealing just which neighborhoods would be "shrunk." The green dots galvanized a potent, citywide opposition. Also, included in the proposals was a four-month time limit for neighborhoods to prove that half the residents would be returning; only then would that neighborhood's future be ensured. Without a 50 percent population return, the neighborhood was toast. Homes would be forcibly bought out (through eminent domain) and the area bulldozed. What better way to kill a neighborhood than to deliver a plan that was equivalent to a death threat? Who would be foolish enough to lift a hammer not knowing if, in the end, the effort would be undermined or wiped out? Unless, of course, you ignored the experts and went full speed ahead to rebuild. And considering the unconscionable time it took the relief agencies and insurance companies to deliver rebuilding support, the four-month cutoff was simply a joke. Any time limit, in fact, meant preordained death.

In the field of urban change, this scenario is called "planners' blight." Setting a new agenda for an area, even suggesting the *possibility* of a new agenda, initiates an array of disinvestment that becomes a self-fulfilling prophesy, inviting a kind of neighborhood-wide demolition-by-neglect that would culminate in bulldozers. Planners' blight has killed neighborhoods and cities across America. But post-Katrina New Orleans would defy this oft-repeated process, as many citizens ignored the experts and went full speed ahead to rebuild.

In an attempt to put a positive light on all of this, maps were created for "neighborhood investment zones" and for areas to be "closely studied" where owners could be bought out at pre-Katrina, rather than replacement, values. What would anyone think "closely studied" could mean, other than to assume the neighborhood was on life support and in need of a miracle? Then there was the proposal for the mayor to appoint an "independent" redevelopment authority, the Crescent City Rebuilding Corporation, with power over all land-use policies and the ability to force a sale (i.e., through a Quick-Take process, a more streamlined way of expropriating property for a public purpose) by property owners in designated areas.[22] The state-legislated authority template was what building czar Robert Moses perfected and used decades earlier to confiscate private property and bulldoze neighborhoods all over New York State throughout the 1950s and '60s. Of course, a referendum would be required to change the city charter of New Orleans, even though such a referendum was guaranteed to fail anyway.

In addition, the ULI report called for the mayor to declare a moratorium on rebuilding permits until redevelopment plans were drawn up and approved at some unspecified time, putting residents of the city in limbo indefinitely. But what about the neighborhoods given four months to prove their future viability? How was that possible without building permits? Included in this reimagined and reengineered city was to be a string of parks and retention ponds linked by pedestrian malls and bike paths. This seems appealing at first—think of the Emerald Necklace and Olmsted parks in Boston and Buffalo, for instance. But if your house is in the way, the appeal turns into a nightmare, especially if you have already begun to rebuild. As Jed Horne reported:

> "I gut my house already," a diminutive, round-faced member of the Mary Queen of Vietnam congregation said when asked what had brought her to a land-use committee meeting way back in November. "Now they tell me I can't live there? No way they can tell me that." Her pastor, Father Vien, put it this

way, and there was no answering him: "We cannot leave this area; we have buried our dead here."[23]

Essentially, the ULI report revealed a detailed road map for usurping any semblance of a public process. The report was so overreaching, so absent of legitimate local input and disdainful of the democratic process that it served as a startling wake-up call regarding the new elite agenda for the city. And it was only January at this point, less than five months since Katrina and Rita. Clearly the citizens had no choice but to develop their own battle plans. The report energized nascent local organizations all over town that were ten steps ahead of officials and already jump-starting the process of rebuilding their city.

• • •

Within five years after Katrina, New Orleans was defying so-called expert predictions, especially the one that expected the city's population to be 50 percent of its pre-storm numbers, as reported often in the press. The first paragraph of a joint report by the Greater New Orleans Community Data Center and the Brookings Institution Metropolitan Policy Program in August 2010 read as follows:

> Nearly five years after the levees failed and flooded 80 per-cent of the city, New Orleans has regained the vast majority of its population. The most recent official population esti-mates from the Census Bureau peg the New Orleans popula-tion at 354,850 in July 2009 up from 208,548 in July 2006, but still 100,000 persons fewer than in July 2005, when the Census estimated the population at 455,188. By June 2010, 66 of New Orleans' 73 neighborhoods had recovered well over half of the number of households they had prior to the catastrophic flooding.[24]

This, the report acknowledged, despite the two additional shocks the city had experienced: the economic recession and the BP Deepwater Horizon oil disaster. Of course, the Katrina funds from government and insurance companies softened the recession. Even the number of blighted and vacant properties had dropped by 35 percent, although the 43,000 remaining ones continued to pose a great challenge.[25] The report also noted the "unprecedented rise in community engagement after the storm, strengthening the reserve of social capital." It went on:

> In general, higher numbers of New Orleanians are participating in public meetings and processes, and are now more likely than residents of other cities to attend public meetings where city affairs are discussed. Neighborhood and grassroots organizations have demonstrated increasing organizational capacity and autonomy, such as the rise in nonprofit housing advocates and developers. Individuals and groups have become more strategic and sophisticated. And there is great cooperation between groups and individuals, including the emergence of new umbrella groups.

If all that was needed was the will and energy of the shell-shocked but determined residents, New Orleans would recover quickly. That was not to be. The impediments over which citizens had no control were endless. The overall sense of uncertainty for everyone was pervasive. What the citzenry would be allowed to do and what the city's new agenda would look like were so much of a question that those forging ahead were doing so on blind faith. The combined effects of impediments created by the insurance industry, FEMA, Road Home, city agencies, and private contractors chosen to perform the government's responsibilities were not for the faint of heart. It is astonishing that more Orleanians didn't just throw up their hands and move away.

For some time after the storms, city agencies appeared para-lyzed at best, incompetent at worst. There were so many city-staff layoffs for lack of city funds that it was miraculous for the city to be functioning at all. As Mike Davis pointed out in *The Nation:*

> An early deadly blow was Treasury Secretary John Snow's refusal to guarantee New Orleans municipal bonds, forcing Mayor Nagin to lay off 3,000 city employees on top of the thousands of education and medical workers already job-less. . . . In stark contrast to its neglect of neighborhood relief, the White House has made Herculean efforts to reward its own base of large corporations and political insiders. Rep-resentative Nydia Velazquez, who sits on the House Small Business Committee, pointed out that the SBA has allowed large corporations to get $2 billion in federal contracts while excluding local minority contractors.[26]

If you quickly gutted your house in order to rebuild, the first hurdle was a permit. Was there a moratorium or wasn't there? Confusion reigned. If you were lucky enough to get a permit, you then needed an inspection from one of just six, very busy city inspectors. Even before Katrina, when there were eight inspectors, a backlog plagued builders and homeowners. FEMA added to this state of semi-paralysis by taking considerable time to update flood maps[27] that determined whether houses needed to be either razed or raised. Federal regulations required that a house more than 50 percent damaged be either demolished or raised above the Base Flood Elevation (BFE). Residents learned to game the system, claiming less than 50 percent damage if they wanted to rebuild or more if they wanted to demolish. If unsure how it could go, you got your property "grandfathered" under the old FEMA maps in order to proceed. Insurance issues were an end-less nightmare. Flood insurance was not required unless you had

a mortgage (banks insisted on this). Worse, even if you had it and
had been paying your premiums over the years, insurance companies figured out how to deny claims. It was a veritable catch-22. As
Horne noted:

> Katrina wasn't a hurricane, it was a flood, the private insur-
> ance companies argued. Homeowner policies did not apply
> to floods. Wind damage? Yes. Rain damage? Maybe. Flood
> damage? No. That's what FEMA's flood insurance was for.
> In an age that had made a mantra of privatization, the pri-
> vate insurers were trying to lay off the storm's cost on the
> public. With good friends in Washington and battalions of
> skilled lawyers on the corporate pad, there was every reason
> to assume the insurers would succeed.[28]

If you were lucky enough to have federal flood insurance and
a qualifiable claim, your maximum collectible would be $250,000.
And even if you got that much—which was unlikely—it almost
certainly would not cover the rebuilding of your house. Receiving
an actual check took forever. The question of whether damage
was caused by flooding or by catastrophic winds enraged many
citizens. Most of the damage resulted from flooding, but wasn't it
fair to argue that the cataclysmic wind and rain of the hurricane
caused the flooding? Without the hurricane, flooding would not
have occurred. That logic did not persuade insurers.

If insurance issues didn't defeat you (assuming you had
insurance), Road Home could do the job. Road Home was a federal funding program, the "largest disaster recovery program in
U.S. history," reported David Hammer, former *Times-Picayune*
reporter and current WWL television reporter, who covered much
of Road Home's troubled history.[29] The money goes to the state
and is then contracted out to a private company.[30] The first contractor was ICF International of Fairfax, Virginia, which was "run
out of state on a rail in 2009 when its contract ended," Hammer

told me. "The company is generally reviled by Louisianians," he wrote, "and essentially banned from new business with the state, but walks away $900 million richer and holding lucrative contracts with governments across the country." David went on to say that "[t]he replacement company, Hammerman & Gainer International (HGI), hasn't fared much better because it used massive change orders to go from a minor company to the company in charge of the whole thing."

Road Home was inequitable from the start. The amount a homeowner qualified for was based on the value of the home before the storms, not on the cost of rebuilding. The same shotgun house appraised at $400,000 in the Garden District would be appraised at $75,000 in the Lower Ninth Ward, thereby automatically ghettoizing the house. Since the Garden District didn't flood, only the shotguns in the Lower Nine would require a hefty new investment. However, an appraisal determining that the damage to each shotgun was 50 percent would yield only $37,500 in the Lower Nine but the full $150,000, the maximum allowable, in the Garden District. Further problems arose from the state's decision to release the money only upon the provision of receipts for completed work. Coming up with front money for the work was near impossible for most low-income owners. The banks deducted the balance of a mortgage, if there was one, sometimes leaving nothing for the owner. The banks lost nothing. For any homeowner of limited means, this meant defeat. Unquestionably, government needs to be vigilant, but these outcomes went far beyond what could be deemed fair and equitable. *Times-Picayune* columnist Jarvis DeBerry wrote:

> From the very beginning of the Road Home, it was clear that the creators of the program had condescension—if not outright contempt—for the dispossessed people who would apply. As if they were perps being booked with a crime, Road Home applicants had their mug shots taken and had to

provide an electronic thumbprint. They were there for help but were greeted with an introductory slap of humiliation.

Mississippi didn't require all that, but Louisiana's then-Gov. Kathleen Blanco, who seemed to think her folks were inclined toward fraud, was unmoved by complaints that the already damaged applicants were being more damaged by the process. Blanco told me during a June 2007 phone conversation that the Road Home was parceling out a bit of money at a time to homeowners because she didn't trust them with one lump sum.[31]

What seemed to be forgotten in the midst of all this vigilance and red tape was that this was a humanitarian crisis of unprecedented proportions. The impediments toward a speedy recovery continue today. In 2014, Road Home sent out thousands of letters demanding repayment of Road Home grants. Almost 24,000 people got letters claiming that their files were missing documents, but the homeowners kept arguing that they'd sent in those documents. Road Home was notorious for losing documents. It never demanded money back from contractors who misspent or failed to spend money given them.

Shrinking government and letting the private sector take over have been the standard operating procedure of national, state, and city administrations for nearly four decades. As Lawrence Powell observed during a symposium at the University of South Alabama:

From the Richard M. Nixon presidency to the [Bush] administration, the watchword has often been wealth more than commonwealth. Jimmy Carter's conservative presidency did not reverse the trend. Nor did the centrist Clinton administration, with its zeal for downsizing, deregulation, and globalization. While the federal payroll may have shrunk, not so the cost of doing the public's business, which has been outsourced to the point that "contractors have become a virtual fourth branch of government."[32]

Outsourcing the government to the point that little is actually run by the government has its own momentum. According to orthodox economists and mainstream political pundits, the private sector is infinitely more efficient, less prone to corruption, and less expensive. One can always find a $435 hammer or a $640 toilet seat in the Pentagon budget or in another agency budget to prove the point.

But upon careful examination, what shrinking government really means is privatizing a government function to the huge benefit of the private contractor and the occasional, minimum benefit of the public. When politicians rant about cutting government spending, this rarely applies to cutting the pork out of the private contracts that are the bulk of government spending.

Mike Lofgren is a former Republican congressional aide who spent twenty-eight years as a congressional staff member. He retired in 2011, articulating resounding criticism of both political parties as "rotten captives to corporate loot." In a TV interview with Bill Moyers on February 21, 2014, Lofgren noted that "70 percent of the Pentagon budget" goes to "private contractors." Author of *The Party Is Over: How Republicans Went Crazy, Democrats Became Useless, and the Middle-Class Got Shafted,* Lofgren told Moyers that "a hybrid entity of public and private institutions is ruling the country" and is "unrestrained." That hybrid is visible in the operation and financing of the official post-Katrina recovery operation.

In contradiction to our so-called free market system, competitive bidding post-Katrina was either nonexistent or a sham. One had to be living in Alice's wonderland to believe efficiency and diminished cost were deliverable through private-sector contracts. Central to the contract story is Joseph Allbaugh, who first worked for George W. Bush when Bush was Texas governor, then managed his 2000 presidential campaign, became FEMA director in February 2001, and resigned in March 2003. Michael Eric Dyson noted:

> Allbaugh timed his resignation to take effect on March 1, 2003, the date that FEMA would be downgraded from a cabinet-level agency and folded into the Department of Homeland Security. He immediately set up a consulting firm to advise companies doing business in Iraq. Allbaugh was succeeded by his former college pal and FEMA deputy Michael Brown, who, like his boss, had no previous experience in disaster relief and emergency management.[33]

A flurry of news reports about contracts appeared not long after Katrina.[34] Analyzing these reports all together was shocking and enraging. Consider, for example, the purchasing of items that simply weren't needed. FEMA rushed out and bought 24,000 body bags after Katrina struck, even though hundreds of thousands were already stockpiled at army bases around the country and 1,000 were on hand at the coroner's office right there in New Orleans.[35]

Another example: While the American Bus Association, whose members include Greyhound and Coach, was trying unsuccessfully to reach someone at FEMA to offer help transporting evacuees, a deal already had been struck. As Dyson pointed out:

> FEMA had outsourced the job of transporting the evacuees to Landstar Express America, a trucking logistics firm with a federal contract worth up to $100 million annually. Landstar Express in turn hired a limousine company, Carey Limousine, which hired a travel management company, Transportation Services . . . whose specialty is arranging buses for big events.[36]

According to the *Chicago Tribune:*

Over the next four days, those companies and a collection of Louisiana officials cobbled together a fleet of at least 1,100 buses that belatedly descended on New Orleans to evacuate residents waiting amid the squalor and mayhem of the Superdome and the city's convention center.[37]

Throughout the aftermath of the storm, a huge number of contracts were given to the politically well-connected—at extraordinarily inflated prices—who then paid peanuts to the actual workers who performed the work. And, worse, most of those scandalous contracts went to companies out of state. All levels of government claim to have invested heavily in New Orleans's recovery. This is an out-and-out lie. When you contrast the contract amounts and the money actually paid out, what actually went directly to recovery work probably amounted to pennies on the dollar. In fact, it is not far-fetched to estimate that only 20 percent—if that—actually went into recovery work.

No less prestigious a public figure than retired Lieutenant General Russel L. Honoré expressed outrage at some of the expenditures he witnessed. Honoré served as commander of the Joint Task Force responsible for coordinating military relief efforts across the Gulf Coast. "More money than you can imagine did not hit the ground," he said in a phone interview. "Companies [getting contracts] looked good on paper but didn't have the capacity."

Dyson noted that "a month after Katrina struck, more than 15 contracts had been awarded for more than $100 million [each]. . . . More than 80 percent of the $1.5 billion in contracts awarded by FEMA were no-bid or limited-competition agreements."[38] He also specifically pointed out that "costs claimed for debris removal was the $568 million awarded to AshBritt, a company based in Pompano Beach, Florida, and a client of the lobbying firm to which Haley Barbour was connected before he became Mississippi's governor." Ashbritt, Loyola law professor William Quigley points out, citing reports in the *Miami Herald*, "didn't own a single dump truck but had paid a GOP lobbyist firm $40,000 right before the storm and another $50,000 directly to the GOP the year before."[39] Bechtel Corporation was awarded $100 million despite raising concerns with its oversight of a Boston "Big Dig" construction project. And KBR (formerly Kellogg, Brown, and Root) has been criticized by federal auditors for billing $100-per-bag laundry service and for overcharging its Iraqi reconstruction.[40]

The list goes on but the favorite example cited by several reporters reflects the overall pattern—the blue tarps used for "Operation Blue Roof."[41] These bright-blue plastic sheets, installed to keep water from penetrating where parts of the roof had blown off, covered the majority of houses after Katrina. When you drove into the city on the I-10 and saw the whole landscape, blue was more visible than anything else.

Here's how the tarps were put in place.

Step One: FEMA bought $6.6 million of the material, "a standard item in the disaster tool kit," from All American Poly of Piscataway, NJ, "without full competitive bidding."[42]

Step Two: FEMA paid the Shaw Group in Baton Rouge $175 per square (100 square feet) to install the tarps, with FEMA providing the material.

Step Three: Shaw subcontracted to A-1 Construction and Roofing for $75 a square.

Step Four: A-1 subcontracted to Wescon Construction for $30.

Step Five: Wescon paid $2 to small local contractors or other local individuals eager for the work, the only ones based in New Orleans. Many locals had been doing the same kind of work before the storm. Their earnings were the only ones that went into the local economy. In other words, a mere $2 of the $175 in "disaster relief funds" actually went to New Orleans. This process was repeated many times over throughout the federal disaster funding food chain.

Shaw's contention was that its superior management skills and cash reserves were critical to the success of an emergency operation mounted on the fly. But a roofing contractor, not involved in this federal funding food chain, told Russell and Varney of the *Times-Picayune* that he charges between $170 and $180 per 100 square feet (equal to one square) for a basic "three-tab" asphalt-shingle roof, about the same as a tarp job.[43] A basic new roof for the cost of a tarp installation! Shaw was apparently the highest-paid tarp contractor. Two others were paid $172 or $149 a square.

This pattern was repeated every time another contract was scrutinized. Former Mayor Nagin, who had his own record of allegedly giving away gouging contracts even for work not done, actually refers to the contracts for debris removal in his book:

> The federal government controlled these essential cleanup functions through four separate $400 million no-bid contracts that were released right after the storm hit. The beneficiaries were several giant engineering firms like KBR, one of Dick Cheney's Halliburton subsidiaries, and the Shaw Group, a Baton Rouge firm that was very close to the Blancos. . . .
>
> They [KBR & Shaw] both were awarded debris removal contracts that the Bush administration agreed to pay $44 dollars per cubic yard for debris removed from areas affected by Hurricane Katrina. These companies would then subcontract the work for $27 per cubic year. At this point neither Shaw nor its first sub had pushed a broom. Their subcontractor would then contract with someone local or a hungry out-of-town firm at around $7 per cubic yard. Sadly, the $7 firm is the only one who actually did any real work. The other two firms just pushed paper and waited for big checks to arrive in the mail. Tragically, the profits of companies at the bottom of this distorted recovery food chain were later squeezed financially with slow or no payments, and as a result, most either filed for bankruptcy or just went out of business.[44]

Charles R. Babcock of the *Washington Post* reported on October 5, 2005: "The recipient of the largest contract in the Federal Emergency Management Agency's hurricane recovery efforts doesn't have a license to build manufactured housing in its home state and has been the subject of dealer and buyer complaints, according to a Georgia regulator. Circle B Enterprises won a $287.5 million FEMA contract last month to supply temporary housing for victims of Hurricane Katrina. The actual manufacturing is being done by several other companies, including Cavalier Homes Inc. in Alabama and Patriot Homes Inc. in Indiana."[45]

So FEMA paid about $70,000 each for thousands of flimsy, formaldehyde-laden trailers (plus contracts to connect the electric and plumbing) instead of buying temporary Katrina cottage kits at $67,000 that numerous local contractors were anxious to build. FEMA maintained that the Stafford Act "limited the agency to funding only temporary housing (Katrina cottages could be permanent), just as it had made funds available for only overtime, to be earned in municipalities that no longer had the wherewithal to pay straight time."[46]

But it was nearly impossible for people in need to get trailers in the first place. Many of them remained parked for months on end outside the city. The cost of the trailer was only the beginning of the wasteful spending food chain. Recall from the Preface the two homeowners I encountered in January 2006 who had trailers delivered to their front yard but couldn't use them. One was waiting endlessly for a FEMA plumbing contractor to connect the water for the trailer, a task that his licensed plumber friend was willing to do for free; he would have been trespassing if he'd allowed his friend in. The other was waiting for a FEMA electrician to do a job that was his own profession to do. Neither of these homeowners would get a key before the contracts were fulfilled and inspected. Both had already waited weeks.

"Contract nesting" is what Russell and Varney called it. "FEMA buys trailers from brokers, who bump up the price per unit by thousands of dollars. And for the housing inspection contract, the federal government paid The Shaw Group nearly $80 an hour, city officials said, for building inspectors who earn about a quarter of that amount, according to city inspectors."[47]

Van Heerden, then deputy director of the Louisiana State University (LSU) Hurricane Center, had suggested putting up tent cities within fifty miles of the city during the preparation test run two years earlier, but he was laughed out of the room.[48] Tent cities, he observed, had been established time and again by the Armed Forces during war or in response to disaster. They would have been quick, cheap, and efficient and surely Louisiana's climate was conducive. A ready workforce of residents would have been available for cleanup work. Of course, a desire for the return of local workers had to exist first. Unfortunately, it didn't among the city's elites. The closing of the public housing that was either not flooded or only lightly so was another indication of the preference to keep the local, primarily African-American workforce dispersed and unavailable. Instead, mostly undocumented immigrant workers were welcomed. Fliers offering jobs were strategically distributed in Houston. The ones who came were then housed in tents and worked under appalling conditions. As Mike Davis noted: "[E]very aspect of the catastrophe was shaped by inequalities of class and race."[49]

Concern is often expressed about the corruption in this famously corrupt city and state. But even by local standards the padding built into FEMA's contracting practices was a scandal. And where were the "efficiency" and "cost-saving" promised by the private market?

Naomi Klein, in her brilliant and perceptive book *The Shock Doctrine,* cites numerous examples of bad contracts in New Orleans during this time. Some of these have been presented here, but she includes an additional gruesome one:[50]

> Kenyon, a division of the mega funeral conglomerate Service
> Corporation International (a major Bush campaign donor),

was hired to retrieve the dead from homes and streets. The work was extraordinarily slow, and bodies were left in the broiling sun for days. Emergency workers and local volunteer morticians were forbidden to step in to help because handling bodies impinged on Kenyon's commercial territory. The company charged the state, on average, $12,500 a victim, and it has since been accused of failing to properly label many bodies. For almost a year after the flood, decayed corpses were still being discovered in attics.[51]

It gets worse. To offset all these expensive giveaways in the name of reconstruction and relief, the Republican-controlled Congress in November 2005 demanded $40 billion in cuts from the federal budget. What programs were cut? Student loans, Medicaid, and food stamps, among others intended to help the same people who were shortchanged by the contracting process. Meanwhile, the "unregulated corporate handouts" provided neither decent-paying local jobs nor functional public services. And, surely, only a few drops of those funds "trickled down" to the local economy.

Lieutenant General Russel L. Honoré observed that so much of the economic impact of the Katrina recovery expenditures benefited people from other cities and states. The people profiting the most were middlemen supervisors. "That's the side of recovery you don't hear about," Honoré told me. The local businesses were "victimized by the process." In the future, he added, a way must be found to avoid generating big profits for the wrong people. "We have to find another way that is more sustainable, with local companies participating in recovery, and make sure the money is invested in people who do the work locally."

What the story of the post-Katrina contracts shows is that the citizens of New Orleans rebuilt their city *in spite of* such intrusions as the private sector cashing in, the insurance companies making sure that their interests came first, and the contractors taking over for government bureaucracies whose primary interest was profit. Indeed, the unfathomable burdens thrust upon them by the storms were made even worse by elites determined to set a new agenda for the city.

Yet, throughout this period, many generous and good-spirited outsiders and locals were contributing creatively, financially, and energetically to the genuine regeneration of the city. What they accomplished was nothing short of one miracle after another; but, it is apparent, volunteers, not-for-profits, and well-meaning businesspeople were allowed to touch only what didn't infringe on the territory of a disaster capitalist. These local efforts were minuscule relative to the big government contract jobs out of their reach. But, in the end, they added up to the real regeneration of a city.

Chapter 3

The Grassroots
Take Charge

One reason that disasters are threatening to elites is that power devolves to the people on the ground in many ways: it is the neighbors who are the first responders and who assemble the impromptu kitchens and networks to rebuild. And it demonstrates the viability of a dispersed, decentralized system of decision-making. Citizens themselves in these moments constitute the government—the acting decision-making body—as democracy has always promised and rarely delivered. Thus disasters often unfold as though a revolution has already taken place.[1]

—Rebecca Solnit, *A Paradise Built in Hell*

On January 12, 2006, more than two hundred bright-eyed, plaid-skirted high school girls showed up in Jackson Square wearing life jackets and carrying oars, with flood lines painted on their foreheads.[2] There they were, holding signs that read "Thomas Jefferson Thought We Were Worth It," "France Take Us Back," "Coastal Restoration for Our Nation," "Party Affiliation:

Louisianian," and, the core message, "Category 5 Levees and Coastal Restoration."

"Do what it takes, do what it takes," they chanted in the most historic location in the French Quarter.[3] Passing cars honked in support. On this day in January they were getting all the attention President Bush was supposed to have received during his second visit to New Orleans after Katrina.[4] The location for his public address on the 12th of the month had been changed at the last minute. So, in the president's absence, all cameras were focused on the girls from the Academy of the Sacred Heart, a private high school.

Shawn Holahan could not have imagined receiving such attention when she cooked up the idea of an "issues only, no politics" demonstration for the president. It was just a simple way to express public anger. Darryl Malek-Wiley, organizing representative for the Sierra Club, stood nearby, stunned. "I've been doing this stuff for twenty years," he told Shawn, "and I've never succeeded like this."

Shawn's predominantly white, affluent Lakeview neighborhood had been decimated by floodwaters as high as those in the Lower Nine. Like the Industrial Canal in the Lower Nine, the nearby 17th Street Canal had collapsed—though without the help of a barge. Close to the Lakeview breach, some houses took fourteen feet of water and were pushed off their foundations. Shawn and her family were only blocks away. Her three-bedroom Lakeview home was wiped out, as were her sister's and parents' homes nearby and the four investment properties her father had bought and managed. All of Shawn's siblings—she is the oldest of six—remain in the New Orleans area. Shawn is a soft-spoken lawyer and divorced mother of three, her Irish ancestry clearly written on her creamy skin. She and I talked over cups of tea in an uptown coffeehouse. Six years after the storm, the pain of it still stings. Her shoulder-length wavy reddish-blond hair frames her deceptively calm face. It is difficult to imagine the rage she felt after Katrina.

In the months following the storm, President Bush had committed to spending $2.9 billion on levee restoration but made no commitment to the additional money needed for Category 5 hurricane protection.[5] "The message I was hearing was the government could restore the coast or fix the levees," Shawn said; one didn't need to be any kind of expert to understand that "they need to do both."

The idea for the "issues only, no politics" demonstration did not come to her instantly. She had initially done a lot of thoughtful exploration and research. "I'd go to the location of the breach, like the scene of a crime," she said, describing her gradual transformation into an "accidental activist." Her voice remained quiet only a short while longer as she explained: "I'd sit there asking 'How did this really happen?' I was so unnerved. I didn't think I was getting the right story. The more I dug, the more I found out, the angrier I got."

Shawn's animus toward the Army Corps of Engineers is understandable and was widely shared, but the levee boards were hardly blameless. Indeed, some of these boards had come to epitomize the famously corrupt "Louisiana way." Like other boards and authorities, they were contractor pork barrels and patronage gold mines removed from democratic control—places in which to park cronies and political hacks with a sharper eye for profit than for the public good. Levee board members were not required to have any knowledge of flood protection, and the boards themselves—the New Orleans board in particular—were distracted from that primary responsibility by unrelated burdens and opportunities: examples include filling in cypress swamps in the 1920s to develop high-end lakefront real estate, building and running an airport on the Pontchartrain Lakefront in the 1930s, and managing a yacht harbor and a casino boat. As independent legal entities answerable to no public review process, authorities are notorious for taking on projects, usually real estate–related, that have nothing to do with their assumed responsibility.[6]

New Orleans chauvinists were reluctant to admit it, but twenty-five years before Katrina, the Corps proposed to build closable gates at the mouth of the lakefront canals instead of building the floodwalls along the canals that failed catastrophically after Katrina passed over the city. The local levee board had maneuvered deftly to avoid the gates, fearing added maintenance costs. Closable gates were also rejected by the electorate based on projected harsh environmental impacts. The gates, a far more effective mode of flood control than floodwalls alone, were rushed into service after the Katrina disaster.

An early post-Katrina reform eliminated the old levee boards and created new public authorities, larger entities that conformed with geographical and hydrological realities. The Orleans levee board, for example, was made part of the tri-parish Southeast Louisiana Flood Protection Authority–East (SLFPA-E). In a major departure from past practice, board members were required to actually know something about flood protection. The new authorities were supposed to be insulated from political meddling.

That insulation vanished when, in 2013, the SLFPA-E sued ninety-seven oil, gas, and pipeline companies—a broad representation of an industry to which Governor Bobby Jindal (elected in 2007) has loyally pandered and from which he has come to count on campaign donations. The lawsuit was an attempt to secure damages to finance repair of a coastline ravaged by oil and gas extraction. Each drilling permit included an obligation to repair the areas that were damaged, such as backfilling canals created for passage to an oil well when the oil well was finished. The companies had never complied. The shockwaves from the legal challenge reverberated statewide and even nationwide. Such a direct challenge to the invincibility of the oil and gas industry was unheard of. The leader of the suit, John Barry—historian, flood expert, and author of *Rising Tide*—as well as two other members were removed from the authority at Jindal's and the legislature's behest.[7] Jindal appointed three new members, expecting that they would withdraw the suit. Instead, the remaining majority voted to keep the suit alive. Barry had, in fact, been appointed to the reconstituted levee board after Katrina because of his extraordinary expertise but was thrown out because of politics.

The levee board history fed Shawn's anger. Not long after the storms she started a blog.[8] Her entries are clear and to the point: nonengineers supervise the Corps of Engineers; local supervisors have only a one-year assignment, so there is never one person to blame; the Corps picks the blue-ribbon review panel that oversees it, leading to "omissions, errors, bad design, misjudgments"; nonengineers decide what projects to fund. The blog was not enough. "I'm fomenting over this like crazy," she said of her mood back then. "This has nothing to do with my house. This is so much larger."

Thus the demonstration idea, which was meant to express outrage. But it was not originally Shawn's idea to bring students. It was a school day. She sent out e-mails to friends and kept repeating the primary ground rule of "no politics." "On a lark," she e-mailed the principal at her daughter's school, Pat Brechtel, a friend, who she thought might be interested. An e-mail came back saying "We're coming." Brechtel brought her students to the site of the demonstration. She didn't think about how their parents would react, "mostly affluent, uptown Republicans not affected by the flooding." Sacred Heart is a magnificent early-twentieth-century complex, situated behind ornate iron gates uptown on St. Charles Avenue. An elite, mostly white institution, it is one of the high-status schools in a city where the question "Where did you go to school?" refers to high school, not college. In Sacred Heart's mock 2004 election, Bush won big.

In a story about the demonstration, *New York Times* reporter Adam Nossiter observed:

> Anxiety for the future and pain over the past cuts across class, race and economic lines here. . . . The high turnout—230 students out of the pre-Katrina enrollment of 269—was further

evidence that the better-off in this city have had a far easier time returning than inhabitants of poorer neighborhoods. At a protest over demolitions in the Lower Ninth Ward last week, there was hardly a single local resident.[9]

Did she think the protest made a difference? "Maybe. It brought attention to the real issue, [being] to correctly rebuild the levees, and it got heard from the mouths of kids with national coverage." There were unexpected bonuses. Shawn's daughter, Charlotte, thought her mom was making something happen. And there were unanticipated—or, maybe, expected—negative reactions. "Some conservative Republican school parents misinterpreted the action. They thought it was anti-Bush when in fact people from both parties are to blame. Some people from uptown could care less about coastal restoration and levee repair. 'I'm fine,' they think. The oldest, affluent uptown crowd is very insular. It's real uptown grandiosity." But then Shawn smiles again. "For the kids, it was the pinnacle of their Sacred Heart education. They learned there could be power in what they do."

• • •

Until the late nineteenth and early twentieth centuries, Lakeview was mostly swampland along Lake Pontchartrain. New areas for development were made possible by the newly installed drainage system at the turn of the century.[10] Lakeview's settlement—reclaimed swampland—started slowly with modest bungalow-style cottages. This style, inspired by the Arts and Crafts movement of the early twentieth century, is also known as the California Bungalow—popularized by artisan Gustav Stickley's *Craftsman* magazine. Usually built with plaster and flood-resistant cypress, like earlier shotgun styles elsewhere, these homes were meant to be durable and low maintenance, a stark reaction against the highly ornamented Victorian styles in older parts of the city. After World War II, everything changed. Development accelerated as the nationwide move out of center cities began. But Lakeview is a white suburban enclave with an important and unique characteristic: it is within city limits.

As new as Lakeview is considered to be in this three-hundred-year-old city, it illustrates how even relatively new communities have deep, rich histories. Lakeview sits roughly between 1,500-acre City Park, the fifth-largest urban park in the country, and the 17th Street Canal not far in from Lake Pontchartrain. The canal, built in the mid-nineteenth century, is the border between the city and the suburb of Metairie, in neighboring Jefferson Parish. With no breach on the west side of the canal, the Jefferson neighborhoods contiguous to the canal were not flooded. Today, one can hardly comprehend the degree of devastation Lakeview experienced, at least not from viewing the mostly rebuilt houses.

During Katrina, floodwaters rose in Lakeview and upended houses off their foundations. Many Lakeview residents had already left, but the devastation was still life-changing. Katrina's carnage revealed both comparable and contrasting impacts in the two levee-breached neighborhoods, Lakeview and Lower Nine. Shawn's story reflects some of those similarities and differences.

"It's all about pigs at the trough," she said, referring to the abysmal response from all levels of government. "Not about what makes sense or is right." It is early in our first conversation in 2011 and Shawn displayed that calm demeanor of many Southern women, though her passion and anger were still palpable. Deceptively reserved, she echoed the refrain heard in the Lower Nine and elsewhere: "It's really all about contracts, who is going to make the money. . . . It was about systematic bi-partisan neglect. That's when I realized we were all on our own." I have heard this sentiment expressed many times since.

Shawn was born in New Orleans, where she married and stayed. Divorced in 1996, she remained in the family's house with two daughters and a son. She was there when word of the oncoming hurricane was first heard. "I told the kids to find four things to take" and, with the cat and dog in their arms, they headed out in the car toward her best friend's house in Grand Coteau, a small farming town not far from Lafayette. "I put a note on the door: 'God Bless This House.' We had lived through many hurricanes but I just knew this was different. I took a last look at my favorite old Live Oak towering over the house with massive arteries hovering over it, insulating, so protective. After my divorce, I felt so alone but that tree watched over us. I related to that mother tree. I was confident it could stay strong." What should have been a two-and-a-half-hour drive took eighteen hours.

Her parents, twelve blocks away and closer to the breach, chose to stay. "My father thought hurricanes were nothing but media events, which they often were. 'Everything disaster, all the time,' he'd say." He had bought four rental properties in Lakeview, "nothing special," she said. "He planned to leave them for us. That was to be his legacy." The mortgages were paid off; thus flood insurance was not required. Because they were not his primary residence, Road Home paid nothing for the properties—yet another oft-heard story that crossed class, race, and economic lines. By denying value and assistance to nonprimary residence property, FEMA wiped out in one fell swoop the accumulated equity of many Orleanians who, like Shawn's dad, had invested their savings in rental properties.

Finally, Shawn's very-pregnant younger sister, Meghan, convinced their parents to leave. Her mother went with Meghan to Memphis to be near a hospital, and there they stayed past the birth. Their father joined Shawn. The rest of the family scattered. The Holahans are a typical large, extended, white Catholic New Orleans family; many of their forebears had migrated out of the city to nearby Jefferson and St. Tammany Parishes during the middle-class exodus from the city.[11] Those who settled in Lakeview constituted an important part of New Orleans's middle class.

In the safety of Grand Coteau, Shawn and her father stayed glued to the TV during the storm. "My brother had driven by after the worst of the storm passed and said the houses were fine." As in the Lower Nine, things were fine and floodwaters were receding, but then the levee breached. "The next day, I saw a shot of Lakeview that told me things were not fine. My father didn't believe it and repeated the media was exaggerating. I knew the worst had happened."

This is where the parallels between Shawn's middle-income Lakeview story and the story of anyone in the Lower Nine or other damaged low-income neighborhoods diverge.

Sacred Heart is what Shawn described as a "network" school. A place was immediately found at a Sacred Heart out of state for both daughters. The youngest attended one in Grand Coteau, where she and Shawn were living. The older one, Bridget, went to Greenwich, Connecticut, with five friends, staying with a host family. A "rat pack," Shawn said with a smile. "It delayed their response to Katrina. What's not for them to like? It was almost like a vacation." Her son, Duke, went to a Jesuit school in Houston and lived with a host family. Duke was a star lacrosse player, and he and other teammates stayed near one another in Houston so they could keep training for the Louisiana state championship. No hurricane was going to stop them. The Jesuit High lacrosse team won the state championship the next spring. For Charlotte, the eighth grader who would demonstrate at Bush's visit, it was tougher. She "bounced back and forth, reacting differently. We moved around a lot among friends. Without my knowing it, she went over to our house, climbed up into that great Live Oak, and just stared below. The house looked like it had been through a blender." When Shawn went to view the house after the water receded in October, residual water remained. "It looked like it had been marinating," she said with a grimace. "Everything corroded. What was in that taupe-brown water? There were no bugs, no roaches, no anything living. Yet, outside was the strangest thing. Watermelon, berries, flowers were in bloom. Even pot." She had not planted any of it.

Shawn really liked Lakeview, "maturing as a long-standing place, finally coming into its own, not just an extension of uptown." But it is a neighborhood of married people, and as a single woman "I didn't really want to rebuild the house by myself." From the day after the storm, Shawn, like all flood victims, was tortured with paperwork. An energetic lawyer, determined and still seething, she filed the forms for the whole family. Road Home lost her records, including her father's application. Trips to Baton Rouge, two hours away, were repeatedly required to deal with the bureaucracy of the private company contracted to administer Road Home. Phone conversations with impassive people, either of questionable competence or simply overwhelmed, resulted in endless frustration. Then, in February 2007, her father landed in the hospital with septic shock from a bacteria infection. He died the following April. "His resistance was shot. When faced with the enormity of it all, he couldn't make a decision about his houses. No one could give him clear answers."

Shawn told me that the Road Home rules were social engineering at its worst. "If you took Road Home money, you had to live there for three years. What difference does it make to you, Uncle Sam?[12] It's a repaired house; isn't that what counts? All those kind of things rankled my father. He could not think his way out of this. He was always strategic. Do you rebuild behind a floodwall? How do you answer that so quickly? It was horrible for the elderly. For three years you have to stay in place just because you get money?"

Talk with anyone willing to recall their post-Katrina fate and you'll find common threads, regardless of race, class, or income: the irrationality of the rules, the impossibility of the process, the injustice of it all. No alternative was clear. Yet, shouldn't the government have been able to exercise some flexibility when rules and reality clashed? By "flexibility," of course, I mean the kind that doesn't disintegrate into corruption. Many things go wrong even with inflexible rules, so what's to lose by adjusting them? All kinds of rules appear throughout this book that are enough to challenge many and, not surprisingly, defeat some.

Shawn's world and her onetime Republican politics have been shaken to the core. "I'm a moderate without a home," she said. After a long pause, she smiled. "What doesn't kill you makes you different, not stronger."

When Shawn's father died, there was no home to gather in for the reception after the funeral. He was one of a group of long-time friends that included former mayor Moon Landrieu.[13] The reception was held at the Landrieu home in Broadmoor, centrally located in the city. At one point, Shawn stepped out in front of the house for a breath of fresh air. Down the block she noticed about twenty kids playing in the street instead of being in school. Few schools were even open. "It brought home what a difference it makes when resources are in place," she said. "Those kids' parents were probably still in Houston, hopefully with a job, all living in suspended animation. Imagine. Two years out of school. How do they ever catch up? How do they regain stability? If it weren't for my kids' network, where would they be? It saved my children's future. You struggle without that connection. You will be fine, I kept telling them. They had a future to look forward to. But those kids I saw down the block, a lost generation. Where are they now? Killing each other."

• • •

The Lakeview rebuilding effort probably wouldn't have occurred as rapidly or as effectively if not for one of those accidental citizen-leaders. Denise Thornton, a West Texas native, is a slim, bright-eyed, energetic woman with reddish-brown hair. At first glance, nothing about her suggests more than a pleasant suburban housewife. In fact, Denise told me that before Katrina "there was nothing very meaningful in my life outside of my family, nothing to remember me for." She devalues herself. Denise is the classic American entrepreneur who started a small business in her garage with a friend—a fellow Lakeview resident. Four years before Katrina, they started Ming Products, creating potpourri and other scented gift products. Their holiday stock had been delivered just before the hurricane and, of course, was wiped out. Still, the business grew nicely and survived Katrina for a while, but Denise eventually closed it down. By her own definition, she is a "worker bee." She was never a community activist and rarely participated in community activities outside of her church.

Katrina changed all that.

Denise's husband, Doug Thornton, manages the Superdome, built in the early 1970s—the world's largest steel constructed space unobstructed by posts or pillars. He and Denise evacuated to the dome, along with the thousands of people seen in TV footage after Katrina. While there, Denise volunteered in the special-needs area, where about five hundred mostly elderly and disabled evacuees were brought. "We operated on generator power, no windows, no sockets to charge cell phones or plug in fans or anything," she recalls. "When the power went out, we only had exit lights and glow sticks. I was helping bring people in and feed them. People would swim up or float up in things like an ice chest. The stench was unbearable. I felt so alone. I had a camera and my dog but no conversation. Doug was elsewhere. You start talking to yourself. I remember thinking that if I get out of here safely I promised God I would do something meaningful in my life."

After being there a week or so, Denise left the dome to live with her sister in Houma, sixty miles away. Before evacuees were officially allowed to return, she snuck into her neighborhood, walking along the railroad track that runs between Lakeview and Metairie. She hailed an ASPCA[14] boat that was out rescuing animals and got a ride to her house. Her 1970s two-story brick house with graceful columns up front was, needless to say, in shambles from the first-floor flooding. She came back with her husband on September 15, when they could drive in, to take out valuables. She started coming in at dawn each day to begin cleaning out the house. Alone, she experienced a new kind of trauma. "I was really alone," she recalls. "There were no crickets, frogs, not even mosquitoes" (an experience other returnees had described). "It was dead silent."

Denise grew up in a construction environment, the daughter of a lumberyard owner and builder. "I was not a girlie-girl growing up," she told me with a smile. After Katrina, she was ready to get to work. "I was so discouraged. I didn't know what I was doing, just randomly throwing out, gutting. I cried my eyes out, wishing I had the camaraderie of at least one female. I kept thinking if I could only get help. I knew it was not going to happen." But it did. Three people walked up—a husband, wife, and father. "They were fishermen, shrimpers, with construction experience. They offered help. They broke up the slate, hung sheet rock, painted for six weeks."

As work progressed, Denise started thinking of how the things she was learning could be helpful for others to know when they returned. She created a website in October 2005 and started posting "contractor tips." She told people to save their rugs and wood floors that came with twenty-year warrantees. She gave building-permit advice and answered questions for people walking by. By December 17, she had temporary emergency power—one socket—and was able to get even more done. Even though the Thorntons could not move back until full power was restored in March 2006, on Valentine's Day of that year Denise formally started the Beacon of Hope Rescue Center out of her house.

Denise was immediately inundated with people coming in to seek help. Ray Wooldridge, part owner of the NBA Hornets[15] and a friend of Denise, offered to help. With his $50,000 check, she bought lawn mowers, tools, and a pressure washer and started loaning them out. A subsequent grant from the Blue Moon Foundation in Charlottesville, Virginia, allowed Denise to hire an executive director. She put up a big sign with the words "Beacon of Hope" on it, received meals from the Red Cross, and gave visitors a tour of what she had accomplished.[16] "They figured if she could do it, they could," she said. "It was an oasis in the middle of utter destruction." As people used the services and got involved, she gave them signs to put in their front yards that read "Coming Back." A year later, Beacon of Hope had five centers around Lakeview and the adjacent neighborhood of Gentilly. Denise and her colleagues dispensed various types of assistance, including tool lending, and became a hub for visiting volunteers coming to help gut houses.

Denise looks back with appropriate satisfaction: "[Beacon of Hope] gave my life new meaning. When you're in the middle of it, you're driven by the feeling that you know you're changing the course of someone's life. It's almost an addiction to keep that feeling going. Although it was so hard, it was a magical time. I didn't have a plan, figured things out day by day. We didn't know what people's needs would be. We were very agile, providing cars, landscaping help, advice on cleaning, gutting, Road Home bureaucracy." It wasn't long before City Hall took note and Beacon representatives began to call there and get action. They focused on installing streetlights, getting rid of trailers, and dealing with blight issues. "We felt after three years that work should be going on, trailers should be gone, property should be maintained. We provided help for free."

• • •

During the tumultuous years after the storm and up to today, the lives of New Orleanians have been transformed. What happens to people in a crisis of this magnitude is unpredictable, among both the privileged and the unprivileged. Shawn channeled her rage into writing a blog, organizing a public demonstration, and fighting red tape on behalf of her whole family. Denise was determined to put her house and family back together and wound up initiating a self-help effort that spread well beyond Lakeview. And more recently another citizen-leader, LaToya Cantrell, found herself heading an effort she never would have imagined possible before the storms. She got ahead of city officials and made sure that it was her community's agenda that led the recovery of her neighborhood.

When LaToya won her seat on the City Council in 2012 after a hard fight with the city's political leadership, the first call she made was to Mitch Landrieu—the current mayor of New Orleans. LaToya, a woman of average height with short-cropped hair, and a patient listener who chooses her words carefully, had a well-earned reputation as a community activist who was unafraid to speak truth to power. The mayor had vigorously opposed her candidacy. With the mayor's help, her opponent raised a war chest three times as big as LaToya's. "You can't hold grudges," she explained over lunch in the spring of 2014, speaking with a clear firmness that serves her well. "It's not my style. But I had beaten the mayor's machine," she added with deliberate emphasis, exuding an energy and determination that one recognizes as critical for a determined activist. "I knew he didn't like to be beaten, so I called him first. 'Man, you tried to kill me,' I said. 'I did, but you won,' he answered."

No one, not even a mayor who famously does not like people to disagree with him, could underestimate the well-earned reputation LaToya had gained by leading the heavily flooded Broadmoor community in a post-Katrina comeback—one that has received national attention for its grassroots-generated rebuilding plan.

Broadmoor is in the heart of the city. Probably more than any other New Orleans neighborhood, it is a microcosm of the larger city, reflecting both its racial and economic diversity—68 percent African-Americans, 26 percent whites, and 48 percent homeowners.[17] Before Katrina, the neighborhood exhibited a high poverty rate of 31 percent, poorly performing schools, and many vacant properties. But the diversity of the neighborhood worked in Broadmoor's favor, LaToya explained, when the community needed to create the kind of partnerships among its residents that appealed to foundations and academics who would help in the recovery process. "Funders have to trust that you can get things done," she observes, noting that when *everybody* is represented at the table, truly listened to, community-wide acceptance and forward movement become more likely.

Like the Lower Nine and Lakeview, Broadmoor was submerged by Katrina. At an early point during the post-disaster planning process, this historic district with a pre-storm population of seven thousand was famously marked on a map with one of the green dots by Mayor Nagin's Bring New Orleans Back Committee, designating it as a prime candidate for partial conversion to a drainage park. "All hell broke loose when we saw that green dot over Broadmoor," recalled LaToya. There is nothing like the threat of demolition to galvanize and unify a neighborhood. "We immediately put up signs saying 'Broadmoor Lives' and mobilized in a big way." That became their mantra. Membership in the seventy-five-year-old Broadmoor Improvement Association (BIA) jumped from two hundred to six hundred after Katrina and became the primary vehicle for organizing the recovery.

Karl Seidman, senior lecturer in Economic Development at MIT, details the community process at the heart of Broadmoor's recovery in his book *Coming Home to New Orleans: Neighborhood Rebuilding After Katrina*. Despite its high poverty rate, he notes, "its residents were more stable—almost 61 percent lived in the same house in 1995 and 2000, and it had a lower incidence of vacant homes than the entire city."[18] Once part of the city's back swamps, Broadmoor had swelled into a lake during heavy rain, attracting fishermen. After drainage canals and early pumping stations were installed, development began. Boasting two streetcar lines, the 150-square-block area experienced a development boom in the 1920s. Today, the area is rich in Arts and Crafts bungalows, along with a heavy dose of Spanish Colonial, Mediterranean Revival, and classic shotgun houses—an assortment as varied as the population. A synagogue built in 1948 attracted a Jewish community that comprised an estimated 30 percent of Broadmoor's population in the 1950s and '60s. Closed in the 1990s, the synagogue now houses a Baptist congregation.[19]

Like other urban neighborhoods, Broadmoor started losing population to the suburbs during the 1950s and '60s. That was when the area experienced "blockbusting," a common phenomenon in cities nationwide whereby homeowners were scared into selling by real estate brokers warning that African-Americans were buying up homes and killing property values. Brokers would buy low from alarmed white owners and sell high to African-Americans. The Broadmoor Improvement Association, founded in the earliest years of home building, fought blockbusting and maintained the neighborhood's stability. It could easily have gone the other way. That same BIA rallied to save the community after Katrina.

LaToya had moved from Los Angeles to New Orleans in 1990 to attend Xavier University and then worked as manager of the Greater New Orleans Education Foundation. In 2000, she and her husband, Jason Cantrell, an attorney, bought a house in Broadmoor. LaToya's activist instincts were immediately energized. "I had never seen poverty like I saw here," she said. "It was so in your face. The needs were so great that any effort could have immediate impact." In her area of Broadmoor she founded the Louisiana Avenue Parkway Area Association to fight drug trafficking, slumlords, and speeding traffic. "I didn't see the BIA meeting the needs of our area," she said. LaToya organized one of the biggest neighborhood cleanups the city had ever seen. "This caught the attention of the BIA and they asked me to join the board," she added. "Things changed just by my being at the table."

In 2004, LaToya was elected BIA president. A year later came Katrina. From her evacuation point in Houston, LaToya tracked residents to see who was where, doing what, and planning to return. As Seidman observed:

> Broadmoor was better positioned than other flooded neigh-
> borhoods to attract residents back to the area. It is centrally
> located in New Orleans and was close to the non-flooded
> Garden District and Uptown neighborhoods, which gave resi-
> dents better access to stores and services. Broadmoor also had
> many homes with raised basements and two stories, which
> lessened the impact of flooding on living spaces and made it
> possible to start repair work on these homes more quickly.[20]

It didn't take long for energetic residents to spring into action, especially following the "green dot" fiasco. Rallies followed. Resident Virginia Saussy organized a demonstration to fight the BNOB plan, draped a large "Broadmoor Lives" banner on the front of her house, hired a brass band, and alerted the press. Three hundred residents signed a petition stating that they were returning, as a signal that not rebuilding Broadmoor was not an option.[21]

Soon after, early in 2006, another rally was held on the lawn of New Orleans native Walter Isaacson's father, Irwin Isaacson. Walter—former editor of *Time* magazine, a Harvard alumnus vice-chair of Governor Kathleen Blanco's Louisiana Recovery Authority, and current head of the Aspen Institute—would become an important link to the professional and funding sources that came to Broadmoor's assistance. At a BIA meeting early in 2006, resident Hal Roark proposed that the community come up with its own recovery plan. The BIA Board agreed. Out of that initiative came the nonprofit Broadmoor Development Corporation, with Roark as executive director.[22] Derelict properties were bought, renovated, and put on the market.

The community was fiercely determined to keep control of the recovery planning process, something all neighborhoods tried to do. And when help was offered from the outside, it was never accepted unless the community's control was guaranteed. The plan was completed by July 2006, less than a year after Katrina, and eventually accepted by the city. While the City Council was trying to develop its own rebuilding plan, recalls journalist and Broadmoor activist David Winkler-Schmit, the Council held a meeting to hear from the "wet" neighborhoods—the forty-nine out of seventy-three that had flooded. "Somehow," David told me with a laugh, "they forgot Broadmoor but LaToya showed up with a Broadmoor crowd and a bullhorn and we got heard."

At the heart of the recovery plan were some daunting projects, including the renovation of the badly flooded local school that reopened as a neighborhood-run charter school, the Andrew H. Wilson school; the renovation of a treasured library and community center housed in a spectacular Arts and Crafts mansion donated by the family of Rosa Freeman Keller, civil rights activist and library integration pioneer; and the establishment of a neighborhood health facility, South Broad Community Health. All of these goals were achieved.

The community's impressive accomplishments could not have come about without outside help, but it was help that responded to the successful organization of the community. Harvard University's Kennedy School of Government sent a team of students and staff to help research and draft the recovery plan and to give it the professionalism useful for gaining official and popular acceptance and following up implementation grants. This inaugurated a partnership that carried on for several years with the assistance of a $1 million grant from Shell Oil.[23]

The Clinton Global Initiative donated $5 million to fund the plan's implementation. The Carnegie Corporation gave $2 million for reconstruction, restocking, and refurnishing of the library and community center.[24] The flooded Andrew H. Wilson school was being looted, so the community, with the help of Bard College volunteers,[25] cleaned out and gutted the school, making it ready for reconstruction. Enough work was done so that when the Recovery School District designated one school to be rebuilt and reopened in each of the five council districts, Wilson was selected. And as initially planned, the spectacular Rosa F. Keller Library and Community Center embodies the neighborhood's spirit. Inside is the appealing, independently run coffee shop, the Green Dot Café—a clear reminder of the community's hard-won battle.

Yet the recovery plan was almost lost. Not long before LaToya wound up running for City Council, she caused an attention-getting fuss on behalf of Broadmoor. While Nagin was still mayor, the community had won a firm commitment of $1.2 million in public funds from the New Orleans Redevelopment Authority (NORA)[26] to implement the community's plan for the educational corridor plan. The community had leveraged that commitment to raise $15 million in private funds. But final city approval was needed from the mayor (by now Mitch Landrieu) and members of the City Council, who were trying to renegotiate the amount instead of just formalizing the commitment. "The city was dragging its feet," LaToya recalled. "Our private funding was about to fall apart and I was desperately trying to get the attention of the administration. The banks were pulling out. The city was using intimidation tactics and not doing its job. I was upset but respectful. Being the loudmouth that I was, I told them all I can kick ass barefoot, if I have to." She does not mince words.

Broadmoor got the funding and, in short order, the community gained a beautiful renovated school, a fabulous restored library (both of which some officials had said should be torn down), and a community health facility in a former bank. As David Winkler-Schmit observed during our conversation: "Usually in public-private partnerships, the lion's share of the money comes from the tax payer. In this case, the private share is much larger."

Beyond measure were the beneficial effects of regular BIA meetings, occasional potluck suppers, considerable neighbor-helping-neighbor activity, and the energizing impact of seeing things happening all around. A rebuilding guide entitled "I'm Back Now What?" was prepared and distributed by the BIA. The rebuilding slogan, "Broadmoor Lives," was put on bumper stickers, lamp posts, and lawn signs, the kind not normally seen except during elections. At one point, LaToya saw lights on in every house in the upper-income area of the neighborhood. It was "a key indicator that people were choosing to come back," she told me. "I knew Broadmoor had won the war."

What the successes of Lakeview and Broadmoor prove is that the most effective strategy for regenerating cities comes from the grassroots—and when it does, widespread acceptance and support within the community are assured. This strategy is implemented in communities all over the country but is rarely understood or recognized by local planning officials and city elites who insist that they are the experts. LaToya's explanation was quite straightforward: "We knew *we* were the world's greatest experts about our neighborhood."

Chapter 4

What Katrina Couldn't Destroy

New Orleans is irrepressible, and it has come back. Slowly, but with its soul intact.[1]

—Walter Isaacson, *American Sketches*

One of the charms of New Orleans is the surprising variation in size and individualized style of homes in so many neighborhoods. "You can't make a wrong turn in this city," observed a friend, marveling at how every block is different and equally interesting. Actually, wrong turns are the easiest things to make because of the city's crescent shape. The twists and turns of the Mississippi make this street grid one of the great challenges of urban America, defying normal compass-based directions.

Every turn reveals new discoveries and surprises: a small house among bigger ones, a big house among smaller ones, the corner store, a small factory, a restaurant tucked away in a residential district, the endless variety of small businesses. And, of course, the varied and splendid architecture. In its totality, New Orleans is a low-scale but dense cityscape of distinctive neighborhoods, each with its own personality, providing interest and delight to residents and visitors alike. It is urbanism at its best.

The overall look of the city is quite deceptive. An "illusion" is what former City Planning Director Kristina Ford called it during a conversation. New Orleans appears to be a city of mostly one-story, single-family houses. But many homes that one would assume are single family—whether shotguns or large Victorians—often actually contain one or more households. Some even have an extra small dwelling in the rear. In addition, as Kristina points out, scattered around seemingly single-family neighborhoods are small apartment houses of maybe three or four stories fitting comfortably among the predominantly smaller-scale dwellings. Combine this arrangement with the city's especially tight development pattern, whereby houses are barely a few feet from one another, and you end up with a density far greater than appears at first glance.

"This is a very intoxicating city," said Charleston-born architect Mac Ball. Mac told me that on his first visit during Mardi Gras in 1975, he knew he wanted to live here. "Part of the intoxication is the plan form, the radial geometry of the street grid," he added. "You have to pay attention in a new way when you move around the city. It makes you more aware of your environment. It's wonderfully confusing. There are no straight streets. It's very mysterious and made more interesting because grids collide."

Great cities have great grids: Paris, Rome, Washington, New York, London. They offer people and vehicles multiple options, adding a layer of convenience not possible with limited-access streets and highway driving. Miraculously, the crazy grid of New Orleans wasn't wiped out or drastically compromised in the 1950s and '60s by traffic engineers hell-bent on widening streets and narrowing sidewalks. Many American cities were hollowed out in this fashion. If ever there was an excuse to deviate from the grid—namely, those crescent curves—New Orleans had such an excuse and didn't take advantage of it. This street grid turns out to be one of the great secrets behind the city's charm and enduring urbanism. It is also a fascinating lesson for other cities to learn from, especially those that were taken in by Urban Renewal's false promises of building superblocks and erasing streets. These are the cities now struggling—like St. Louis, Buffalo, Tulsa, and San Antonio—to revive downtowns and neighborhoods that have more parking lots and empty spaces than buildings or reasons to visit. "New Orleans grew one neighborhood at a time along the oldest light-rail line in America," said land-use lawyer Bill Borah in an interview. "The neighborhoods were often mixed income and definitely mixed use. When planners come in to tell us about models for development, I say the best model for New Orleans is New Orleans itself."

After the storms, this tight grid of mostly short blocks served the recovery momentum well. A short block with only a few houses does not look as hopeless as a superblock with only one or two dwellings. On the short blocks, one occupied house was often enough to encourage the next resident to rebuild—and so it went from there. The fact that many of those blocks still have one or two unoccupied houses has not slowed down the return of neighbors.

Not that New Orleans escaped Urban Renewal, highway building, and wasteful, speculative demolition for parking lots entirely—or that it avoids this problematic tradition in the present. But, broadly speaking, the city wiped out a chunk of its central business district in the 1950s for a new train station,[2] a modernist City Hall complex, and blocks of parking lots that become full only for events at the Superdome. Unfortunately, parking lots or recent new apartments now sit where some of the most significant early history of jazz took place.

Before the Civil War, New Orleans, besides being the infamous center of the slave trade, was one of the richest cities in the United States. It was spared the destruction that so many southern cities experienced during the Civil War because it capitulated early. After the Civil War and Reconstruction, the city exploded in new growth with shipping on the Mississippi. The years from 1880 to 1920 marked the height of that expansion. This is the city most visible today outside the French Quarter. Throughout the 1920s, New Orleans was still the richest city in the South and remained so until World War II, when it was deemed the largest and fastest-growing southern city. Some splendid 1920s-style bank towers are now pricey condos.

In the oil bust of the 1980s, the dramatic exodus of corporations and employees pulled the rug out from the New Orleans economy. It was primarily the lack of money that averted further Urban Renewal mistakes (until the present, as we will see later). Many people in New Orleans attribute this lucky happenstance to an inherent conservatism among the bankers and moneyed class of the city. "New Orleans is an ultra-conservative city," one businessman told me. "That is what saved it. Banks wouldn't lend money and politicians couldn't get their act together. Only simple interventions succeeded. So much context is left here that a unified quality survives." When banks did loan, they loaned only to blue bloods.

The late Savannah civic leader Lee Adler explained a similar pattern in that city's history: "Savannahians resisted Urban Renewal as a Communist plot."[3] Some of this same instinct saved New Orleans as well, and explains why, today, the past lives comfortably with the present.

Theories abound as to why New Orleans has held on to so much of itself, perhaps more than any other city. Mac Ball offered an interesting perspective: "When New Orleans was settled, it was divorced from any other urban area. Here it is at the end of the river. The nearest city was Houston, a cow town, or Atlanta [a depot city originally]. The house forms and buildings are found nowhere else in America. The influence came mostly from the Caribbean. New Orleans continued to exist by itself. The eccentricities became pronounced and not affected by elsewhere." More common theories tie New Orleans's economic and land development patterns to its unique societal structure: decisions about what city-changing projects to take forward emanated from a closed circle of insiders for whom protecting the status quo was a key goal.

At the center of the city's wealth and power were the exclusive luncheon clubs dating back to its earliest days. An individual had no social standing among the elite without membership in one of them, and all the money in the world could not buy membership.

As Randy Fertel notes:

> Club members ran the city. . . . The undemocratic, aristocratic traditions of colonial France and Spain shaped New Orleans's social structure. When newly prosperous Americans built their mansions in the Garden District, they modeled themselves on a society stratified by parentage rather than merit, a society of exclusion, not inclusion. The blue-blood members of the Rex and Comus Krewes, of the Boston and Pickwick Clubs, led the southern resistance to Reconstruction in the 1870s and resistance again to integration in the 1950s and 1960s.[4]

And as *Times-Picayune* columnist James Gill writes: "New Orleans was largely untouched by the rapid industrialization that elsewhere wiped out the social customs of the 18th century."[5] When big corporations moved to New Orleans over the years, the CEOs of these companies expected to be warmly welcomed into the social hierarchy, as they were in other cities. Not in New Orleans. During the big oil boom of the 1970s, all the major companies had offices here. New towers went up along Poydras Street. But in the '84 crash, it didn't take much for oil executives to move their offices to Houston, though it is impossible to know how much of an impact the social issue had. The importance of the clubs took a backseat during the recovery after Katrina. Shell Oil is celebrated in New Orleans as the one that stayed and supported the city. In terms of measuring a city's economy, it is unclear whether the absence of big corporations truly undermines a city's economy, as conventionally thought.

New Orleanian Jews also experienced exclusion, despite the many generations of their forebears who declared the city home and the expansiveness of their inherited wealth. This gave rise to the awkward tradition whereby wealthy Jewish citizens went on ski trips with their families during Mardi Gras to avoid the embarrassment of not being invited to one of the balls. Ironically, Randy Fertel pointed out, "Jews had been founding members of the Boston Club, and in 1871 Louis Solomon, the first Rex [King of Carnival] was Jewish (though, some argue, a fully assimilated Jew)," yet by the twentieth century they were excluded. Even the dashing young Baron Edmond James de Rothschild, who had been welcomed in the royal courts of Europe, was not invited to New Orleans's balls.

"It's not how much money you have, it's who your daddy was," a New Orleanian friend once told me. By definition, this tradition narrows the loop within which new, bold, and innovative ideas can take hold. "Venture capital is hard to come by in a society built on simply protecting inherited wealth," one resident observed. And as James Gill told me, "There's no innovative thinking." But he went on to ask: "Is that a symptom or a cause? Decline was inevitable. The old advantage of controlling everything that went in or out of the Mississippi valley diminished. We were overtaken by Atlanta and Houston." Then he laughed, not wanting me to think he meant that becoming Atlanta or Houston is something to aspire to, and said: "At least we have a funky city. The question is, Can you have both? The answer is no." Perhaps this is true; but my feeling is that there needn't be a choice between the corporate city and the lively funky city unless creative economic thinking is truly absent.

Before Katrina and Rita, the club-based, behind-closed-doors decision process was largely left unchallenged. Some observers believe the grip is loosening. But, since the storms, many big decisions—the closing of Charity Hospital, streetcar extension routes, the demolition of public housing, the fate of the I-10 elevated highway—are still being made out of public view and without a public process. Public meetings provide an illusion of public influence but are really about public comment, *not* public input. The grip of the city elites may be loosening, but it is still very much there.

• • •

Many cultures came together to shape New Orleans's spectacular architecture, yet the richness and breadth of this architectural legacy are not widely recognized. The French Quarter with its mix of French and Spanish influences (mostly Spanish because a massive fire in 1794 destroyed much that the French had built), the wrought-iron balconies and ornate cornices, the densely filled shotgun and double-galleried neighborhoods with their endless variety of Greek Revival, Italianate, and Creole cottages—all of this architectural diversity gives credence to the common observation that New Orleans is the only European or Caribbean city in the United States. Indeed, waves of immigrants—Alsatians, Croatians, Italians, the Irish, and German Jews—left their mark on the city's landscape.

Much of the city was rundown even before Katrina and Rita: crooked walls, peeling paint, and half-broken shutters were more or less accepted as part of the landscape. Purity of conditions now mix comfortably with frayed elegance in most parts of town— "the tattered fringes," as Dorothy Parker described the Garden District when it had turned seedy. But beyond the French Quarter and the Garden District are neighborhood after neighborhood full of architectural gems. Walter Isaacson describes the city as a whole as a "distinctive mix that makes even the uncelebrated neighborhoods of New Orleans so seductive."[6] In a conversation with me right after Katrina, Reed Kroloff, formerly the dean of the School of Architecture at Tulane University, asserted that "New

Orleans—along with San Francisco—has the greatest collection of eighteenth-, nineteenth-, and early-twentieth-century residential architecture in the United States." And as Mac Ball put it: "We're talking about miles and miles and miles of historic properties. The shotgun is the brick of New Orleans, beautifully simple, sustainable, high ceilings, floor raised off the ground to let air circulate underneath [as well as tall windows and doors with shutters to let breezes flow through]. Every house has a unique mask, an architectural veil, a public face, and a public space. Everyone has a front stoop or a porch."

Clearly, the three-hundred-year-old city has a texture and an exuberance seen in no other American metropolis. Every cornice, every ornamental detail, every roofline and front porch is different from every other in its arrangement of elements, selection of detail, and paint scheme. And so many are handcrafted with singular individual touches.

Adding to its uniqueness is the fact that New Orleans personifies author Jane Jacobs's definition of *mixed use*. Jacobs is considered one of the most important urban thinkers of the twentieth century, and her ideas are what many urban planners, developers, and designers aspire to. Jacobs observed that the presence of mixed primary uses were the necessary condition for successful streets and neighborhoods. In her classic *The Death and Life of Great American Cities,* she writes:

> The district, and indeed as many of its internal parts as possible, must serve more than one primary function; preferably more than two. These must insure the presence of people who go outdoors on different schedules and are in the place for different purposes, but who are able to use many facilities in common.[7]

Today, *mixed use* is conventionally defined as residential, retail, and commercial. That is an oversimplification. Jacobs's definition was much broader. Primary uses were varied and intricately connected. All could serve as "anchorages" such as dwellings; offices; factories; certain places of entertainment, education, and recreation; and some but not all museums, libraries, and galleries. Her definition, she explained, was conditioned by scale and design—namely, a scale that does not overpower its neighborhood and a design that keeps it integrated and not isolated from it.

New Orleans is rich in mixed-use neighborhoods that meet this description. Schools, churches, libraries, occasional galleries and small stores, cafés and restaurants, bars and music venues, and small factories are scattered in residential communities all over town, exhibiting a scale comfortable with their neighbors. A more specific example is that the popular single-screen movie house located in an upscale, uptown residential neighborhood has no designated parking lot; cars park throughout nearby streets, and people walk to the theater or take the St. Charles streetcar, which is just a few short blocks away. The vast number of locally owned businesses is astonishing. They survive despite the full measure of available big-box stores. More big boxes keep coming as the city government inappropriately keeps offering incentives that make it even more difficult for the local stores to compete and survive. At the end of 2013, Mayor Landrieu boasted of seeing sixty-one new retail stores open during his tenure, almost all of them national big-box chains.[8]

New Orleans is one of the few cities in the country that have not lost their corner-store tradition. And while many of those corner stores have long been out of business, both before and after Katrina, the City Planning Commission is wisely honoring the desire of certain neighborhoods to let them be revived, as entrepreneurs seek to reactivate those spaces. Slowly but surely they are being reopened as new businesses.[9] The corner store was an integral part of the evolution of American cities. With its commercial use at street level and its housing use above, the corner store served a nearby residential population and was often the business of an immigrant family where several relatives shared responsibility. For new arrivals especially, it served a multitude of financial, familial, and space needs. But more so than commercial ventures and family residences, corner stores were invariably the gathering place of the community, the local hangout, the physical anchor around which everything else took place. And while a streetcar was most likely available a short walk away, giving access to downtown, the corner store was the neighborhood staple for a primarily pedestrian society.

The 1920s and the emerging era of the automobile began to change all that. Modest-scale local chain stores were slow to compete. After World War II, the national focus turned toward reliance on the burgeoning car industry to convert the economy from a military to a domestic one. Federal funding of interstate highways and suburban development followed. Chains got bigger and the local stores suffered. In fact, some corner stores turned into chains. The corner stores withered in use and in many places were torn down along with the neighborhoods they served. Most urban zoning codes were fatally adjusted to total accommodation of the car, providing for vast parking lots and big stores. In many cities, however, one can spot the leftover corner store, either empty or converted to residential use.

Here again, New Orleans escaped the wipeout of an important urban form—one that contributes to its uniqueness. Corner stores in the form of delis, restaurants, clothing boutiques, food marts, antique shops, and bakeries are continuously reemerging here. Yet despite their economic, social, and urban value, corner stores are rarely found in new developments seeking to create "new neighborhoods." Financial institutions that fund these new developments won't allow them, even when an enlightened developer knows their value. They don't fit the formula of the financiers.

Beyond the corner store there are a number of small, Main Street–style commercial neighborhoods—Oak, Freret, and Maple Streets uptown, Louisa in the Marigny, Oretha Castle Haley Boulevard in Central City—where a seamstress, shoemaker, and laundry can still be found among clothing stores, hardware stores, and small restaurants and cafés. On-street parking seems to be sufficient for most of these establishments, especially since many of the nearby houses date from the early automobile era of the 1920s, with driveways to the side and the front door still oriented toward the street. Older buildings were not built with driveways at all and are closer together.

World-famous Magazine Street is a national treasure, a remarkable six-mile stretch that, like the rule-defying traffic patterns of the city streets, contradicts many assumptions about shopping streets. It has rebounded in full force since the storms and serves as the model for shorter, more localized streets where rents are lower. It is the largest of the local shopping streets, passing through several different neighborhoods and attracting shoppers from out of town as well. This shopping street evolved without big plans, large developers, or cookie-cutter formulas.

In the 1950s and '60s, when the car became more important than the pedestrian, many cities turned their primary shopping streets one-way—yet another of those mid-century trends intended to speed car traffic, to which New Orleans did not succumb. Only minutes from the central business district, Magazine is a two-way traffic street with only one lane each way, giving the street an intimate feel. Metered parking spaces line both sides. Pedestrians cross comfortably. Cars coming from the side streets edge across carefully without the help of traffic lights. Major thoroughfares with traffic lights cross at half-mile intervals. These are the signature New Orleans boulevard-like streets with two lanes of traffic each way separated by a median—the "neutral ground," which is landscaped differently in each neighborhood. In its entirety, Magazine Street epitomizes what Jacobs describes as a "close grained diversity of uses that give each other constant mutual support, both economically and socially."[10]

A post-Katrina rebirth of neighborhood streets beyond Magazine is noticeable everywhere in New Orleans. St. Claude in the

Marigny and the Bywater is attracting small, funky art galleries and similarly small entertainment venues.[11] Harrison Avenue in Lakeview and Oak and Maple Streets uptown have all recovered nicely. Freret—in bad shape before Katrina and known for prostitution, empty storefronts, and drugs—was transformed into a lively, vibrant fourteen-block area, with dog-grooming entrepreneur Michelle Ingram spurring the robust revival. She worked hard to organize property owners and the community to improve conditions.

Oretha Castle Haley Boulevard was named in the 1990s after the Louisiana civil rights leader in an effort to turn around the deterioration of the street that had been occurring since the residential out-migration undermined this once-thriving commercial corridor. Formerly known as Dryades Street, it evolved from the mid-nineteenth century with a robust concentration of African-American businesses ranging from life insurance companies to retail stores. By the 1930s, with an additional concentration of East European Jewish immigrants who operated clothing and furniture establishments, Dryades had become a shopping and entertainment alternative to the racist Canal Street where the main-line department stores clustered. Here, on Oretha Castle Haley Boulevard, black residents could try on clothes, which they were not allowed to do on Canal.

In 1998, author and entrepreneur Carol Bebelle and visual artist Douglas Redd founded the Ashe Cultural Center in the former Kaufman's Department Store. This nonprofit arts center was an anchor already in place that, after Katrina, helped initiate a gradual revival of the street's arts and entertainment legacy in what was the heart of an historic black neighborhood. "We create programs and theater," Carol told me, "that help raise consciousness and help us see ourselves in a more objective state. When we see onstage the issues we are grappling with—whether race, violence against women, or literacy—it leads to new understanding. Down the street is the Zeitgeist Theater, an art gallery, and Café Reconcile, which trains young people for the restaurant industry.

Ten years after Katrina, this hub is seeing new additions regularly, such as the Tulane City Center in the former Kaufman's Department Store and the Southern Food and Beverage Museum. A parallel renewal project is the Felicity Street Development (FSD), a not-for-profit preservation effort spearheaded by New Orleans native Louise Martin. Starting in 1998, FSD has bought, renovated, and resold more than fifty properties along the O. C. Haley corridor, recruiting new homeowners and businesses to the area.

All of these varied streets reflect the steady comeback of a flooded city, but what has received the biggest welcome and represented the biggest vote of confidence in the city's future is the opening of significant food emporiums. Famously expensive Whole Foods opened in a former streetcar barn in the Uptown area. But Langenstein's, the oldest full-service grocery store in New Orleans (starting as a corner store) and fifth-generation family-owned, had already reopened with little fanfare. Langenstein's is just one of the many locally owned businesses that either survived Katrina or opened soon after, long before major chains entered the picture.

Michael Langenstein, the founder, was a truck farmer in the Uptown neighborhood when he opened the first corner store in the 1920s "as a way for his two sons to make a living," according to Michael Lanaux—a great grandson, who with his brother has owned and operated this store since 1991 and a suburban store in nearby Metarie since 1994. "There's a lot of family pride here," Michael said in an interview. "I grew up down the block and was exposed to the business from birth, starting as a bagger when I was a kid." He and his family grew up with many of the customers, and thus the relationships are personal. Since Langenstein's has never asked for the kind of tax or development benefits that the city has lavished on out-of-state-owned big boxes since the storms, Michael explained, he doesn't feel the obvious lack of a level playing field. "Those stores are just smarter than the city," he chuckles. "I don't blame them. They don't need those breaks but they know they can get them, so why wouldn't they?"

The 2012 opening of Rouse's supermarket, a Louisiana chain, at the edge of the Warehouse District was a clear signal that the momentum of downtown's residential population post-Katrina was on the rise. Of even greater significance was the restoration of the iconic, locally black-owned Circle Food Store, since 1938 a treasured resource for the 7th Ward black community at a central location at the corner of Claiborne and St. Bernard Avenues. A distinctive white stucco building with a round cupola and red tiles on the roof and an arched arcade around it, the Circle miraculously survived the neighborhood destruction caused by the construction of the I-10 in the 1960s, as well as eight feet of Katrina water. Eight years and multiple grants from different levels of government later, Circle Foods reopened in 2014 and is once again an anchor for the black community.

Fortunately, none of these neighborhood shopping streets or singular stores seem to be losing a battle against suburban chains. That could change as city leaders continue to fall for the illusory benefits of superstores like Walmart, Costco, and Target, all of which have discovered New Orleans since Katrina. The city tax incentives these companies receive are unavailable to small local entrepreneurs, and they always promise more jobs than they ever deliver (at minimum part-time wages).

Many civic and business leaders are dismissive of the importance of the local economy. The strength of the local economy of New Orleans—with its impressive mixture of local businesses—is never officially measured and is consistently undervalued by pro-corporate civic and business leaders. Ask any of them what the impact of local businesses is and they will either profess ignorance, say it is too small to matter, or refer you to Dana Eness, director of Stay Local—if they even know about this useful organization.

Stay Local is a nonprofit program of the Urban Conservancy that brings attention to the importance of local businesses and works to keep them stable and growing. It connects local, independent businesses to resources, new markets, and each other.

Quantifying the local economy defies easy statistical measurements, Dana explained to me. City records, she added, are poor and scattered. Various studies around the country, however, have shown time and again the larger financial and job-creation benefit of investment in local businesses over chain stores. This reality, however, never seems to have an impact on local development policies.

In 2009 the Urban Conservancy engaged an Austin strategic planning firm, Civic Economics, in a New Orleans study referred to as "Thinking Outside the Box." This was an expansion of research begun in 2002 that evaluated the comparative economic impact of local businesses and their chain competitors. Prior studies had shown that locally owned businesses generate as much as two to three times the local economic activity as chains. The new study compared the recirculation of dollars in the local economy by fifteen Magazine Street merchants with that of a large general-merchandise store such as a SupercenterTarget. The merchandise offerings were comparable.

The findings were stunning:

> The study shows that local retailers, when compared to leading chain competitors, generate twice the annual sales, recirculate revenue within the local economy at twice the rate, and, on a per square foot basis, have four times the economic impact. Investing in locally owned businesses is a cost-effective way to grow the New Orleans economy and is compatible with development patterns in existing commercial districts.[12]

Bear in mind that the average SupercenterTarget, which occupies 179,000 square feet in one concentrated traffic-collecting place, achieved sales of $282.51 per square foot, yielding a total annual store revenue of approximately $50 million; in contrast, the participating Magazine Street businesses reported total sales per square foot of $587. It follows that 179,000 spread-out square feet of

Magazine Street businesses would generate an estimate of $105 million in annual sales across as many as one hundred individual stores. Total recirculation of dollars in the local economy was 16 percent for Target and 32.1 percent for Magazine businesses. Studies examining local businesses elsewhere in the country reveal similar findings.[13]

The study also addressed an important land-use consideration, one with particular significance for New Orleans's dominant grid. Whereas Magazine Street merchants mostly utilize on-street parking, a SupercenterTarget (like other superstores) requires roughly 300,000 square feet just for parking—nearly seven acres in a surface-parking configuration. One would think this kind of study would generate policies favoring local retailers and avoid excessive tax breaks and zoning concessions for big boxes, but unfortunately not.

The ongoing strength of the local economy, despite the two hurricanes, is observable in ways that statistics and studies can't show. "Just look at our ads, all local and no nationals," said Clancy DuBos, political editor of *Gambit,* a weekly local news magazine with a circulation of forty thousand that is distributed free to outlets all over the city. Restaurants, stores, services, movies, and much more are reflected in the ads. "We are a true barometer of the local economy. Our biggest year was 2007 before the economy declined but we have never lost money." The *Gambit* ad lineage seems to reflect the state of the local economy: "Local businesses watch every dollar," Clancy told me. "They don't spend easily and certainly not when business is bad."

Clancy described an instance involving the *Gambit*'s managing editor, Kandace Graves, and the resumption of its publishing activities nine weeks after Katrina. Graves and her family were having breakfast at a local eatery. "It was a Monday," Clancy said, "and *Gambit* always hits the stands on Monday. In the middle of breakfast, the *Gambit* delivery arrived for the first time since the storm and everyone around them cheered. The newspaper is part of the cultural fabric, a habit like red beans and rice." For everyone there, it was a sign of post-Katrina recovery and renewal.

• • •

The physical uniqueness of New Orleans and the enduring charm that accompanies it go beyond the city's architecture and culture. Indeed, transportation is also key: the lifeblood of urbanism. Streets, traffic, and streetcars combine in New Orleans in a way different from other American cities. Most significantly, elements of this traffic and transportation system defy the experts. Everything that professional transportation planners say can't happen not only happens here but works well and explains why the city is so pleasant to be in and to maneuver around. My favorite is the network of narrow streets. Most of the city's traditional neighborhoods, the ones developed in the nineteenth century up to World War II, have streets that are just about wide enough for three and a half cars. Yet, contrary to every transportation rulebook, most of these streets are two-way. In some neighborhoods, where one-way streets dominate, two-way streets are placed at occasional intervals.

But here's what makes New Orleans unique: parking is allowed on *both* sides. What this does to traffic is amazing. To say it "calms" traffic is an understatement. When two cars are coming from opposite directions without enough room to pass each other, one or the other simply pulls over slightly, usually in either an empty parking space or a free space in front of a driveway. No competition ensues. It is an unspoken custom that people seem to embrace easily, usually with a wave and a smile as the two cars slowly pass each other. This is a rare, car-based politeness. Of course, New Orleans has major avenues that serve as both shopping and residential corridors. None are without occasional traffic lights. Only one of these thoroughfares has six lanes, with three heading in each direction.

The wisdom of the surviving street grid offers drivers multiple opportunities to turn at specific destinations, spreading traffic out, never overloading particular streets and neighborhoods with traffic passing through that occurs when roads limit access. In this way, traffic is totally dispersed, concentrated in only a few places at rush hour. The I-10 and 610 highways attract the heavy traffic and daily tie-ups despite the tremendous capacity on city thoroughfares. This is how an effective urban grid works. Many streets change direction at certain points, making them useless as through-streets and guaranteeing destination-only traffic. This long-standing arrangement is being adopted in many forward-thinking cities; it is now called "traffic calming."

What makes all of these conditions remarkable is that New Orleans is actually a very car-dependent city. True, the biking population continues to grow. Yes, many people live within walking distance of certain destinations and amenities, minimizing their need to drive everywhere. And, yes, the limited-service streetcars are a treasure, as is the limited bus service. But the car remains the essential mode for getting around. A taxi infrastructure exists, too, so it is possible—especially if you are going into the French Quarter—to leave the car home and take a taxi. But again, New Orleans is like no other car-dependent city. The grid allows traffic to be widely dispersed and avoids a congestion burden.

New Orleans is one of the few American cities that did not lose all of its streetcars, even though it lost all but one before Katrina. That streetcar today is a distinguishing "picture postcard" feature of the Crescent City, but instead of serving as the foundation for rebuilding a more transit-dependent city, it is almost a toy—an unreliably slow one at that, there to serve tourists, the elderly, and sometimes students. Without dependable and expanding transit, New Orleans is becoming more car-dependent just when most cities across the country are gradually becoming less car-dependent. Car dependency erodes the vibrancy of urban downtowns. This observation is embraced elsewhere but not taken seriously here. Post-Katrina federal transit funding was not invested wisely in New Orleans, at least not to the benefit of residents for whom it could be an alternative to the car.

Consider for a moment how important streetcars were in the tight, walkable development pattern that evolved in all American communities in the late nineteenth and early twentieth centuries. Streetcar suburbs were the earliest developments spreading out from all the growing downtowns.[14] Developers often built the lines to service the new housing they were building. Most houses were within a fifteen-minute walk from the streetcar. The thriving Garden District, home to the St. Charles Streetcar, is a classic example of this.

New Orleans had multiple streetcar lines, with neighborhoods up and down the river evolving along them. Across the country, these neighborhoods evolved in similar organic patterns. The distinguishing features are visible today: tree-lined streets, tightly developed houses, an occasional small apartment house of a compatible scale, a local business, small front yards, and driveways at the side of houses.

During World War II, trolleys and streetcars reached their highest use. But by war's end, all systems were overused and in disrepair. After the war, dismantling—instead of repair—began.[15] Mass transit disappeared from most downtowns; the purposeful reconfiguration of the landscape to accommodate the automobile gained full speed. The automobile, steel, and other rubber tire–related industries conspired to remove streetcars and trolleys to make way for rubber tire vehicles, highways, and auto production.[16] This trend overtook New Orleans, with one exception: the St. Charles line.

In 1962, the streetcars came off of Canal. Jack Stewart—an urbanist, passionate preservationist, brilliant historian of all things New Orleans, and professional contractor—recalls fighting bitterly to avert this loss. "I fought for two and a half years to save it," he told me. "I was in junior high. I produced a slide show for the City Council to show why it should be saved. I borrowed a slide projector and bought a $35 camera in a pawn shop. A Save the Streetcar group coalesced around me." They lost. But finally, forty years later in 2002, the campaign was revived and the fight continued. The Regional Plan Association wanted a new line on Poydras, a parallel street of high-rise office buildings, instead of the former location on Canal.

The 150th Anniversary of the New Orleans St. Charles Streetcar—the oldest continuously operating line in the world—was celebrated in 1985.[17] But this did nothing to bring about the realization that an expanded streetcar system should be a convenience and travel source for local residents, rather than tourists. A Riverfront extension was built for the 1988 Republican Convention but was of no use to residents. "I argued until I was blue in the face," Jack recalled, "that this would do nothing for the residents of the city. Supposedly, it was considered to be part of the revitalization of Canal." In truth, the revitalization of Canal began after Katrina, and the Convention Center spur did nothing to facilitate this process. Historic department store buildings were adapted to hotels, and some old hotels were revived and upgraded. Downtown buildings are continually being renovated and repurposed.

After Katrina, it took three years to bring back the flooded Canal streetcar line—clearly not a transportation priority. In July 2009, the city privatized its entire transit system. The Regional Transportation Authority contracted with Veolia, a French transportation company, to run the system. This did nothing to advance a more public-transit-focused city policy.

The most effective streetcar lines run on dedicated traffic lanes, trigger stoplights to turn green, and follow a reliable schedule. Most modern lines also include a pre-pay system to facilitate passenger boarding. But when it came time to add the next leg to the streetcar after Katrina, again the tourist was the priority and widely accepted efficiency standards were ignored. Critics insisted that connecting the Canal Street line to the little-used Union

Passenger Terminal along Loyola Avenue was of minimum value; the real need, they argued, was to extend the Canal Street line out to the neighborhoods of Marigny and Bywater, which were experiencing an unparalleled post-Katrina regeneration. Officials claimed, however, that the Loyola Street line had won a competitive Federal Transportation grant of $45 million based on 2010 engineers' estimates and would cost taxpayers nothing.[18]

If the resident population were more important than tourists, this would not have been the first submission. Of course, unexpected conditions and the usual reasons for expensive change orders raised the final price tag of more than $60 million, as David Hammer of *Eyewitness News WWLTV* reported in the spring of 2014.[19] Hammer also noted that the extra $15 million was coming out of a "$75 million pot of local bond and reserve money that was originally set aside to extend the Loyola spur" along Rampart, at the northern edge of the French Quarter, to the neighborhoods of Marigny and Bywater. The loss of the $15 million now meant that the extension will go only past the Marigny and not into the Bywater—yet another clear sign that residents' needs come second to those of tourists.

Transit ridership has diminished over the years, Jack pointed out. "In the early 1960s," he added, "New Orleans's local travel was 75 percent transit and 25 percent automobile. By the mid-1970s, the split was 50/50. By the late 1970s, the split flipped back to 75/25 in favor of transit. Now, it is 88 percent car, 12 percent transit. Before Katrina it was still 75 percent transit, 25 percent car."

What makes this bad situation worse is that ridership claims on the Loyola line have been inflated through changes in the larger system. Some bus routes have been shortened, forcing riders to switch to the streetcar to get all the way downtown. Some riders have ceased making the trip by transit altogether. "What we're doing," transit advocate Rachel Heiligman told Hammer, "is really just shifting the ridership from one mode—the bus—to the streetcar."

Cities all over the country—Dallas, Salt Lake City, Los Angeles, Denver, and many more—are re-creating piece by piece the streetcar system they once had. Accompanying those re-creations are new investment and economic activity. Either by luck or sheer resistance to change, New Orleans did not lose the whole system, but recognition of its potential value has yet to be officially recognized.

From the street grid to the streetcar, from the architecture to the network of local and corner stores, New Orleans's urbanism is indeed unique. Katrina damaged but could not destroy this distinctiveness, and so far, the people of New Orleans are trying hard not to let official policies and new agendas do the job instead.

Chapter 5

The Bells Keep Ringing

New Orleans' culture is of a piece. You can't really lose one
part of it without losing the whole thing.

—Tom Piazza, *Why New Orleans Matters*[1]

G iven all that makes New Orleans unique, all the richness of
the architecture, music, food, and culture, one would expect
the presence of a fierce protectionist bent—a public and a set of
policies that would do everything possible to ensure that new
development does not erase historic buildings. But this is not the
case. In fact, a fierce protectionist bent is stunningly absent from
official and socially prominent circles. Each preservation conflict
is a battle. And given all that the floods ruined or severely damaged, one might expect a new and deeper appreciation for what
still exists. Also not true. "New Orleans doesn't have the fight in
it of a Greenwich Village," observed an ardent preservationist.
"It is death by a million nibbles with considerable neighborhood
erosion, made worse by Katrina." A more cynical view holds that
much of New Orleans's history survives because no one has sought
to demolish it, yet. "Preservation by neglect"—a phrase long used
in the preservation field.

Enter Karen Gadbois, a weaver turned award-winning journalist and staunch preservationist—an extraordinary example of the many local citizen-activists without whom New Orleans would be in terrible shape since Katrina. Karen became an activist in the typical way—she got angry. After Katrina she observed innumerable houses being needlessly demolished, so she started a blog to document what she was discovering. She pored over FEMA's demolition lists, ferreted out buried information from hard-to-locate city files, drove around taking pictures, and put all of her findings on the website. In particular, she uncovered official plans to expropriate and demolish the homes of people who were unaware of the impending situation; these residents were either planning to rebuild or in the process of doing so but had yet to return after the storms. She discovered homes being demolished by the city that were not flooded nor badly damaged. And she found houses untouched that contractors claimed were being fixed up with public funds they had collected. In fact, contractors had billed the city for gutting work done by volunteers as well as for "remediation" of houses that they then got paid to demolish.

Karen was essentially a newcomer, having moved to the city with her artist husband and young daughter from Mexico in 2002. The outsider's passion for local heritage is a common phenomenon in many cities, New Orleans included. New residents take nothing for granted, unlike longtime residents, and their sense of appreciation for what exists is often sharper. They have a certain naiveté about how things work and are not as reluctant to advocate for preservation. Karen's understanding of historic preservation and identity goes to the heart of what it means to have a real attachment to a place, and to appreciate what exists while accommodating appropriate change. In November 2008, she posted this personal story on her website:

> In 1988 I moved to a small village in Mexico. The church which is located in the main square defines the town itself.

It is a compass and a gathering spot. . . . The original was built in 1683 and completed by Zeferino Gutierrez in 1880, inspired by postcards from Europe.

My husband's family had moved there in 1968 when there were 6,000 people. By the time I came, the population was 25,000. It was still a small and very personal space. Most everyone at some point in the day met in the park which faced this Church. On Sunday young men and women parade counter-clockwise in the square in a courtship dance and each hour of the day was marked with a manual tolling of the bells.

One day the bells began to ring and did not stop. After a full half hour of calamitous ringing I walked to the square to see what was going on. When I arrived I saw a small Bobcat and a crowd of furious residents. It seems that the City government had decided that a lower portion of the Church property should be demolished to build a new sales area for street vendors.

The bells continued to ring and people kept coming. There was no talk about "historic" preservation, instead the talk was about identity—about ownership and pride and self determination. It was about a spatial connectedness that would not be destroyed that day. The citizens prevailed, the Bobcat left and officials figured out how to get the space they wanted and not destroy one tiny bit of the Church. I always find myself caught in this narrow confine of historical preservation when it is a much larger social and political issue. If we, the citizens, are not given the most basic voice in issues of self-determination, how will we see ourselves?[2]

Historic preservation concerns so much more than saving a single architectural treasure, as Karen's story illustrates. By tolling the bells through her website, she brought people together to resist thoughtless public policies, to force attention to cultural and social values, and to demand citizen input in shaping her village's future. Today, Karen waxes equally poetic about New Orleans:

> This city is visually lyrical. To walk along the street, the more attention you pay, the more is revealed, the more you see. At first you just see a bunch of pretty old houses but each neighborhood reveals itself in a nuanced way, also lyrical. Each has its own signature. Each is different because of the human touch. You notice how each house catches the breezes differently, how the rooflines sometimes adjust to fit into a tight space. This is such a physically democratic city that you see not just where people live but how they live, how they concentrate life in the front of the house, congregate on the front porch. That's why I call New Orleans a "chattering" city. People face the community. You see them being talky, chatty, a very social city.

This emphasis on the front of houses leads to what many local residents identify as "keeping up with appearances." If you are short of funds, you simply paint the front of the house, your highly valued face to the community.

As Karen was growing up, weaving and printing were her primary interests; she commuted to Massachusetts College of Art in Boston, the first public school in the country dedicated to art. In the 1980s, she drove to Mexico "to study textile design, soak up the culture, and learn Spanish." There she met her husband, Jon Schooler, an American painter living in Mexico. They loved to travel together. One trip took them through New Orleans. Karen was convinced that at some point they would move here. When their daughter, Aida, was in seventh grade, they did just that.

In 2002, the family moved into a raised cottage in New Orleans with a colorful decor reflective of their artistic talent and taste. The house contains many intriguing objects imported from Mexico, found at flea markets, and produced by individual artisans, as well as Jon's paintings and Karen's own diverse creations: pillows with mixed-fabric covers, rugs, pottery, and neck scarves. Carrollton, her diverse, working-class neighborhood, reflects the demographics of the city: 60 percent black, 40 percent white and "other"—a mix of professionals, blue-collar workers, and subsidized renters. The house had taken four feet of water during Katrina, ruining the rental apartment downstairs. During the storm, Karen, Jon, and Aida relocated to Houston. They were grateful for the refuge provided by friends in the new city, but the lifestyle choices there were "not how we envisioned our life to be," Karen told me.

One of the remarkable occurrences after the storms was how school parents, neighbors, friends, and strangers rallied to help each other even while struggling to rebuild their own houses and lives. This happened at Ben Franklin High School. At the time of Katrina, Aida was attending Ben Franklin, the most prestigious public magnet high school in the city and long ranked one of the best in the country. Ninety-nine percent of the graduates go on to attend college. The school has been integrated since its founding in 1962. During a Thanksgiving visit back to New Orleans in 2005, Karen and Jon found that post-Katrina conditions there were still dire. At a school meeting, parents were told that if they didn't come back, the school couldn't reopen in January. The first floor of the school was flooded but upstairs was functional. The principal, Carol Christen, a former nun, was tenacious in her determination to reopen, so she got approval to convert to a charter school and secured the necessary funding. Enough families returned. The school reopened in January 2006, one of the few to do so.

Few other houses were occupied in Karen's neighborhood when the three of them returned permanently on the New Year's Eve after Katrina. "There was only one house in each direction," she recalled. "We used to aim flashlights at each other from a window just to say hello." Her blog started getting attention, but she didn't know what to call it. "I was acutely aware of the importance of the environment and historic preservation but not any school of thought about either. It was visceral." She had read a series of articles by Pulitzer Prize–winning architecture critic Blair Kamin of the *Chicago Tribune* entitled "Squandered Heritage." That sounded just right and so the website got a name. "The political indifference and squandering of all we had—culture, built environment, place"—would be the subject. No resident organization had existed in Karen's neighborhood before Katrina, and she could see the handwriting on the wall. By December 2006, "developers were proposing typical anywhere-USA, big-box, parking lot projects, formulas they build everywhere, the cheapest possible, what I call from the 'garden shed' school of architecture. It was all political but we didn't know who or how to fight."

Karen and a friend started passing out flyers. The first fight was around the plan that broke the zoning code for a large Walgreens. Many people believed that developers and city officials assumed not enough people had returned to organize a resistance. But neighborhood residents coalesced, won a redesign of the building, and evolved into the Northwest Carrollton Civic Association. They didn't stop Walgreens in the end, but they did have a significant early victory. A developer had proposed that a long-unoccupied white stucco house with arched windows and terra cotta tile roof—a common local Mediterranean style—be demolished and replaced by a Dollar General store. The house stood alone among empty lots, orphaned by surrounding development.

Karen described the events that followed:

> We learned there was this little committee representing four or five city agencies that met in the back room of City Hall, literally, to decide these things. It was run by a city employee and there was no hint how things got on or off the agenda. A representative from the Preservation Resource Center (PRC), Michelle Kimball, attended. She occasionally informed our group of something important in our neighborhood. We went

before the committee to strenuously oppose this demolition. They were so surprised. Who were we? The developer didn't know this house was special and that it was in good shape. Eventually, he paid to move it to a vacant site, fixed it up and then sold it. The Dollar General got built. It was our first success.[3] No one could figure how this little neighborhood committee with no staff and no money could do it. The last thing that committee wanted to do was deal with a community. They tried to act fast, before people really came back.

Karen's "Squandered Heritage" work progressed throughout 2006. She scrutinized city lists and found multiple instances of "predatory demolition" whereby homeowners were led to believe that they had to demolish because of black mold, without receiving advice on how to get rid of mold instead and preserve the integrity of the house. In addition, she and a friend found endless false records, including paperwork pertaining to houses classified as blighted that actually had been restored. "The first day we went out," she told me, "there were ten properties marked remediated that were just not done. Some houses didn't even exist." The story was getting too big for just her website. She brought her findings to local WWL-TV reporter Lee Zurik and then partnered with him to air these revelations.

Karen's work had "set off a bomb that has exploded in slow motion here in the last three weeks," Adam Nossiter reported in the *New York Times*.[4] "Largely thanks to Ms. Gadbois: the federally financed program to gut and repair the storm-damaged homes of the poor and elderly, on which the city spent $1.8 million, has been exposed as—at least partly—a sham." Forced to hold a press conference to address all of this, Mayor Nagin dismissed Karen's "amateur investigations," accused her of hurting the recovery, and criticized Zurik for being "reckless" in following up on Karen's discoveries. But apparently the FBI and the US attorney for the Eastern District didn't think he was reckless. An

FBI investigation led to the conviction of the former head of the New Orleans Affordable Homeownership (NOAH) program[5] for taking $350,000 in kickbacks from contractors.[6] Two contractors pleaded guilty and were sentenced to prison terms of six months and two years, respectively.

Karen's success didn't stop there. She had become friends with a young news blogger, Ariella Cohen, who had moved to New Orleans from Brooklyn. Ariella had joined the staff of New Orleans's *CityBusiness* and observed what Karen was doing. Together they conceived of *The Lens,* an online investigative journalism news site first focusing on land use and then expanding into broader city matters. *The Lens* was officially founded in November 2009.[7]

The Lens evolved into a major news source in the city, and today, with nine employees on a budget of only $700,000, this public-interest newsroom exposes financial wrongdoing, backroom dealings, fraud, political intrigue, and more. Its focus on underreported stories about land use, criminal justice, education, and City Hall activity has had a major impact on the city.

• • •

The story of Karen Gadbois and "Squandered Heritage" brings to light a fundamental New Orleans conundrum, serious enough to diminish the strengths of the city over time, nibble by nibble. The problem is that there exists both a deep pride and an equally deep ambivalence regarding the city's cultural heritage. So much of the culture is rooted in the African-American community. Certainly a general citywide agreement exists as to the value of traditional, indigenous New Orleans culture; but that culture is not always sufficiently recognized as a complex web of interrelated parts, each depending on the existence and strength of the others. The culture, like the city itself, is an ecosystem whose strength depends on the continued viability of *all* its parts: architecture, music, food, Live Oaks, Mardi Gras Indians, and more. And as with a truly organic ecosystem, new things are forever being added to old ones without necessarily replacing what came before. Remarkably, for example, New Orleans has more restaurants and music clubs now than it did before the storms. In an interview, actor, musician, and radio host Harry Shearer, who lives in New Orleans part-time, noted that "this is a port city that has always accepted new things. It is contrary to the city not to embrace the new and incorporate it into the culture. Contrary to what people outside think, there is enormous music and audience variety every night. It's not just about jazz."

• • •

What makes New Orleans culture unique and durable is this web of inseparable elements that are all connected. Second-line parades in which friends and others follow the first-line band—part and parcel of the traditional jazz funeral and a staple of social aid and pleasure club calendars—keep music flowing despite patently unfair official treatment. They pay at least three times what Mardi Gras parades pay for permits while creating only a fraction of the trash from Mardi Gras. New Orleans culinary traditions always continue undisturbed in home kitchens, on the neutral ground during Mardi Gras and other celebrations, and in backyards at family gatherings.

The Mardi Gras Indian tradition is indestructible no matter how hard officials try to tame the public expression of this tradition on St. Joseph's night and other occasions.[8] Bourbon Street may continue to offer only what tourists want to hear, but all over town, in darkened dives and private venues, authentic New Orleans music wins out. And at Jazz Fest every year, the purveyors of singular culinary specialties as well as craftsmen continue to test their new creations—jewelry, art, hats, hand-hewn furniture—in preparation for a potential expanded future entrepreneurial endeavor.

An endless number of individual property owners continue to take up the restoration challenge and prove over and over again what really has lasting cultural and economic value. The culture of New Orleans is, as Tom Piazza put it, "all tied up with the rhythms of life" in a way that promises a long continuum, despite harmful blows along the way. Sadly, the importance of each part of the cultural web is unrecognized until one of the critical parts disappears.

In September 2012, Lolis Eric Elie wrote an op-ed for *The Lens* about a parking lot that reflects this kind of loss—a significant loss because of the area's connection to Louis Armstrong, probably the city's best-known and most celebrated son.[9] Soft-spoken and mild-mannered, Lolis in many ways embodies what makes New Orleans special. The son of Lolis Edward Elie, a lawyer and notable civil rights leader in the 1960s,[10] young Lolis is a former *Times-Picayune* columnist, author of several books on the culture of cooking, and one of the writers for the brilliant HBO series *Treme*—a fictionalized version of post-Katrina New Orleans. His article about the 100 block of South Rampart Street[11] exhibited his disgust with the city's lack of concern for preserving its cultural landmarks.[12] He described frequently driving past the empty downtown corner where, years earlier, five historic buildings had been torn down to make way for a nine-story garage that has never been built.[13]

> In the case of the buildings in the 100 block of South Rampart, a devil's bargain was reached in 2000. The city ruled that "the developer of the parking building must replicate the appearance of the demolished building in the design of the new building." Thus, the parking garage structure shall incorporate salvaged ornamentation from the original buildings, as well as replicas of those items that were too fragile or difficult to save, in a design that closely mimics the historic buildings. In addition, the first-floor commercial space in the

parking garage will incorporate an area to commemorate the history and culture of the site. Plaques will also be installed on the exterior to mark the site and briefly relate its history.

Facades are, of course, bogus almost by definition. Even one that provides an accurate sense of the building behind it can't begin to convey the richness of the history destroyed in its creation. But in the compromise that paved the way— quite literally—for a parking lot, there was at least the possibility that passersby would catch a whiff of the time when that block was a cornerstone in our city's long-forgotten Chinatown.

In the city of New Orleans, there is no consequence if a developer tears down a historic building and then fails to develop the project he tore down the buildings to develop. No mayor in my lifetime has seen fit to secure a performance guarantee to insure that the promised work ever gets done.[14]

Virtually nothing remains downtown of the great era when jazz was born here.[15]

Not far from the French Quarter but very distinct architecturally and historically separate from it, the South Rampart corner was what was left of the African-American side of town where music history was made. Here was "the epicenter of an artistic whirlwind destined to change world culture," Randy Fertel writes. "South Rampart Street became home to jazz when the whorehouse district Storyville, only three blocks away, closed in 1917."[16] One of the five buildings that stood on this corner was the Morris Music store, once owned by Armstrong's friend and mentor Morris Karnofsky, a Lithuanian Jew, whose parents informally adopted Louis as a young boy. They helped nurture him and loaned him the money to buy his first cornet.

Lolis points out that many landmarks associated with Armstrong and the whole famous jazz era had been torn down over the years—including, in the 1950s, Armstrong's boyhood home.

Others are threatened with demolition by neglect.[17] If that sorry record were not the case, he writes, maybe this would not have been such a big deal. "But it is a big deal," he adds, "for at least two reasons: First, we've lost a priceless landmark that could have informed scholars and attracted the ever-important tourists in ways that would both maintain the city's architectural identity and generate the tourist revenue that seems to be City Hall's most cherished commodity. Second, we repeated a pattern whereby we demolish architecturally significant landmarks to make way for projects that never get built."

Nowhere in the city is the lack of cultural respect more apparent than in Treme—the oldest continually occupied free black community in the country. Treme is a center of the New Orleans culture still celebrated today and as significant a birthplace of American jazz as can be found anywhere. In this neighborhood, across from the French Quarter, there is a gated, underused thirty-two-acre park named Armstrong Park. Ten blocks of Treme were demolished for this thankless park in the 1970s. As writer, jazz clarinetist, and educator Tom Sancton puts it, the ten blocks "were flattened and over one thousand residents displaced to build— irony of ironies—a cultural center."[18] In familiar Urban Renewal fashion, this heart of a significant black community was destroyed to make way for a New Orleans version of Lincoln Center.[19] Not surprisingly, the money ran out after the Mahalia Jackson Theater was built and the remaining land was turned into a heavily gated park that effectively keeps out the very community its creation tore apart.

As Sancton notes:

> This project put millions into the pockets of contractors and corrupt politicians, but did little for the city residents or the tourists it was supposed to attract. The park, which looks like a Disneyland stage set with its cutesy fountains and bridges, quickly became a venue for muggings, murders, and drug

deals—a strange way to honor Armstrong, whose own childhood home on Jane Alley, by the way, was demolished in the
1950s over the protests of jazz lovers who wanted to turn it
into a museum.[20]

Lolis wrote and coproduced with director Dawn Logsdon a
2008 PBS documentary on this deeply historical neighborhood,
Faubourg Treme: The Untold Story of Black New Orleans—a
wonderful exploration of the area's little-known history. As Lolis
points out, "Treme was home to a large, prosperous and artisti-
cally flourishing community of free black people . . . where the
19th Century Creole Music tradition and 20th Century brass band
tradition were born." It was a mixed community where "rich and
poor co-habitated, collaborated and clashed to create much of what
defines the New Orleans culture we know today." At its most basic,
Lolis maintains, Treme is the "capital of New Orleans culture."

In his 2012 op-ed, Lolis places the South Rampart parking
lot, a few blocks away from Treme and Armstrong Park, in the
context of the city's devaluation of the architectural heritage so
inextricably linked to its cultural history. He writes:

Because the destruction of these landmarks happens so often,
I see it not as a group of isolated incidents, but as a pattern of
behavior rooted in a mentality that is fundamentally at odds
with the character of our city. No matter how many times the
politicians invoke gumbo or jazz or streetcars, I find very little evidence in their behavior to suggest that they understand
the essential function these cultural icons play in maintaining
whatever greatness the city can lay claim to.

Rather, what I hear when they speak and what I see
when they act is a generic mindset, the kind of thing that
you would expect if the brain of a politician from Arkansas
or Arizona or Alaska was placed in the body of a politician
from New Orleans. Our "leaders" embrace a one-size-fits-all

capitalism that destroys our most valuable resources in the pursuit of trinkets that have proven profitable in places that have nothing else to sell but office towers, parking lots, and easy highway access to suburban enclaves.[21]

Evidence of the generic mindset Lolis refers to is emerging on the downtown parking lots, which, decades earlier, replaced an intricate network of small retail shops and residences developed in the jazz era of Buddy Bolden and countless others. Recently built is an apartment complex with ground-floor retail and generous parking. This design is the contemporary era's standard answer for "pedestrian-oriented development." It would fit comfortably in any no-character downtown. It is a ubiquitous design that historians in the future will identify as "Early Twenty-First Century Generic," reflecting absolutely nothing identified with New Orleans. As Tom Sancton's father, Thomas Sancton, Sr., said to him with obvious bitterness:

> These neighborhoods were a hundred years in the making. Then came progress, and all these blocks, and the life they contained, were gone in an instant. The earth-devouring greed is in all of us, Tommy, but it becomes terrible when it's backed by government power and demagoguery. It gets into City Hall, then moves into the funding phase, the cutting in of contractors, suppliers, bond lawyers. The next thing you know, a whole layer of culture is stripped away.[22]

Another egregious example of devaluation of the city's architectural richness and social fabric was the destruction in 2012 of an entire twenty-seven-block, Mid-City neighborhood to make way for the unnecessary replacement of Charity Hospital (more on this in Chapter 9). In this working-class neighborhood of small businesses and residences, 165 houses were deemed architecturally significant, dating from the late nineteenth and early twentieth centuries. As a concession to preservationists, Mayor Landrieu allotted $3.2 million in city funds to move 81 or more of these houses (originally 100 were announced) to empty lots around the city.[23] It could have been a historic preservation win if done in earnest and with care. In the end, it was a disaster. So that the houses could be moved under wires and over city streets, the roofs were shorn off and, in some cases, the second floor as well. If there was a projecting side gallery, that went too. Architectural details were removed and sold. The houses were relocated helter-skelter. Many of the houses had been fully restored with federal Road Home or insurance money and even some government preservation grants. But in the end, they were mostly destroyed in the move. They were left uncovered, open to the elements, prey to wind, rain, and vandals for years afterward.

Preservationists were constantly bringing attention to this sorry state of affairs. To say that this irritated Mayor Landrieu is to put it mildly. He insisted that preservationists should applaud his effort to save the houses, regardless of the poor implementation and failure to save them. About 21 of the 73 houses were plopped down in a small neighborhood wedged between Broadmoor and Central City, known as Hoffman Triangle. Severely flooded during Katrina, this neighborhood rallied, formed its first neighborhood association, staged cleanup drives, and worked assiduously to increase homeownership. Residents of Hoffman Triangle were not consulted nor pleased to have these newly blighted, unrestored houses near their own front doorsteps, creating more public-nuisance problems than they already had.[24]

In April 2011, Landrieu held a press conference to announce another demolition—this time, of an intact row of classic but dilapidated bungalows used in the promotional materials for *Treme*. They were a perfect representation of the city's distinctive architecture. Why a press conference to announce the demolition was thought appropriate is hard to figure. Intended or not, the effect was clear: it was salt in the wound of preservationists.

At the press conference, Landrieu seemed to take pleasure in taunting some of the preservationists present. Singling out Sandra Stokes, the leader of the fight to save Charity Hospital and the houses demolished for the new hospital complex, he said, "You don't even live here. You live in Baton Rouge." In fact, Sandra had moved to Julia Street in the downtown Warehouse District shortly after Katrina six years earlier. Landrieu then turned to Brad Vogel, a young lawyer who was spending a year in New Orleans working for the National Trust for Historic Preservation. Brad did extraordinary work as an advocate for saving Lower Mid-City. "I don't know where you live," Landrieu said. Brad was stunned by these angry outbursts. Sadly recalling the incident, he told me: "I live in St. Roch [a regenerating neighborhood close to downtown]. I thought to myself, here I am, a resident of four years who came to the city post-Katrina, living in a neighborhood still very much on the edge. I'm here putting down roots to help stabilize the shallow soil of this place at a critical time and the mayor is slinging xenophobic statements at me in front of the press because we disagree on something." It was hard to tell whom Landrieu appreciated less: preservationists or newcomers helping rebuild the city. The houses went down, and the lot remains empty to this day.

The demolition of the various houses and businesses was a big loss for the community, but scores of smaller instances of architectural and cultural destruction go unnoticed—the nibbles that add up to big bites. The "blight fight" is a good example of this. Nine years after Katrina, the city still has thousands of so-called blighted houses—empty, deteriorated structures waiting to be processed.[25] Some, while not architectural masterpieces, certainly are of consequence, having been built with quality materials not available today and in a style that fits their surroundings. Diminishing populations in many cities since the 1960s and the mortgage default crisis of the early 2000s resulted in large numbers of abandoned, deteriorating, blighted properties. This is a national problem because the federal funds available for blight elimination are not available on an either/

or basis of demolition or reconstruction. If the same amount available to a demolition contractor were available to the many home seekers willing to do most of the rehabilitation work themselves, many blighted houses would be speedily picked up at city auction. But, unfortunately, securing federal demolition funds trumps preservation when it comes to blighted properties.

For example, in April 2011 more than a thousand people showed up to bid on approximately one hundred vacant houses and empty lots with an average of seven bidders per property. Officials were astounded by the turnout. Since the city keeps no real records of renovation permits for blighted properties, and since there are more hurdles involved in property reclamation, this auction spoke volumes, challenging official assumptions that there is little market for these homes.[26]

Actually, rescuing worthy structures easily demolished by the city's blight-removal program is one area that has seen some improvement during the Landrieu administration, according to Michelle Kimball, senior advocate on the staff of the Preservation Resource Center. Here again, the improvement results from a vigilant civic watchdog function that, if absent, would lead to a considerably greater loss of the city's historic fabric. Michelle is probably the only paid staff member of a preservation organization who has a watchdog function among her responsibilities. She monitors all demolitions, code enforcement, and land-use and zoning procedures, with the goal of preventing needless demolitions and inappropriate land-use and zoning decisions. To the disappointment of the preservation fighters on projects like the demolitions of the Mid-City houses, Charity Hospital, and public housing, the PRC has been a bystander. But in the day-to-day business of city government where preservation nibbles frequently occur, Michelle is there.

On the blight-fight issue, Michelle told me, "there has been a tremendous learning curve. It seemed at first that Mitch [Landrieu] was ready to demolish everything that was remotely blighted. The system isn't perfect now, but it is much better than it once was." Significantly, she added, the director of code enforcement informally sits down with the director of the Historic Districts Landmarks Commission (HDLC) and "together they make judgment calls about what should be sent to Sheriff Auctions and what to send for demolition review. Mistakes are made from time to time, but typically I just make one phone call and a property is taken off the agenda." She acknowledged that the courtesy paid to the HDLC is a major advance.

Michelle pinpointed a problem universally found in cities and towns where code inspectors have limited, if any, technical knowledge of historic structures. "City code enforcement staff and hearing officers need some serious preservation sensitivity training," she noted. "I'm still hearing plenty of stories about folks who go to a code enforcement hearing and they are told that their best option is to demolish their house, when this is far from true." As Michelle observed, many neighborhoods in New Orleans are on the rebound. People are buying homes that were blighted even before Katrina. Values are increasing in many neighborhoods, and gentrification is occurring in some areas. Clearly, more structures could be reclaimed and turned into tax-paying properties instead of being lost.

Yet official recognition of the overall value of preservation—from providing local jobs for the economy and raising property values to the repopulation of neighborhoods and saving the city's famous aesthetic—remains lacking. "People take preservation for granted because they are surrounded by so much historic fabric," Michelle said. "There is an apathy, a self-imposed pressure to continue 'progress,' to keep up with other cities like Houston and Atlanta even though they have nothing we want to aspire to." Ten years after Katrina, preservation remains a constant struggle.

No one is more disheartened by the lack of a strong preservation advocacy community than Bill Borah, a white-haired, blue-eyed land-use lawyer who was born into the upper echelon of New

Orleans's social strata. The son of a federal judge who was Rex, King of Carnival (a major social coup), Bill participated in all the classic social rituals of Mardi Gras balls and garden parties. To the manor born by birth but not by temperament, Bill forged a divergent path and was a key leader in the most significant preservation battle the city has ever witnessed: the successful fight in the 1960s to stop the planned six-lane elevated highway through the French Quarter that would have eviscerated the historic neighborhood. To this day, fifty years later, the social and business establishment of New Orleans continues to question what he did and why. He is seen as the errant son when, in fact, he should be celebrated as a civic hero.[27]

Fresh out of Tulane Law School, both Bill and his close friend Richard Baumbach, Jr., worked to kill the elevated highway, designed by Robert Moses in 1946.[28] For this battle, Bill had the enthusiastic support and total financial backing of the Stern Fund run by Edgar Stern, Jr., a highly respected Jewish businessman in a town that accepted Jews—no matter how successful or wealthy—in only a limited and restricted way. Stern, for example, was a member of the most prestigious, WASP-dominated Rex but not the exclusive Boston Club.[29] At one point, Stern was invited to join the Boston Club, but when he asked if the invitation included his closest friend, Monty Lemann, he was told no.[30] Stern declined the invitation.

Stern, noted Bill, "was the establishment," not just because of his Rex membership. "He brought the first television station to New Orleans, was a generous philanthropist, and was on all those business community boards," Bill said. "He had to sit in meetings with highway proponents and this was a guy who did not like conflict." What grated on the establishment even more about Stern was his and his parents' (Edgar and Edith Stern) advocacy of racial integration. Edgar Sr. and Jr. built the Royal Orleans Hotel at the Canal Street edge of the French Quarter (Edgar Sr. died before it opened in 1960). The first year it opened, they threw a Christmas party. Bill recalled: "Richard and I walked in and immediately went 'Whoa!' Every black hotel employee was there, along with everyone else. We said to ourselves, 'These people are really serious.' That just was not done. Edgar was a gutsy guy. He knew how destructive that highway would be and he was willing to oppose it despite the unhappiness of the business community." Establishment friends of Edgar urged him to fire Bill and Richard, but instead Stern funded their involvement, starting in 1966 until the actual defeat of the highway in 1969.

The business community, the political establishment, and the newspaper, the *Times-Picayune,* all enthusiastically supported the highway—as similar establishment groups and newspaper editorials supported highways and Urban Renewal in cities across the country, in cities where population was beginning to move out. "They sold it as the key to the city's future," Bill explained. "The *Times-Picayune* continually published front-page stories about other cities building highways. They wouldn't publish the other side. We couldn't even get a letter published. That's why we distributed flyers neighborhood by neighborhood." The greatest appeal of federal interstates everywhere, surely including New Orleans, was the 90 percent federal funding coming to the city to pay for the highway construction. Oh, the contracts—construction, legal, financing, insurance, banking, design, engineering—and the 90 percent federal financing: like sugar plums they always danced in the heads of the local political and economic circles. Many cities cashed in on that federal largesse and now struggle to put back an urban fabric of assorted buildings and streets, not just isolating towers amidst parking lots, in their downtowns.[31]

But in no other city, perhaps, was the social and economic price to be paid as great for standing up to the establishment. "New Orleans's social structure is so interwoven and interconnected," Bill said, "all a spin-off of Mardi Gras with the Dukes and Duchesses giving parties, always kissing, always serving great food. If you're born in the right family and keep your mouth shut, you can feed off the economic trough and social scene for life. You can ride it from cradle to grave.[32] New Orleans politics is part of this extended family. When we fought the highway, what we were really doing was challenging the way things were done, the way the power structure worked. We knew this issue was key to New Orleans's future. We set an example for the rest of the country, but it was not what the business and political elite wanted."[33]

But Bill never expected the level of ostracism he experienced. "Many of my parents' generation just stopped talking to me," he said, and later his fledgling law practice suffered. The message was clear: "If you straighten up, we'll love you again." He didn't, of course. The highway was defeated. The French Quarter was spared the dismal fate of the demolished ten-block heart of Treme, where the I-10 was built at the behest of the business community. Today, the same business community and political groups that promoted the highway feed off its absence through the tourism economy centered in that storied historic quarter that would have become a shadow of its former glory. "It's frightening," Bill said. "They misunderstand the concept of progress and think it always has to be new. They don't make the connection to the proven source of economic development that preservation has been in so many ways."

Katrina changed this dynamic, at least for a while, Bill said. "It opened the city up to the nation. Before, outsiders couldn't get anywhere here without a connection to the local establishment. They wouldn't then, but after Katrina all that changed; even the language changed with talk of needing a comprehensive master plan and with a need to clean up the corrupt levee boards. But now [nine years later], things are drifting back." Bill led the successful post-Katrina effort to amend the City Charter to secure for New Orleans a Master Plan with the Force of Law. This was a significant change that required the zoning ordinance as well as all capital expenditures to be consistent with the Master Plan. "If followed," Bill explained, "it would undo the system of corruption and favoritism normally followed in this town." Although the ordinance passed, it is not enforced.

New Orleans was substantially spared that highway disaster, but, as Lolis pointed out in his op-ed, the city still does not appropriately value its unique traditions and expressions of its culture. "Why else would you consistently arrest jazz musicians playing our music in our streets for our entertainment?" he asked. "Why else would you harass Mardi Gras Indians on such a regular basis? Why else would you try to enforce a noise ordinance on jazz musicians in Jackson Square while allowing Bourbon Street night clubs to blare rock and roll without regard to decibel level? Why would you raise parade fees on second-line organizations to such an extent as to threaten the continued viability of this emblematic parading tradition?"

Alison McCrary, a young nun who works with street musicians and Indians, had another take on the devaluing of the heritage: "When Indians practicing on Sunday nights are arrested for loitering, this criminalizes a tradition. This reflects a lack of basic respect and engenders no trust. Racial profiling is so obvious in the enforcement of the French Quarter rules," she explained. "For example, during the French Quarter juvenile curfew in 2013, 750 arrests were made, 704 of which were African-American, or 93 percent." Then she asked: "Does a curfew really work? Was juvenile crime the real problem? Is this the best use of police manpower? Selective enforcement only continues to erode trust in the NOPD. The police are criminalizing youth." As author Jason Berry said to me: "The race and class issue is jagged and deep."

For what value and for whom is the culture considered important? "The irony," Lolis noted, "is that outsiders value the culture that no politician, black or white, really does."

• • •

On every level, it seems, the commitment to saving New Orleans's culture and keeping it strong is ambivalent at best. "A lot of people like to rhapsodize about jazz and the Indians," said Tom Piazza, "but when it comes to threats to their existence, an odd civic passivity is deeply ingrained in the culture, if it is in fact passivity and not a kind of hostility."[34] Official efforts to limit music in the streets, or to restrict the Indians' flow of movement, are met with a public outrage that is muted at best. "It is easier," Tom continued, "to pay lip service to that culture and let it help brand the city for tourism." Tourists come and go, but without a solid and committed resident population the tourist city becomes an empty suit. If you do it for the local, the tourist will come. If you do it for the tourist, you will lose the local, and eventually, you will lose the tourist as well. Only the local gives a place character.

The physical manifestations of the culture—specifically, the historic architecture that Karen Gadbois and occasional bands of preservationists struggle to keep standing—elicit a parallel ambivalence. New Orleans music, traditions, and food can be discussed in the same breath, but the physical manifestation of all of it— the architecture and physical environment—is not automatically included in the image. Yet if New Orleans's interrelated past is not well represented in the present, how does one make the connection between its music and food, on the one hand, and its historic buildings, on the other? "Architecture *is* part of the culture," Lolis said with emphasis. "The mayor and City Council don't understand that. The mayor talks about how these dilapidated buildings are killing us. Well, they're so valuable that we should figure out how to put them back together. You have to ask whether the buildings have killed more people than the cops have."

Karen identified a profound irony here, also inextricably bound up in race: "This town," she said, "is renowned for being built by craftsmen, not architects. Mostly black craftsmen. It is not a parallel culture. The tradesmen *are* the musicians and the Indians. They *are* the cultural standard-bearers." They were and are the lathers, plasterers, carpenters, welders, painters, iron workers, stone cutters, and more.[35] The late Chief Allison "Tootie" Montana, for example, was for decades a New Orleans cultural icon as the Chief of Chiefs of the Mardi Gras Indians.[36] As Big Chief of the Yellow Pocahontas Tribe, "Tootie" is also credited with ending the culture of violence in the 1950s between Indian tribes, largely by making the competition among them a matter of pageantry and amazingly artful costumes. Above all else, he was a master craftsman specializing in the installation of lath for fancy plaster work.

In 2002, the New Orleans Museum of Art presented an exhibition entitled "Raised to the Trade: Creole Building Arts of New Orleans," which celebrated the "rich legacies of artistry and craftsmanship of many generations of master builders."[37] Here again is one of those intricate and fundamental threads in the inextricably linked fabric of New Orleans culture, unknown to so many. Noting that many African-American skilled craftsmen brought their trades to New Orleans from Santo Domingo (Haiti) at the close of the eighteenth and early nineteenth centuries, John Ethan Hankins, the exhibit curator and author of the accompanying catalogue, wrote: "[T]he unheralded legion and tradition of highly skilled trades people have, with their hands, created the celebrated architectural landscape of New Orleans."

Indeed, the exhibit and its beautifully illustrated catalogue persuasively link "fine art" and the "craft" of building arts. Noted American artist Jacob Lawrence celebrated the work of the craftsmen in a series of paintings in the late 1940s. Lawrence wrote a caption for *Builders,* a painting he completed in 1947: "In New Orleans, the Negro has made his greatest step toward economic security. He has large membership in trade unions (A.F.L. and C.I.O.) and representation on the executive board of the Louisiana State Federation of Labor."

Many African-American craftsmen lived in the 7th Ward, considered the heart of black New Orleans. Yet the talents of this population have not been passed on in any significant way. To do that, John initiated a modest program in 2007, the New Orleans Master Guild, but noted: "There are incentives to demolish homes, presumably to be replaced by houses requiring a minimally skilled workforce not rooted in the fabric of the New Orleans culture. There is even workforce training money for low-skilled construction workers. But there has been no assistance from the city, state, or federal government to help the celebrated master craftsman to train apprentices in our renowned building arts techniques." This kind of serious training could be a great job-creation project if appropriately supported. The need for these skills will never die in New Orleans, as long as so much of its architectural legacy remains standing. The late Irving Trevigne, a master carpenter from the 7th Ward who restored Lolis's Treme house, put it nicely in Lolis's PBS documentary, *Faubourg Treme:* "Anybody can build a house, but not just anybody can bring an old one back."

There is yet another layer to this overall conundrum. Tom Piazza identifies it as "a peculiarly Southern shame at seeming backward." Longtime New Orleanians look at the supposedly up-to-date, "modern" southern cities of Atlanta and Houston or even Charleston and Savannah—what Tom calls "the jewel boxes of the South"—and see themselves falling behind, although one could easily be forgiven for asking "Behind what?" After all, those "modern" cities laid waste to many of the historic neighborhoods and traditional downtowns considered so desirable today. And while those "jewel boxes" surely have exquisite architecture, they don't have the depth of culture found in New Orleans.

As Karen told me with the tone of a cynic: "When New Orleans lost out to Atlanta and Houston and other great cities of the South, it was assumed that it was because New Orleans is old. Preservation was the easy whipping boy. I don't know the last thing that preservationists stopped from happening, but when anybody stands in the way of a developer, preservationists are to blame."

The truth is that developers have the political clout to halt or derail potentially beneficial projects in New Orleans. As this book illustrates, preservationists have been powerless to stop some of the city's biggest mistakes. The closing of Charity Hospital, the demolition of the red brick/tiled-roof public housing projects, and the destruction of hundreds of architectural gems all over town happened despite them.

Yet even in the face of significant opposition, there are still numerous examples of successful preservationist projects. Since Katrina, the Canal Street theater district has revived thanks to three restored theaters—the Saenger, the Civic, and the Joy—that attract visitors and locals alike. In Treme there is the restored 1950s Carver Theater, built as a movie house for blacks during Jim Crow; in other theaters in the city, they were restricted to the balcony. Appealing new hotels have emerged from the restoration of legendary Canal Street department stores like D. H. Holmes and Maison Blanche. Commercial towers from the 1920s, such as Hibernia Bank, are now upscale condominiums. A handsomely restored district of old industrial and warehouse buildings is now one of the city's growing upscale neighborhoods. And the former 1920s Morton's Auction House building on Magazine Street was converted to the Intellectual Properties Building, which rents office space to start-ups that will help grow the economy. Indeed, on many commercial streets all over town there are splendid examples of restored buildings converted to new uses. No assemblage of new construction can match the style, character, and appeal of the city's array of reclaimed buildings.

In New Orleans and elsewhere across the country, restoration and conversion of historic buildings have catalyzed regeneration and new growth far more effectively than the glitzy replacement structures that promise the world but deliver little, and expensively at that. Preservationists are rarely acknowledged for their achievements. They should be celebrated, not castigated.

While individuals continue to value and restore architectural treasures in every neighborhood and while the lure of living in such restored gems attracts a new population to the city, the record for the official city leadership and larger business community, as Lolis has argued, leaves a lot to be desired.

"We're like no other place," said Karen. "But we'll become like all other places if we don't preserve what makes us like no other place."

Chapter 6

Building New, Restoring Old

They [Make It Right] are the only people who really hung in with the Lower Nine and are making things happen.

—Pam Dashiel, former head of the Holy Cross
Sustainable Development Organization

This is a proving ground for a bigger idea that could work globally. . . . This project is not mine anymore. It is so beyond me.[1]

—Brad Pitt

Make It Right is building 150 safe, sustainable homes in the Lower Ninth Ward, the neighborhood most devastated by the flooding from Katrina. They are called the "Brad Pitt Houses" for obvious reasons, but the real story of Make It Right is even bigger than Pitt's celebrity and could help change the way other American cities and towns are rebuilt, and not just after disasters. Pitt and a multitalented group of like-minded individuals effectively defied conventional planning norms, rejected the goal of city leaders to thwart the return of homeowners in this most devastated section of the Lower Nine, and eschewed assistance from Road Home because of the government's endless restrictions on the applicants. They took on the community as a full and equal partner in what may be the largest, greenest development of single-family LEED (Leadership in Energy and Environmental Design) Platinum houses in the United States. In fact, Make It Right actually dealt with individual low-income homeowners as clients, rather than just as beneficiaries of their designs.

Immediately after Katrina, Pitt wanted to help in some way. He happened to meet Matt Peterson, national president of Global Green. The mission of Global Green is to make the world of construction more ecologically sustainable. With Pitt's support, Global Green initiated a project in 2006 whereby five new houses and a small eighteen-unit structure were built using the best green techniques. The site is located at the natural levee in Holy Cross. The houses are presented as twenty-first-century shotguns with environmentally certified wood, energy-saving technology, ground-source heat pumps, and solar-paneled roofs. Many residents of the Lower Nine resented the location of these houses. Holy Cross itself is easy to love, easy to defend. But the most vulnerable area in the city, where the barge landed, was on lower ground far from Holy Cross. That's where the community sought help.

Pitt wanted to expand beyond Global Green's project plan. While he was on the architectural jury[2] for the Global Green houses, he contacted his friends at the architectural firm GRAFT.[3] It was a year after Katrina, architect Thomas Willemeit told me in an interview, "and Brad said the city was still devastated. 'This is not my country,' he said. 'Nothing is happening. No one can tell me where the people are or what is being done.' He was frustrated with government and convinced that Americans have to prove that people can come up with solutions." I was sitting with Thomas in his Berlin office, a sunny atelier filled with energetic young architects. GRAFT is a firm where the term *starchitect* is alien and where teamwork and "mutual inspiration" prevail. That is what the firm name refers to: "grafting" ideas together collaboratively. A number of years ago, the three partners at GRAFT—Thomas as well as architects Wolfram Putz and Lars Kruckerberg—designed a studio for Pitt and became fast friends with the actor. Pitt is a modern-architecture buff, a rebel of sorts with an architect's sensibility who once aspired to be an architect himself. "At some point, he realized his talents lay elsewhere," noted Thomas.

"We went to the site," recalled Thomas. "I was shocked. I can still see the 'X' signs on houses indicating how many were found dead. There seemed to be no sign of hope. We had no plan. There was no precedent. We were starting from scratch. The first set of goals was to rebuild a community and to do it at a higher standard than it was. We knew it had to be the Lower Nine."

The GRAFT team recommended working with environmentalist Bill McDonough. The goal was to incorporate the principles of *Cradle to Cradle,* a book written by McDonough and German chemist Michael Braungart, by designing beyond what is normally considered sustainable and making the management cost of the homes affordable, selecting materials that resist moisture and require minimal maintenance, utilizing sunlight, and using fixtures with low water use.[4] "Pitt and I talked about what was possible and how sustainable principles could be applied," Bill recalled in an interview. Initially, Bill created a "Be Native to Place" framework that is climate- and location-specific. Then he brought in his friend Tom Darden, chairman of Cherokee Investments, a company that started out as a brick manufacturer but evolved into a major mitigator of brownfields.[5] Darden became the fourth partner in the effort, along with Pitt, McDonough, and GRAFT. Make It Right (MIR) officially launched in 2007.

The group met with local architects John Williams and Steven Bingler. At their first meeting over lunch at Antoine's Restaurant on St. Louis Street, they soon realized that many questions needed answers before any concept could be developed: what was feasible, how to choose the site, how to find displaced families, how to fund, what was the condition of the levees, and, most critically, do the people who lived there want to come back? "I said we had to first meet with the community to learn what we can," recalled Steven. Enter Tom Darden III, who had heard about the effort from his father. Tom, a young partner in a North Carolina development company, had long been interested in land-use and environmental issues. He was the first to volunteer at Make It Right, eventually becoming executive director. He volunteered to do the on-the-ground research, along with his North Carolina partners, all of whom were looking for a way to help after the storms. Their observational and listening skills were put to a strong test.

"We knew we wanted to be in the Lower Nine," Tom recalled, "so we started to talk to people in the community. We considered developing around activity hubs like the school. But we kept hearing people say they wanted to rebuild where their homes had been. They were all tied to their own area. Brad pushed for where it would make the biggest statement, have the biggest impact, and be inspirational for the community. We evaluated the additional risks associated with building there [at the levee break] but thought that if we built the houses off the ground, additional risks would be outweighed by the symbolism of building in that area."

Considerable public debate swirled around the issue of residents returning to the Lower Nine. Even before the floodwaters disappeared, I was stunned that so many nonresidents had an opinion on whether or not the Lower Nine should be rebuilt—not just New Orleanians from other neighborhoods but even strangers who had never visited the Crescent City, let alone the Lower Nine. Usually, the opinion was a definitive "Don't rebuild the Lower Nine." I had never heard such reactions to other disasters, natural or man-made. But here I was hearing about how "those people" should be relocated to a site on high ground instead of rebuilding their own residence in place. The "Don't rebuild" view was countered by dynamics and sentiments at the heart of the New Orleans way of life: strong familial and social ties, cultural attachment, and deep commitment to place.

Environmentalists raised legitimate concerns that every homeowner needed to take into consideration, but Lower Nine property owners needed to make their own choice to stay or go.

The idea of building at the worst site had not occurred to the team—Pitt, McDonough, GRAFT, and Darden—until they heard local voices passionately speaking their minds. "We told them that we needed them to go where officially no one wanted us to return," recalled Tanya Harris. And so eventually they did. "It is a small act of disobedience," Pitt said.[6] "It was all Brad's idea," said Tom. "If we went to the weakest spot, if we figure out how to build in the worst area, then we could do it anywhere. The flooding risk is there. Fewer services exist. But we weighed the symbolic importance of that site, too. If 150 homes were achievable, it could be catalytic. And this particular area is actually two feet above the base flood level."

The first public evidence of the effort was a clever, large-scale public art project. In December 2007, Pitt and the architects at GRAFT randomly placed 150 odd-shaped frames covered with shocking pink fabric around the designated building zone. This "Pink Event" symbolically represented the destroyed homes and signaled to displaced residents that something was happening to bring them home. The idea for the pink houses emerged while Pitt was shooting *The Curious Case of Benjamin Button* (filmed in New Orleans), in which a two-story fluorescent-pink silhouette of a house was used on the set as a placeholder for a computer-generated house that would be inserted in the editing studio. "He was mesmerized and called to say we should do something like this," Thomas told me. "It would be like Monopoly houses, and Brad said the fabric color should go well with green so we chose pink. We used a sustainable fabric and when the exhibit came down after four weeks, we used the fabric to make bags to sell for more fundraising." The project worked. The world paid attention, displaced residents got interested, and funders came forth.

The trust of the community did not come easily, and it didn't happen overnight. The team scrupulously avoided creating a formal Master Plan because the fears of gentrification and land grab were so great. "From the start, the neighborhood understandably feared a land grab," Tom points out. This meant not doing anything in a way that would look as though control was being taken away from the residents. Definitely a challenge. "So, when we acquired a property," he explained, "it was clearly a temporary acquisition. We acquired it, built a house on it, then sold it to a family, either the one whose house was there originally or one who lived nearby."[7] The strategy was to concentrate the density. The houses were not necessarily contiguous, just near one another. "So we've proven over and over again," Tom added, "that we were building for a family who lost their home."

The process of figuring out the design of the homes started in an unusual way. The group wanted to move quickly, so they talked to leaders around the world and collected names of fifteen architects, hoping to end up with six or seven, but "everyone said yes," noted Wolfram in a phone conversation. "It was to be a donation. All we offered was a plane ticket and two nights at a hotel." An internal debate was whether to pick one or two designs and build fast or "show we could have good design and meet all the goals," recalled Thomas. The "go fast" route was rejected. The Make It Right team selected thirteen final designs. A conventional competition would have then appointed a jury to decide on a smaller number of final designs, but Pitt wanted to discard that idea and instead let the homeowners pick which ones they want. This resulted in an interesting variety among the built houses. Before designing anything, the architects had to meet several times with the potential homeowners to hear their wishes and with the larger community to hear their expectations.[8] Most residents wanted the space under the raised house to be usable for more than just parked cars, such as crawfish boils and other social gatherings, and many didn't want any flat roofs.

"Architects are used to presenting to professional juries," noted Thomas. "They had to change the words they usually use and use straightforward and simple words. And they had to learn to really listen. We tried to prepare them for the chaos of open discussion. They got instant feedback, more direct than they were used to. We were surprised. Nobody ever asked for traditional New Orleans homes, never said the designs were too interesting or the wrong color. That shocked us. The professionals got used to it and eventually got excited."

Make It Right exhibited innovative environmental thinking inside and outside each house. Mistakes were made and lessons learned along the way, as expected of cutting-edge work. At one point, a special glass-infused wood that had been used, especially on exterior stairs, started rotting despite a forty-year guarantee. The wood was immediately replaced and the manufacturer was held accountable. In addition, the building process was slow—too slow for some critics. But as Tom explained, each house was a single development. Changes were made based on the client's requests or lessons learned from other houses. Make It Right broke all the conventional rules. Rarely, if ever, have low-income community residents had the opportunity to be fully engaged in the redevelopment of their community, given a choice in the design style of their subsidized house, and then allowed to tweak the design instead of having a design jury make that choice for them.

As of this writing in 2014, more than 100 houses of varying shapes and pastel colors occupy the corner of the Lower Nine where the barge came through. Eventually, there will be 150 houses. Individually they look very avant-garde, with odd shapes and unconventional angles. Traditional New Orleans features like front porches, balconies, and front stoops have been reinterpreted and placed on houses in varying configurations. "We've cracked something here," Pitt told *Architectural Digest* on the fifth anniversary of the project. "These houses redefine affordable housing."[9] Lolis Eric Elie agrees. "It doesn't look like architecture for poor people," he observed in conversation. "It's simply affordable housing. The Lower Nine is like a suburb. So devastated, this area was a blank slate. Architecture appropriate here may not be appropriate uptown." But many people have critiqued the designs, architects especially. The houses have been described as "too contrary to New Orleans traditions," "outrageously inappropriate," "ugly," and "weird." Outsiders may say what they will but the homeowners, in fact, love these houses.

While the story of Make It Right unmistakably starts with Pitt, it includes in equal importance a cast of citizen-activists who had an extraordinary impact on Pitt and helped shape the project. Charles Allen, a young environmentalist resident of Holy Cross, was one of them.[10] At first, Charles worried about whether Pitt and his colleagues would stick around and see things through over the long haul: "People were suspicious of all the organizations who parachuted in after the storm. Being rational, people always wonder: What's in it for these groups? Why would they be doing this?" As Charles came to understand the project, it became clear that "Brad was the first person the community really believed. So many people came to study, question, promise, and disappear—but he seemed real." A Xavier University graduate with a biology degree and a master's in public health from Tulane, Charles keeps pushing the envelope of expectations for what can be improved environmentally in the neighborhood, throughout the city, and along the Gulf Coast.

Until Make It Right came on the scene, Charles didn't know anything about architects and planners. "I knew more about scientists, coastal use permitting, brownfields, energy efficiency, and things like that," he said, laughing. He got involved through Pam Dashiel, then head of the Holy Cross Sustainable Development Organization they started together. Pitt had reached out to Pam. "Pam told me they wanted our help," he recalled.

Charles is tall and thin with a warm smile and moves easily from the lighthearted to the solemn, but he is always seeking a deeper meaning in the subjects that he is discussing. He frequently shares wisdom he learned from his parents and grandparents. "I'm always impressed," he said, "by people who are very smart or know how to give. My mother told me: 'A lot of love has been given to you, and you must always feel you can give it back.' This is not easy in this dog-eat-dog world. Someone must have done the same thing for Brad. He knows how to give." Charles also likes to cite a particular observation of his father, a retired state education administrator, high school sports coach, and longtime Lower Nine resident who has little patience for the critics of Make It Right: "I don't know what they're squawking about," the senior Allen has said. "Every period and place has its own style. Those houses represent the post-Katrina period like stone houses in other cities."[11]

"[E]very time I come back you can see the neighborhood grow a little bit more. And coming over the Claiborne Bridge is my favorite sight," Pitt has said. "[T]his is such an emblem of change and survival and resilience and putting your life back together and putting together a new way." Pitt laid out the goals of Make It Right in contrast to other rebuilding efforts:

> [W]e're after something different. And that is—how do we define our neighborhoods for the future? . . . We want to see, with the community here, if we could build . . . a house that was a home with dignity—dignity for the family, their paycheck, their health, their kids' future, and . . . we've had amazing, amazing results. And I think this goes so much, so much further beyond just one neighborhood.[12]

• • •

Robert Green, a fifty-nine-year-old retired real estate agent and accountant, is an MIR homeowner. A tall man with a salt-and-pepper beard, Green is a bundle of energy, always willing to tell his and the neighborhood's story to passing tourists or the TV cameras. He counts Anderson Cooper, Tavis Smiley, and Spike Lee as memorable visitors. Green's story is a microcosm of the disaster. Green lost a granddaughter to Katrina's floodwaters. His mother died on the roof, waiting to be rescued. A memorial sits in the small front yard of his new house, the site of his former home.

Like thousands of residents, Green at first heeded the call to leave. He and a car filled with his family—including his elderly mother, a mentally challenged cousin, a daughter, and grand-daughters—left the Sunday before Katrina hit and headed to his brother's place in Nashville. They were on the road for hours, but eventually ended up where they started. "My mom was so sick we had to turn back," he told me. "We headed for the Superdome and tried to get her to the special-needs section. They told us to go home and come back tomorrow. They couldn't take her then."

"We didn't expect the storm to be so big, so fast," Green recalled of the next morning. "The water rose twenty-five feet in twelve minutes." Green led the family up into the attic and broke a hole in the roof to pass everyone through. He put three-year-old Shanai on the roof and reached down for the next two children. When he looked up again "she was gone." The house was lifted off its foundation and floated from 1826 to 1617 Tennessee Street with the rest of the family on the roof. His mother died from dehy-dration and exposure. They had to leave her body on the roof.

Eventually, neighbors in boats came to the rescue. "Neigh-bors were the only first responders," he said with an edge in his voice. "They took us to the Claiborne Avenue Bridge [nearby] but we were told we had to go to the St. Claude Avenue Bridge [a siz-able distance] if we wanted to be rescued. When we got there, hun-dreds of National Guard and state troopers were standing around just talking and watching. I told one of them about my mother's body and he said, 'What are you telling me for?'" Her body lay on the roof for 120 days. No search effort seemed to be able to find her. "I found her myself on December 29th," he said. "Her body was so exposed and visible on the roof anybody should have been able to find her." He found Shanai's body in October.

Tennessee Street is two blocks in from the levee breach. The remains of Green's house were a "concrete pile, a toilet, a burnt car, and a sofa." As with many houses in the neighborhood, the three front steps remained in place, standing alone as if to attest to the former presence of a dwelling.[13] Green had moved there with his mother and three brothers as a twelve-year-old, in 1967, when "Tennessee Street was all white." His mother had been an Air Force WAC in the 1950s. By the '60s, she was working two jobs, one in an Army mailroom and the other as a key-punch operator for Cooper Data Systems. They were living in the Desire Housing Project on the other side of the Industrial Canal, known as the Upper Ninth Ward. The family was forced out because his mother was making too much money. Moving to Tennessee Street, however, was surely considered a move up from the public housing.

After Katrina, Green had settled in Nashville near his brother and was planning to stay and open an accounting and real estate office. When he returned in order to find his granddaughter's body, he changed his mind. "I knew I had to come home," he said, shaking his head. His words came forth slowly for the first time and with a tinge of emotion. "This was a family house. I had played football in the streets. My kids played football in the streets. I had regularly walked around the neighborhood with my young kids to say hello to our elderly neighbors. We knew everyone." Green had appealed to FEMA for a trailer on behalf of his mentally challenged cousin, who died, subsequently, in 2008. His FEMA experience was just one more bizarre screw-up experienced by Katrina victims all over the city. "At one point, the FEMA agent told me that my mother *withdrew* her request for a trailer," he said with a chuckle. "I told him that if he had had a communication from my mother, I wish he would tell me how because I would love to speak with her again, since she's dead." He eventually got the trailer. For a long time, his was the only presence in the neighborhood, and he became a favorite media interviewee.

At first he had planned to build a new house himself. Architectural students from Georgia Tech drew plans for him. He got permits to build, but then he reconsidered: "Make It Right sounded like a big opportunity. They were the first ones anyone could trust. You have to believe in something, and I believed from the beginning." Unlike many homeowners, Green was able to prove ownership of his house. He could produce his mother's deed and tax receipts, unlike others whose grandparents had built the family home and never created a deed. He had to pay $6,000 for a succession attorney to establish this fact. "Because I was in real estate, I knew real estate attorneys and abstractors and could get help." His three brothers signed over to him their ownership share.

Green's experience with Road Home was also quite typical.[14] Road Home bureaucrats estimated it would cost Green $167,000 to rebuild. They offered him $700. "What did you expect?" he said. "They had every incentive to save money: $700 to replace but $150,000 to go away! They offered everyone $150,000 to go away, more than they offered to stay. Well, if you're elderly and you have difficulty proving ownership, what would you do? You get more money to leave than to stay, and plenty did. You wonder why so many didn't return? If you had to live somewhere else for two or three years in the meantime and spend money doing that, it was a hard choice."

Green appealed the ridiculous $700 offer, and even that dragged on for months. The process discouraged many others. Eventually, he got $125,000. His Make It Right house cost $166,000 to build; he paid the $125,000 from Road Home and was given a grant of $40,000 from Make It Right. Donated or reduced-cost components helped keep the total construction expenses down. Some homeowners got bigger grants and a soft second mortgage, if they qualified.

Green's MIR house was designed by Thaddeus Zarse of the New Orleans firm Eskew + Dumez + Ripple. It is a two-story, pale-green variation of a shotgun with the same open flow between rooms. This house is 1,700 square feet in size; the one destroyed was 1,100 square feet. It has four bedrooms and is a family home, with two sons living there full-time. Other children come and go and often stay for long periods of time. All of Green's children were involved in the process of picking a house design and worked with the architect to make little adjustments.[15] Contemporary versions of shutters and grill work served the same traditional purposes of shade and air circulation. A porch, ground-floor bench, shaded space, and small garden area continued the traditional connectedness to the street and community. His old electric bill used to average $250 a month. When he lived in a FEMA trailer, it was $170 a month. Here in the MIR house it is $120 for both electric and gas—about $90 for the electric alone. And, he pointed out, he is home all day and there are four computers and four TVs. McDonough and Braungart's *Cradle to Cradle* principles are apparent in the house's water and energy-saving systems and in the use of permeable materials out front such as gravel, gardens, grass, and stone rather than concrete pavers.

Meanwhile, with all the new state-of-the-art green technology components in each house, residents have been trained in new skills and some have started their own businesses. Incremental steps and micro-planning are very much part of the strategy, which includes an organic approach, learning as the process unfolds.

The innovations that don't necessarily attract the spotlight are often quite small but, when added up, contribute significantly to the repair of the city's ravaged fabric. In the Lower Nine, for example, a number of minimal efforts emerged that contributed to the restored-housing inventory. The twentieth restored SUN (Southern United Neighborhoods)[16] house was intended for a low-income resident who had not been able to return to New Orleans until this house was completed in 2014. In addition, the Greater New Orleans Foundation (GNOF) Community Revitalization Fund is doing great work.[17] The list of grants given out in just over three years includes more than fifteen neighborhood-based housing efforts aimed at low-income residents.

In the late 1970s and early 1980s, when I was observing similar endeavors in places like the South Bronx, Savannah, Pittsburgh, Brooklyn, and Cincinnati, such local efforts were a novelty. Experts dismissed them as too small, too ad hoc, and not meaningful, although collectively they added up to real change. While they were rare back then, today every city has some kind of neighborhood-based renovation/reconstruction effort, sometimes several. To be sure, some of those efforts have been co-opted by conventional developers and contractors in ways that undermine their quality and spirit, and others are more about producing tax credits for investors than providing appropriate quality housing for the locality. But overall, the efforts of community-based organizers working to make local improvements add significant momentum to renewal.

• • •

Outsiders, too, are making such efforts in New Orleans. Consider the story of Anne Van Ingen and Wes Haynes, both New York preservation experts, who decided after Katrina to make a contribution to the rebuilding of the city by restoring a small shotgun house in Holy Cross and then selling it at no profit, just covering their costs. Anne and Wes bought the damaged 1,100-square-foot shotgun with one bath in August 2008, a few months before the economy fell apart. They finished restoring the house in 2009 but couldn't sell until 2012. Banks weren't lending. An inventory of similar houses, restored by the Preservation Resource Center, was also on the market. Eventually, a young contractor from Texas bought it and started a new contracting business. "We just wanted someone who would be a good neighbor," Anne told me. The buyer fit that requirement.

This one restoration had a major impact on its block and beyond. When Anne and Wes started working on it, only two of the thirteen houses on the block were occupied. Those two houses, and others nearby, were restored with preservation grants administered by the State Historic Preservation Office (SHPO).[18] "They illustrate the advantage of being in a designated historic district," said Anne, who had worked in the field in New York State as director of the State Council on the Arts Architecture and Planning Committee. "It is quick, nimble, smart, and thoughtful money administered by people in the state historic preservation office who knew the neighborhood and had long-standing relationships there. This was in contrast to FEMA, which took forever and was administered by people who knew nothing about the place. FEMA money was hard to draw down. This money was not only quickly received but well targeted and easier for the homeowner with less paperwork."

Anne and Wes's work was like a beacon for the block, a sign of renewal momentum beyond the two houses. A neighbor across the street gained confidence in the prospect that the area had a future and began to rebuild. Two more neighbors soon followed his lead. Nearby streets were regaining occupants, too. It is impossible to calculate the cumulative impact of those early rebuilders. Surely, no statistic can capture the snowball effect. Today that block has only one blighted property out of thirteen, and it is hard to know which of the many possible explanations apply. Restored historic gems are scattered everywhere in Holy Cross. Ten years after Katrina, the market is up and grievances about gentrification are being discussed.

Then there is another outsider, Leonard Riggio, who, like Brad Pitt, stepped in to help after the storms. But he had a different strategy. Riggio is best known as the head of Barnes & Noble, the world's largest bookseller, which until he acquired it in 1971 was primarily a college textbook company. Riggio first grew a book exchange business he founded as a student at New York University in 1965, acquired Barnes & Noble along the way, and developed that combination into the major force it is today. A serious modern art collector and former chairman of the Dia Art Museum in Beacon, New York, Riggio has long been involved in civil and human rights efforts. "My ancestors came here at the turn of the century," he told me, "making me third- or fourth-generation American. African-Americans came generations before that, and the idea that this group has to continue to fight for its rights troubles me today."

During our conversation, Riggio was sitting in his Fifth Avenue office surrounded by art books as well as contemporary artworks and furnishings. Like so many Americans, he was "transfixed watching the storm. The pictures of the Superdome really got to me, so many poor people living in low-lying areas and treated like second-class citizens. I always loved the city of New Orleans and loved to visit," he explained with the passion so common among distant fans of this city. "While it still experiences racial tensions," he added, "there is no other city where the mix of races works so smoothly, even with rough spots."

Riggio "hatched a plan never done before" to help repopulate a working-class area of the city through construction of replacement homes on single sites. Along with his wife, Louise, he made a donation of $20 million—the largest housing-related contribution by an individual after Katrina—to start Project Home Again. The foundation underwrites all staff and soft costs. Money spent on each house goes only to construction.

Getting the project off the ground was no easy task. First, in an attempt to work with the city, Riggio explained his idea to then-Mayor Ray Nagin. Riggio asked for help from the city to acquire vacant land: "We wanted a piece of land for a hundred homes in one spot to create density. It was going to include a major work of art, maybe a general store and a community center. But Nagin asked, 'How are you going to make money on it?' and what was

in it for him. He brushed us off to a deputy, who proceeded not
to help." Riggio went on to say that "Catholic Charities was no
help, either. We spent eighteen months banging our head against a
wall and were turned down at every corner. Everyone wanted the
money or for us to do something else. In frustration, we turned to
a real estate broker."

In hard-hit Gentilly, Riggio found property large enough for
twenty high-profile homes on a major thoroughfare. Gentilly is
a working-class community that reminded Riggio of his Brooklyn neighborhood near Coney Island where he grew up and where
cab and truck drivers, electricians, and sanitation workers all
owned their own homes and shared a great sense of community.
"A busy and visible street would be a beacon for the community,"
said Carey Shea, who became executive director of Project Home
Again in 2008. Carey had come to New Orleans from New York
City, where she worked for Habitat for Humanity because, as
she noted in an interview, she "wanted to be part of the recovery focused on affordable housing." In 2006, she administered
and coordinated the Rockefeller Foundation–funded Unified New
Orleans Plan process that had been designed by Steven Bingler,
who was chief planner of the process. After that, Carey worked on
developing a community revitalization fund at the Greater New
Orleans Foundation, where she was discovered by Riggio. Carey
recognized that Riggio was having trouble getting his project off
the ground. "I was scared they would get frustrated and leave."
Carey had a history of success in the affordable housing field,
starting as a defiant homesteader on Manhattan's Lower East Side
in the 1980s after college. She made Project Home Again work.
"People saw our houses," she said, "and were reassured if they
were on the fence."

Homebuyers for the first twenty houses had to have lived
and owned a home in New Orleans before Katrina. They had to
swap their irredeemable house to buy the new one. Twelve buyers
were from Gentilly. Eight properties were traded with the city for

vacant parcels in Gentilly. After that, Project Home Again was off and running and the swap system continued. The damaged houses received were then deconstructed and parts were sold through the PRC salvage store. The organization focused on dense blocks with a missing house. The build-and-trade process continued until the first one hundred homes were finished early in 2012. Houses sold for their appraised value, which typically was $20,000 below cost. The gap was made up by a city-funded Neighborhood Stabilization Program (NSP2) that funds the difference between the building cost and sale price.

Gentilly is a sizable neighborhood with both new and old sections. No historic architectural style dominates the newer section where Project Home Again was building. The new homes are two- to four-bedrooms in a modest Craftsman style. An "architecture compatible with the culture" was the aim, with energy efficiency as part of the design. "We actually built a very simple but livable house," Riggio told me. "It was the way my family lived with my grandmother. My father was a taxi driver." Each home was slightly modified by the new owner and came furnished. The owner chose the furniture.

After the first hundred homes were built, the Riggios committed to another hundred, to be finished by the tenth anniversary of Katrina by means of a grant of $44,000 toward each house. This time, moderate-income buyers who hadn't owned a home in the last three years as well as newcomers to the city were eligible.

It is unclear what the future will hold for Project Home. "With each twenty to thirty houses," Carey said, "we learned to make the homes greener and less costly, added a focus on landscaping and storm water run-off, and shifted parking to the rear." The best part, she added, was "watching the neighborhood come back and gain its own renewing momentum." The work of Project Home Again is another valuable contribution to the sustainable rebuilding of New Orleans. The catalytic impact of each house is hugely significant.

Yet not every new house is a plus for the city. Habitat for Humanity is building numerous houses, for example, but not necessarily to the good. Habitat is a worldwide Christian housing ministry founded in 1976 by Alabama entrepreneur Millard Fuller. After a life-changing experience, he and his wife gave away all their worldly possessions and refocused their life to apply Christ's teaching by building housing for the poor.[19] The program was made famous by former president Jimmy Carter and is loved by the volunteers who hammer in nails and feel good about their contribution; it is similarly loved by big donors looking for an easy, familiar way to make a contribution (even though a contribution in response to a disaster like Katrina does not always go entirely to the site of that disaster).[20]

Sadly, the poor quality of Habitat's houses causes resentment among those who see it as "poor people's" housing. As one local resident observed: "They are so obviously cheap in looks and materials that they actually bring down the values in the neighborhood. And they don't offer the homeowner long-term equity growth because the quality is bound to diminish, not appreciate." A former employee of Habitat told me that, sometimes, after the volunteers are gone, their work has to be ripped out and replaced by professionals. Another critic added that it is "a condescending view of what poor people should be allowed to get—1,100 square feet, one bathroom, tiny rooms, and a porch hardly deep enough to rock a chair on. And God forbid the future owner of the house being worked on drives up in a late-model car: all feeling of charity among volunteers goes out the window."

In 2006, I remember walking in the Ninth Ward past the construction of Musicians' Village, which includes the fabulous Ellis Marsalis Center—an entertainment venue and multifaceted music school. Volunteers from Habitat were happily nailing up the walls and laying floors. Yet right across the street were homeowners struggling to repair their badly damaged houses with help from family and friends. Several of these homeowners were elderly. I asked one of them if anyone from Habitat had offered any help. One elderly gentleman replied: "They don't even say hello and, you know, in New Orleans, we all say hello, even to strangers."

• • •

Fortunately for New Orleans, historic preservation has offered the strongest appeal to a handful of dedicated civic adherents since as far back as the 1920s, when a group of formidable women—whom we will learn about later—fought to save the French Quarter, at the time a virtual slum. Rarely in any US city have preservation advocates been as successful, despite some big losses—probably because they started so early in the twentieth century. In most cities, a preservation movement didn't take hold or gain many adherents until after the Urban Renewal losses of the 1960s. Although the preservation tradition isn't as widespread as it could or should be, there will always be a dedicated group of citizens who will fight for the preservation of the city. Through the decades many individuals have contributed to the preservation tradition, usually by battling official plans to demolish historic areas for one misguided project or another.

The best-known preservation organization in New Orleans is the Preservation Resource Center. Established in 1974 with a $45,000 grant from the Junior League at the height of demolitions, the PRC soon pursued a catalytic project. In 1976, PRC saved and restored a very important but derelict 1832 row house, one of the so-called Thirteen Sisters on downtown's Julia Row. That street was then the heart of Skid Row. To observe that Julia Street neighborhood now, between the Warehouse District and the Central Business District, one would be hard-pressed to understand how deteriorated it had been. Investors follow, after preservationists have shown that a market exists. This preservation work served as a critical regenerative catalyst early in the city's history.

PRC programs went into high gear after the storms, with many volunteers coming from around the country to help. They painted houses in failing neighborhoods to give the area a facelift. They led tours of restored homes to inspire prospective homebuyers. *Preservation in Print,* a highly informative monthly magazine inaugurated in 1988, kept people informed and gave them cause for optimism. Through Operation Comeback, PRC restored and sold approximately 100 houses—more than half of these since Katrina. Through Rebuilding Together, PRC repaired approximately 1,300 homes occupied by low-income, veteran, and elderly owners—about 350 of these since the storm. After Katrina, with the help of the National Trust for Historic Preservation, another 25 houses were restored and reoccupied. PRC deconstructed and salvaged close to 200 structures that were beyond repair. Salvage parts are sold in their salvage store. With tours, events, ever-changing programs, and workshops on such things as mold remediation after Katrina, PRC has made an impact comparable to that of major developers and is considered a model nationwide.

PRC has not done as well in the advocacy department, however. For the huge, politically fraught fight to save Charity Hospital, the battle to save the Mid-City neighborhood, the intense fight to save the historic red brick/tiled-roof public housing projects, and the most recent fight over a Holy Cross development, PRC was absent.

Patty Gay, PRC's tireless director for more than forty years, cites several threatened smaller properties that PRC advocated to save mainly by publicizing the threats and bringing attention when needed. Over the years the organization has championed the rescue of some uptown properties and three nineteenth-century buildings on Canal Street owned by a Minneapolis hotel developer.[21] And PRC joined the successful citywide outcry in response to the mayor's proposal to tear down the World Trade Center building and replace it with an iconic waterfront sculpture and new development. "New Orleans is a poor city," she said in an interview, "and whenever a developer comes up with a big development, it's hard. The important thing is that preservation comes up with solutions and our programs do that." Patty pointed out that PRC's educational role is a form of advocacy.

But this is not enough for serious preservationists. Early PRC founder Mary Lou Christovich has never lost her feisty "can-do" spirit. Expressing a sentiment echoed by many, she said: "I admire all they do with volunteers but they have become a bureaucracy within themselves with a board of socially prominent men and women tagging along to be identified with a successful organization but who don't have the needed fire in the belly for historic preservation." The unhappiness with PRC's limited advocacy efforts was summed up by author Fred Starr in conversation: "Of course, the PRC is a noble organization, but it is too gentle to engage in the kind of head-bumping and arm-wrestling that is sometimes called for in order to turn back the enemies of historic preservation. Perhaps PRC should consider hiring a couple of in-house pit bulls."

Another well-known preservationist organization is the Louisiana Landmarks Society. Organized in 1950 to prevent the demolition of the nineteenth-century City Hall designed by noted architect James Gallier, Sr., Louisiana Landmarks over the years has been involved with the effort to save the 1854 Jefferson Parish Court House, the fight against the French Quarter Expressway, the lawsuit against closing Bayou St. John from Lake Pontchartrain, and many other issues. In 1971 it restored the Pitot House— an eighteenth-century Creole plantation house overlooking Bayou St. John—and opened it as a museum. Early in the historic preservation movement, national house museums were of utmost importance. The Pitot House Museum remained the focus of the Louisiana Landmarks Society for years. More recently, the Society initiated the Nine Most Endangered List to spotlight the most critical New Orleans landmarks threatened with loss; it also stepped up its advocacy work, participating in the lawsuit to keep the moratorium on more hotels in the Quarter and joining the fight to save Charity Hospital, the Mid-City neighborhood, and the historic public housing. In 2014, it sided with the community of Holy Cross to stave off a most inappropriate development proposal that had become a very contentious citywide fight.

Easy development money is made with big, new construction projects involving big contracts, big tax incentives, political influence, and efficiency of scale. None of that is true of genuine restoration projects. Fortunately for New Orleans, a few preservation-minded developers are doing well just by restoring blighted vintage houses. This entails incremental change with immediate and significant impacts in one neighborhood that triggers upgrades in other neighborhoods, cumulatively adding up to big change.

Neal Morris is an exemplar in this group. A graduate of Tulane with degrees in business and law, Neal restored his first house while still a student. From then on he was hooked. He picks the "worst of the worst" to restore, and he does this in neighborhoods where not much upgrade activity is occurring or where the upward trend is still modest. The best part of his work is that the restored homes become long-term low-income rentals, a resource in short supply. Even in cases where a surrounding neighborhood has gentrified into a middle-income enclave, the low-income tenants are protected.

"Infilling our historic density should be the priority," Neal said in conversation, "before adding new megaplexes. Rare is the building that can't be saved given the will, ingenuity, and determination." By layering available tax incentives—federal and state low-income and historic rehabilitation tax credits, and the city's Neighborhood Stabilization Program incentives—Neal has restored 450 units since founding his company, Redmellon, in 2000. Redmellon is a made-up name purposely meant to differentiate it from typical development companies. "The soul of New Orleans is our historic structures," Neal said, reflecting his passion for preservation.

All of the efforts described in this chapter are interesting in their own right, but even more fascinating is the fact that nothing like this took place in New Orleans before the storms. Few neighborhoods, and even fewer not-for-profit organizations, organized around uplifting an area—an important aspect of the city's recovery. Before Katrina, no one officially seemed to care about blight and surely nothing was done about it. Since the storms, it is front and center. Indeed, this rebuilding is being undertaken all over town by community-focused organizations and small developers.

Unfortunately, the significant, citywide impact is unheralded by the Landrieu administration, one preservationist told me. No recognition is apparent as to how much these efforts are contributing cumulatively to the elimination of blight. Individually, the programs are welcomed, applauded, and celebrated in almost heroic terms. But acknowledgment of the big-picture impact is missing. One of the program participants noted that while all these efforts have been helped by various government programs, no city agency has sought to bring representatives of these efforts together in one room to discuss their work, their strategies, what resources they have or need, and how things could be better.

The mayor's anti-blight policy seems largely focused on code enforcement and demolition[22]—an emphasis that is common in many cities long experiencing population loss. The primary driver of this anti-blight focus is the availability of federal funds. Federal blight-removal money is inappropriately available only for demolition. Cities want those funds, but if flexibility allowed some of that money to go to homeowners or developers wanting to renovate, the impact would be a more positive one. "The mayor doesn't quite realize how much is being done positively out here," one activist told me. "We are, in effect, his troops on the ground."

The two factors driving New Orleans's revival most of all are the widespread renovation of damaged homes—some ordinary and some of historic quality, some by nonprofits and others by small developers or homeowners themselves—and new infill houses that strengthen existing communities. These factors are decidedly not part of some grand plan that came off any professional drawing board. The gentle repairing of the urban fabric has evolved organically, but within a framework in which expectations and limits are set—a framework that makes possible a rebirth without a grand formal vision. Simply put, this organic process is working better than any citywide plan would have been able to, in a reasonable amount of time, allowing as many different individuals or groups as possible to participate. The rebirth is being planned and implemented *by* the citizens from the ground up, not *for* them from above. Ten years after Katrina, the results are remarkable.

Chapter 7

Inside and Outside the Levee

If Texas annexed 50 square miles of Louisiana Coast, we would go to war! Yet, the political community doesn't even notice as it sinks away.

—Oliver Houck, Tulane Law School professor

A t the northern edge of the Lower Ninth Ward, not far from the Butler/Harris compound, is a seemingly insignificant but historically rich body of water, Bayou Bienvenue.[1] Dead tree stumps stick out of this once-thriving 433-acre cypress swamp. The water appears motionless. Dense greenery that once filled this space now only hugs the far shore and, somewhat amazingly, an egret or pelican occasionally passes through. This urban coast meanders out to the state coast. It is part of a whole geographic system that serves as a buffer for storm surges and is critical for flood protection, fisheries, and flyways for migratory birds. All the elements of the big picture are here.

Up through the 1920s, Bayou Bienvenue was a robust cypress swamp with dense woods and plenty of fish, alligators, and lily pads. The nearby Lower Ninth Ward population, still rather small at this time, fished from handmade pirogue boats in the fertile waters.[2] Today, a twelve-foot steel wall runs in front of an earthen levee along the Lower Nine shore, erected after the heavy floods caused by Hurricane Betsy in 1965. Until 2012, tall grasses and weeds grew along the wall, so thick that the steel barrier was hardly visible. A rail line parallels the water's edge, once a busy freight route from the Industrial Canal that winds around the Lower Nine border to the Mississippi River wharves. Breaking this visual and physical barrier is a single oasis-like clearing. A modest wooden overlook stands there, with a pergola and steps down to the water. The simplicity of this overlook obscures its immeasurable significance. One walks up a path through a modest landscaped area, across rail tracks, up the incline with crushed oyster shells underfoot, and then up steep wood stairs to the overlook. A surprise awaits. To the northwest, a snapshot of the environmental degradation of the Louisiana coast over the past century spreads out before one's eyes. Usually, one needs to fly over land or take a boat tour to see firsthand what were once dense wetlands protecting the Lower Nine's shore and serving as a buffer against high hurricane winds.

Looking back from the platform landward south toward the Mississippi River, one takes in the slow but steady house-by-house regeneration of the Lower Nine. Here, close to the bayou, is the least rebuilt area. The density emerging from the Make It Right houses is a considerable distance away. New or rebuilt houses are randomly set in open fields and much of the stretch bordering the bayou feels like rural farm country. It was so quiet, when I first visited the site in 2007, that I could hear voices from the front porches of one rebuilt house three blocks away. Each year since, a few more houses appeared haphazardly. Some were built and owner-occupied; others were built on speculation for rent. Density increases toward the river, many blocks away. The feeling of emptiness, however, still prevails. When I first went there, the landside view was as desolate as the world imagined the whole Lower Nine to be. But then I remembered Josephine Butler's determination, her disregard for the emptiness around her, and her confidence that others would follow. There was nothing specific to inspire my own confidence other than having observed for decades the kind of resilience that is part of the DNA of so many communities. Sure enough, the positive change began to emerge slowly, under any official radar, and still is emerging.

In 2012, a long-fought-for park was rebuilt across from the overlook, bringing back more life to this northernmost section of the Lower Nine. A few more new or rebuilt houses appeared. More people came to the overlook. Many hands made the overlook happen, but the dedication of one person in particular was the thread that tied it all together, transforming this singular site into part of a larger vision. This person was the late Pam Dashiel, a black, Boston-born environmentalist who lived in the Lower Ninth Ward for close to twenty years. Her mother grew up here, and for years Pam heard great stories about the place, people, and culture. She knew at a young age that she wanted to move here.

Pam understood community engagement. As Jacques Morial, a public policy analyst and civic activist, told me: "Pam was central to holding the various groups of the Lower Nine together. Under Pam's leadership [that community] led in civic engagement after Katrina. They are the model. They met weekly. They were self-governed. They built a lot of trust among themselves, so that if someone didn't get his way, that was okay because he knew he had been heard and that another time he would get his way."

In 2007 Pam cofounded, with environmentalist Charles Allen in Holy Cross, the Center for Sustainable Engagement and Development to focus on coastal rehabilitation, greening the built environment, and increasing food security.[3] The idea of initiating a catalytic project at the most challenging site of the Lower Ninth Ward would not have occurred to most people. But Pam had an expansive vision of urban and environmental rebirth, a vision that started in the Lower Nine but fed the health of the larger city and region, including the dangerously eroding coast. She understood that any minimal intervention could trigger larger impacts. The overlook is a by-product of Pam's vision. A force of nature in her own right, Pam represented the will of this community not just to survive but to grow back stronger in an environmentally conscious manner. Almost a human embodiment of the Live Oak, Pam was resilient, firmly connected, and deeply rooted in her community with a broad influence reaching out around her. She stood strong and firm, determined to survive the ill winds of government neglect and absence of support.

"There was a vacuum," Pam noted in a conversation with me after Katrina, a few years before she died suddenly of a heart attack in 2010. "The Lower Nine was always ignored, so people always had to do for themselves." Quiet-spoken with short-cropped hair and a winning smile, she deftly spread environmental awareness without making anyone feel uneducated and inspired everyone involved to believe that their effort was as important as her own. "She'd ask your opinion and you didn't realize she was pulling you in," said Warrenetta Banks, office manager for the Center. "Everybody has a passion. Hers was the environment and this community. She had a subtle, calm way of getting you involved."[4]

Sometimes it was not so calm, nor subtle. And that is where the overlook comes in, an accomplishment way beyond its modest appearance. Architect John Williams, whom Pam often called with her newest challenging idea, recalled: "She'd start out by asking me, 'John, have you ever done' whatever new idea was on her mind. My response was always the same: 'No, but I have a feeling I will now.'" That was how the overlook came to pass.

The effort to restore the bayou had been initiated by the Center under Pam's and Charles's direction. The idea was quite serendipitous. Austin Allen—now head of the LSU Landscape Design Program but, at the time of Katrina, teaching at the University of Colorado at Denver—came two days after the storm to help in the Lower Nine. He had brought his graduate landscape design students and was looking for a project. He reached out to Jacques,

who took him to see the bayou. Lower Nine third-generation resident Steve Ringo came along. "We piled up rocks at the wall to
stand on and look over," Jacques told me. "I knew that was where
the water came from before the levee broke. That bayou once softened the storm surge in a hurricane. It needed restoration." For
Jacques and others of his generation, the bayou was a playground,
if they were willing to somehow climb over the floodwall. When
Jacques was six years old, in 1967, his day camp came here for a
nature walk. When he got older, unbeknownst to his parents,[5] he
and his friends would bike down on their own from Pontchartrain
Park at Lake Pontchartrain.[6] "They wouldn't have liked that we
crossed three highways and a bridge," he recalled with a grin. "It
was a unique experience for a kid growing up in the city" and, in
his case, the "pseudo-suburban community" that was Pontchartrain Park. "There was cool stuff there. One friend brought a box
and caught turtles to sell for home aquariums for ten cents."

In 2006, at a community meeting about rebuilding efforts,
Pam solicited ideas from the audience. Steve Ringo said: "Mayor
Nagin told us to 'think outside of the box,' so how about restoring
the bayou?" The bayou? Few but the old-timers knew the bayou
even existed beyond the wall of steel that cut it off from view. As a
group, they went over to look, leaning ladders against the steel to
get a view over the wall, surprised at what they saw. Sure enough,
they all recognized a valuable asset and multiple opportunities.
"The larger community vision Pam had initiated already embraced
the idea of solar and other green technology," noted Darryl
Malek-Wiley, a Sierra Club organizer for New Orleans who has
worked on Gulf Coast environmental issues for more than thirty
years and moved to New Orleans in 1982. "But she recognized
that rebuilding green wasn't enough, that we needed to take care
of our portion of the coast as well, and here was the opportunity
to do it."

As with hundreds of other local rebuilding efforts all over
New Orleans, volunteers came from around the country. Austin

has spent his life here since Katrina and lives in the Lower Nine. The challenges are daunting, he admitted, but "you have to start somewhere." His Colorado students signed on to the platform project. Four faculty members and twenty-eight students met with the community, researched the challenges, suggested plans, amended them after local comments were offered, and designed the platform that became a community priority. In addition, students from the University of Wisconsin provided valuable studies of the bayou water.

The idea for the platform was the easy part. The students raised the money and bought the materials or got them donated, but the Wisconsin professors insisted on getting a permit. What may appear to be a normal expectation elsewhere is never normal in New Orleans.

The stories about permits range from jokes to tales of horror. In this case, it was a horror story. Pam called John, figuring that he could secure the permit. "That's impossible, I told her," he recalled. "You need permission from six agencies—the levee board, the Corps of Engineers, the Coast Guard, the Department of Public Works, the New Orleans Belt (the local railroad that runs along the bayou shore), and the Department of Environmental Protection. And it would need handicap access. Impossible!" The Corps had informally approved the plan, but the levee board said that the plan did not conform to guidelines. The Wisconsin professors, however, made it clear that the platform would not get built without a permit, so Pam was relentless. Eventually, John called Pam back and told her again that this was impossible. "But I told her I would be personally liable if they went ahead, and I asked her if she needed me to tell them she had a permit. She said yes, so I said, 'Pam, you have a permit.' Then I asked her if she knew what civil disobedience was. 'Tell them you have a permit. It's the right thing to do.'"

She did just that. The platform got built.[7] No permit was ever issued. The delays involved just in trying to get the permit took so long that the students graduated but came back on their own in the summer to build the platform.

On one occasion, Jacques was at the platform with Malik Rahim, legendary community organizer, former member of the Black Panther Party, and founder of Common Ground in New Orleans—an organization that helps residents rebuild. On this day, a railroad official drove by and stopped to tell Jacques and Rahim that the platform was illegal, that they were trespassing, and that they had to leave. Rahim replied, "If you so much as touch that platform, no train will ever be able to pass here again." No further problems ensued.

Even in the beginning stages of the platform construction, the significance of the site and its hopeful story of environmental and community renewal was clear. I kept coming back to this site. Pam's platform initiative became another one of those New Orleans stories that serve as a metaphor for the slow but solid forward-moving rebirth process. It is another example of a local initiative pursuing a seemingly impossible goal with minimal official, financial, or technical support, yet with dedication, modest foundation support, perseverance, and the critical assistance of volunteer expertise. The story of the regeneration of New Orleans after the storm is filled with tales of the impossible being accomplished by those too naïve to know that it "can't be done," or those determined to just do it and ask permission afterward. This is a common theme in the regeneration successes in every city. Sometimes, the effort is labeled a "demonstration project." It's amazing how many outside-of-the-box "demonstration projects" succeed and eventually become the norm. Over time, many of these modest beginnings mature into major results; that is the way of effective, enduring change on any scale.

The goal of restoring Bayou Bienvenue started receiving official attention from the city, state, and the Corps of Engineers. To facilitate the renewal process, the city's Sewerage and Water Board initiated a pilot project at the East Bank Sewage Treatment Center just downriver: clean effluent from two ten-acre zones is being pumped up into the bayou to help fill it back in. It's working. Slowly, this body of water is coming back to life. "Salinity is actually down," Darryl reported in early 2012. A heavyset man with a Santa Claus–style beard, Darryl is a self-taught environmentalist who worked with Pam on a variety of projects. "Pelicans are back. So are osprey, herons, egrets, and Black-bellied Whistling-Ducks." A rock dam was constructed, as was a thirty-two-foot surge barrier with pilings going two hundred feet deep. Darryl explained that this is why—with the closing of MR-GO—the saltwater flow into the bayou is diminishing and fresh water is increasing.

"We're inventing the strategy as we go along, monitoring the progress, and learning from each step," Darryl told me. "The gradual progress of the bayou is emblematic of both the Lower Ninth Ward it borders and the city that is almost oblivious to its existence. The Lower Nine is the only community with the deep sensibility to rebuild sustainably. Others are building back the way they were, and some didn't experience as much destruction." More solar panels are installed in the Lower Nine than anywhere else in the city.[8] Recycled and sustainable materials and historic preservation—the greenest form of construction—are widely embraced here. Make It Right and Global Green houses are at the cutting edge of the sustainable new design and construction in New Orleans. Vegetable gardens abound. Dozens of community groups are busy assisting local residents in myriad ways.

By 2012, word began to get out about the bayou. Curious residents, bike-tour participants, and visitors stopped by. Some came with pirogues or kayaks and set off from the rocky beach created below the platform. By December, I saw that the overgrown weeds and tall grass that hid the bayou for so long had been cleared out and mowed. The steel fence had been sandblasted and repainted. A walking path along the top of the earthen levee had been cleared. Volunteers had planted marsh grass and young cypress trees in boxes to protect them from nutria and rabbits. Life was indeed returning to the bayou.

• • •

John Taylor, a lifelong resident of the Lower Nine, grew up spending most of his time in the bayou. "They used to call me Daniel Boone or Davy Crockett 'cause I was always in the bayou, coming out of the woods with turtles, nutria, rabbits, and alligators," he told me. "I took orders. While everyone else was dancing, I was out there. It kept me out of jail and from being rich. The only thing I understood was nature." Until fur coats went out of fashion, John would earn money by catching nutria, an invasive species originally imported from Argentina.[9] You can still earn $8 a tail because the goal is to diminish their number, but no one wants the fur.

John was a classic victim of Katrina. He was the only occupant of the Lower Nine house that had been his parents' home and was still in their name. The house was destroyed. John and his ten siblings inherited ownership. "You can't get three of them to think the same on anything," he said, so they walked away from the property. The only damages he was able to collect on were for the three trucks he owned. With the $21,000 he was paid for the trucks, he bought a blighted house at auction that he could fix up himself. But he can't afford both a licensed plumber and an electrician. Without work done by both, he can't get a certificate of occupancy. In the meantime, his savings dwindle as he pays to rent a place and hopes he can save enough to renovate the house. Thin and weatherworn at sixty-six (as of 2013), and a definite wetland specialist with a self-taught PhD-level knowledge of zoology, biology, and delta ecology, John can attest to the return of wildlife in the bayou.

Bayou Bienvenue is more than just a metaphor for the slow but steady regeneration of New Orleans. It is a symbol of the urgent but potential rebuilding of the Louisiana coast. The destruction and potential regeneration of Bayou Bienvenue connect the two overarching environmental issues that will determine the future of New Orleans. First, the eroding coast is increasingly close to the city. The Mississippi River Delta loses the equivalent of "one football field" of marshland per hour.[10] Over the last seventy-five years, according to Randy Fertel, "we've lost the equivalent of the state of Delaware to erosion."[11] Second, the city itself is sinking. Vast pumps remove rain and floodwaters, weakening and compacting the soil below. Call it outside and inside the levee: outside is the delta, inside is the city.

Outside the levee is the failing coast of Mississippi, Alabama, Louisiana, Florida, and Texas—the 6,000-square-mile delta built up from the sediment overflowing from the extraordinary Mississippi River, whose inextricable connection to so much of the country is little understood. John Barry writes:

> The river seemed the most powerful thing in the world. Down from the Rocky Mountains of Colorado this water had come, down from Alberta and Saskatchewan in Canada, down from the Allegheny Mountains in New York and Pennsylvania, down from the Great Smokies in Tennessee, down from the forests of Montana and the iron ranges of Minnesota and the plains of Illinois.[12]

The creation and sustenance of the coastal delta was wholly dependent on the nourishment from the annual spring floods of the Mississippi and the rich soil left behind. Without that nourishment, starvation has been the delta's history.

As Bob Marshall, a reporter at *The Lens,* explains:

> Scientists point out that the Mississippi deltas are notoriously complex. Laid down by the river 6,000 years ago, they are a wild weave of countless layers of material, ranging from highly

organic marshes to heavy clays, old woody swamps and pow-
dery alluvial sediments—all of which vary in thickness, rising,
falling and sometimes intertwining to depths of hundreds of
feet. Those layers decompose, compress and sink at varying
rates and are sliced by a web of faults. That makes predicting
future rates of subsidence a nightmare for planners.[13]

The causes of sinking are many. All the mechanisms meant to
tame the river over decades—flood control levees, spillways, locks,
jetties, canals dredged for transportation and for 10,000 miles of
oil and gas pipelines—combine to starve the Gulf of nourishment.
The pipelines crisscross, interlock, and overlap throughout the
marshes; all are connected to wells scattered about. These same
marshes are, of course, both a nursery and a source of food for the
indigenous aquatic species. Since the discovery of oil in the 1930s,
oil and gas companies have built their own canals; permits, initiated in 1972, required remediation of land—which they ignored.

Over the decades, residential communities; important migratory bird breeding grounds; shrimp, oyster, and fishing waters;
and estuaries of all kinds have vanished into oblivion. The rich
alluvial sediment from the Mississippi that once maintained and
renourished the delta and the inland landmass is falling off the
continental shelf into the Gulf. Algae blooms accumulate at the
mouth of the river, creating an annual dead zone of 6,000 to 7,000
square miles, the second largest in the world.[14]

Stemming this environmental disaster and reversing it to the
extent possible are critical to the survival of the southeast coast of
the country, a story stubbornly unknown to most Americans.

This is not merely a southeastern US issue or a New Orleans
issue but one that affects the entire country. Since 2001, R. King
Milling, as head of the American Wetlands Foundation, has made
it his mission to alert the nation to the threats to the Mississippi,
the devastation of the coast, and the resulting financial impacts.
King, the former head of the Whitney National Bank, is also one

of New Orleans's and the state's leading businessmen—about as far from the typical environmental advocate as one could be. He got involved in coastal issues because "this is about business and the enormous potential loss to the country," which is why the American Wetlands Foundation, along with other organizations, has been taking the issue up the river to Memphis, St. Louis, Chicago, and other places. "The whole country has a stake in the coast where five of the country's fifteen largest ports are located," he said in an interview. "Frankly, the worst thing about Katrina is that it became all about New Orleans. It's much larger than that."

Soon after Katrina, political scientist George Friedman wrote a cogent article, "The Ghost City," emphasizing this point.[15] The funding of American industrialization, he pointed out, came from the wealth produced in America's farmland—all made possible by "the extraordinary system of rivers that flowed through the Midwest and allowed them to ship their surplus to the rest of the world. All of the rivers flowed into one—the Mississippi—and the Mississippi flowed to the ports in and around one city, New Orleans." New Orleans was, and still is in many ways, the "pivot of the American economy." Without the New Orleans–area ports, Friedman added, "the very physical structure of the global economy would have to be reshaped."

According to King, the connections of forces working inside and outside the levee could not be clearer. "With the deterioration of the coastline," he said, "and as the erosion continues in the delta, the mouth of the river becomes vulnerable. Ultimately that damage exposes the levee system to direct assaults by the storm surges and waves. More breaches are likely to occur." Southeast Louisiana's national importance, he added, can't be overemphasized. Some people around the country and in Congress appreciate the importance of this region, but we're not setting aside enough money to address the urgent issues: "We happen to be in the center where the climate issues are felt directly, but we're talking about

events affecting the whole country that just happen to be occurring in southeast Louisiana."

The potential national impacts are clear. Coastal Louisiana by itself accounts for 26 percent of America's annual seafood harvest, measured by weight,[16] and is the nursery for much
of the Gulf; southern Louisiana has 40 percent of the country's
coastal marshes[17] and 70 percent of the country's outer continental
oil, and 90 percent of its gas comes from the Louisiana coastal
zone.[18] Accounting for 20 percent of the country's maritime shipping,[19] the New Orleans port connects to six national railways.
The southeast coast constitutes the central flyway for the annual
migration of songbirds and waterfowl (353 species); roughly 5 million migratory waterfowl winter here.[20]

In addition, the southeast coast is the largest and most productive fishing grounds in the continental United States. Thus
the Louisiana license plate: "Sportsman's Paradise." Beyond the
numbers, it is difficult to measure the richness of the wetlands.
And furthermore, southeast Louisiana is home to one of the last
regional cultures in a nation once full of them. The Louisiana
Cajuns are totally dependent on the Gulf-based food economy and
oil economy. There's the rub. If that coast disappears, so do they.

As if rapidly rising seas and Hurricanes Katrina, Rita, Isaac,
and Gustav were not enough, BP's Macondo well and Deepwater
Horizon platform fifty miles off the Louisiana coast exploded on
April 20, 2010, killing eleven men and spilling 210 million gallons
of oil into the Gulf.[21] Oil and gas gushed for months. Residue from
the spill remains to this day. A bigger setback for the recovery of
the Gulf Coast and the city could not have been imagined. Before
that fateful day, New Orleans's recovery was slowly happening,
citizen empowerment was gaining strength, small initiatives were
showing results, and the new mayor, Mitch Landrieu, was two
weeks away from his May 3rd inauguration after having won election by 67 percent of the vote with broad support across racial

and geographic lines. What should have been a time for optimism turned into another period of doom and gloom.

In a perceptive article about the experience of trauma, Randy Fertel discusses the pre-BP state of resilience: "Working together, community action groups re-created, as [Harvard trauma psychologist] Judith Herman describes, 'the psychological faculties that were damaged or deformed by the traumatic experience [including] 'the basic capacities for trust, autonomy, initiative, competence, identity, and intimacy.'"[22] All of this was undermined by the BP disaster. The damage from the spill was not just widespread but painfully long-lasting, with new devastations exposed in a steady flow of revelations that continue today.[23] Then came the disclosure that BP had deployed an illegal toxic dispersant without permission—"not to cure the harm," Randy noted in the same article, "but to hide it from view and thus causing more harm, as corporations and government agencies and leaders covered their asses."[24]

In the fall of 2011, while BP was claiming that the beaches, the water, and the seafood were safe, Naomi Klein accompanied a scientific expedition revealing that the "good news story" BP was telling was demonstrably untrue. What she learned was profoundly discouraging:

> Among the most striking findings are graveyards of recently deceased coral, oiled crab larvae, evidence of bizarre sickness in the phytoplankton and bacterial communities, and a mysterious brown liquid coating large swaths of the ocean floor, snuffing out life underneath. All are worrying signs that the toxins that invaded these waters are not finished wreaking havoc and could, in the months and years to come, lead to consequences as severe as commercial fishery collapses and even species extinctions.[25]

The real impact on the fisheries, and on the local birds diving into the contaminated water for food or the migratory birds needing to eat on their route, is yet unknown. One great concern is that carcinogens may have settled on the marsh floor where a whole range of creatures live, including shrimp, crabs, and oysters. A 2011 study of a 35-square-mile area of the ocean floor found the floor "covered with a blanket of dead bacteria, much of it oily and sticky . . . bottom-dwelling invertebrates—worms, starfish, even coral—were dead."[26]

In April 2013, journalist Bruce Alpert wrote an article with the headline "Watchdog Group Reports Health Problems from Dispersant Use During BP Oil Spill."[27] This piece exposed numerous health problems related to the use of Corexit: "Cleanup workers, doctors, divers and Gulf Coast residents interviewed by [The Government Accountability Project] have reported health problems . . . including blood in the urine, heart palpitations, kidney and liver damage, migraines, memory loss and reduced IQ." But health problems were not the only consequence, as Alpert wrote:

> Federally required worker resource manuals detailing Corexit's potential health hazards were either not delivered or removed from BP worksites early in the cleanup, as health problems began. . . . A government agency regulation prohibited diving during the spill due to concerns about potential health risks. Yet, divers contracted by the National Oceanic and Atmospheric Administration were told it was safe to go deep into Gulf waters without protective equipment. . . . Nearly half the cleanup workers interviewed reported that they were threatened with termination when they tried to wear respirators or additional safety equipment.

Predictably, BP's response, according to a spokesman, was to argue that the "use of dispersants . . . was coordinated with and approved by federal agencies. . . . BP is not aware of any data showing worker or public exposures to dispersants at levels that would pose a health or safety concern."[28]

The aftermath of the Deepwater Horizon disaster cast a pall over recovery projects throughout the Louisiana coast. As Bob Marshall ominously reported in *The Lens*: "Recent studies . . . confirm that hydrocarbon toxins remain in marsh sediments and continue to cause biological impairments that were precursors for species-wide collapses in Alaska after the Exxon Valdez spill."[29] In 2014, there were "dying dolphins, bluefin tuna embryos with heart defects and hundreds of dead sea turtles washing ashore. The oil is not gone and the impacts to wildlife are ongoing."[30]

After the storms and levee failures, the devastation and subsequent problems were, if not always obvious, at least concrete; but after the BP oil spill, everything was uncertain and ambiguous. "With Katrina, rebuilding began perhaps with picking up a hammer," Randy Fertel wrote. "After the BP oil spill, how does an individual have any impact on 210 million barrels of oil and 1.8 million gallons of toxic dispersant?" Add to that the complete and well-earned distrust of the oil industry and the government agencies that are theoretically supposed to monitor its work, and you have an unending specter of doom that was hard to shake. After the oil spill, Congress passed the Restore Act providing that 80 percent of BP's penalties will go to the Gulf's restoration[31] in the five affected states; but given the trail of broken promises, few people expect this to occur as promised. The act doesn't even kick in until 2017.[32]

The best way to see and feel the damage done by the spill is by boat. The visual reality is frightening. Bob, a tall handsome man with a head of thick graying hair and an engaging smile, confronts the reality regularly. On a boat ride, he points out the devastation at every turn. We pass houses on stilts in deep water that not long ago rested on an island. We glide over former landmasses with only shadows visible below. We travel vast open water that used to be dense marshes. We view small, rock-laden spits of land that continue as nesting places for pelicans but are constantly needing to be sustained and rebuilt by dedicated private organizations.

Amidst all the negative scenes is the federal/state Lake Hermitage diversion and marsh restoration project, replenishing one critical area with river sediment and water as it could be doing in so many other places. This is not just a sign of hope but clear evidence that solutions exist to be implemented.

In the toolbox of solutions, the diversion is significant; sediment is dredged from the nearby Mississippi and piped into the sinking marshes. Some diversions have been accomplished; others have been approved by the state but not yet funded. With the funding, however, comes a web of problems exposing endless conflicts and contradictions that make attacking the problems exceedingly difficult.

As we wended our way by outboard through canals and along the coast about thirty miles south of New Orleans, Bob explained, in exasperation, that the ability to make diversions happen "is mired in private interests and local politics, and by extension state and federal politics as well." Residential communities have been built in recent decades along the canals. Sportsmen occupy many of these second homes and cherish the availability of speckled trout and red fish that flourish in the brackish water. Some of these sites are not more than a stone's throw from the Mississippi, often just across the road.

Each diversion crosses multiple parcels of privately owned property. Approval is needed from each property owner (an estimated 80 percent of the wetlands in Louisiana are privately owned).[33] Some of the owners want only part of the diversion's beneficial consequences, but "many want the land rebuilt," Bob told me. "They don't care what it takes to save the marsh, it should be done. Others only want the slurry pipeline that brings sediment to rebuild or fortify the wetland, but they don't want the brackish water to change (it would be freshened) because it may interfere with the fishing they come for." And, of course, petrochemical companies want to protect thousands of miles of pipelines and service canals that might be closed off with new sediment.[34]

Real estate developers want diversions to happen in someone else's backyard. Fishermen don't want their fishing grounds disturbed. The oystermen, back in 2002, went so far as to convince a state judge that freshwater diversion projects ruined their oyster grounds. They won in the lower court but were overturned by the Louisiana Supreme Court.[35]

Bob laughed at this dilemma, noting: "This is a microcosm of what positive change means and the pushback that comes with trying to advance it. This is what planners have been facing for twenty years. People take what they need for commerce or recreation from the already degraded system. Any urgently needed improvement would interfere with their current use." But here's where the local and state politics come in. "On principle, this state hates to interfere with private property," Bob explained. "Eminent domain is time-consuming, complicated, and can get stalled in courts, anyway. But what's available is a Quick-Take Authority [a streamlined way of expropriating property for a public purpose]. The state doesn't want to use it in order to advance any of these projects. However, utilities, oil, and gas companies have this authority [given them by the state] and use it all the time. Okay for them [private purpose] but not for the state [public purpose]."

This complex web is so tangled, it's hard to imagine coastal restoration moving forward. It makes the accomplished levee rebuilding look easy. The $14 billion rebuilding of the levee system after Katrina was completed by the Army Corps of Engineers. Observers caution, however, that the "rebuilding" was only for the levees that failed, not for others that might fail in the future. This means that uncertainty still defines the future of the southeast coast of the country.

• • •

"Inside the levees"—the protected side—presents a whole different series of complications. As urban soil dries out, it sinks, or subsides—just like the vast expanse of delta marshes outside the levee. This natural process of subsidence is accelerated by pumps and drainage canals created a hundred years ago.[36] Streets buckle. Building foundations shift. Walls crack. Worse, the city is easily flooded during periodic torrential rains. Without storage capacity in the system, the water has nowhere to go until the pumping process runs its course. New Orleans has 129 miles of levees to keep water out and 22 pumping stations to drain water from heavy rains or storms.[37] How the city of New Orleans confronts subsidence will determine how well, and how smartly, it will recover.

The fundamental problem is this: Since the onset of levee building after the 1927 flood, all these coastal and inland challenges have been met with highly technical, exceedingly expensive, politically chosen engineering projects. That engineering paradigm, it is slowly being recognized, is not sustainable. Engineering solutions have their limit. But they are now built into a system of politics, public policy, contracts, and the economy, all held together by an intransigent politically supported bureaucracy. An illustrative parallel is the post–World War II onset of massive highway building as the cornerstone of a fifty-year transportation policy. Highways are huge engineering feats involving many technical challenges and lots of concrete—all big solutions. For fifty years, highway engineers tried to build the country out of a mushrooming traffic-jam and air-pollution nightmare. The failure of this effort has been a painful and expensive lesson, whereas more recent alternatives like mass transit and traffic calming have slowly gained favor.

The parallel to the highway lesson is clear.

When it comes to accommodating water, whether brought about by floods, hurricanes, or torrential rains, the New Orleans paradigm remains primarily stuck in a century-old engineering mode that means higher levees, higher poles for power lines (which should be buried instead), and bigger pipes for the pumping system. These are all more of the engineering paradigm that needs drastic change. Like the overbuilt, overengineered, overpaved high-way system, the engineering solutions have surpassed their limit. Unfunded but creative incremental solutions are readily at hand as alternatives to the excessive engineering paradigm inside the levee. The most significant of these is Living with Water (LWW). Under the LWW alternative, water storage capacity is built into the urban landscapes in projects that serve as appealing amenities when dry. But modifying an entrenched paradigm is difficult.

David Waggonner, a slight, bespectacled man with a soft voice, is a Louisiana-born architect with the New Orleans firm of Waggonner and Ball, whose work ranges from historic preservation to environmental design. Not long after Katrina, David traveled to the Netherlands with Senator Mary Landrieu (D-LA) to explore how that country survives and thrives below sea level. He witnessed remarkable strategies for converting excessive rainfalls and floods into dual-purpose recreational and landscape assets. In countless ways, the Dutch accommodate water instead of just fighting it.[38]

Out of that trip came a partnership with the Dutch embassy in Washington and a series of workshops that focused on how canals, for example, can become amenities: doubling as water parks and pathways—that is, with seating, park, and active sports areas along the way, and filling up when storm water storage capacity is called for. With the assistance of a multidisciplinary team of Dutch planners, engineers, urban designers, and soil experts, David has incorporated some of these ideas into designs that are intended to drastically reduce the subsidence of the city's soil, save money, and create new public amenities.

LWW strategies would not replace the existing pump system but only supplement and balance it, thereby easing the strains already on it. Studies show that the pumping system, for example, has become ever more expensive because of its high energy consumption. Energy use "is off the charts because we expel storm water through this high-energy-consuming system instead of reusing it in the landscape," David told me, making reference to studies that show high consumption. Reduced energy consumption would occur as the pumping diminishes. According to the aforementioned studies, David added, the ambient temperature of the entire city was raised by the creation of the drainage system because water is a cooling medium. New or enlarged water features, on the other hand, could act as a natural air-cooling system. Indeed, Living with Water features would ease city flooding and retain water beneficially—and with less pumping and a more stable water table, city land would subside less. Great opportunities have been missed as the city rebuilt, David said. No mechanism, policy, or budget exists to incorporate LWW strategies into the recovery effort, even as millions of dollars flow for street, drainage, and utility work. Living with Water adjustments could have been designed into any or all infrastructure improvements, new schools, housing, hospitals, big boxes, and street repairs.

Driving around the city with David in the spring of 2013, I heard some of the same frustration conveyed to me by Bob Marshall. We drove along Napoleon Avenue, one of the city's several boulevard-like thoroughfares with a broad grassy median, known as the neutral ground. "Look at how high the [neutral] ground is, which means water pours from it into the street," David said. "It should be the reverse. It could retain water, spare the streets from flooding, and be an attractive landscape at the same time. Instead, the Army Corps of Engineers is building a giant culvert underneath, bigger than the existing one, to store and then pipe water out to the lake without rebuilding the neutral ground atop it to reduce runoff and enhance surface storage." This is one of a series of similar projects in the uptown area. The LWW alternative, on the other hand, eliminates the need for the more expensive, bigger culvert and creates a new amenity.

This "lost opportunity," David explained, is compounded by what he calls a "criminal act" committed by the utility company Entergy. As the Army Corps digs up the full length of the neutral ground for the culvert, Entergy could "easily be burying their adjacent power lines." Instead, with generous reimbursements from FEMA, the company installed new, taller poles along the street to rise above the gracious Live Oaks that line the avenue. But to install those poles, Entergy is hacking off a substantial portion of the tree limbs that create the canopy that helps cool the streets in summer. Clearly, considerable money is to be made from repair reimbursements after disasters. In fact, Entergy's New Orleans unit filed for bankruptcy after Katrina, slowing the repair process until a $171.7 million award of Community Development Block Grant money from Washington was granted to it.[39]

As David put it, refusing to change the water and power paradigm condemns this city and other flood-prone cities to continued devastation from floods. The alliance of the Corps and Entergy with complicit city agencies is a powerful one in which the "local has little say. The Corps is a military organization doing civil works with a rigid chain of command. The bureaucracy is all-powerful. A discussion of alternatives is too limited within this framework."

When David first toured around the city with his Dutch colleagues, one said to him: "You say the Army is in charge of this?" Another asked: "Why hide the water? It's a great amenity. Everyone loves to see it."

We drove on to a blue-collar neighborhood, Hollygrove, which borders a cement-laden outfall canal—an ugly conduit for water to get to the lake. Here is another obvious missed opportunity to create a park-lined waterway that would immeasurably improve this amenity-deprived community as well as the one on the other side of the canal that happens to be in the neighboring Jefferson Parish.

A bit further is another blatant case. Costco, the giant retailer, is building a huge facility including a nonpermeable parking lot. That big box, unlike surrounding residential developments, is elevated above potential flood levels, thereby ensuring that water runoff will go to the surrounding neighborhood; it may even overflow the adjacent drainage canal "already severely challenged to convey water from further 'upstream,'" David said. This was a controversial project that Mayor Landrieu pushed through the City Council with a sales tax forgiveness of $3.3 million and $2 million in city investment in street and infrastructure improvements.[40] This despite a lot of community opposition, David noted, and also "without extracting even a storm water runoff, flood-abatement, landscape-amenity in exchange. Instead, its design makes conditions worse at the canal and in the system for the next deluge." A spokesman for the mayor noted that mitigation is designed to "discharge storm water to historical locations." He also noted that the city worked with Tulane University on a new football stadium "so that they created a retention pond under a practice field."[41] None of these "offenses," David pointed out, are without alternatives that "improve safety, represent a better economic investment, and improve the quality of life." Mayor Landrieu has publicly praised LLW's ideas, but he always notes the absence of money.

Along the Lafitte Corridor, acres of fenced-off grass fields sit adjacent to a cement-walled, litter-filled drainage canal, where the Carondelet Canal once connected a turning basin at the French Quarter to Bayou St. John and Lake Ponchartrain beyond. Excavated in 1795 for navigation and drainage, the canal stimulated economic growth and the expansion of the city; but with the advent of the railroad and modern drainage techniques, it was cemented over. "This canal is so important to the city's whole water system," David told me. "It was the first canal dug in one very vital place. It is the one entrance into the whole canal system." The potential transformation of this blighted landscape is easy to see. David's face lit up as he described the potential of a ribbon-park of attractive water features that would effectively extend Bayou St. John down to the French Quarter—a new waterfront within the city. He called it the "Lafitte Blueway Amenity." "This is the life blood, not just an amenity. It's empty along there. One can envision more people living along the waterway in high-value real estate. The highest-value real estate in Rotterdam is along the canals. This is a huge real estate opportunity."

Waterfront parks, biking trails, kayaking or canoeing opportunities, and cafés could line the waterway. Vacant industrial properties along the shore would be ripe for new development. But the key is excavating the canal, removing the cement, deepening the waterway—in fact, making it a real waterway.[42] According to David, this would "create passive stormwater storage and conveyance within the Lafitte Corridor. Fifty percent to 70 percent of the adjacent neighborhood flooding would be mitigated ([resulting in] thirty-five to fifty acre-feet of storage capacity) during a ten-year storm event." Water flowing from Bayou St. John would ease pressure there, and, as David put it, "soft edges and shelves would provide habitats for native plantings and fauna." The bio-swales along the edges would remove pollution from the street runoff.

This kind of strategy can improve public life, public space, and the landscape at a fraction of the cost of repairing hurricane damage.

After Katrina, a dedicated group of local residents formed the Friends of the Lafitte Corridor to advocate for the Lafitte Greenway within the Corridor. The city began work on the Greenway in 2014, but it is not a genuine Living with Water element. It is not a "Blueway" but a "Greenway." The city has initiated some of the amenities attached to the excavation plan without the excavation of the canal. Plans include soccer fields, bike paths and bike racks, improved street crossings, and 542 new shade trees, mostly oak and cypress, planted along the way.[43] This 2.6-mile corridor extending from Armstrong Park to City Park is currently planned, but it's unclear how much more of it will be completed anytime soon. This welcome amenity omits the most important element— excavating the canal and removing the cement—that would make it a Living with Water storm water mitigator.

Of course, the Army Corps would rather put billions into increasing the height of these same ugly floodwalls and deepening the litter-strewn concrete canals. It continues to increase the size of the pipes taking water to the lake but can't find the money to let a more effective, landscaped-based, beautiful alternative happen. In contrast, as David points out, the New Orleans Redevelopment Authority (NORA) is advancing the LWW ideas working with the neighborhoods of Gentilly Woods and Ponchartrain Park— together known as Pontilly—to convert into rain gardens properties NORA already owns. Individual property owners may be inspired to do the same. Eventually, some of these NORA-owned properties can be combined into parks, serving the same purpose in a larger way. With the idea of "Retain, Detain, Drain," this neighborhood-scale storm water management plan has garnered FEMA funds to diminish future FEMA flood insurance claims and Sewerage and Water Board funds to start the creation of rain gardens. This might turn out to be the right project to show what can happen when LWW principles are appropriately applied.

Bob Marshall and David Waggonner are demonstrating flip sides of the same coin. If the delta outside the system of levees that protects communities is not stabilized and rebuilt, cities like New Orleans could be waterfront within decades and smaller port cities like Houma, Grand Isle, and Lafitte could disappear altogether. Numerous sites were already taken off the map in 2013. If an LWW strategy is not adopted, the kind of storm flooding witnessed in recent years will drown and remove from maps a greater number of communities than have been submerged so far. In the reality of rising sea levels, the window of opportunity gets shortened to get things turning around.

The recovery of New Orleans provides a showcase for a new direction for many waterfront cities. New Orleans is leading the way, at least in terms of the strategies devised by individuals— even if such strategies are not yet embraced in any meaningful way by policy makers and elected officials.

A major statewide rethinking was initiated in 2000 with the establishment, by former governor Mike Foster, of an independent

commission headed by R. King Milling to bring together industry, environmentalists, scientists, and cultural and community
interests to reorganize the state's plans and structures. Out of that
came the Coastal Protection and Restoration Authority (CPRA),
which brings "all interested agencies and parties" under the juris-
diction of one committed agency, noted Garret Graves. (Formerly
a member of Senator David Vitter's staff and CPRA director in
2013, Graves resigned in 2014 to run successfully for Congress.)
There now exists a state master plan filled with projects that could
replenish the delta. The greatest significance of the plan, observers
note, is that it is based on science and not politics. Funding seems
elusive but, insisted Graves, "we have forty innovative funding
sources," including the BP spill settlement, to pull from.

Today, a definite momentum of support is building for Living
with Water. Graves told me the state sees Living with Water "as an
important complementary tool never before utilized in Louisiana."
New Orleans's leadership may be slow to sign on, but as Graves
put it: "If you don't make it visible in New Orleans, no one will
understand it."

Chapter 8

Environmental Connections

Billions have been spent on failed infrastructure and very few paradigms have shifted, except, perhaps, the dynamic of citizen activism.

—Jim Dart, architect

Katrina was a wake-up call for the country. Studio classes in architecture schools across the country took up the post-Katrina challenge defined by the final, widespread recognition that climate change requires new approaches to building and landscape design.[1] Students were designing "Katrina Cottages," demonstrating what could be built quickly and simply after a disaster. Reliance on the super-sized, highly engineered infrastructure to control the environment was finally recognized, in some quarters at least, as a paradigm that had run its course.

While politicians and city officials debated the merits of Living with Water, small-scale variations of LWW emerged right after the storms from the citizens themselves. In communities around the country, homeowners converted thirsty lawns to native flora and fauna, as concern focused on the shortage of water and not just floods. Some localities offered tax incentives to do so. In flood plains, the goal was to install porous surfaces to absorb water. Porous driveways and parking lots replaced blacktop. Small rain gardens increased in popularity. Even backyard cisterns enjoyed a comeback.[2] Trees were planted to shade streets. In the western deserts, where sprawling suburban cities and towns consume more water per capita than anywhere else in the world, citizen groups are finding ways to restore and preserve buried waterways, a process known as day-lighting.[3]

On the Gulf Coast, people are taking matters into their own hands in small but meaningful ways. Collected Christmas trees are woven into the marsh, attracting silt and helping grow new grass. Groups and individuals are planting new grass in all sorts of places. Picket fences are erected that build sand dunes along threatened beaches. Artificial reefs are constructed by sinking boats that are supporting marine life. None of it adds up to a substitute for the big work that needs to be government funded, but at least advances are being made while big plans stall.

Architects Jim Dart, a New Orleans native teaching at the New Jersey Institute of Technology, and Deborah Gans, teaching at Brooklyn's Pratt Institute, teamed up to show the possibilities of incremental adaptations that could be interconnected on either a block-by-block or neighborhood-by-neighborhood level. Individually or collectively, these adaptations would diminish runoff. Jim and Deborah have long histories of working directly with communities on regeneration issues on both design and planning challenges, and they were particularly experienced in first understanding the social and physical geography of a community before putting pencil to paper.

Jim and Deborah's original assignment was part of the Department of Housing and Urban Development–funded study that assigned architecture teams to various neighborhoods after Katrina. Their location was one of the least sustainable areas of the city, New Orleans East, located at the easternmost end of the

Lower Ninth Ward. New Orleans East was as heavily flooded by Katrina as the Lower Nine and Lakeview, but its profile is quite different. Known just as "The East," this area saw minimum development early in the twentieth century, mostly on the narrow road of higher ground along Gentilly Road; this road becomes Chef Menteur Highway after crossing the Industrial Canal, following the natural levee of the old bayou and along the shore of Lake Pontchartrain. Farms, small villages, and plantations emerged in the early 1900s. "Fishing cottages built in the '30s," Deborah pointed out, "just occupied land. The owners didn't buy the land so the titles are dicey. They never had an incentive to sell," which would have been a way of normalizing the ownership. The postwar era of suburban development emerged here, especially following the newly laid highways. Development surged in the 1960s as whites migrated out of the city. The growth in the 1960s and '70s followed the carefully zoned and planned patterns that reflected the new era of the automobile and the carefully separated uses.

After World War II, the residents of New Orleans East were primarily whites who had moved out from the core city. The opening of the I-10 Highway, development of new port facilities, and the establishment of the huge NASA Michoud plant[4] added to this eastward development throughout the 1960s and '70s. The 1950s ranch-style "slab on grade" was the dominant style of choice at first. These houses were different from the city's predominant architecture in several ways: larger front yards instead of porches, car ports and eventually garages, site emphasis on width rather than depth, backyards where kids can play (these are even more important than front yards), shallow pitched roofs with deep overhanging eaves. Today many houses are substantial in scale, with brick facades, spacious interiors, and well-tended small-scale landscapes.

In the 1960s, a 20,000-acre land development scheme emerged that would collapse in the oil bust of the 1980s and effectively cool the market there. Abetting the diminished market was the accelerating white exodus as many oil company operations and jobs shifted to Houston and elsewhere. Quickly, New Orleans East became a favorite destination for middle- and upper-income black entrepreneurs, lawyers, teachers, doctors, and other professionals. In 1965, the population there was approximately 75,000; and by 2000, 95,000. By the time Katrina hit in 2005, The East was overwhelmingly African-American, and although it has pockets of poverty and high crime, it probably has the largest concentration in New Orleans of upwardly mobile and high-income African-Americans. It is also home to one of the city's two largest Vietnamese settlements.

"It was nirvana," said Bernard Charbonnet, Jr., a true New Orleans native whose ancestors "came to New Orleans *before* the Haitian revolution."[5] A heavyset man with an endearing manner, he described the city's onetime biggest shopping center in The East with "top-tier" stores, a popular ice-skating rink, and all kinds of appealing amenities. A prominent lawyer, Bernard, known to his friends as "Bunny," had a client list mostly based in New Orleans East. Katrina devastated not only his home but also the small downtown commercial building where his office was located. Many of his clients did not return after Katrina, so he had to build his practice all over again. "They were doctors, lawyers, teachers, nurses and wherever they evacuated to, they were welcomed and found jobs and schools open for their children," he told me. "With schools and hospitals closed here and their houses flooded as badly as in any neighborhood, they had little to return to." For those who did return eventually, it took forever to go through the rebuilding process.[6]

The East, Deborah observed, "represents the dominant suburban housing type and also the most vulnerable" because of lack of any elevation. Known primarily as a ranch house in wood or brick, this model faces an additional challenge in The East: because the ground is mostly a former wetland, what Deborah calls "ooze." Beams at the edges of the slab require supporting pilings. Equally as drowned as the Lower Nine and Lakeview, The East "had no poetic narrative like Holy Cross's nineteenth-century shotgun" and it was by no means rich. In fact, she added, it reflects "the misconception that all suburbs are rich places."

Interestingly, two environmental advantages exist in The East that are not found anywhere else in New Orleans. All the installed utilities are buried underground, a requirement since the 1960s and Hurricanes Betsy and Camille. Furthermore, several of the subdivisions were built around small lakes, providing both an assist to drainage and a scenic backdrop for backyards, a kind of "living with water" drainage resource—just the type of amenity David Waggonner advocates.

When Deborah and Jim took on the assignment in The East to figure out where and how to rebuild, the lessons they learned were received directly from the community on the ground. According to Deborah, "The first thing we learned was the area looked like a developer subdivision, but we discovered that it wasn't. A number of generations lived there, people who built their own suburban house before the developers arrived. We found a twelve-block area owned by four extended families with a deep family network. This kind of relational context is strong in southern Louisiana, not just New Orleans. When we got there, we recognized that we were not looking at a devastated neighborhood now abandoned but one that was actively being reoccupied by the property owners. This meant planning and rebuilding simultaneously. The East is idiosyncratic. People were going to rebuild; the question was how."

Jim and Deborah set out to reimagine the brick ranch that is particularly challenging for a subsiding landscape. They designed "wetland landscapes" to be created on an ad hoc, site-by-site basis that "could be stitched together over time across a neighborhood." They met with local property owners shortly after the storm, provided information on flood-proof construction and best practices, and created a brochure entitled *Retrofitting the Rancher.*[7] What they presented in person, and in the brochure, was a way to

visualize the environmental transformation of an entire neighborhood through individualized features such as the addition of attic
refuge spaces, solar roofs, cisterns, green walls and fences, porches
for shade and ventilation, and sustainable features like rainwater catchments, lawn-free lots, and wind-loving plants and trees.
They used actual homes for their designs, indicating the address,
so that residents could imagine such transformations concretely
and aspire toward them. They called it "reframing the suburb."

This kind of cross-disciplinary design thinking in which
environment, architecture, technology, and landscape are all of
a piece is readily replacing the silo approach whereby each discipline focuses only on its own concentration. "Today, the urgency
of climate change compels us to understand place systematically as
the foodies do," Jim told me. The organic farmers, proliferation of
markets, local food restaurants, and localized small agricultural
efforts, he noted, all have environmentally conscious activists
behind them who understand how interconnected everything is. In
the case of New Orleans, of course, this means understanding and
making the connections that go from the Gulf and all its bayous
across the landscape to backyards, markets, and gardens.

The environmental dimension of the New Orleans recovery
is multilayered and endlessly diverse. From the urgent restoration
of the wetlands in the Gulf to the citywide strategy of living with
water, the biggest picture is covered. But here again, initiatives
bubbling up from citizens—such as markets and gardens—contribute in small but dynamic ways. As they grow and multiply,
these small efforts contribute significantly to a more sustainable
lifestyle and help spread awareness of the accumulated impact of
modest and manageable solutions.

Richard McCarthy, an accidental environmentalist, recognized this early and helped put New Orleans at the forefront of
issues connecting food, environment, and place. Richard is legendary for jump-starting the farmers market movement in New

Orleans with the establishment of the Crescent City Farmers Markets that he cofounded with civic activist Sharon Litwin in 1996.[8] McCarthy ran it for seventeen years. He left in 2013 to become executive director of the national Slow Foods Movement, headquartered in Brooklyn.

Born in 1966 of a British mother and a New Orleans father whose family went back generations here, Richard studied sustainability issues in the developing world for his master's degree at the London School of Economics. Richard has big cheeks, a receding hairline, and an easy smile. He overflows with enthusiasm for using food to connect the environment, the economy, and sociability. But he didn't make those connections immediately. He returned to New Orleans from London and got involved in the grassroots effort to derail the then increasingly popular David Duke, the former Grand Wizard of the Ku Klux Klan who held political office in the late 1980s and almost became governor by fanning the flames of divisiveness and hate. To some, Duke's rhetoric made him look like a defender of the "little man." It was "always about what he was against," Richard recalled in an interview. An alliance, including "mad leftist political activists," mounted a campaign—the "Truth About David Duke"—with Richard embarking on "guerilla journalism" and writing in social justice publications at Loyola University New Orleans.

Richard found himself confronting a variety of disturbing issues. Environmental justice was a particularly strong one in Louisiana, where the power of the oil and gas industry trumped everything. "It was about big oil and big sugar and no one had a vision of what the local economy could or should look like. There was no investing in natural assets." Richard saw a need to "try being creative with developing a real local economy versus one dependent on big oil and outside national chains." A hodgepodge of issues swirled around in his head—issues that now seem mainstream. Today, there is growing recognition of how interconnected everything is—the environment, the economy, poverty, food, housing, transit—but in the 1980s this was not at all the case. As Richard put it, "civil society in New Orleans had shrunk to a narrow scope."

Included in that assortment of issues was the recognition that "safe civic spaces didn't exist in the city." The incidence of high crime had long been a fact of life in New Orleans. That led Richard to organize with his wife, Bonnie Goldblum, the cleaning up of garbage-filled empty lots in their Carrollton neighborhood in 1992—a good example of people coming together in new ways, and that activity jump-starting new neighborhood connections. Then, Richard reached out to farmers to bring in fresh local food and the market idea was hatched. Or, more accurately, rehatched. "The city's once-thriving public market system was a distant memory," he told me. Over time, the Crescent City Farmers Markets network has grown to thirty-two markets around the city, open on different days of the week, with a combined economic impact of more than $10 million.

The national farmers market movement in cities had been building slowly since the 1970s but has rapidly accelerated since the 1990s. When New York's first Green Market was proposed for Union Square in 1974, city policy regulators resisted it vigorously. A considerable civic effort was necessary to gain official approval. It was such an outrageous idea and few expected it to succeed. But succeed it did, as did others.[9] Today, across the country, so many farmers markets are taking root, with such great success and so many benefits, that one needn't go very far to find an example of a market that is regenerating a downtown or neighborhood.

When the first Crescent City Market tried to open in 1995, bureaucratic roadblocks and regulations such as those besetting the Union Square Green Market stood in the way. "The state health department wouldn't let us open," Richard recalled, "because we couldn't sell fresh food in the open air, only packaged." It took the enthusiastic intervention of then-Mayor Marc Morial and City

Councilman Oliver Thomas to overcome this notion, as well as others. "It was presented as a 'demonstration' to get around all sorts of roadblocks," Richard added.

The multiple levels of value of farmers markets have become increasingly clear. "The sight of tents and umbrellas gives the impression of informality and insignificant economic activity," said Richard, but that is deceiving. "In fact, it is highly efficient, enterprising, and democratic," he added. "Markets actually fulfill an ancient role of bringing informal businesses into the formal economy. It also connects farmers with their customers, helps them learn what new things they should grow, makes them feel valued, and makes them feel connected with, if not part of, New Orleans."

The economic impact goes way beyond what most people assume. Markets provide new local jobs, avoid taking jobs away from somewhere else, and bring customers to nearby businesses. This "multiplier effect" is an important economic attribute. Such markets have brought life back to and spurred the rejuvenation of innumerable failing downtowns, from Madison, Wisconsin, in the 1970s to Roanoke, Virginia, in the 1980s. The most famous one, perhaps, is Pike Place Market in Seattle; though threatened with extinction during the Urban Renewal days, it is now a notable tourist attraction that caters to locals but is irresistible to visitors.

The environmental connections between climate change and farmers are equally compelling. Climate change is having direct impacts on farmers, whether in the form of drought, new weather patterns, too much rain, or hurricanes. And since farmers' customers recognize the effects of disasters immediately, it can be argued that disasters sometimes force them to take notice of things they had not thought about before. Case in point: When shoppers can't get the produce they are used to, they are forced to understand why. The same is true with the fish, oyster, and shrimp businesses in the market, all extremely sensitive to environmental irregularities that customers can't miss.

Needless to say, Katrina upended everything and everybody associated with the markets, vendors and customers alike. Painfully, Richard recollected:

> It took ten weeks to come back. We felt lost until then. We couldn't find farmers and fishermen. We deputized Poppy Tooker [the popular radio-food-show host] and others to find them. And when we reopened, it was the happiest place in New Orleans, an early indicator that we would be okay. We became the "office of homeland serenity" where people could break from spending every minute fighting insurance companies or FEMA. Our reopening accelerated a return to normalcy in what was a dark, vulnerable time. We showed we could get commerce back and used the market as a defiant place of recovery. Farmers were in tears when they returned. They thought they had lost the city they had adopted.

Books can and should be written on the endless positive impacts that farmers markets have on their communities. One of Richard's favorite market outcomes was "the wave of younger chefs driven by a commitment to regionalism and forging new relationships with growers." All over the country, local farmers markets expanded and changed the restaurant business. A new wave of restaurants sprang up around Union Square in the 1970s after the Greenmarket opened and chefs could buy directly. Union Square, before the market, had become a place to avoid—more a hangout for the homeless than for anyone else. Today, Union Square is a magnet for everyone and is surrounded by high-end destination restaurants.

The same dynamic emerged from the Crescent City Market that is located a stone's throw from so many restaurants. There are more restaurants in New Orleans today than before Katrina, and new food styles keep emerging. "The market opened the way to a new direction in restaurant cooking," Richard told me. "A break from just the canon of Creole cooking. It gave chefs more options." Perhaps even more significant to the "big picture," Richard noted that the "creative content" of the markets sent a strong signal to influential sets of capital investors that good things can happen here.

After the long dominance of a car-dependent lifestyle, people seem to relish the face-to-face opportunities provided by farmers markets. Indeed, the conversations and connections at markets lead to an endless variety of new opportunities. The proliferation of farmers markets in the post-Katrina city is clearly one of the great bottom-up success stories.

• • •

Farmers markets are particularly significant in the poorest neighborhoods, like Hollygrove uptown and the Lower Ninth Ward, where "fresh," "local," and healthy food options didn't exist before Katrina.

Hollygrove is a primarily African-American working-class community at the far end of Uptown at the Jefferson Parish border. It was as flooded by a breach in the 17th Street Canal as the Lower Nine was by a breach in the Industrial Canal. Once an integrated community, its white population exited starting in the 1960s. Also like the Lower Nine, Hollygrove has a high percentage of people born and raised there, and unable or unwilling to go elsewhere. Thus, it has many elderly residents. But under a joint effort by the local Trinity Christian Community and AARP, with many volunteers, programs were organized right after Katrina focusing on house renovations, crime, health, and encouraging new local businesses. More than 1,600 homes were rehabbed, an extraordinary number for a community-based effort.

Hollygrove is also home to an unusually large, innovative farmers market complex. For example, the Hollygrove Farm and Market, started in 2008 by Paul Baricos, has become an important Food Hub that aggregates the crops of small farmers to sell directly to the public, whether local hospitals, consumers, or restaurant chefs.[10] Food Hubs are expanding rapidly across the country, offering marketing and other support to local farmers, and helping to develop regional food-supply systems. An attractive Growers Pavilion on-site was designed and built by the Tulane City Center, an impressive program whereby modest but significant community projects all over the city are assisted by Tulane School of Architecture students.[11] Included in this multipurpose structure is a storefront selling food, slanted roofs that collect rainwater used for irrigation, and a shaded section for lectures and workshops.

For Hollygrove, beyond the welcome change of fresh food in what was a "food desert" before Katrina, the market "helped rebrand the community as representing something more than crime," noted Karen Gadbois, who lives in the Carrollton/Hollygrove neighborhood. The market also brought people together as a community in a way it wasn't before the storms.

Some markets and gardens have become integral to school programming, with gardens cropping up at many schools where blacktop doesn't preclude that possibility. Their uses are almost endless; not the least of these is a water retention function denied by paved parking lots. Probably the earliest significant effort was the Edible Schoolyard, a program integrating an organic garden into the school curriculum in a broad way; indeed, the initiative has had a far-reaching impact. Many of the more recent New Orleans school gardens were inspired by this most successful catalyst.

Cathy Pierson, an energetic Uptown woman with penetrating eyes and an inquiring mind, is a longtime gardener. The first woman chair of Tulane University Board and a founding board member of the Louisiana Children's Museum, Cathy is the classic Garden Club member who translates her passion for the particular into a societal contribution of broad impact. In 1998, she and her friend Karin Geiger, another garden enthusiast and also a Louisiana Children's Museum founder, wanted to share their garden interests with the public schools. They offered their services to Outreach, a privately funded after-school enrichment program offering opportunities to public school children. Thus was born "the Propagators" at the Samuel J. Green Middle School, an Uptown charter school.[12] In a once-a-week activity, Cathy and Karin taught kids not only how to grow food but how to do things with it. They started simply, by actually making lemonade from lemons. "We [also] taught flower arranging with the flowers they grew and we placed flowers around the school," Cathy told me during a lunch interview a few years ago. "We just planted stuff for fun, like roses at the fence, and it totally beautified the school." Dr. Anthony ("Tony") Recasner, the principal, noticed that the kids benefited in a variety of ways.[13] "Some loved the digging or the growing or the arranging, but the positive effect was across the board," Cathy said. "There was even less trash around." The program was expanding and the Garden Club had hired some part-time instructors.

Then Katrina hit.

In so many instances, post-Katrina coincidences led to new innovative efforts. Four months after the hurricane, in December, Randy Fertel—philanthropist and early supporter of rebuilding New Orleans schools and the delta after Katrina—was attending the annual dinner of the Nation Institute;[14] also present was legendary chef and organic food activist Alice Waters. Their mutual friend, writer Calvin Trillin, introduced them. Alice told Randy that years earlier New Orleans chef Paul Prudhomme had done her a big favor that "helped save my career," so she had a soft spot for the beleaguered city and wanted to return the favor. She asked Randy: "What can I do to help?" So Randy told her about "this small school with a garden" that he supported.

In 1995, Alice had worked with the principal of the Martin Luther King Jr. Middle School in Berkeley to convert an empty lot into the country's first Edible Schoolyard.[15] This program covers all aspects of food growth, preparation, and consumption while weaving in discussions of land stewardship and environment. Alice was intrigued with the idea of initiating one in New Orleans, and before the evening ended, the idea of bringing an Edible Schoolyard to the city was hatched.

Tony was already an avid supporter of school gardening and experiential learning. By March 2006 Randy had taken Tony to Berkeley, and by April he had brought Alice to New Orleans. Randy gathered together a task force consisting of faculty members as well as community leaders with landscape architecture, gardening, and farmers market expertise—and "the immediate response was 'let's do it.' There was a total buy-in, and since Cathy and her friends were already involved," Randy said, everything worked even better. Ironically, in the 1990s, when Cathy and her friends first got their little garden started, the School Board resisted. After Katrina, new things were possible.

Today, this one-third-acre lot at the middle school generates three thousand pounds of produce a year. The garden includes an outdoor classroom, a wetlands area, a composting station, a butterfly garden, a greenhouse, and several benches. A sizable kitchen brings the lessons indoors for food preparation classes. First Line, the charter company that runs this school, has introduced similar programs at all five of its public charter schools.

In City Park, a 1,300-acre municipal park that is 50 percent larger than New York's Central Park and one of the oldest municipal parks in the country, Grow Dat Youth Farm occupies a small 4-acre corner where it built on the lessons of the Edible Schoolyard to create a program for high school students.[16] More than just a youth development program, Grow Dat offers the social support so badly needed by this poverty-ravaged, Katrina-surviving youth population. This kind of program addresses many needs of New Orleans youth that never got attention before. Growing food becomes the same kind of educational opportunity as the Edible Schoolyard, but for older kids. This effort also has an entrepreneurial learning aspect by enabling the kids to sell 60 percent of their produce at a nearby farm stand, in markets around town, and to restaurants and corner stores. The remainder is donated to hunger-relief sites.

Our School at Blair Grocery in the Lower Ninth Ward is another example. Started after Katrina by former New York City schoolteacher Nat Turner, it has incorporated sustainability and environmental issues in its curriculum from the outset. It, too, provides students the opportunity to earn money by selling their produce. They not only take regular classes in English and math but also learn economics by figuring the costs, sales, and profits of the garden. They carry the produce, such as various unusual sprouts, and sell directly to a dozen of the city's high-end restaurants. On top of their education, they earn $50 a week. All such programs are, in effect, escape routes from an otherwise heavily problematic life. Like so many seemingly small efforts, the school-garden idea spread throughout the city.

From the Gulf to inside the levee and Bayou Bienvenue, and down through the farmers markets and school gardens, an environmental sensibility has grown since Katrina. These small efforts—which are fundamentally about environmental stewardship, about paying attention to and improving the environment—started small and continue to illustrate how much creativity can come from the ground up. Individually, they bring to bear a particular set of contributions, but together, they add a significant environmental dimension to the city's rebirth. The initiators of all these efforts are not waiting for someone high up on the chain of command to repair the environment of their city—they are doing it themselves.

Chapter 9

The Demise of Charity Hospital

As through this world I've wandered, I've met lots of
   funny men,
Some will rob you with a six-gun, and some with a
   fountain pen,
But as through this world you travel, and as through
   this world you roam,
You will never see an outlaw drive a family from their
   home.

—Woody Guthrie, "Pretty Boy Floyd" (1939)

Army Staff Sergeant John Johnson cuts an impressive figure. An imposing six feet four inches, with ebony-hued skin, Johnson sports a uniform laden with colorful campaign badges and meritorious awards reflecting his thirty-six years of service in every known conflict around the globe—Iraq, Afghanistan, Kosovo, Somalia, Grenada, and more. One of six children, Sgt. Johnson was born, raised, and still lives in New Orleans's 7th Ward, long considered the heart of the African-American community in the city. He talks as passionately about his native city as he does about his service in the armed forces. A self-described "proud hawk," Sgt. Johnson thrives on pressure. Give him an impossible assignment and not enough time to do it and he'll accomplish more than asked and in less time than anticipated. That is exactly what he did within days after Katrina, when he was recruited by Colonel Douglas Mouton of the Louisiana National Guard to help reopen Charity Hospital.[1] Charity was flooded during Katrina but it also happened to be the most critical hospital in the city, the one most people depended on.

Charity was the second-oldest continually operating public hospital in the country, founded only months ahead of New York's Bellevue in 1736.[2] Its trauma center was the envy of cities everywhere, second in status only to Cook County Hospital in Chicago. Considered one of the most vital and successful hospitals in many respects, Charity was a critical center of medical care in New Orleans, particularly for poor people and the uninsured.[3] Johnson was happy to sign on to the mission of reopening this vital institution. He is a little hazy on the chronology of events between September 7 and 19, because everything happened so fast. Trained as a master electrician, Sgt. Johnson had become a power distribution specialist, having accomplished some staggering challenges over the years in various battle zones.[4] So when told that officials didn't want to reopen Charity unless repaired in a week, Johnson got it done in three days.[5]

Under impossible circumstances, with no official support and no budget, Johnson restored power through a complicated rerouting of the electricity from the nonflooded generators on the loading dock. He worked around the clock to pump water out of the basement using high-powered German pumps that he found unused at the Superdome. More than two hundred volunteer doctors, nurses, technical professionals, citizens, and military staff—including National Guardsmen, Seabees, and personnel from a Navy ship docked at port as well as from the 82nd Airborne—worked nonstop to get the hospital up and running. They not only decontaminated the first floor, including the emergency room, but also removed debris from the upper floors, making the hospital cleaner than it was before the storm.

Within two weeks of the storm, the 82nd Airborne declared Charity Hospital ready for patients.[6] "I lived to do this," Sgt. Johnson explained with deep passion over coffee in a neighborhood hangout a few years ago. "I'm in full war mode, waiting for years to serve what I was trained to do. I wanted to be that guy, John Wayne, Harrison Ford, who in a clutch didn't panic and made it happen. I was gung ho. No stopping me. I don't ask permission; I ask forgiveness afterwards. I'm fifty-six, no rank, just an old soldier not afraid of too much and on the brink of retirement, but ready for what in many ways was my most important assignment."

Nothing, in his view, was more important after Katrina than reopening Charity. Sgt. Johnson was born in Charity. Years later, doctors there saved his mother's life. He has six grown children—including a chemical engineer, a pharmacist, an auto mechanic, and an air traffic controller—and he cares deeply about his injured birthplace. It was beyond the personal: for Sgt. Johnson, Charity defined the soul of the city. "It's part of what made us great," he said. "It served the poor throughout their lives, cared for their wounds, understood social issues, and didn't let a patient leave unless sure he or she could handle it. Patients weren't a product but human beings." That was the heart of Charity's mission.

What never occurred to Sgt. Johnson was that public officials from the city and state and, more importantly, the leadership of Louisiana State University had no intention of letting the hospital reopen in its iconic home. Long before Katrina, LSU leaders had another agenda that would have been difficult to pursue if Charity had survived; it was another one of those post-Katrina "opportunities." The only thing standing in their way was Charity's incomparable medical reputation and the immeasurable attachment of the city's population to the historic institution. As we've seen before, the storms made possible what could never have happened politically and financially without the disaster. The hospital in fact did not reopen, but not because it wasn't ready and functional, and not because it wasn't desperately needed. Rather, Charity did not reopen because LSU leaders and state officials had a different agenda in mind—a big, expensive, new hospital, something that could not be gotten if Charity were up and running again.

It is difficult to comprehend the full measure of this tragedy without a clear understanding of the significance of Charity Hospital to the history and fabric of the city. Generations of uninsured New Orleanians relied on Charity's services. Indeed, considering how many underpaid musicians, cooks, and hotel workers there were throughout the city, the social-safety-net function of Charity cannot be overstated. Nor one can even begin to estimate the number of Katrina victims who did not return because they were worried about their access to healthcare now that Charity was closed. In its place, a scattered, severely limited assortment of services was spread around town—a mere shadow of its former capacity.

Indeed, Charity doctors had achieved celebrated medical successes. Maxwell Wintrobe made major advances in the diagnosis of sickle-cell anemia. George Burch made diagnostic advances in the understanding of blood circulation. Rudolph Matas was the first doctor in the United States to perform curative surgery for an aneurysm, the first to operate on a patient under spinal anesthesia, and the first to identify appendicitis as a condition that could be treated by surgery rather than by administration of opiates. "Charity was one of the best teaching hospitals in the country, where students from Tulane and LSU did their training," noted Dr. James Moises, a former Charity emergency-room physician who participated in the post-Katrina cleanup of the building. The hospital served 100,000 patients a year prior to the storm.

Virgil McDill of the National Trust for Historic Preservation wrote: "In addition to its social role, the architectural prominence of Charity also stood out. In a city known internationally for its diverse architecture—from Colonial to Creole to Victorian—Charity stands apart as the premier example of art deco architecture. Classically designed with streamline elements by Weiss, Dreyfous, and Seiferth—the firm that designed Louisiana's Capitol—the H-shaped structure incorporates several innovative elements of early 20th-century design, including glass block windows and aluminum sculptural detail."[7]

Until 1997, the Charity Hospital System with ten hospitals around Louisiana was publicly owned. Governor Bobby Jindal was then head of the state's Health and Hospitals Department. He turned management of that system over to Louisiana State University. LSU had wanted a new hospital—and, in fact, had been planning one since 2003, unbeknownst to many outsiders.[8] It was also looking to restructure the hospital's core mission in order to bring in more full-paying patients. In 2004, an entire wing had been converted to private, single-patient rooms for patients who were not publicly funded. The intended trajectory was clear: fewer poor people, fewer uninsured patients, and more conventional service. What a lucky break for Louisiana State University: the new mission could get a strong head start with the money LSU would claim from FEMA for the contrived excessive damage caused by Katrina. "I was one of the first state officials to tour Charity after the storm," then–State Treasurer John Kennedy told me in the winter of 2011.[9] He saw that it had been made ready for service. Kennedy said he asked LSU hospital CEO Don Smithburg, "Why not move back in at least temporarily?" According to Kennedy, Smithburg responded, "If we do, we will never get a new one."

On September 19, 2005, less than three weeks after the storm, Sgt. Johnson and the army of volunteers were told "by LSU officials that they were arranging for our removal from Charity and intended to shut the building permanently." Entergy, the local power company, had concluded that it could put Charity back into service "in just ten days." The 82nd Airborne, the famed disaster relief unit, was also pulled off the job. To be summarily removed from a post-disaster mission was a first for these volunteers, Sgt. Johnson noted. Reluctant hospital police locked out the rest of the volunteer workers as well.

Even seven years after Katrina, Sgt. Johnson was still feeling the shock and pain of the betrayal of the people of New Orleans and the many volunteers who had endeavored under extraordinary conditions to get Charity reopened. Having reengineered the hospital's power network for the basement and floors 1 and 2, he then secured the use of powerful state-of-the-art generators from General Electric with the capacity to provide long-term power to floors 3–19. In his presence, LSU officials refused to accept the generators. General Electric subsequently took them away.

In order to qualify for the maximum compensation from FEMA, the hospital had to demonstrate more than 50 percent damage. But only the hospital's basement flooded during the storm and was rapidly repaired to a "medical ready" condition. Initially, in the fall of 2005, FEMA's estimated damage was $9.5 million. Every step of the way, LSU challenged FEMA's numbers. Under pressure from LSU, FEMA first escalated its estimate to $23 million. By 2008, this number had magically climbed to $150 million and, finally, $475 million through a newly devised process called FEMA Arbitration. FEMA's Project Worksheet #PW2175Ver3 documents the back-and-forth arbitration dispute over the reimbursement amount, which went from $23 million to $475 million. According to Jan Moller, writing for the *Times-Picayune,* FEMA told an arbitration panel that "the private firms commissioned by the state to review hurricane-related damage to Charity Hospital made a series of errors that helped produce over-inflated estimates of how much Louisiana should be reimbursed."[10]

Reportedly, FEMA also alleged "that the three consulting firms hired by the state to perform damage estimates were not truly independent" and had ongoing financial relationships with the state.[11] Much of the hospital's post-storm condition, FEMA claimed, was due to years of neglect. The arbitration hearing was closed to the press and the public, despite protests from citizens and reporters. Prior to the hearing, FEMA staff members who had opposed LSU's damage estimates were transferred or reassigned. FEMA attorneys failed to call credible witnesses to testify. Sgt. Johnson submitted a sworn, notarized statement contradicting information provided by LSU to FEMA. He was never called by FEMA to testify. Inexplicably, none of the witnesses interviewed for this book and who had submitted damaging reports in their FEMA depositions were called to testify.

Firsthand confidential reports from participants in the cleanup—with photos as backup—suggest outright sabotage in order to meet the FEMA requirement to qualify for full compensation: After the storm, bathroom doors were locked and needed to be kicked down by police, who discovered that the faucets at each bathroom sink had been left running full blast with folded sheets in the sinks to block drains. An electrician found fuel lines to the generator disconnected, reconnected them, and connected the restarted generator to the building's distribution system; he was then chastised by LSU officials and ordered to disconnect. The street grid connection was subsequently ordered cut.

• • •

In 2006, the Louisiana legislature charged the Foundation for Historical Louisiana (FHL), based in Baton Rouge, to conduct an independent study to determine Charity's structural soundness and potential reuse. Enter Foundation Board member Sandra Stokes, another accidental civic leader. The study was overseen by Sandra, a video and film production manager, who eventually became the primary leader of the effort to save and reopen Charity and spare the city one of its worst planning and financial disasters in decades. Without her, there would not have been a well-organized fight.

Sandra is slim, energetic, and personable with flowing blond hair. Born in Covington, Louisiana, on the north side of Lake

Pontchartrain, she graduated from LSU in the mid-1980s with a degree in civil engineering. She was one of three women in a huge graduating class. Engineering jobs were scarce because the oil companies had left New Orleans for Houston. But she realized quickly that the field was not for her. "I didn't want to talk about the torque on the bolt on a bridge," she told me. "I didn't think I could be that boring." She landed a job as office manager in an advertising agency and wound up as producer and director of broadcasting for the agency. After seven years, she went freelance and has been keeping busy since.

"I was invited to be on the board [of the FHL]," Sandra continued, "but I told them I don't have money and I'm not a muckymuck but I give 200 percent to anything I do." The response was: "We need doers." It was the first board she had ever served on. "I was naïve," she said with her frequent throaty laugh, "but I loved old buildings." At the first board meeting she attended, doctors came to explain the legislation that named FHL to conduct an architectural study of Charity that was intended to determine whether the first three floors could be reopened temporarily. "They only wanted us to look at the first three floors," Sandra recalled, "but we looked at the whole building and, without asking [the legislature], did a concept plan that fit all the requirements. We didn't tell them until the morning of the presentation."

The FHL board had passed a resolution to do the study, but some board members were nervous. "We could lose occupancy in the building," one member said anxiously, referring to the old governor's mansion in Baton Rouge in which the FHL office was located rent-free. Built in 1929 by Governor Huey P. Long and modeled after the White House, the mansion was used by the state government until 1961, when a new one was built. Even more critical was what another board member said: "If we are held hostage from doing our mission by the building, then we're not doing our mission." Sandra had no idea what she was in for—but then, accidental civic leaders never do. If they knew at the beginning what they know by the end, chances are slim they would have the guts to jump in at the start.

The legislature had not funded the study, Sandra noted, "probably not expecting us to pull it off." But the foundation did pull it off, raising the $600,000 cost and withstanding considerable outside pressures. The foundation solicited by mail five thousand graduates of the School of Nursing and twenty-one thousand Louisiana doctors, raising over $1 million. "We stuffed the envelopes ourselves," she told me, seeming still amazed at the result.

RMJM Hillier, one of the country's leading architectural firms, was engaged by the foundation to conduct the study.[12] Well known for both its hospital and its preservation work, the firm has several successful renovation-modernization projects to its credit, including the US Supreme Court and the Virginia State Capitol. RMJM's analysis was exhaustive, including unearthing the building's original blueprints and analyzing the structure with the latest tools, such as thermal imaging and impulse radar assessment. Charity was found to be architecturally exceptional and "ahead of its time," perfectly suited for renovation into a first-rate, state-of-the-art medical and teaching facility—exactly what LSU claimed it wanted. Colin Mosher, an RMJM Hillier partner, was amazed to find such a great building. "The six-foot walls you could never afford to build today," he told me. "The building lent itself to a great retrofit and a new atrium with a fresh modern look." The structure was ideally located, with the first floor already three feet above the flood plane, and adjacent to I-10. A renewed Charity would have enabled the Mid-City neighborhood to continue reviving, and it would have retained the kind of downtown anchor other cities dream of having to give strength to the larger district.

Building a new modern hospital in the shell of Charity for an estimated $550 million—thereby saving 34 percent in construction costs pertaining to the hospital portion alone—was found to be the most cost-effective way to return quality healthcare at considerably less expense; in addition, it could be accomplished in three years of construction time.[13]

LSU ignored all of the study's facts and figures and plunged ahead with its own agenda—namely, to leave Charity closed and build a new hospital on a new site.

Sandra would find herself overwhelmed by the absurdity of what was transpiring and the injustice that went with it. She stayed with the unfolding drama for years, attending every kind of meeting, boldly speaking out about inconsistencies and false-hoods, writing letters to the editor, testifying before the legisla-ture, calling reporters to give updates. Her outrage and frustration were palpable but she stayed on top of every detail, and still does. She managed, as well, to laugh at some staggeringly ill-conceived decisions and falsehoods. "You can't make these things up," she said. "Besides the issues of sustainability and the reuse of histor-ical buildings, I was concerned with returning healthcare faster and cheaper and hated watching government waste and the social inequity of what was happening. We could have had everything faster at less cost plus genuine economic revitalization."

LSU refused to reopen Charity and made clear that only a new building would do. The nearby VA hospital decided that it, too, wanted a new hospital. Most of the several hundred homes and businesses that were demolished for the two projects were on the site the city offered for the new VA hospital. To avoid demol-ishing a neighborhood, opponents of the new plan identified a nearby thirty-nine-acre site that was perfectly suitable for a new VA hospital. The alternative site was the former Lindy Boggs Hos-pital, which was closed after the storms.[14] This alternative site could have fulfilled all the specified requirements, cost less, and avoided wiping out a neighborhood. The VA seemed poised to accept this proposal, but LSU and the city stood in the way.

Civil rights lawyer Mary Howell was one of the key individ-uals battling to save the homes of people who were struggling to rebuild their lives. She told me that "the city and LSU used the VA as a stalking horse. If the VA moved and built farther out from downtown, the new LSU hospital could fill the gap—even though it didn't have the money to build it." Effectively, this pushed the VA into the occupied neighborhood and left more room than needed for an expansive, new LSU University Medical Center.

The feds required that the city adopt a neighborhood-based recovery planning process before storm compensation and replacement money could be approved. This requirement was fulfilled by the Unified New Orleans Plan (UNOP) of 2006.[15] Under that plan, the two hospitals were supposed to share thirty-seven acres closer to the downtown business core. All public meetings about the hospital—not hearings—were based on the UNOP plan.

To be clear: The federal government required the city master plan to approve funding. What LSU was making happen—leaving Charity closed and building a new hospital on another site—contradicted that city master plan. But the federal government funded it anyway. The combined thirty-seven-acre plan won approval for use of $75 million in HUD Community Development Block Grant (CDBG) funds for site preparation.[16] But that thirty-seven-acre shared plan is not what got built.

To the surprise of everyone, through a series of singular moves led by former mayor Ray Nagin's recovery czar, Ed Blakely, that additional $75 million in HUD CBDG funds was instead used to coerce the Veteran's Administration to move its facility to a completely different, densely populated thirty-acre site even farther from the downtown core—in other words, to the Mid-City neighborhood subsequently demolished.[17] At an August 11, 2008, public meeting, Blakely said: "We think it's important for you to understand that the City of New Orleans is pledging its resources to purchase only one site, the site that we proposed originally—that is, the site that we think makes the most difference for the people now and in the future."[18] Thus it was obvious that if the VA chose the Lindy Boggs site, or any other—which it reportedly was seriously considering—the city would not give it the $75 million. Blakely made it clear: do what the city wants or no money. Thus, the VA was shifted to the densely populated Mid-City site. LSU then obtained the original thirty-seven acres that the two build-ings were supposed to share. LSU needed only about one-third of those acres for its actual hospital complex.

What had been a joint complex with some shared facilities on thirty-seven acres ballooned into two totally separate stand-alone hospitals on sixty-seven acres (twenty-seven blocks) through a pro-cess shielded from the required citizen participation and public approvals. The new site is now on the other side (the lake side) of the elevated highway, clearly separated from the downtown core it once anchored. "Alternatives were never thoroughly and publicly discussed," State Treasurer Kennedy told me. "From day one, it was clear the powers-that-be were not going to consider any alternative."

The replacement plan and site were totally excluded from the final city master planning process. In fact, Goody Clancy, the planning consultants who were brought in to guide that final mas-ter plan process in 2010, were specifically instructed to stay away from both the hospital issue and the site.[19] So that final master plan—with no reference to the hospital site—was approved by City Council and the city's planning commission in 2011, follow-ing several years of varied, cumulative planning efforts. It was as if the area and the planned hospitals didn't exist.

Certainly the public review process was nonexistent. In Sep-tember 2008, then–City Council president Arnie Feilkow prom-ised a public hearing in ten days. It never took place. During the entire process, no elected body of government was called upon to approve the overall deal. Nor did any elected body take respon-sibility for the loss of the neighborhood. Pieces of the deal were approved by elected officials (an old Robert Moses strategy called "segmentation"), including the closing of streets, the approval of a flawed business plan, and the appropriation of state funds. But each was a separate element, never the whole project. While perfunctory public "meetings" were held regarding specific aspects of the hospital plan, a real examination of the true costs and benefits never occurred. Proof that the money was available to build both facilities was never provided. And surely a full discussion about the impact on the future of the city never occurred either.

The excessive waste of federal, state, and city funds for this project seemed criminal, especially considering the human needs of this storm-decimated and infrastructure-failed city. And there were enough instances of questionable procedure, backroom dealing, falsehoods, sabotage, and manipulation of federal regulations to prompt a congressional inquiry.

This demolition-and-rebuilding project demonstrated incontrovertibly LSU's domination over everything else in Louisiana. No elected official or other institution had the political power and the claim to state funds that the university appeared to possess at the time. As they say in Louisiana, "There are four branches of Louisiana government: executive, legislative, judicial, and LSU." When Sandra talked to state legislators, she was told about the four branches "with a smile." One legislator said to her: "Sometimes we think LSU has the most power."

Even the Department of Housing and Urban Development seemed to be under LSU's thumb. An Administrative Complaint filed by Mary on behalf of two longtime residents of Lower Mid-City in June 2010, with HUD secretary Shaun Donovan, faulted HUD for permitting funds to be spent on a project for which those funds were not approved, and the city's application to HUD itself included "false and misleading information." The complaint cited "altered documents which were submitted in order to obtain access to these funds for a purpose which is apparently not within any of the three national objectives Congress has defined as the statutory basis for HUD's authority." The funds were used for land acquisition, demolition, and relocation costs related to the VA hospital.

"The application makes it look like the new VA was part of the recovery plan approved by the city with citizen participation—and it wasn't," said Mary. HUD's response was to refer the complaint to the state. After a long delay, Mary received a reply from the state. As she pointed out: "I filed the complaint with HUD complaining about the state. HUD referred it to the same state agency that wrongfully approved the grant in the first place. Needless to say, the state responded that everything was basically okay. Ridiculous."

This is the kind of irreparable tear in the social and physical fabric of the city that can never heal. And the lives that were torn asunder by the demise of Charity Hospital can never be fully repaired.

• • •

Bobbi Rogers did everything right. She and her husband, Kevin Krause, came to New Orleans as volunteers six months after the storms, landed in Lower Mid-City, and fell in love with the people and the neighborhood. They bought and restored a house—in part, through a state historic preservation grant—and committed to make the damaged city their home. A year later, they found themselves in the middle of a losing battle to save their home, their neighborhood, and, indeed, the soul of the city.

Wally Thurman is a New Orleans treasure. A slight man in his eighties, a World War II Air Force veteran, he is living proof that the people of this city are just as special as its unique architecture and history. In his Mid-City neighborhood, he knew everybody, helped neighbors, loaned tools, and cooked for volunteers after Katrina. He was considered the neighborhood's unofficial mayor. He, too, lost the battle for his family home and the only life he knew.

Deborah Brown-Cassine, a New Orleans native whose African-American ancestors date back to the early days of the city, bought her first house while she was single in Lower Mid-City. Over the years she married, had kids, walked many times to the

Canal Street streetcar, staged birthday parties in the backyard, and hosted Mardi Gras parties to watch the Endymion Parade go by on Canal Street. Deborah had planned to pass on her house to her children and future generations. She was the last holdout to live in the neighborhood of the proposed hospital complex neighborhood.

Bobbi, Wally, and Deborah are among the more than six hundred people whose lives were uprooted and homes were unjustly taken away. Emerging onto the flattened landscape that was their community is a mega-scale two-hospital complex built on lies and half-truths, and through a process that on every level failed to meet democratic standards. "This was a neighborhood of people who cared and looked out for each other," Mary told me. "After Katrina, they shared kitchens, took showers in each other's homes, and watched out for each other's property. Many of them came back after the hurricanes and rebuilt because the city asked them to."

Mary's law office occupies a small camelback[20] house a block from the footprint of this doomed neighborhood. She recognized "the relentless juggernaut" approaching the neighborhood before her neighbors did. "I never knew anything about this stuff," she said with a spirited laugh, speaking about historic preservation and environmental law. "I was used to the relatively simple world of police killing people."

Well known for her work in the criminal justice system, Mary was truly mystified and overwhelmed by the injustices being perpetrated in Lower Mid-City. As she related to me:

> In the civil rights world, I understand the roles of all the players but here, all those men in suits, those developers, contractors, politicians, it was all about process, not content. "Listening to concerns" means nothing because people have no power.
>
> This racially diverse, predominantly African-American community essentially had no legal protection. Community

is not a value deserving protection. The significance of the neighborhood had become larger than race and class. After the first few residents were picked off and had made deals, the others got scared. This struggle had everything: process, social justice, historic preservation. The opposition was a broad-based, integrated movement, a great combination of people. But the powers-that-be understood how vulnerable it was. People were exhausted. They had returned, rebuilt, and were now under siege, already fighting insurance companies, government recovery agencies. The more I found out, the more horrified I was at all the same cynical decision-making and sheer cowardice of the entire political leadership that knew better. The absolute silence on every level was inexcusable.

Before Katrina and the neighborhood's subsequent demolition, Lower Mid-City, with Canal Street and Tulane Avenue as its central arteries, was filled with predominantly workforce residential housing and a smattering of commercial and industrial businesses. Lacking tourist attractions, it maintained a quirky local flavor with a barbershop, remnants of the early German culture (such as Deutsches Haus and Dixie Brewery), and an 1879 French Second Empire–style school, McDonogh No. 11, which, after the storms, was expensively restored with federal funds as a special high school for architecture and construction. The school closed to make way for the new hospital. There was even a Banksy mural—Abe Lincoln as a homeless man—on a brick building in the area.[21]

After the storms, Lower Mid-City exhibited the resiliency and defiance that are the hallmarks of so many beleaguered city neighborhoods nationwide. It was the site of one of the first and most vigorous revivals in the city. Residents and businesses existed comfortably side by side in this economically and racially integrated neighborhood. At the heart of communal life was a local gathering place called the Outer Banks Bar. After the storms this bar became an unofficial, street-level recovery center where twenty rebuilding volunteers at a time slept upstairs and communal cookouts were a recovery staple.

That sense of community is what inspired Bobbi Rogers and her husband to buy a house and stay. "We loved the porch sitters, the friendliness," she recalled during a conversation in March 2011. "In Phoenix, we lived in a subdivision with houses as close together as here, but we never knew our neighbors or their names. Lower Mid-City was not too sanitized. Eclectic, a good mix, and so easy to get to know everyone."

Approximately 265 houses in the neighborhood were taken by the state through either forced purchase or eminent domain. Many of these had been restored with federal hurricane recovery funds and then demolished. Further, over 50 functioning businesses were dislocated, some going out of business due to the disruption. More than 165 homes in this historic district were built with old-growth cypress trees, which are rare today. After preservationists protested, approximately 77 houses were moved, although shorn of the details that had made them worth saving.[22] "Cypress, the quality of the buildings, and the character of the neighborhood—these are things you won't get back," said Brad Vogel, then a young attorney working as a fellow for the National Trust for Historic Preservation.

A tireless and dedicated group of citizens tried everything to bring attention to the people, businesses, and architecture endangered by the expansive hospital plan. A booklet entitled "Can We Save These Historic Homes . . . Before It Is Too Late?" was prepared with photos of a sampling of the 140 properties in the VA Hospital's footprint dating from the late nineteenth and early twentieth centuries, all contributing to the Mid-City National Register Historic District. The selection reads like a catalogue of classic New Orleans architecture, with Mediterranean Revival and Craftsman Cottages included in the mix: "1895 double shotgun with apron gallery, pierced work spandrels and spindle frieze"; "1910 Edwardian cottage designed for a garden with classic rounded Doric columns and dormer"; "1890s double shotgun with apron overhang, jigsaw brackets and gable with fishscale shingle"; "1900 corner store house with prominent traditional beveled entry, show window, family entrance, overhang supported by turned colonnette."

New Orleans's architectural richness can blind citizens to the value of what exists and could be endangered. Erosion of place is a slow process easily unrecognized. "I compare it to the passenger pigeon," Brad told me, specifically referring to shotgun houses. "In the short term, no one notices when one or two disappear; but when enough disappear over time, people ask where are the passenger pigeons?"

Most of the owners in Lower Mid-City learned about the planned destruction of their homes when they opened the morning newspaper to read about the new VA hospital planned for their property. Some were subsequently denied access to the appraisals on which compensation was based. Others were denied hearings to protest the compensation amount. Their files were sometimes lost. Residents were faced with expropriation by the government when they contested compensation. They were threatened with having their utilities cut off when they continued to press their legal rights. They were promised "comparable" relocation choices that were painfully not comparable. Deborah, for example, was offered "comparables" in high-crime neighborhoods or those with heavy vehicular traffic, including one site near the jail. Homeowners were assured that they could stay within the Mid-City area but were then told it was too expensive. "They never saw us as people, families," observed Deborah wistfully. "The goal was just to clear property." In the end, homeowners even had to pay salvage contractors if they wanted to remove any exterior or interior ornamentation for themselves.

After the storms, Deborah and her husband were able to cobble together enough money to completely restore their camelback house built early in the twentieth century with $47,000 from Road

Home and $80,000 from insurance. Like many homes of this vintage in Lower Mid-City and all over New Orleans, Deborah's house had two original fireplaces, custom molding throughout, and wide pine floors. Theirs was one of eleven houses on their block. Before the forced displacement in 2011, six other families had came back. Two houses were still unrestored. One elderly lady had died. Another house was in progress.

Wally lived in the same house he was born in, just a few blocks from the Outer Banks Bar. The house was built by his grandfather shortly after arriving from Germany. A retired steam-fitter, Wally was one of the first residents back after the storms. He snuck in after Katrina before the city was officially open and got right to work. He was there to greet each returning neighbor and, of course, to help—including running extension cords from his house to provide neighbors with power. "We [the neighbor-hood] were like a family," Wally told me. He walked around the neighborhood checking to see that everything was in order. And if the occasion warranted, he would bring someone coffee and a snack. He spent two years and $50,000 restoring his Arts and Crafts house himself and rented out another house he owned to volunteers working in the neighborhood. He cooked for them, too. "Monday was red beans and rice but spaghetti was my best dish." Now, he lives in a suburban subdivision where nobody walks, people drive into and out of their garages, neighbors rarely talk to each other, and nobody needs him. This suburban house was all he could afford with the compensation he was given for his demol-ished house. Photos and mementos fill his walls and he depends on long-distance visitors for company. He no longer has any reason to walk around the neighborhood.

What is never calculated when an entire viable neighborhood gets wiped out for so-called economic development projects is the tax income lost to the city from the former residences and busi-nesses. Forget that the city has given away taxable land. Just con-sider the lost taxes from the demolished structures. Bill Reeves, who researched just 54 properties of the more than 140 parcels on the VA site, told me that the taxable assessed value of the 54 properties totaled $701,830 annually. Recall that this was not the site where the VA was originally willingly planning to build. In fact, the city did not need to lose that income, including the lost jobs and businesses. This was a self-inflicted wound of the worst kind.

The bottom line is that two mildly damaged hospitals—Charity and Veterans Affairs[23]—could have been renovated and upgraded into state-of-the-art facilities. Viable alternatives that would have saved homes, taxpayer money, and time were dismissed. As Adam Nossiter wrote in the *New York Times*:

> The long shadow of this city's recent natural disaster has redrawn the odds on even the most unassuming districts, promising obliteration for some, like this composite of ghostly wrecks and painted shotgun-house gems a single room wide, adjacent to downtown. Even acknowledging that Katrina upended everything in New Orleans, many residents are mystified by this logic, in a city with vast stretches of underused, unused and downright derelict property. New Orleans has an ample supply of vacant office buildings, vacant hospitals, vacant storefronts and vacant lots, many conveniently located downtown.[24]

Charity could have been reopened; but, instead, a reported $101 million from FEMA[25] was pumped into the renovation of another hospital, Hotel Dieu, which was formerly run by the Daughters of Charity.[26] Hotel Dieu had been sold to the state in 1992 and renamed University Hospital as part of the Charity System. It was the worst-flooded hospital facility in New Orleans, but in place of a permanently reopened Charity, it was renovated and opened for temporary use meant to last five years. So University Medical Center, formerly Hotel Dieu, is still functioning ten years later. It is scheduled to be torn down eventually.

What has been lost here is difficult to measure. To accommodate this massive sixty-seven-acre complex—two hospitals and acres of parking—twenty-seven square blocks of street grid were erased in a city whose extensive, exquisitely functioning grid is a national marvel. The whole site will be car-dependent, with a projected eight thousand to eleven thousand cars a day. The Anywhere-USA buildings exhibit a monotony that New Orleans architect Steven Bingler likens more to a jail than to anything else. In a weak attempt at accommodation, Eric Hansen, the project manager for NBBJ (a Seattle-based architectural firm), told Jed Horne of *The Advocate* that the skinny windows that look like slits are "a salute to the tall windows and French doors characteristic of New Orleans homes."[27]

For just the LSU site, only about one-third of the site was needed for the 424-bed hospital; the considerable extra acreage will contain surface parking, temporary green space, and future profit-making commercial development by LSU. New Orleans now has a second business district, which is emerging as new development gravitates here on the other side of the highway and away from the core.

And for what? A quintessential New Orleans neighborhood has been destroyed, its inhabitants scattered to the wind.

• • •

LSU was never successful in raising the $1.2 billion to build the new hospital, now called the University Medical Center, and this new University Medical Center has been taken away from LSU management and given over to Louisiana Children's Medical Center Corporation (LCMCC) to manage. This is good news, according to doctors who say LSU was a poor manager and LCMCC is a good one so far. Massive layoffs of state health workers and major service cuts occurred during the years of construction. In 2011, in fact, the state had to absorb huge LSU Charity hospital-system losses. The federal government had ruled that the state must repay $239.5 million in Medicaid money that was misspent between 1996 and 2007.[28] In effect, the state overcharged for payments to the LSU Charity hospital system to cover the uninsured. More federal cuts came in 2012. Governor Jindal used those cuts as an excuse to move toward privatizing the entire statewide LSU Charity system of ten hospitals. As Sandra Stokes noted, Jindal needed LSU in place in order to invoke eminent domain to take private property. In Louisiana, unlike many states, taking private land under eminent domain is legal only for public purposes. Once he had the land, he could proceed to privatize.[29]

The LSU Board members resisted privatization, but Jindal replaced those members with others favoring it. The legislature opposed privatization as well and voted it down, but then a clause was snuck into later legislation providing the loophole that Jindal needed. Over the years, much of the hospital system's services have been contracted out. Many of the contracts went to out-of-state providers.

"The failure to reopen Big Charity was just the beginning," commented Jacques Morial, a healthcare financial specialist and a member of the citizen-team that fought to reopen the hospital after the storms. "The system we had that worked so well for seventy years is no longer." Jacques points out that Jindal refused Medicaid expansion, thus ensuring that the "state will pay an increasing share of acute care. People who don't have access to preventive care will wind up in the hospital more often." Sixty-three thousand poor people, Jacques noted, now receive care in the neighborhood health centers initiated by Dr. Karen DeSalvo after Katrina, while she was vice-dean of Tulane Medical School.[30]

Immediately after Katrina, Karen got permission from Tulane president Scott Cowan to use the Tulane resources to set up sidewalk treatment services for people remaining in the city. Starting out with medicine-filled ice chests on card tables, this ad hoc operation eventually grew into the citywide network of healthcare centers that exists today. Many of these centers are one-stop health centers offering primary care, optometry, dental services, and pharmacies and, as such, have become the location of choice for low-income residents. It was clear to Karen and others that this community-based, decentralized system focusing on health-care and prevention could be the model of the future, lessening the burden on overused emergency rooms and other hospital services.

"The data shows that if you have a healthcare system grounded in primary care and prevention and you give people quality care," Karen said, "you get better healthcare, more efficient and less costly, and definitely fewer deaths." The more readily accessible system of ninety-three local health centers, run by a variety of providers, is probably the only positive outcome of the Charity closing. But there is no guarantee that the federal and state funding for them will survive. "That system was meant to be a bridge to healthcare reform and Medicaid expansion," Jacques explained. But without the expansion, who can predict what will happen?

The legislature could force the governor to sign on to Medicaid expansion, but bills to do that in 2014 failed. Since that legislative session, Jindal's popularity plunged to a "net negative of 24 percent in the polls, the most unpopular governor in the country," Jacques noted. It is possible that the next governor could change direction on the issue.

Meanwhile, Charity remains empty to this day. The art deco landmark is so big, so perfectly suitable for hospital use, that it has been nearly impossible for a new use to be found. The state was supposed to market the building, but it held off while Mayor Landrieu tried to work out a deal to move City Hall and the Civil Court into the building, despite the resistance of the judges. During that time, developers made inquiries about redevelopment proposals but were never permitted to present proposals while the mayor's plan was alive. That plan finally collapsed in the spring of 2014. The state was supposed to keep the building secure but people have easily gotten in to take pictures and film footage, and the copper wiring has been stripped methodically throughout.

An interesting proposal has been put forth that would utilize at least a portion of this 1-million-square-foot building not only for a long-term mental health facility, which the city desperately needs, but also for clinical research, affordable housing, and more.[31] Since the proposal is not coming from conventional circles, it is hard to know whether it's being taken seriously.

"We never did get half of what was promised would happen after Charity was closed," said Brad Ott, an adjunct sociology professor at Southern University–New Orleans (SUNO) who expertly tracked the history of Charity in detail and is one of the key members of the citizen-opposition group. "All the healthcare was supposed to be replaced when Charity closed," Brad told me. "Instead, obstetrics and pediatrics have been given to other hospitals and are not provided for in the new University Medical Center. Charity's much-used community care units were cut drastically, from about 160 to now less than half. A confusing system of new clinics, some for-profit and some not-for-profit, have partially filled the vacuum in the almost ten years since Katrina and no one can predict how many will remain open once the new hospital opens."

One of the early rationales for two new hospitals adjacent to one another was that they would be able to share physical plants, power, emergency rooms, and equipment. *None* of that actually happened. When both are opened, some doctors may serve in both—but that's the extent of the alleged potential synergy.

Probably the most devastating outcome for the city has been the almost total elimination of mental health services. Charity's entire third floor was devoted to such care. "Charity's psychiatric services included a dedicated crisis center that included detox facilities," Brad said. "Now there is nothing and there won't be. The only facility will be the Orleans Parish Prison."[32] The situation is even worse for children with mental health needs. Tragically, these children are suffering terribly as a result of the trauma caused by the storms and their aftermath. In her 2013 book, *Hope Against Hope,*[33] author Sarah Carr took a detailed look at this traumatic impact in the context of the post-Katrina school system of New Orleans. And more recently, in a 2014 article for *The Hechinger Report,* she notes: "A 2010 report by the Children's Health Fund and Columbia University's Mailman School of Public Health found that children displaced by Hurricane Katrina were 4.5 times more likely to have symptoms of serious emotional disturbance than a group of demographically comparable children in a national survey."[34]

The current mazelike healthcare system provides for only one to three days of treatment (a time period that is insufficient for proper testing), offers no therapeutic group homes, often sends children to hospitals in other cities (parents without cars have no way to visit), and is very challenging for parents who don't know how to navigate the maze. As for the charter schools, some offer counseling but many do not—and problem children often wind up dropped or pushed out of their school. The charters, Sarah writes, have "no central office to rely on for social and counseling services. Because [students] are judged solely on test scores, some schools have neglected mental health and counseling." Jay Altman, cofounder (with Dr. Tony Recasner) and current CEO of the First Line Charter School network, considers the closure of New Orleans Adolescent Hospital (NOAH) to be a travesty. "The absence of this kind of support is one of the great current tragedies in the city," he told me. But the Recovery School District (RSD) and the charters are "not waiting for the state to provide what should be basic therapeutic support services." The RSD is piloting a therapeutic support program for the coming year, and charter networks are beginning to create their own programs. This does not mean the city is off the hook, but at least the RSD and charters are moving ahead.

The mistakes—medical, civic, and financial—seem endless. One has to ask: Where were all those fiscal conservatives during this exhaustive battle to do the right thing at less cost?[35]

In the story of Charity Hospital, the primary culprit is clear: LSU. But many other power centers have been complicit: former mayor Ray Nagin and, especially, his recovery czar Ed Blakely, who initiated this inexcusable project; current mayor Mitch Landrieu, on whose watch it continued; Governor Bobby Jindal, who has made a bad situation desperately worse; the Obama administration, particularly HUD secretary Shaun Donovan,[36] on whose watch the plug could have been pulled; Senator Mary Landrieu, who understood what was going wrong but gave up after her attempt to bring about the redesign of the VA project was summarily dismissed; Senator David Vitter, who is supposed to be a fiscal conservative; and the members of the New Orleans business community who chose benefits that would accrue to them rather than to the well-being of the community.

The lack of a transparent public process exhibited throughout this saga shows no sign of improving. Planning and development policies continue to provide best for the well connected. A quintessential neighborhood—filled with high-quality historic houses—has been obliterated. The 1960s Urban Renewal–style hospital project was initiated by the Bush administration and continued with the blessing of the Obama administration, which had said that this scorched-earth demolition approach would no longer happen. And there is no assurance that a similar scenario won't be repeated. Throughout the Charity Hospital controversy, virtually every system institutionalized to protect citizens' rights failed to fulfill its promise. New Orleans is certainly not the first city on which this antidemocratic insult was imposed, but given the fragility of its post-storm condition, the severe damage done to it will be long lasting.

"New Orleans has a history of bad luck with big projects," observed Jacques. "The 1984 World's Fair was meant to recapture New Orleans as the Gateway to America. It went bankrupt in three months. Eight years later, New Orleans got a casino promising 20,000 jobs. It has gone bankrupt three times and produced

1,900 jobs plus corporate employment support. It was supposed to pay the state $100 million. It paid $28 million. New Orleans is totally vulnerable to pedaling the last worst thing."

Mega-projects like the new hospital complex are notorious for costing more than anticipated, destroying more than required to meet a deceptive goal, and moving ahead outside of a genuine public review process. This could never have happened if disaster had not struck. The final result: sixty-seven acres for two hospitals and the destruction of an integrated, working-class neighborhood to make way for what didn't need to happen.

In the end, the city will spend more than it gets, the number of jobs will be smaller and less local than promised, and the healthcare system that finally arrives will come at a stiff price. Facilities and services that have emerged to fill the vacuum will be shuttered, and jobs will be lost and then counted as "new" jobs with the shift over to the new medical complex. By the time the truth is clear, the destruction will be history and irreversible.

Chapter 10

Crime, the Jail, and the Police

[Y]ears of stagnation . . . have permitted Orleans Parish Prison to remain an indelible stain on the community.

—Federal Judge Lance Africk[1]

N ot every aspect of New Orleans life since the storms has seen improvement.

Recovery is not a linear progression. The city's jail, police department, and overall crime rate are probably the toughest challenges. The jail, known as the Orleans Parish Prison (OPP), and the police department (NOPD) are both under Federal Consent Decrees, strong measures meant to force improved conditions in both. Debate has raged for years over these institutions, but the post-Katrina spotlight helped advance the cause of reform. How far the momentum of reform will go is too soon to tell, and whether any of these efforts will affect the crime rate is an open question. As of summer 2014, the number of murders was down substantially, but it is unclear whether that was due to improved conditions or to a smaller post-Katrina population. It is worth noting that crime rates have also dropped nationwide. Despite fluctuating crime rates, New Orleans consistently ranks among the most violent cities in the country.

Norris Henderson served twenty-seven years in the Louisiana State Penitentiary (also known as "Angola Prison") for a murder he did not commit; upon his release, he founded a not-for-profit organization called V.O.T.E. (Voice of the Ex-offender), which he still runs. The organization works to "create a space and a voice for people impacted by the criminal justice system in the United States."[2] In a conversation with me, Norris put bluntly what many people believe: "If we want to do something about the crime problem, we have to do something about the jail." Stories of rapes, stabbings, beatings by prison guards, poor sanitation, and inadequate medical care are constantly in the news. In 2013, *Mother Jones* completed a three-year study of prisons around the country and concluded that OPP was among the ten worst, describing it as "barbaric."[3] The problems and complexities of this jail are seemingly endless. With a consent decree in place and federal justice department officials struggling to enforce agreed-upon changes, conditions don't seem to be changing with any reasonable speed.[4]

In a peculiar arrangement, while the jail is mainly funded by the city, it is run by the sheriff—an independent, elected official. His employees serve "at his pleasure," without civil service protection, giving the sheriff a potent political constituency and patronage base. There is no effective oversight of the jail operations by the mayor or the City Council; under Louisiana law, the operations of the jail are solely the responsibility of the sheriff, Marlin H. Gusman. A former City Council member, Gusman took office in 2004 and was reelected as sheriff several times, the last time in the spring of 2014. Sheriff Gusman argues that improvements at the jail will take place once a new jail, built with FEMA funding, is fully functional. He claims that the new jail will be roomier, more modern, and easier to supervise and that it will have better recreation facilities and visiting areas.

The size of the new jail has been one of the most contentious post-Katrina issues. Before Katrina, the OPP consisted of numerous buildings, holding about 7,500 prisoners, spread over several city blocks. These buildings experienced severe damage from flooding. Gusman initially planned for a new replacement, capable of holding up to 10,000 prisoners, funded by FEMA. Such a large jail would ensure the flow of revenue from the feds, the state, and other parishes that have dumped their prisoner overloads in New Orleans—a long-standing practice that predates Gusman. Instead, citizen groups fought back, with some success, against rebuilding the deeply flawed system. A city ordinance passed after Katrina capped the newly built jail to a population of 1,438 prisoners, but Gusman did manage to get FEMA to pay for construction of a brand-new kitchen with the capacity to serve almost 25,000 meals a day, based on a prisoner capacity of 8,000.[5]

In 2012, the Southern Poverty Law Center sued Gusman, alleging that he is running a jail so devoid of human decency and security that it is unconstitutional.[6] The Justice Department civil rights division agreed, called OPP "a violent and dangerous institution,"[7] and joined the lawsuit. Dr. Jeffrey Schwartz, a nationally recognized expert in security and operations in jails and prisons, testified in federal court that the jail was "plagued" by "suicides and other in-custody deaths, rapes and other sexual assaults, stabbings and severe beatings." Schwartz, who has evaluated some three hundred prisons and jails, added flatly: "The OPP is the worst jail I've ever seen."[8]

In response to the many reports of prison violence, Gusman observed during an interview in the spring of 2014: "This is a violent city. The jail is a mirror of the community. We have the worst. We have difficulty retaining staff. It is a competitive market. Personnel are hard to hire. We are at a thirty-year low. We can always get better and we have to ramp up hiring." He said he has "a hard time believing" some of the alleged atrocities reported in the jail, such as the number of sexual assaults, "unless they are confirmed by my staff." And he noted the distinction between "reported and confirmed" crimes. At the time of the interview, a debate between Mayor Landrieu and Gusman had been long active over who was responsible to pay for improvements. The sheriff made it clear that much could be improved but the city has to come up with the money. Meanwhile, the prison population has dropped in the past few years—with an average of 2,200 prisoners per year through 2014—and the budget deficit increased.[9]

In 2013 the city sued, seeking financial relief from two federal consent decrees covering the prison and the police department that would cost the city a lot of money. At the same time, Gusman blamed Mayor Landrieu for the lack of funds to improve conditions, prompting Clancy Dubos to write in his weekly *Gambit* column: "That argument is laughable in light of the fact that Sheriff Gusman maintains ancillary operations that include motorcycle, mounted, K-9, search and rescue [operations] and security/patrol units. He spends more on fuel than the Fire Department, EMS, the district attorney's office and the coroner's office combined."[10]

Dubos also noted: "The relationship between a violent jail and a violent city cannot be denied. After prolonged abuse inside the jail, is it any wonder they come out angrier and meaner than when they went in?" Probably the most important criticism came from Norris, who observed "that the reason there are so many people in jail is that we're arresting people we shouldn't. Low-level offenders, who could be cited, bonded, and released, are instead thrown in jail and kept for too long. They come out worse. If they had a job, it's now gone. If they had housing for which they were the supporter, that's gone. Now they return to the street."

Valuable insights can be gained from the story of a prison survivor.

Calvin Duncan spent twenty-eight years in jail for a murder he did not commit, and yet he can still exhibit a positive attitude and talk about his time in both the OPP and Angola Prison with clarity. He is passionate about changing the system for those still in it. There is a sweetness about this man with his chubby cheeks, round face, and penetrating eyes. His warm and easy smile makes it easy to forget the travesty of justice he has experienced.

Angola Prison, where Calvin spent twenty-four years of his life, used to be one of the country's most notorious prisons; but for Calvin, Angola was "paradise"—with interesting activities and educational opportunities—in contrast to the OPP in New Orleans. "I grew up and was educated in the Parish jail," he said, referring to his most impressionable years. "I was still young there, seventeen and eighteen. I reached Angola in my twenties and learned how to deal with anger. At Angola you don't always respond violently; you walk away. You learn different methods." In the parish prison Calvin met guys just like him "coming from families living in poverty with jobs that didn't pay enough to live on and no benefits, living from paycheck to paycheck. They had been living messed up lives. Then Katrina wiped out what little they had. Their children are either killed on the street or in prison." As Calvin sees it, the whole system is not only "messed up" but stacked against guys like him. "A black kid was killed the other day," he told me during a March 2013 interview. "But that didn't make the news. It happens every day. But a white lady was kidnapped and raped in the Garden District and it was all over the news."

Calvin's story has elements that are seen in many cases of the innocent found guilty: a court-appointed lawyer who knows nothing about the case and no time to investigate it, the lack of DNA or any substantial evidence, a misidentification by the witness, the inability of the accused to secure accurate reports, information withheld by the state, no access to case documents, a misstatement by the reporting officer, and the limitation of one year to obtain a new trial with new evidence. These patterns have been unchanged since Katrina.

In 2001, the New Orleans Innocence Project took Calvin's case. The Project seeks to prove the innocence of prisoners in

Louisiana and Mississippi, the two states with the highest incarceration rates in the world.[11] "They gave me hope," Calvin told me. "When I gave up on myself, they didn't. I lived for them." In 2011, he got his day in court. There was no way for him to win a new trial because the one-year limitation to present new evidence had long passed. If he maintained his innocence, nothing would change for him. So Calvin had no choice but to make a deal to plead guilty to manslaughter and attempted robbery, for which he received twenty-one-year and forty-nine-year sentences, respectively. "Or I would spend the rest of my life in jail. It was clear the judge was not going to give me a new trial."

"Good behavior," rather than innocence, was used as the rationale to release him. "Innocence is not something you get out of jail for," he said with a wry smile. "Every day I was in prison I kept saying I didn't commit the crime, but never got out. The one day I said I did, I went free."[12]

Calvin's story is not uncommon in New Orleans or, for that matter, anywhere else in the country. Calvin always read a lot and most of the time managed to get good grades, especially in math. But when he arrived at Angola Prison and started taking educational classes, "I found out I hadn't really learned anything." The New Orleans public schools were well known for their low standards and for advancing students beyond the level they had actually achieved. "Where and how they're living is the real problem," Calvin said, referring to the students. "If you're abused at home and hungry, it doesn't matter what school you're in. These kids need a mentor, someone to sit down and talk to them."

Calvin had a strong mentor, an uncle who'd served in the Korean War; as long as he was in Calvin's life, Calvin did well. "'Calvin, stay in school, be smart,' he would tell me over and over and he helped me with my homework. He had never been exposed to thug life. He had never been in prison, and he wouldn't believe today that prisons could be privately owned. He came out of the war an alcoholic and died of cirrhosis of the liver when I was fourteen. When he died, I died. I had no one to guide me. I was living a messed-up life. I shoplifted for clothes, then burglarized houses. I was like a time bomb, like what you're seeing today, over and over. Society is saying, 'We're not going to help you but we'll take your children and raise them in prison.'"

Fighting on the street was never frowned upon when Calvin was young, but there were no weapons in those days. "Now, kids are coming into jail who can't fist-fight. They only know weapons. It broke my heart. These were good kids who made mistakes, disillusioned with life but couldn't defend themselves. Raised by their moms, they were never taught to just fight. So they don't fight when there is a disagreement, they kill each other." Bitterness is totally absent from Calvin's comments and observations. "I'm really angry at myself," he said, "because I was so naïve. I thought it was all a joke. I blame myself because I wasn't educated. That's why I like to talk to kids. We can do better with education. It's wrong not to do better. People want their children to be safe, want someone to come talk to their kids, talk to their daughter about getting pregnant. They want help. Kids need mentors. Nothing is as effective as a mentor. Too many of these kids assume they will end up either in prison or the graveyard."

• • •

In post-Katrina New Orleans, it is difficult to see how a turn for the better can occur for the poor. Living conditions remain ceaselessly challenging, what with a police department trusted by few residents, a "reformed" school system that still seems to fail those most in need, an economy dependent on low-wage jobs, and a rental housing market beyond reach to most low-income residents. Before Katrina and since, too many factors can lead to lives of either meager subsistence or crime.

"When you have a kid whose father is in jail and his mother can't earn enough to put food on the table, you give him no choice but to be a dealer," Reverend Dwight Webster told me. His Christian Unity Baptist Church serves several neighborhoods not far from the French Quarter. "Drugs are how he earns for the family and to pay for his sister's school uniform for charter school. When you adjust for factors like that, you understand the problem better."

The economy of New Orleans depends on the low-wage tourist industry in a big way. The out-of-state hotel chains and club owners can get away with wage scales in this city that they wouldn't dare try in others. Efforts to pass a living-wage law are consistently derailed. Thus, poverty is an overwhelming fact of life. It is no secret that poverty and the absence of decent-paying jobs fuel crime. But a real change in the culture of crime won't happen without a fundamental change in the NOPD.

In New Orleans, fear of and disrespect for the police have been facts of life for a long time. As Dan Baum wrote in the *New Yorker* in January 2006:

> New Orleans disrespected its police, and often the police seemed to disrespect themselves. Even the department's official history reads like a multi-count indictment of graft, ineptitude, and brutality, as far back as the Louisiana Purchase. The first police force in French New Orleans was organized in 1803, but after "numerous complaints" the entire unit had to be dismissed, and that set the tone for two centuries of bribe-taking, drug-dealing, beatings, torture, and murder of civilians and fellow-officers alike.[13]

For many African-American youth in New Orleans, the journey that leads to jail begins with the police department, which has a reputation for brutality and corruption. NOPD's longtime, deep dysfunction has had a profound impact on the community it is supposed to "protect and serve." Corruption is found in many police departments, but New Orleans takes it to another level.

Civil rights attorney Mary Howell described the conse-quences of this estrangement between community and police: "You can't fight crime with a police department which is corrupt and brutal or is perceived by a significant part of the population as corrupt and brutal. Victims don't report crime, witnesses don't testify, jurors don't convict because they don't believe the police. You slide into vigilantism; people take things into their own hands because the system is so dysfunctional."

Mary, a slight, slim woman with short cropped hair and an infectious smile, attended LSU as an undergraduate and, later, Tulane Law School. She opened her practice in 1977. At first it was a diverse civil rights practice, including cases involving housing and employment. "Quickly, the problems with the police took over everything," she told me with a discouraging tone. "And since, it has been almost relentless. Sometimes it seems as though the police department is impervious to change." Her current caseload reflects this reality: police misconduct, prisoners' rights, victims of hate crimes, government whistle-blowers, and street musicians and parading Mardi Gras Indians harassed by the police.

The 2013 intervention by the Department of Justice was the first time the NOPD was under such a "consent decree." While it is commonly held that the bad cops in the police department are in the minority, their influence is felt throughout the department. Silence and cover-ups preclude plucking out the bad apples. As one astute observer of the police noted: "About one-third of the police force are good guys, one third corrupt, and the last third easily influenced by the bad ones." In 1994, Congress passed a law giv-ing authority to the DOJ to file civil lawsuits against police depart-ments, jails, and other law enforcement agencies that engage in a "pattern and practice" of unconstitutional behavior. Typically, the cities targeted would enter into a "consent decree," with the DOJ granting a federal judge authority to oversee reforms of the agency.

The lack of public confidence in the city's police department stems from an extensive and gruesome history of police violence.

As far back as 1980, when a white police officer was shot and killed in the predominantly black neighborhood of Algiers, on New Orleans's west bank, the police went on a terrifying rampage for a week; according to press reports, they staged mock executions, marching young black men with their hands behind their heads and guns to their heads, torturing some and killing four. Historian Leonard N. Moore's *Black Rage in New Orleans* masterfully recounts the history of the NOPD and the accompanying politics.[14] Of the Algiers case, Moore writes: "The urban guerilla tactics of the thug cops put the city on the verge of a race riot."[15] Somehow the city did not explode, even though urban riots were occurring in Overton, Brownsville, and other poor neighborhoods during that period.

Seven officers were indicted, not for murder but for civil rights violations. In 1984, after an exhaustive trial that relied on the testimony of a fellow officer, three homicide detectives were found guilty and sentenced to mandatory five-year prison terms. No one was charged with murder. Two years later, the city paid $2.8 million in settlements to the victims. The cops were dubbed the "Algiers Seven." All were white. The Algiers case clearly reflected a culture of corruption, use of excessive force, and a lack of leadership. That pattern persisted. Periodic police shootings of civilians erupted into major cases. In the mid-1980s, the number of civil rights complaints made against the police to the Justice Department was higher in New Orleans than anywhere else in the country. The 1980s were not kind to New Orleans. White flight, urban disinvestment, Reaganomics, crack, and an oil bust all hit the city in short order. More than 60,000 people lost their jobs, including 184 police officers.[16] Unsurprisingly, the incidence of police shootings and subsequent complaints continued to increase.

Then, on March 22, 1990, a popular and well-respected police officer, Earl Hauck, was shot and killed by a man identified later as Adolph Archie—an African-American with a petty criminal record. Archie had served time in prison and subsequently walked away from a work release program. According to news reports, he tried to steal a gun from a security guard at the Superdome. He was chased through City Hall and ran into Officer Hauck on the street. It appeared that Archie shot Hauck and took off running. Police were immediately in pursuit. Archie was shot in the arm and, through a complicated string of events, was taken to Hauck's police station instead of to a hospital. "Over the police radio," Mary told me, "cops were saying 'Is he dead yet?' 'Kill him now,' 'String him up by the balls,' 'We've got to start killing them,' but no command voice intervened to say 'Stop this. This man is under arrest. He's in custody. He must not be harmed.' That voice never comes. That tape is just chilling."

Eventually Archie was taken to the hospital and died from injuries allegedly due to his attempt to grab an officer's gun and escape. The initial coroner's report stated that his injuries were consistent with a slip and fall. But Mary ordered a follow-up autopsy, which showed that "he had a fractured larynx, injuries all over his body from being kicked and beaten and hemorrhages in his testicles." The coroner ultimately changed his report to homicide, due to intervention by the police.

Mary, who represented Archie's children in a federal civil rights lawsuit, noted that "no police officers were ever indicted. No one was ever held accountable. I think the killing of Archie was the beginning of the end for this police department, that this could happen in broad daylight, openly. It has always felt to me like there was a blood stain on the city from this incident that has never gone away. After that, it was 'anything goes' where the police were concerned."

In 1994, New Orleans was the nation's homicide capital. The NOPD solved only 37 percent of the murders committed that year, about half the national average, and "solve" meant only that the suspected perpetrator had been identified, not arrested or prosecuted. Federal officials estimated that 10–15 percent of the force was corrupt.[17] During this time, the *Times-Picayune* reported, the police department was "reeling from several years of corruption, with more than 30 officers arrested in connection with a variety of crimes. Convictions had been obtained against officers for bank robbery, bribery, theft and sexual offenses."

Then came the murder of Kim Marie Groves by order of police officer Len Davis in October 1994.[18]

Davis seems to have been the ultimate corrupt cop, running a drug and protection operation out of a warehouse stocked with cocaine. In an undercover operation ongoing for ten months in 1994, the FBI had wired a number of police officers. As reported in the *Times-Picayune*, "federal law enforcement officials have described the case as one of the most shocking they have seen, sources said."[19] The drug operation and warehouse were located in the Lower Ninth Ward. "He was terrorizing people there," Mary said. "Kids were pulled over and beaten. There were constant threats against people. They would complain and nothing would happen. It was a really dire situation." In October 1994, during the investigation, Groves—a thirty-two-year-old mother of three in the Lower Ninth Ward—complained, supposedly confidentially, about Davis and his partner mistreating a seventeen-year-old boy. Within twenty-four hours, she was shot and killed by a hit man at Davis's behest.

Because of the drug probe, Davis's phone had been tapped, so his ordering of Groves's death by a hit man was heard in real time and recorded. Mary summarized what the press reported at the time: "The evening of Kim's complaint, he's patrolling her house and sees her. He calls the hit man, who is running late. 'Come do her. Come do her now.' Finally, the hit man just says, 'All right, I'll do her now,' drives there, shoots and kills her. Her children are inside the house and hear gunfire. They go running outside and see their mother dying in the street." When the public learned what happened, "there was such a chill through this community," said Mary, who represented Groves's children. "It's the first time in all the years I'd done this work when it really felt like there was

a wake-up call happening. The combination of New Orleans leading the nation in homicides and the revelations about the extensive
corruption in the police department resulted in 1994 being a very
scary time to be in this city." Davis reportedly was the first police
officer in the history of the United States who was convicted and
sentenced to death for violating the civil rights of a citizen who
was killed for complaining about police misconduct. He remains
on death row.

The savagery of Groves's slaying and the audacity of Davis
and his drug partners left the city shaken. Mary described what
happened next: "Her murder was so outrageous that for the first
time in decades of civil rights work around the police, finally, for
one brief moment, we were out of denial. There was a recognition
by the powers-that-be that something had to be done." US Attorney Eddie Jordan said that this was not a question of bad apples;
that the corruption inside the police department was systemic,
pervasive, and rampant.[20] Mayor Marc Morial made the first and
most successful effort to "clean up" the NOPD. He broke with
tradition and recruited a police chief from outside the department
and the city, selecting Richard Pennington, the African-American
commander of the force in Washington, DC.

Mary continued: "Pennington was the ultimate outsider. At
his swearing in, the FBI took him aside and the FBI told him about
the corruption and the big cocaine investigation inside the department and told him to trust no one. It was good advice." Pennington made no attempt to be "one of the boys" and came down hard
on everyone. He set a twenty-hour-a-week limit on "detail work"
(i.e., private security employment supposedly done during off-duty
hours), prohibited officers from working at bars and strip joints,
and stopped hiring officers with criminal records or bad credit.
He also imposed higher admission standards for new recruits and
persuaded the City Council to approve a substantial pay raise for
New Orleans cops, who were considered significantly underpaid
by national standards.

Pennington's major initiative was "community policing," an increasingly popular strategy around the country that got police officers out of their cars and on bike or foot, thereby increasing their familiarity with the community and fostering mutual understanding. Mary reflected on the events taking place at this time: "There was a brief moment of respite from the enormous problems with the police. For the first time in the history of the city, you had a mayor, a police chief, and a US attorney who 'got it.' We were out of denial. We recognized that we had a serious problem that would take a systematic and dedicated effort to transform."

"This is during the Clinton administration, so actual resources were available," Mary added. "Pennington was in an unusual situation. One, he had a Justice Department who was actively prosecuting and investigating police misconduct; a lot of federal money was pouring in through the COPS [Community Oriented Policing Services] program for training and community policing. The DOJ was going all over the country suing police departments and getting consent decrees with federal court oversight to reform police departments. A lot of similar reforms had been instituted here voluntarily, under Chief Pennington, but in other cities you had court orders with monitoring to make sure they were doing what they were supposed to do."

During Pennington's administration, crime rates began to drop, including those for murder, rape, and armed robbery—although the same was true around the country. Officers were more visible in the public housing projects. The number of homicide detectives increased by 40 percent. Police admission standards became stricter, and there was tougher training for new recruits. Most compelling was "a 28 percent decrease in civil rights complaints to the FBI and a 23 percent drop in complaints against officers for illegal activity. A house cleaning of corrupt officers investigated by the public integrity division [resulted in] 38 arrests or indictments, 89 suspensions, 18 dismissals, and 24 resignations or retirements from officers under investigation."[21]

In the end, "Pennington either arrested, fired, or replaced 350 members, roughly 20 percent of the 1,750-member force, and he had also made history by asking the FBI to scrutinize his own department."[22] He took a very strong and direct stand that he was going to clean up the police department, and he did. Pennington was unburdened by personal ties to any officers, which gave him a critical advantage, Mary noted: "He didn't know officers' families, their mothers, their preachers. He didn't have the old school ties, the neighborhood ties. He had the backing of the DOJ, the FBI, the mayor to do what needed to be done. And he was very straight in doing that, from what I could see."

Pennington was warmly embraced by the people of New Orleans, and at a certain point he assumed he could translate that popularity into political power. He decided to run for mayor in 2002. Things started to "fall apart," Mary said, during the last two years of Pennington's term while he was running for mayor and then even more seriously under the next chief of police, Eddie Compass. "We used to say that people were more afraid of the police than the criminals—and it was hard to tell the difference," Mary added. "That's the way it became again," as shootings once more increased.

Ray Nagin, a businessman, emerged as a candidate favored especially by the uptown white business elite. He appeared out of nowhere, having no public involvement in government or politics. A nominal Democrat who supported Bush in 2000, Nagin was elected in 2002 with 85 percent of the white vote and the support of police unions. Five candidates emerged to replace Pennington, all career officers from the NOPD. Police experts around the country, all of whom told Mary that with a department as deeply troubled as New Orleans's, "you have got to follow an outside reform chief with another outside reform chief to show that this is not just a question of a specific administration, [a specific] mayor, or a specific chief, but this is about a paradigm shift; it's about a culture change; it's about a real transformation." But unfortunately, that is not what happened.

Nagin drew from within the NOPD to appoint Compass, who made it clear that he would "not forget his roots" as a policeman. As Mary put it, with obvious disappointment in her voice: "He mostly wanted to be loved by his fellow officers and almost immediately you saw discipline stopped, accountability stopped. The good ol' boy network was back."

• • •

After 9/11, the Department of Justice turned its focus toward homeland security and the civil rights staff in the department was shifted to antiterrorism. In 2004, the same year Eddie Compass became chief of police, the feds pulled out of civil rights oversight. The unique oversight of the NOPD in place since the '90s simply stopped.

A month before Katrina, the spotlight was once again on a dysfunctional police department. On July 30, 2005, forty-eight-year-old Raymond Robair was severely beaten by the police and dropped off at Charity Hospital by the same two officers who reported to the hospital that they found him on the ground suffering from a drug overdose. As the press reported, this false information guaranteed Robair's death. Charity Hospital, famous for its effective treatment of trauma victims, focused on the false drug-overdose report instead of on his ruptured spleen; if the latter had been attended to, his life might have been saved.

Robair died in front of the home of his childhood friend and neighbor, Merline Kimball, in Treme. Six generations of Merline's family have lived between the 1100 and 1600 blocks of Dumaine. She can tell you each house in which her grandma raised her kids, her great-grandma raised her kids, and other family members grew up. "My great-grandfather was a German Jew who married an illiterate black woman," Merline told me. "She learned to speak seven languages. We heard French, German, and Italian growing up but only learned English." Scores of children lived on Dumaine, all of whom played together in the street. Robair and his brothers—Charles (the city's first black fireman) and Benny (a construction worker)—lived across the street, and Merline and her siblings played with the Robair brothers when they were kids. Many children still play on Dumaine, including Merline's six grandchildren. "My house is always filled with children of all ages, and toys are everywhere," she said with pride. Over the years she has raised many children from the community. "The oldest is fifty," she added. "I mentored them when they needed it."

Merline talked about Robair as well. "Raymond was a skilled roof man. Katrina's wind couldn't remove the roofs he installed. My roof was half-gone but the two down the block that Raymond installed are still there and never had a leak." Many of New Orleans's roofs have a metal vent at the peak that facilitates air flow in the attic. The vent on Merline's roof fell onto the ground one day, narrowly missing several children. Robair was there and told Merline he had material left from other jobs and would fix it. She could pay him when she had the money. He nailed up the opening with a temporary plywood panel and on July 30 came to finish the job. Having taken her grandchildren to school early in the morning, Merline was inside napping. Robair sat on the front stoop to wait.

That's where police officers Melvin Williams and Matthew Dean Moore found him. For no reason, according to subsequent investigations, witnesses, and trials, Williams brutally beat, cursed, and kicked Robair, press reports noted.[23] According to press reports, Moore "slammed" Robair to the ground but mostly stood by watching as Williams kept beating and kicking him. Robair was howling in pain. Merline told me that Williams, known in the neighborhood as Flat Top, was widely reputed to be dealing drugs for over twenty years. He intimidated people to get them to deal for him. Williams had a "reputation for violence and dirty deeds."[24]

Merline actually felt sorry for Moore. "I did not want him to go to jail," she said. "He was a good man. He rescued people during Katrina, used his own money to buy food for people. He came to make a difference. He was a rookie assigned to Flat Top, but he participated in writing the report. He could have been free if he told the truth."

The police were not always feared, Merline said. "In the '50s and '60s, police walked the neighborhood, were friendly and helpful. My brother ran away once when he was a teenager. They found him and brought him home, warning him not to try that again. He didn't. Police would take the bullies to court to let them see bad people getting convicted and crying when sentenced to life in prison. They would even come to our block parties, eat with us, and just be there." She doesn't know why, but things changed in the '70s. "The police became criminals, scared everyone. We never ceased being afraid, looked at them as serial killers, did our own policing, never called the police. We patrolled ourselves, had our own judge, our own prosecution, and we punished ourselves."

Robair could have been just another victim of the police, who—again, by 2005—had no fear of getting caught. Merline would not let that happen. "I spoke out everywhere," she said. "If the City Council had a hearing on fair housing, I'd go and say 'Raymond Robair doesn't have a chance for fair housing.' If the hearing was on Entergy's electricity work, I'd go to say that 'Raymond Robair won't have a chance to pay his Entergy bill.' I called a friend at the *Times-Picayune* and they did a big story on him. We held rallies in front of my house and kept it in the media. But none of the witnesses on the block would come forward. They were too frightened." What made a difference was an FBI agent named Mike; "drop-dead gorgeous," Merline said. "He was so cool. No one had been accepted by the community like him. Mike told us, 'I'm not the bad guy. I'm here to get the bad guy.' He was so down-to-earth, everyone fell in love with him. He told everyone that if they needed protection to call him."

The day of the beating and murder, Merline called Mary Howell. "We were determined not to let them sweep this under the rug." No one in the city's criminal justice system could be trusted—including the coroner, who always relied on the police report for his conclusions. Mary sought an independent report. "Raymond had a full jazz funeral but the casket was empty," Merline told me with a laugh. "The pathologist was in the funeral home conducting his own autopsy."

Merline waited six years to finally see the two officers convicted and sentenced to prison. Williams was convicted for fatally kicking Robair and got twenty-one years; Moore was sentenced to five years for submitting a false report and lying to the FBI. The case was one of several alleging police misconduct that had come under federal scrutiny. This case was still very much in the spotlight when Katrina hit. Robair's death occurred during the same week as a resentencing hearing for Len Davis. One of the three counts in Davis's original conviction had been reversed on appeal. He was again facing a jury trial to determine whether or not he would be sentenced to death.

By August 2005, a replay of the 1994 collapse of the NOPD with the killing of Kim Marie Groves, the sentencing of Len Davis, and the beating to death of Robair by the police were all in the news. The Katrina police stories were gruesome. An atmosphere of lawlessness overtook the city. As reported in the press, police officers deserted the city in droves, stole people's guns and weapons, looted stores, drove past people dying in the streets, and stole Cadillacs from the dealership lot.[25] Tim Smith (not his real name) retired from the NOPD as a detective after more than twenty years. He went back temporarily after Katrina because the department "had lost half the force." Detective Smith reported that "police cars were driven all over the country. Word went out that if you see an NOPD vehicle to stop and search. They found $140,000 in cash in one and Rolexes and jewelry in another." Stories of heroism occurred as well, with police rescuing people throughout the city—just as you would expect of a police department.

The NOPD's history left the city in the worst possible condition in which to face what the hurricanes wrought. As Mary explained, "We went into that storm with a deeply dysfunctional department. The storm stripped bare any pretense that there was any structure, any accountability, any policies in place, any of the exo-skeleton." Police Chief Eddie Compass's job was already on the line before Katrina hit, and then he broke down crying on TV during the storm. He passed on as fact outrageous unsubstantiated rumors of crimes, distorting the perception of the city enough to scare away rescuers who might otherwise have saved lives. The wanton shooting of unarmed citizens six days after Katrina and the killing of two citizens, including a mentally disabled forty-year-old man, on the Danziger Bridge—as well as the murder and burning of the body of Henry Glover by police during the hurricane aftermath—put New Orleans's police issues back into the national spotlight. Both cases exposed the pattern of police cover-ups. The conviction of five officers in the Danziger case was overturned in 2014 due to prosecutorial misconduct. The DOJ has appealed. The revelations resulted in the resignation of the long-time US attorney, Jim Letten.

Ronal W. Serpas was appointed police chief by Mayor Landrieu in May 2010.[26] Serpas, years earlier, had served in the NOPD, rising to the number two position under Richard Pennington. At the time of his appointment as chief of police in New Orleans, he was serving as chief in Nashville. Serpas and Landrieu were childhood friends; from the start, there were people who raised off-the-record concerns that they were "too close." Serpas was another insider. Questions plagued Serpas's tenure, Detective Smith told me: "Why did the city pick up his Nashville home mortgage that [according to Smith] the city continued to pay during his tenure in New Orleans? Why did Serpas have a rent-free apartment from Catholic Charities (while earning $140,000), a free car, and an expense account? How did Serpas not know about his family connections to the company he hired to administer the red-light cameras?"

According to Smith, the demoralization of the police force was partly due to a pattern of officials promoting only their friends into higher positions—especially those that come with liberal overtime, which helps to inflate pensions. "Captains and higher officials," Smith reported, "make their own hours, sometimes two hours a day. They don't get vacation; they just go. High-ranking officers promote their friends, the ones who will do their bidding."

The department, according to Detective Smith and others, is totally demoralized and down to only eight hundred officers after many resignations as of August 2014. Smith attributes the demoralization largely to the process by which officers are assigned to private security details during their off-hours. The detail system was taken away from the police department in a reform move and is now run by the city, whereby the city gets $3 out of each $25 per hour of detail. The officers complained that they had regular detail assignments where they had an established relationship with a company or institution. Under the new system, assignments are rotated so no one is permanently assigned to the same place and there is no guarantee of a regular assignment. With police salaries at just $30,000 after one year of service,[27] Detective Smith pointed out, officers have to rely on detail assignments for a living wage.

On the street, particularly in black neighborhoods, confidence in the police is still hard to find. Norris told me that police sometimes cruise a neighborhood and park. "People go inside not because they are doing something wrong," he said, "but because they fear being picked up for something made up." And then there is a perverse drug flow, Norris reported. "People have drugs confiscated by the police only to see it back in the streets from the police."

One significant issue not gaining enough attention is the connection between crime and the presence of lead in the soil.

Howard Mielke, a professor at the Tulane School of Medicine, has mapped the city and found a direct correlation between the lead concentration in inner-city soil and high-crime areas.[28] The first connection between lead and crime, he said in conversation, was in the 1980s, but he first got into it in 2000 studying the connection between learning and crime in high-lead-concentration areas. "The police recognize the connection," he pointed out, "and, in fact, use the failure rate of fourth graders, where learning problems are first recognized, to determine how many jail beds they will need in the future." He also noted that the city funded the lead mitigation—capping existing soil, adding clean soil on top—in thirteen playgrounds, out of more than one hundred in the city, until it ran afoul of an ill-conceived state law that requires the use of cement covering, just the kind of approach all flood-prone cities are trying to get away from. A direct correlation also exists, he said, between "a drop in crime rates in high-traffic areas since the elimination of lead in gasoline." None of the programs instituted to "fight" crime have been or can be meaningful without solutions to NOPD's systemic problems. But one overarching accomplishment provides hope for the future: in 2013, the federal consent decree finally went into effect. The 122-page decree is meant to fundamentally alter the police department's policies, practices, and culture. Scores of new policies and procedures were drafted concerning the use of force, searches and seizures, arrests, interrogation methods, discrimination, lack of accountability, failures to investigate serious crime, and more. Unlike many consent decrees signed with police departments everywhere, this one covered an unusual broad array of procedures. Most significantly, the NOPD consent decree is overseen by an independent monitor chosen by the DOJ and the city. Earlier reforms were not subject to a consent decree or court-monitored and, without that monitoring, were ultimately erased.

The black churches in New Orleans are another significant positive. They wrestle with NOPD's systemic problems on a daily basis. Reverend Dwight Webster has taught at several New Orleans colleges—Tulane, Loyola, Xavier, Delgado—and was director of the Southern University at the New Orleans Center for African and African-American Studies. Having done three decades' worth of work in New Orleans, Reverend Webster is in a position to argue that the churches have made a significant impact within smaller segments of the population, working with young people, on reentry programs, getting jobs, and providing shelter. But, he told me, they can't get grants for this significant work that is directly in the community.

"We took our own mission money for summer camp among other things," he said. "From impressions [formed by] listening to colleagues, it looks like the mayor wants it to be his own programs plus those of people who are on his side. In fairness to the administration, the mayor's NOLA for Life is a real effort, and he's hired some talented people. [The program has everything from gang reduction, family violence mitigation, midnight basketball, and job training as part of an overall strategy that includes both long-standing and new efforts.] The problem is trying to come up with a new program instead of refinancing and supporting who were doing it before." Small churches needing funding, Reverend Webster noted, seem to get lost in the larger scheme of things, and the discretionary funds that City Council members had are gone. Those small grants were very helpful, he added.

As Reverend Webster further pointed out, the churches suffered from Katrina in ways that most people don't think about. Their programs were heavily funded by their congregations, so when 40–50 percent of their active membership did not come back, financial support coming from their own members diminished drastically. That left a huge hole. The good news, he added, is that people are still coming back, but that does not mean their budgets suddenly swell. "Almost every Sunday we see someone back," he reported. "Recently, we had a woman who grew up here, moved away, and has now come back with her family."

Regardless of the admirable efforts being made outside the criminal justice system, the burden remains on the inside—and that is where public confidence falls away.

Good news and bad news fluctuate in New Orleans like the ebb and flow of the tide. None of it seems conclusive. There's still a steady flow of unnecessary arrests, and occasional police shootings. Murders seem to be down, but New Orleans still has one of the highest homicide rates in the country. Shootings, rapes, and armed robberies have increased. Changes in EMS care for trauma victims—such as inserting IVs in the ambulance rather than waiting to arrive at a hospital—seem to have made a difference. That probably means more shooting victims survive than used to.

In the final analysis, what small internal improvements might have been made at the jail are not sufficient to diminish the nightmarish conditions there. Sheriff Gusman was reelected in 2014 and still insists that the city needs to contribute more money for improvements. The new jail is not yet complete. Arrests for minor offenses persist, thereby continuing the vicious cycle in lives already challenged by poverty. The NOPD suffers from poor morale and diminished numbers. Conditions at the police department today come nowhere close to the past horrors recounted here, but the general perception is that the city does not seem any safer. Although much of the post-Katrina recovery story is upbeat, the prolonged problems involving both the jail and the police are truly discouraging.

Chapter 11

The Education Challenge

> Looked at one way, this jumble is a classic let-a-hundred-flowers-bloom portfolio system. But in practice, the system is inherently unequal, with each network administered by different rules.
>
> —Paul Tough, author of *Whatever It Takes: Geoffrey Canada's Quest to Change Harlem and America*[1]

Gilbert Julien stands five feet eight inches, is solidly built, and has a dark complexion and natural athletic skills. His family story is fairly typical. His mom and stepfather had low-end, low-wage jobs that kept the family living paycheck to paycheck. His father and two uncles were in prison. The family of five lived in a small shotgun in the Lower Nine. When he was nine, they moved to a similar house in Mid-City. Three kids shared a room. Often, too much was going on for doing homework. The TV was always on. Gilbert could have had the same fate as Calvin Duncan but he was lucky.

Gilbert is intense. Wise beyond his twenty-one years, he has determination in his voice. Over lunch at a popular uptown bistro in March 2013, Gilbert seems both at ease and on guard. His demeanor does not readily betray much of what he saw growing up in a neighborhood where danger lurked everywhere. Nor is he forthcoming about how much negative influences touched him or his family. When things got overbearing at home—too noisy and overcrowded—he went for long walks. Gilbert got through it all, he said, primarily because he loved to read. At sixteen, he dreamed of having a bookshelf. He kept his books under his bed. "That's all I ever did was read—history, Malcolm X, slavery, philosophy, Socrates," he told me. "Sure, there was plenty of violence around me. I got used to it. It was normal. In school, I spent a lot of time in the reading room, staying away, always by myself. You do what you have to do. I don't work hard to be in second place. I want to be better." Gilbert knew what he was missing because he took two summer college preparatory classes at Newman High and "saw past where I was." He makes a distinction between just surviving and living. "My mom worked her whole life to survive. [She has a low-wage job at Ochsner Hospital with a medical benefit covering only her, not her kids.] I don't want to do what she did. I'm big on life. Reading taught me how to think, to think long term, to know there is more out there."

Gilbert went to a string of bad public schools. In third grade, he had the good fortune to have a reading tutor. One thing the city public schools sometimes did well, if funding provided for it, was to hire tutors for students in different subjects. The reading room and college prep course he spoke of would not have been available except for this good turn of events. This unusual program in Gilbert's school was started by Marie Gould. She recruited tutors from the community and among Tulane students. Gilbert would eventually have done well, Marie said, because "he was smart, interested in learning, and had no disability." But so much was stacked against students: "Classes were huge and there was so much chaos in all those kids' lives. But Gilbert had an incredible ability to focus. He was the easiest student I ever taught."

She changed his life.

No one can understand what is meant by "at risk" kids unless one of them becomes part of your life. And every story is different, every obstacle harder than the previous one, each factor complicated. Marie is one of the rare people who take the time and care enough to make a difference and, in the process, gain unusual insights that illuminate how the issues of crime and education are intermingled in New Orleans. Other cities exhibit similar patterns, but in New Orleans, barriers are rarely surmounted, especially as successfully as in Gilbert's case.

Marie is petite and slim and wears her hair short. She never wanted to be a teacher, she said. But as a former reading specialist, a summer Forest Protection Officer in the Colorado wilderness, and now as a kayaking guide to the disappearing Louisiana wetlands, she seems to be doing a good job at just that. It seems fortuitous that she enrolled as an education major in college because it was the path to a scholarship. "I like children but I don't like teaching," she told me. "I don't like to maintain order, to police the classroom. It is a real gift to be teaching a class of difficult kids."

She is soft-spoken and a natural outdoors person. She bikes around New Orleans, runs a business (Louisiana Lost Lands Tours), and loves vacations in the wilderness with her husband, journalist Bob Marshall.[2] Instead of a classroom teacher, Marie became a reading specialist and was immediately overwhelmed by the challenge. "The kids were all failing," she said. "You needed an army. I knew I couldn't fix the problem but I said I would die trying. The whole school was in trouble." With a grant to tutor "at risk" kids, she worked with the school's principal to establish a reading room (a refuge for kids like Gilbert), bringing in volunteers as tutors twice a week. She recruited about twenty-five such tutors from all walks of life, including her husband, a postal worker, lawyers, doctors, professors, even an Academy Award–winning actress. That was the army she knew she needed. Eventually, the program was adopted by Tulane, which enlisted student volunteers.

Gilbert was one of three third-grade boys in Marie's first group in 2001. "Gilbert was repeating third grade because he could hardly read," she told me. "The only reason was because no one taught him. By the end of the school year, he was at a fourth-grade reading level. He improved so much, his teacher didn't want to report it, afraid to be accused of falsifying his test scores." The story was different for the other two boys. One was "as quick as Gilbert but hyperactive, inattentive, and stressed. He could not focus." His father was in prison and his mother had been arrested for shooting someone. The other boy did well and was interested in learning but lacked the ability to relate, although he shared his reading lessons with his illiterate father. "He often said he was just looking forward to growing up to be a street kid and hang out with the guys. He never responded to warmth. I never bonded with him." Both of those boys are now in jail.

"Gilbert was stiff as a board but wanted to be near safety and affection. He always wanted to be under the wing. Both of Gilbert's parents are intelligent. His stepfather was a good man but there wasn't much parenting." Marie managed to get to know Gilbert's family—to gain their trust and, apparently, their appreciation. His parents can't read well. She tried encouraging his stepfather, but education was not a priority for him. Gilbert's mom once told Marie that "nobody cared if I did well as a kid. Nobody checked to see if I did my homework." Marie added: "She always thanks me for Gilbert's progress." For three summers in a row, Marie took Gilbert as a helper when she worked as a Forest Protection Officer for the US Forest Service in the Eagles Nest Wilderness of Colorado. Later, Marie and Bob sent him on a Grand Canyon rafting trip with a diverse group of kids, allowing him to discover how different people can get along. "Gilbert was unusual," Marie noted. "He had a real steady calm, stayed focused, and was safety conscious. He was above peer pressure. He was called a geek when he had a book under his arm. Mostly, he didn't react but one time he punched a guy in the face who was calling him a geek."

Gilbert was with Marie for one year and then Marie's husband, Bob, became Gilbert's reading buddy for the next three years. As he was entering seventh grade, Katrina hit. Marie and Bob lost track of Gilbert. Most of New Orleans's public schools never reopened after the storms, and in those that did, in a reconstituted state, kids were shuffled all over the city, shifted out of their neighborhoods, disconnected from whatever anchors there might have been in the educational system. Gilbert's family home was flooded and they were forced to move around. Then, in 2007, totally by chance, Bob was in Home Depot and he heard a voice saying, "Mr. Bob, Mr. Bob." Gilbert had spotted him. It was a happy reunion. By now, Gilbert was in ninth grade and showing promise as an athlete, though still focused on his education.

Before the storm, Gilbert would occasionally telephone Marie and ask if he could stop by, just to hang out. The frequency of his visits increased after he and Bob reconnected. One night he called just as Marie and Bob were going out and Marie had to say no to a visit. The next day, the school track coach, who was worried about him, called Marie to say, "When Gilbert calls to ask if he can come over, it is because he is in 'trouble.'" Marie assumed that meant danger of some sort, so they never said no again. Gilbert was coming by so frequently that Bob and Marie invited him to live with them in their bungalow-style house in the university district uptown. Bob had two grown children (a son and a daughter) from a previous marriage. There were no children living in the house. Gilbert moved in but frequently visited his family. At Marie and Bob's, he was able to do his homework and, best of all, read. "He read everything," Marie told me with an admiring tone. "*Robinson Crusoe* (children's edition), recently Ayn Rand, Coehlo's *The Alchemist*."

Gilbert has managed to live, in effect, between two worlds, maintaining his individuality while attached to both families. This would be a challenge for anybody, but, of course, race makes it more complicated. Gilbert was torn at times. "You want me to sound white," he accused Marie once. "No," she replied, "just bilingual. He wants us to know he's still black and that we haven't changed him." As a kid, he was not embarrassed to have an out-of-the-classroom relationship with her. "He'd stop by the reading room just to say hi," she recalled. "But by high school, he was embarrassed. I could tell. If I went to his track meets, he'd pretend not to see me. If on a rare occasion his mom was there, he'd go sit with her. None of the kids had moms there. When he was older, I once asked him if I embarrassed him. 'I'm over it,' he said."

Gilbert graduated salutatorian from Cohen High School. The school ranked second from the bottom in the entire state. He gave a rather searing graduation speech, filled with both brutal truths and attempts to inspire: "We lost people we loved. We started wars with our own family. We have been beaten down mentally and physically and no one seems to care, because we are Cohen children. . . . I understand that life gets so hard that you get to the point when you want to give up. I have been to that point a couple of times this year, because no matter how hard I worked I was still one step behind." But then he reminded his audience of the Frederick Douglass quote "Without struggle there is no progress" and beseeched his classmates "not to give up and continue to work hard. You will find success." He received a standing ovation.

Gilbert's status as salutatorian was a cruel joke considering the quality of his education, although Marie says he was a role model for his classmates. His dream was to go to a college out of state. That didn't happen, and he received an athletic scholarship to a state school that disappointed him: "I hung out with the athletes who were either getting stoned or drunk." He quit at the end of freshman year and signed up for the Air Force so that he could learn skills that eventually would lead to a worthwhile civilian job. Too often for young people like Gilbert, the armed services are the only place for a good education.

• • •

Gilbert's story reflects poorly on the New Orleans pre-Katrina public school system, but it reflects even worse on the city itself. This is a city more divided than it is willing to acknowledge, and it's even less willing to do what it takes to change the fundamentals. The story of education in New Orleans is about so much more than what happens in the classroom. Educators like to speak of the whole child but ignore the whole life of that child. After Katrina, the public school system didn't open until January, with few schools opening even then. The Parish School Board fired all the teachers, tore up the union contract, and kids living lives like Gilbert's were set adrift indefinitely.[3] The schools that gradually reopened did not target this challenged population. Recall Shawn Holahan's view from the porch after her father's wake, all those kids playing in the street during what should have been a school day. Who knows how many years it took to place those kids back in school. Today, those are the kids who are killing one another.

By the onset of the twenty-first century, New Orleans schools had gone through the traumas of integration and white flight in the 1960s, budget cuts and deterioration that accelerated in the 1970s, enlarged class sizes and classrooms out of control also in the '70s, and the crack epidemic of the 1980s coupled with increasing poverty and years of mismanagement and corruption. Those troubled decades left the city with often beautiful but ramshackle school buildings, an education system unworthy of the name, and a school population that was 94 percent black. FBI investigations had led to arrests and convictions for all sorts of financial irregularities—salaries going to dead people, for example—and before Katrina hit, the school system was declared bankrupt. Eight superintendents had come and gone between 1998 and 2005. Two years before the storms, the state created the Recovery School District (RSD) for the purpose of either turning low-performing schools into charters or putting them under direct state supervision. Interestingly, improvement under the modestly altered pre-Katrina school system was already beginning to happen. As Sarah Carr, a senior editor at

The Hechinger Report, notes: "Despite chaos at the top, the system made significant academic gains in the years before Katrina."[4]

The school system is now charter-based.[5] Students apply and go through a process that while less complex than at first glance, nonetheless requires a degree of parental sophistication (not to mention literacy) that can be unrealistic. Most schools don't target the highest-need population, which is a continuing problem. And while most schools say they don't "cherry-pick" the best students or "discriminate" against the ones with special needs, they find ways to manage admissions.

Today, in the reconstituted school system with students traveling from all over town, many kids spend three to four hours a day on a school bus.[6] Some have to wake up at five in the morning to make the bus and don't get home until seven. Ideally, kids should be able to walk or bike to school, but under the old neighborhood school system, schools remained "ghettoized."[7] The top schools before Katrina were "magnet" schools that parents from all across the city fought to get their kids into. *Community-based* meant *segregated,* inasmuch as the school population mirrored the surrounding population: if based in a segregated neighborhood, a school was segregated. Many parents, thrilled to be out of the old system, accept the current long travel time as a price to pay. "Post-Katrina, what emerged from open admissions was competition among schools that increased the commitment to excellence," observed Randy Fertel, a supporter of the new system. "Not relying on neighborhoods to populate the schools, the schools had to get better or die. Such a free-market system is not ideal, but neither is the monopolistic system under the OPSB [Orleans Parish School Board]."

Education and criminal justice are probably the two most challenging and contentious issues in New Orleans, both oversimplified by people on either side. Easy analysis of either topic is elusive. Most New Orleans kids—especially the ones who, post-Katrina, are living either in their own or a relative's home—are likely getting a better education than they did before the storm. Many are in refurbished, formerly long-neglected school buildings or in FEMA-funded newly built ones. Class sizes are smaller, bathrooms work, and schoolbooks are new—no longer the ones passed down for decades. Outside resources, privately donated, are supplementing school budgets in a robust way, like never before. One can find classrooms where enthusiastic children are in attendance. One of the biggest changes is that both the white and the black middle class have begun to care about the school system in new ways; indeed, schools are being given attention and funding for the first time in decades.

It is difficult to get a clear picture of what has been gained and lost by the total overhaul of the public school system. Not all the charters or their networks are equal in quality. The situation is constantly changing. As of summer 2014, for example, virtually all New Orleans schools are charter schools. The teachers' union, once a mainstay of the city's black middle class, no longer exists, but at one school—the prestigious Ben Franklin High School—the teachers voted to unionize in 2013. Other schools might follow.

The number of charter schools changes each year; some close and others open, adding to the confusion. A new charter has a five-year opportunity to prove itself or either be taken over or closed. Most charters fall under the state's Recovery School District; most are nonprofit entities with public oversight. In other words, the former public school system has effectively been transformed into a public-private partnership with an assortment of business models, but all privately controlled and publicly funded. Before the storms, New Orleans had the highest proportion of private and parochial schools in the country. It was a divided but easy-to-understand system.[8] Now it is a web of disconnected pieces that do not add up to a comprehensible whole. As Carr puts it in her excellent, even-handed book, *Hope Against Hope:*

Unquestionably, the former system was an utter disgrace. But it is far easier to cite the deficiencies than to understand the causes. Politicians and citizens grandstanded about white racism, the breakdown of black families, the selfish oblivion of the business community, or the intransigence of the teachers' union. More thoughtful observers hesitated to parse the causes of the troubles in New Orleans schools too neatly. Those who sought the education overhaul loved to tell the story of the post-Katrina high school valedictorian who could not pass the state exit exam after multiple tries. But had the system failed her because of low expectations? A racist school accountability structure? Burnt-out teachers? Decades of damaging underfunding? Or some combination of them all?[9]

Today, many New Orleanians believe that the "reform" of the schools is the best thing that happened after Katrina. How this favorable constituency breaks down by race and class is an open question. Cathy Pierson, former chair of the Tulane Board of Trustees, articulated feelings I heard from many New Orleanians on the total makeover:

> We began to believe New Orleans could change. This was a city of such low expectations for itself. Taking over the schools meant we could finally change the system. We went from not thinking the city and schools were workable to a "can do" feeling. New resources and support were available. The new message to our kids was "We would love for you to come home. We're not sure what the job opportunities or crime will be, but there is more opportunity now for a middle-class person. The public schools were not an option before. They are now." Things didn't feel workable before; they do now.

Yes, it is difficult to get a true picture of what conditions are beyond the glowing press releases that the state or the charter schools choose to release. The numbers can be deceptive. If 50 percent of the schools have accomplished something, how many students does that mean? What percentage of the whole school population does that cover? The percentage of students graduating from a school doesn't reveal how many students were forced or "persuaded" or "counseled" to withdraw or were expelled during the year. No one knows how many children with disabilities did not return to New Orleans because schools were not admitting them. Confusion is inevitable within a system in which there are around eighty-eight charter schools with forty-five thousand students (it was sixty-five thousand before the storms[10]) governed by forty-five different autonomous entities.[11] Some schools are a single entity; others are part of a group run by one organization. One fact is clear: New Orleans is the first school system in the country that is virtually all charter.

Attendance, dropout, and graduation rates are all self-reported and most school board meetings are held in private, resulting in an opaque system that is difficult to monitor. Jessica Williams covered all the schools including charters for *The Lens* for four years and now covers the schools in Jefferson Parish for the *Times-Picayune*. She and about twelve reporters covering board meetings often had a difficult time getting charter boards to adhere to open meetings laws. "It used to be that they didn't even let reporters in the door," she told me. "And executive session was a time when some of them discussed whatever matters they didn't want the public to hear, whether those issues were covered under Louisiana laws governing executive session or not."

Jed Horne put this into perspective: "One should not think this is a charter school invention. The resort to and abuse of executive sessions was famously part of the pre-Katrina OPSB approach to school governance. The charters are just yielding to a persistent temptation but are making halting progress toward full compliance with open meetings laws." As a May 2013 article in *The Advocate* noted, an independent report indicated that state oversight of the finances of all the schools was adequate but oversight on all other matters was not.[12] However, a state legislative audit released in December 2014 indicated that $7 million in equipment, such as computers, was missing.[13]

The school situation in New Orleans is a moving target. A genuine assessment requires reflecting on issues larger than just education. After Katrina, the school board waited until January to open a few schools and terminated all the teachers. School officials, like the other "experts" who assumed that few would return, miscalculated. They greatly underestimated how many low-income families with children would return. I remember the chaos in January after the storms when I talked to returning residents who couldn't find an open school to take their kids to (class sizes were limited to twenty-five students)—and surely not one located near a low-income neighborhood. Not enough schools were open.

A dizzying array of arguments—utilizing an arsenal of facts and figures—can be heard from either side of the education debate. But the unanswered question is this: Are the Calvins and Gilberts of the city benefiting under the "reformed" system? How good the current schools are—there are many good ones—misses that most important question. It is vital to understand that the takeover of the school system was another "Katrina opportunity" to complete a transformation that had begun before Katrina but could never have advanced politically without the disaster wrought by the storms. In addition, and most importantly, school issues are harmfully divorced from community and familial circumstances, unrealistically extricating students from those conditions during the day but not improving the conditions to which they return at night.

This takeover represents a complete political power shift. As Carr notes, "Control of the city's schools passed from a predominantly black political class to a largely affluent and white corporate elite."[14] More specifically, Carr calls it "a coalition of local power brokers, backed by several of the nation's wealthiest foundations and top politicians."[15]

Walter Stern is a Tulane-educated historian and former newspaper reporter who ran TeachNOLA for two years and is now writing a book about race, education, and urban development in New Orleans. TeachNOLA is a local version of Teach For America (TFA) that recruits certified teachers with New Orleans experience as well as new teachers from outside of New Orleans. What has happened in the past decade "is a narrow approach to education reform," Walter said. "The focus is a limited one instead of a holistic view that recognizes the problems of the schools are integral to the problems of the city." The emphasis, he added, is "on tests, statistics, and other measurements" to judge success instead of "tying it all to the community—access to jobs, decent pay, housing, health, and mental health services."

No city in America has created a system to judge success in a concerted way, although many have programs that at least try. In a *New York Times* op-ed, Daniel J. Cardinali, president of Communities in Schools, wrote of his organization's attempt to specifically address the social, political, and communal context of students' lives. Research makes clear, he argued, that conditions at home—poverty, ill health, overcrowding—directly affect attendance records, school behavior, and success potential.[16] Organizations like Communities in Schools work with local and state governments to perform the requisite intervention for students in need—a most appropriate program for New Orleans.

Lance Hill, executive director of the Tulane-based Southern Institute for Education and Research, is probably the charter system's harshest critic and most passionate defender of the old system. He noted that "before Katrina, LEAP [Louisiana Educational Assessment Program] scores were improving 3–5 percent a year, starting in 2002. Teachers were probably teaching to the test, and the increase came as they got better at it. By 2005, it was at 5 percent. And by 2012, scores were at 60 and 65 percent in publicly run schools." An improvement for sure, but still not optimal. Five schools had been turned over to charter operators by 2005, but as

Carr points out, "In the wake of Katrina, a small, powerful group of state officials decided they needed to take more drastic action."[17]

• • •

Louisiana is only one chapter in the still-unfolding national story of the ongoing transformation of the public school system into a charter-dominated system. For some fifteen years, three primary foundations—Gates, Walton, and Broad—have promoted this shift and put the kind of money behind it that makes local public and school officials salivate. Katrina was the perfect storm to accelerate this transformation in Louisiana.

First, Governor Blanco turned away from her biggest base, the teachers' union, and by executive order weakened the requirements for charter schools, removing conditions relating to community, faculty, and parental votes. The legislature then passed Act 35, changing the definition of failing school from a performance score of 60 to less than the state average of 87.4. New Orleans was the target and the only one taken over under Act 35. Based on interviews at the time, Jed Horne reported that the Bush administration and the Catholic Church were pressuring the state to adopt a voucher program. Blanco resisted that. Cecil J. Picard, Louisiana superintendent of schools (1996–2007), pushed for a complete charter system. But a full disbanding of the school system would require a constitutional amendment, so New Orleans native and state school board member Leslie Jacobs, a key player behind this plan, recommended that the Recovery School District take over only failed schools. This change in the failing-school definition allowed things to move ahead without that constitutional amendment.[18]

When charter school proponents in New Orleans are asked why they support this new system, they often cite corruption in the old system as well as paralyzing school board politics. Financial irregularities under the new system have been reported also, along with questionably high consultant fees, expensive out-of-state professional training trips, and testing-score irregu-larities—but none of this measures up to the sins of the old way of doing business.[19] Indeed, the old system seemed primarily to be a source of contracts and jobs—in much the same way the storms were—for all those politically connected out-of-state contractors. The irregularities associated with the new system seem to be taken less seriously, but they're still creating unanswerable questions in a less-than-transparent structure.

The key advantage that comes with charter status is the school principal's freedom to hire and fire at will, to create or change curricula, to set salaries, to provide merit pay, and to avoid going through a central bureaucracy for every new book or pencil. For the principal, this allows for individuality and flexibility. Com-petition for students provides the incentive for schools to improve. Teachers, too, gain the advantage of being able to leave one school and switch to another.

As noted earlier, Jay Altman is the cofounder of First Line Schools, a network of five highly regarded charter schools. Alt-man, now First Line's CEO, speaks both passionately and artic-ulately on behalf of the new arrangements. "Governance reform has created a strong positive organizational culture and a positive work environment in which people can be effective," he told me. "One can hire whom you want instead of people being assigned from the central office. Collective bargaining agreements, with job security the priority, unintentionally made handling under-performing employees impossible. The costs to train, mentor, and monitor needy teachers are too high and too much of a hassle." Growth, Jay added, "comes with thousands of little steps and now improvement is possible with thousands of little changes that didn't need central office approval." The old system was "like farming on concrete. Changing the seeds or the fertilizer is not the problem. The concrete is the problem."

Once the transformation occurred, millions of post-disaster money came pouring in, with spending per pupil reaching 65 percent more than before the storms. (The state budget allots $8,000 per pupil but $45,000 per prison inmate.) The national foundations, in particular, provided resources never dreamed of before. Jay explained that this money is now directed to supplementary programs and new initiatives, rather than being relied on for operations. Many civic-minded upscale New Orleanians also got involved, supporting a local school for the first time. Enormous improvements were made possible.

In 2010, FEMA provided $1.8 billion[20] to repair or replace eighty-five crumbling school buildings hardly touched since the days of school integration in the 1960s.[21] But by 2014 it was clear that this would not be enough to make up for the fifty years' worth of disinvestment, and big questions were raised as to how this money was being spent. Reports of shoddy workmanship, questionable hiring practices, work paid for but not done, out-of-line expensive change orders—the litany goes on. None of the questions raised are unfamiliar to New Orleanians, but these are now state-level rather than local-parish questions. As of this writing, and as far as can be learned, the issue of how those FEMA funds were spent has received no thorough scrutiny.

The new system was clearly in keeping with the direction of our increasingly corporate-based American culture. Charter schools embrace the language and principles of corporate America and its great dependence on science, data, outputs, results, and value added.

With the complete transformation of the school system, an incalculable investment also was made to recruit, train, place, and retain scores of Teach For America volunteers, who earn a salary and a stipend toward either their further education or payment of their student debt. The TFA issue is indeed a tricky one, especially regarding the question of whether it is appropriate to suddenly bring in what Jed called "a shaky cadre of bright kids with zero cultural literacy." But then, Jed noted, this is "not the first time the city has had young teacher interns doing a couple of years

here before going off to law school or taking over daddy's firm."
Whether teaching quality is better with credentialed teachers has
not been studied. The first year in a classroom is going to be a
struggle for any teacher. For either the trained or untrained, probably the best learning is as an assistant teacher or intern.

Are recent graduates of graduate schools of education well
qualified to teach in poor neighborhoods? Are recent graduates
of elite schools, mostly white kids from the North, qualified for
this work right out of undergraduate school? To their credit, many
come with a real commitment to make a difference and exhibit
a real sense of caring. The eighty-hour week these kids experience is hardly sustainable, although part of that time is apparently
devoted to taking courses for their own advancement. Understandably, the average stay for TFA teachers is reportedly two and a half
years. Is it really possible to build a new school system with such
short-term commitments?

One of the most contentious issues post-Katrina was the firing of all the teachers. It shaped the perspective of where the school
fight fits into the post-Katrina city. New Orleans is not the first
city to try to lay a large portion of the blame for a failing school
system on the teachers and their union. "The union problem" is
more often than not (inappropriately) the first comment uttered by
public school critics nationwide. Unions are held to blame in other
areas of the economy as well. The middle class, which has effectively been disappearing from US society, was once heavily made
up of union members. While definitely not the sole explanation for
the vanishing middle class, the absence of union-scale wages and
benefits is certainly a contributing factor.

Yet unions have done a good job shooting themselves in
the foot, given their intransigent work rules and their excessive
resistance against allowing the firing of unproductive or poor-
performing employees. However, as one successful teacher, now a
school principal, said to me: "If you've given a teacher the appropriate training, given him or her the resources to do a good job,

provided an amenable physical facility, maintained a reasonable class size, and had that teacher appropriately mentored, if after all that the teacher is still poorly performing, then I'd say you should be able to dismiss that person or give them a nonteaching job." That has not come close to happening in New Orleans. After Katrina the teachers were initially put on unpaid leave. Then, three months later, school district employees were notified by e-mail that they had been dismissed. If they wanted to teach in New Orleans again, they would have to pass a new test. At the time, New Orleans had one of the highest percentages of black teachers of any urban school district in the country, about 75 percent. The OPSB then delivered the final blow by firing all the teachers. As Carr writes:

> Most teachers knew as well as anyone that the pre-Katrina schools failed too many of the city's children. And all but the most extreme would concede that, in some cases, subpar educators were to blame. Taxpayers, state officials, and school system leaders set up even good teachers to fail at times, however, by starving the schools of resources or squandering them. New Orleans public schoolchildren had been criminally neglected for decades. But no single villain perpetrated the crime.[22]

As Jacques Morial put it: "An entire political class was dispersed—people who played a vital role in political empowerment and in the lives of students they mentored for years. Many still haven't returned. They were probably the last block of black middle-class voters. Teaching provided one of the few remaining opportunities for African-Americans to enter the middle class."

Before Katrina, noted Parish School Board member Sarah Usdin, "the school system was the epitome of failure. There were no expectations for the kids, no one lost their jobs for failing the kids, and there was no advocate for the kids. If a student just showed up, he would pass. Twenty-one percent didn't graduate.

We've fixed that, but that is different from saying every high school is doing a great job." Sarah is considered one of the shining lights among charter school boosters. A former Teach For America member and then its executive director in New Orleans, she founded New Schools for New Orleans, a kind of venture-philanthropy that provides encouragement, expertise, programming, and financial support for new charter schools and is credited with infusing the system with new ideas and a high level of energy. She believes that reform has accomplished a great deal, she told me, but it still has "a long way to go to fulfill its goals." The controversy surrounding this transformative change is not too different from what is heard nationwide.

Another exceedingly contentious issue in New Orleans is the school system's intense focus on testing. It would be ideal, Jay said, if a single variable could be used to measure school quality. But testing is only one of several: "The school culture, the atmosphere in the classrooms and in the halls, is another." And "a third is the value-added things—like arts, sports—that help make a school. Testing can serve a purpose, but you have to ask what you want to measure—absolute performance, how much progress students have made, the progress of groups that traditionally have not done as well (i.e., students with language or socioeconomic problems). You want all three measurements to acknowledge progress." Jay acknowledged that testing can lead to "teaching to the test" and that this, in turn, can be "reductionist"—but the "flip side is no measuring of progress."

• • •

Finding a New Orleans voice not passionately partisan on one side or the other is difficult. Andre Perry, however, comes close. A mild-mannered African-American with a clean-shaven head, Andre has credentials on both sides of the debate. He directed a charter school network after Katrina for the University of New Orleans and then was associate director of Loyala's Institute for Quality and Equity in Education, assessing post-Katrina education changes and developing education opportunities for students in the area. In July 2013, he became Founding Dean of Urban Education at Davenport University in Grand Rapids, Michigan. He is now charged with establishing what he promises to be a "ground-breaking College of Urban Education focusing on the development and preparation of teachers and administrators with specialized skills designed to enable them to teach and lead effectively in urban school districts." That sounds like a mouthful, but his words are totally in sync with his views. "With all the resources and training opportunities available after Katrina," he asked pointedly over a downtown lunch, with his obstetrician wife at his side, "why couldn't they have drawn from our own local population? Why did they have to bring in outsiders from big-name schools to teach in and run our schools? Why not invest in local people?" Good question.

In Andre's view, the purpose of an education system is not just to teach students but to advance "community wellness. The goal of reform should not just be to improve schools but to improve the community. We are missing the opportunity to include parents, workers, everyone in a more substantive way. The important goal is to increase the capacity of local talent." When you separate community improvement from school reform, he observed, "both test scores and crime rates go up." Genuine reform in New Orleans is "limited by our own biases about the city based on race and class."

Andre does not dismiss the need for an infusion of "new people and new ideas," but, he asked, "why can't Teach For America recruit the majority of their volunteers from Loyala, Tulane, and other New Orleans schools instead of having only a very small number of locals? They'd gain people who are already part of the fabric of the community, who know the culture and are invested in it. It's expensive to import. Teachers are the most important variable in education. Make them the heroes, not the scapegoats.

Furthermore, the goal of education is not to go to college; the goal is to thrive in the community, to learn self-reliance and critical thinking."

"New Orleans is a city of neighborhood sensibilities but we don't have neighborhood schools anymore," Andre added, referring to another controversial issue concerning the new system. He, like many others, feels that the current system devalues the local culture that grounds the city's students—a culture rich in its own music, cooking, and traditions. Jay Altman told me that a newer shift toward more "career-track" mission schools is occurring, instead of only college-ready schools, and that many schools now reserve a portion of spaces for local, neighborhood students. After almost ten years of scrutiny and sometimes sharp criticism, charter schools are responding in different ways.

Quoting Georg Eliot from *The Mill on the Floss,* Andre said: "I desire no future that will break the ties of the past."

The loss of traditions is a real issue to many observers—especially the role of music. Here again is a fundamental New Orleans contradiction: the culture is celebrated, but it is also being eroded in seemingly small ways. Marching bands, for example, were hugely important before Katrina. Each band proudly identified with a particular school and neighborhood. Students worked hard to participate in their band; learned concentration, discipline, and self-esteem; and took pride in the occasions when they were called upon to march, particularly during Mardi Gras or other parades. Music in the schools was more than just marching bands.

"The public schools had premier concert bands, jazz ensembles, orchestral programs, and marching bands," said Sonya Robinson of Artists Corps New Orleans. "There is no understanding of that history by education reformers who use the word *excellence.* The word is losing its power. These music traditions were markers of real excellence on a national level. They were exemplar programs." Jay Altman agreed that the diminishment of "enrichment programs" is a problem, but he pointed out that there is constant pressure for learning time that requires additional classes and thus some things get pushed out.

Artists Corps New Orleans is trying to reintegrate the music tradition into the school system by placing music teachers in schools and subsidizing the first two years. The receiving school has to commit to hire a music teacher after that. Significantly, Sonya emphasized, they look first for local New Orleans musicians. Local or out-of-town applicants must commit to five years to even be considered. Sonya is not the only person to point out how useful music education is to children, in that it facilitates the learning of cognitive and social skills and inspires a motivation to learn. But as she articulated its importance, she pointed to the contrasting use of the word *culture*. As used in today's revamped system, it seems to mean a "culture of safety and college-bound," as if it can be separated from outside the walls in the street and the neighborhood. "It is a culture of submission, conformity, control—but questioning authority should be part of their education. This is culture with a small 'c.' But what we have in New Orleans is culture with a large 'C.'" Sonya agrees with much of the school-reform effort, but, she added, "one is not allowed to speak from the center. If you question any part of the canon, you are against it and you're immediately put in the other camp. There is no room for nuance."

At the Ellis Marsalis Music Center in the Ninth Ward, director Michele Jean-Pierre sees evidence of the impact on student learning that serious music programs have on children. "When we get a child from an underperforming school," she told me, "we see significant improvement in their schoolwork. Our classes are small, and work is concentrated." It is more than just a matter of the kids enjoying the music program in a comfortable and relaxed setting, she added. "Music is math. Knowing math makes you a better musician. The kids didn't know they would get math here." Indeed, the Center's classroom tests indicate that students in music programs show significant gains in math and reading. One can't miss the feeling of energy, seriousness, and excitement at the Ellis Marsalis Music Center, which was built after Katrina as part of Habitat for Humanity's Musicians' Village in the Ninth Ward.[23] It rivals the feeling of what happens just before the curtain goes up on a real performance.

Fortunately, schools have taken heed of the pressure to bring arts back into curricula heavily focused on testable subjects.

Darryl Kilbert is a three-decade veteran of the New Orleans school system: a no-nonsense teacher and principal who was superintendent of the public schools for six years until 2013. During his tenure as superintendent, student test scores rose above the state average and the school's financial condition went from near-bankruptcy to a top-grade credit rating. Darryl, a bespectacled, bald-headed African-American, knows all too well what was wrong with the old education system—primarily too little discipline and too much truancy. Echoing a bit of what Andre said, Darryl noted that "we were not addressing the real needs of the students that include home, church, and school." Things began to get bad in the 1970s and '80s, "when what we knew as home and family began to change. We had a lot of homeless kids and kids with single parents." The churches began to lose their moral and ethical purpose, he said, "when they turned into businesses and lost touch with the individual needs of their constituents. School then became the social agent, addressing the moral and emotional side of students, which we were not equipped to do." Truancy became such a serious issue that a truancy center with probation officers was established. "Kids were coming to school when they wanted to."

Darryl continued: "The crack epidemic hit in the '80s. Budget cuts eliminated or diminished programs like athletics, arts, and we had to increase the pupil/teacher ratio. Problems graduated from chalk throwing to drugs and crime. Now we were responsible for being the parent, too. We held events with parents to teach them the importance of nutrition, a good night's sleep, and some quiet time." The positive results of these actions didn't have much impact.

How far the new reform system will go depends on a lot more than what happens in the classroom. One wise concept that has not gotten enough attention is a simple plan to use schools as the anchor for other community services to "cluster" around or nearby. With 29 percent of the population without cars and with so many parents working long hours, often at two jobs, basic human needs go unmet. Under a plan, called "Nexus," designed by architect/planner Steven Bingler and his firm, community health centers, libraries, family counseling services, recreational facilities, and the like would be located near schools. After Katrina, Steven, who designed and—with Carey Shea—led the Unified New Orleans Plan (UNOP),[24] also worked on the school facilities master plan. "We looked at the 127 school sites but only 85 were needed for the returning population," Steven said. "The idea was to cluster around the school other community-based activities, not to put the health clinic in the school but across the street." For example, if a parent could get glasses or see the dentist or a doctor after a parent/teacher conference, "there is a better chance for that parent to be more involved in the school and for the child and parent to have other needs taken care of."

The Nexus concept was included in the city's post-Katrina school facilities plan but has so far been used only in Broadmoor, and quite successfully. As described earlier, the Broadmoor community developed the "education corridor" as its defining concept in its master plan with the school, library, and health center, all not far from each other along Napoleon Avenue. "Now connections are being made with Propeller, a social service business incubator," Steven pointed out, bringing together a real nexus of community services and activities more accessible to a larger number of residents than if all were randomly spread out. Propeller, a social-minded nonprofit incubator, is emerging as an important center for Broadmoor.

Whether Broadmoor's version of Nexus will inspire city and school leaders to apply the idea broadly remains to be seen. Nexus is only one modest way to address the larger issues surrounding the ever-changing school situation, but at least it could be a start. At a minimum, it can add something positive to the lives of people who could really benefit.

While using schools as the physical center of communities is an important civic goal, what colors most opinions about the current quality of education is the disastrous circumstances of the former system. Yes, many students are receiving a better education than before Katrina. Yes, students have hope for college who never dreamed of this possibility before. Yes, the new system is enthusiastically embraced by many parents in the African-American community. And, yes, the physical condition of the schools has never been better. But this view of the past nine years of change should not stop there.

Most of the charter schools are constantly changing. The qualitative difference among them can be huge. The travesty of the systemwide firing of the teachers will remain a stain on the city for some time to come. Indeed, serving the students most in need, as was originally promised, requires more aggressive efforts. And providing more slots for nearby students would go a long way toward relieving the long-distance burden on many children, making the charter school for some a neighborhood school.

Most critically, it is time to attune the schools more realistically to the workplace. While it is important to encourage students to aspire to college who may never have thought it possible, that option may not always be the best choice—especially when one considers the financial debt it brings. Given a different opportunity, many students would opt for vocational schools that teach the skills necessary to get a well-paying job in New Orleans. The new opportunities offered in the upgrading post-Katrina economy of the city indicate, more than ever, that workforce development—including living-wage jobs—should be an important goal.[25] How great it would be if a new generation of citizens not only valued the culture that formed them but had the skills and desire to protect it and carry it on. The combination of a good education and a decent-paying job is a starting point for improving the life of students, families, entire neighborhoods, and, as a consequence, the city itself.

Chapter 12

Public Housing and Disaster Capitalism

The great New Deal enterprise to provide decent, stable housing for the lower-income and working classes was gradually
destroyed through mismanagement, underfunding, poor
design, and civic neglect. . . . The initiative to dismantle public housing is misrepresented as an effort to improve the lives
of public housing residents.[1]

—Edward G. Goetz, *New Deal Ruins: Race,
Economic Justice, and Public Housing Policy*

New Orleans was one of the first cities in the country to get
public housing, with four projects in place as early as 1940.[2]
These were solid, well-crafted red brick structures of three to
five stories, often with tile roofs, front-entrance grill work, solid
wood floors, and separate entrances for small clusters of apartments. Many of them stood around courtyards with shade trees
and paths. As a style, they became the model for many private garden apartments that followed.[3] "The bricks," as they were called,
are now gone, save for a few restored legacy buildings, torn down
after one of the most contentious controversies in post-Katrina

New Orleans. They have been replaced with faux-historic, privately built new developments that accommodate only a fraction of their former tenants. This has kept many of the working poor from returning.

In 1997, when *Times-Picayune* columnist Jarvis DeBerry was at Washington University in St. Louis, Wynton Marsalis visited the campus and spoke about his three-hour jazz oratorio, *Blood on the Fields,* for which he had just won the Pulitzer Prize. This extraordinary work chronicled in song and music the history of American slavery through the story of a couple transported over the Middle Passage[4] and their life of pain that followed. As he spoke, Jarvis recalled, Marsalis drew a parallel to "the public housing in my own city." Jarvis had never been to New Orleans but he was "disturbed by the hyperbole," wondering if it was really necessary. Months later, as he arrived to join the *Times-Picayune,* he drove into town past the Fisher Housing Project in Algiers and "burst into tears. It looked like a prison."

Consisting of fourteen three-story elongated buildings with balconies connecting apartments, all arranged in parallel rows, the Fisher Housing Project was built in 1965 at the end of the low point of public housing design.[5] Hemmed in by the approach roads to the Mississippi Bridge, the railroad, and a canal, the Fisher was isolated from other West Bank communities; like many of the out-of-sight-out-of-mind projects elsewhere in the country, it was doomed from the start. Its prisonlike appearance was immediately apparent. "I found it wholly disturbing," Jarvis told me, as we tried to make sense of the public housing issues that caused intense disputes and angry protests in post-Katrina New Orleans.

Not long after his arrival in the city, Jarvis was working on the crime desk at the newspaper when he was sent to cover a shooting at the St. Thomas Project, near Magazine Street and the Lower Garden District. "It seemed like it was half boarded up," he said of the three-story, rundown brick buildings. "I was thinking to myself, 'How do people live like this?'" He continued: "I don't suggest it was misery all the time. I also saw happy scenes like the young woman with a Saints sheet as a cape, broomstick in hand, marching as a drum major at the Lafitte Project [one of the 1940s brick projects that, unlike the Fisher, resembled suburban garden apartments]. There definitely was hope, celebration, and moments of joy. People often reported, 'We had a community.' Poor people more readily share with others their little bit of nothing so there were many stories of great acts of kindness. All of us have focused too much on [public housing's] dysfunction and not enough on its function as a real community." Even in the worst projects, the networks of support needed to survive intense poverty develop with great depth and remarkable humanity.

Jarvis added: "Well-meaning friends ask why people were so desperate to return to the public housing after Katrina. It's their home, I would say. The same reason you would be upset." Then he asked: "I don't know if it is better; is it better?"

Today, walking through or driving by the various New Urbanist–style[6] developments that have only partially replaced the several thousand units demolished, one instinctively believes that things have gotten much better. On St. Joseph's Night in 2014, for example, some friends and I walked through the Harmony Oaks Apartments in Central City on our way to watch the splendid ritual of the Mardi Gras Indian tribes, in full costume, emerging at unknown times and from unknown places to "meet and greet" each other.[7] Harmony Oaks, with its blocks and blocks of two- and three-story houses with front porches and green lawns, replaced the 1,403-unit C. J. Peete (also known as the Magnolia development) with 460 units of mixed-income apartments—one-third of which is supposed to be for displaced public housing tenants. A reported 15 percent[8] of the former tenants relocated here.[9] It is hard to know the exact proportion since both HANO (the Housing Authority of New Orleans)[10] and HUD (the Department of Housing and Urban Development) won't provide specific verifiable numbers.[11] The still-new apartment complex seemed pleasant enough. "This looks nice," one of my friends commented. Another friend noted: "Ten years ago, I never would have walked through that neighborhood."

How can one *not* assume that this visual tableau means things are better? Of course it *is* better for the selected few former public housing tenants lucky enough to live in the replacement housing among middle-income tenants. But an entirely different question is whether wiping out the sturdy, red brick buildings—many of a construction quality unmatched today—really made things better for *all* public housing and middle-income tenants. Likewise, was it truly necessary to scatter several thousand former residents to the winds? Many of these residents were the backbone of the city's low-wage workforce, especially the hotel maids and restaurant kitchen workers. Contrary to myth, most of the people in these communities worked, although at disgracefully low-paying service jobs.

The end results are quite complicated and only a few things are certain: public housing is mostly gone and has been replaced by private developments funded with public dollars and lucrative financing arrangements, including generous tax credits; few former public housing tenants live in new quarters in mixed-income developments; others, specifically those with Section 8 vouchers,[12] have relocated—usually to depressed neighborhoods, renting from landlords not always interested in property maintenance and where carrying costs are more expensive than public housing units. As a report by the Greater New Orleans Fair Housing Action Center revealed: "An alarming 82% of landlords refused to accept the vouchers or added insurmountable requirements for voucher holders."[13]

In addition, not all of the promised replacement units are built yet, even ten years after the storms, and the crime rate has not gone down; the criminal activity is now just dispersed. Sound, reusable, high-quality buildings of an earlier era than the 1960s Fisher Project that alarmed DeBerry were unnecessarily demolished in the name of progress.

The demolition of public housing, as we saw with the closing of Charity Hospital, is a perfect example of "shock doctrine": the exploitation of disaster to achieve what would be impossible through the normal public process.[14] Congressman Richard H. Baker (a Republican from a wealthy area of Baton Rouge) got it right when he was cited by a reporter after Katrina as saying: "We finally cleaned up public housing in New Orleans. We couldn't do it. But God did."[15] God actually had nothing to do with it; rather, the local politicians and power elite of the city, in partnership with the state and federal government, made sure that most of the 5,100[16] mostly well-crafted units were doomed. As *New York Times* architecture critic Nicolai Ouroussoff wrote:

> Billed as a strategy for relieving the entrenched poverty of the city's urban slums, it is based on familiar arguments about the alienating effects of large-scale postwar inner-city housing.
>
> But this argument seems strangely disingenuous in New Orleans. Built at the height of the New Deal, the city's public housing projects have little in common with the dehumanizing superblocks and grim plazas that have long been an emblem of urban poverty. Modestly scaled, they include some of the best public housing built in the United States.[17]

The targets of the destruction were buildings that were broadly recognized for their incomparable quality. Architecture critic James S. Russell articulated this widely held view: "In New Orleans, public housing doesn't mean bleak high-rise towers. The city has thousands of units with Georgian brickwork and lacy ironwork porches that came through Hurricane Katrina barely scathed."[18]

Many units had private or semiprivate entrances, avoiding the often unsafe and space-wasting corridors. And the pitched, terra-cotta roofs outlived most other roofing materials, not unlike buildings in Europe more than a hundred years old. Multipane windows, solid wood doors, and columned entryways completed the tableau. As Ouroussoff notes: "Solidly built, the buildings' detailed brickwork, tile roofs and wrought-iron balustrades represent a level of craft more likely found on an Ivy League campus than in a contemporary public housing complex."[19]

The fight over this public housing was one of the ugliest of the post-Katrina controversies. Minimally damaged, almost all the projects were boarded up right after the storms, enclosed with locked chain-link fences and off-limits to Katrina evacuees; in fact, they were forbidden access even to retrieve their belongings.[20] Marches and protests were ignored since the agenda had been set before the floodwaters drained out of the city. The culmination was a shocking City Council hearing at which the council members voted unanimously to demolish. The City Hall gates were locked. Hundreds of protesters, wanting to testify, were kept out with pepper spray and taser guns. The scene was reminiscent of a third-world revolution.

To many, the planned demolitions were one more indication that the poor, mostly black hurricane refugees were unwelcome home after Katrina. "This is not about [helping] the poor; it is about not seeing the poor," said Ron Mason, president of the Southern University and College System and for four years (1996–2000) executive monitor of New Orleans Public Housing. "Poverty was always so 'in your face' in New Orleans," he continued, noting that the key housing projects were right in the city's downtown, two of them a stone's throw from the French Quarter. "Today the poor are just spread out, less visible." In 1996, under a deal cut by Mayor Marc Morial and HUD secretary Henry Cisneros, Tulane, in partnership with Xavier, took over the administration of the public housing. Mason at the time was senior vice president and chief legal counsel for Tulane and was given the monitor job, supposedly to be half-time for both jobs; in other words, Ron Mason was the de facto head of HANO.

"New Orleans's public housing was considered the worst in the country," Ron continued. "It was a huge organization with highly visible facilities next door to downtown." Nothing had ever really been done to improve things. Historically, he said, New Orleans went through cycles of high-paid consultants coming in to devise half-measures over ten-year cycles. "Public housing was just being used to pay consultants." This pattern seemed to persist until Tulane took the helm.

With $2 million a year in federal funds, a number of programs were initiated under Mason's leadership. "We developed an array of tools to lift people up," he said. Residents were involved in management; some were hired to do maintenance and help with security. Tulane and Xavier students tutored project youth and worked with residents on a community garden. Professionals helped them find jobs. Courses were offered on health, parenting, job training, teen pregnancy, and high school equivalency. Professionals also worked with residents to establish Individual Development Accounts to enable them to buy a car or a house, thus helping some tenants become homeowners. Tulane history professor Lawrence Powell worked with Ron on this program. "Congress was pressuring HUD secretary Cisneros to do something about public housing in New Orleans and around the country," Larry told me over lunch.[21] "In New Orleans, it was corrupt, inefficient; maintenance was failing, money disappearing; it was totally dysfunctional."

Lo and behold, the empowerment programs instituted by the Mason-Powell team actually worked. "Many residents were working off the books doing nails, washing cars, cleaning houses, and were not in networks to hear about regular jobs," Larry said. "Our people helped them find jobs, got them credit counseling and basic financial education. We connected them to mainstream financial institutions so they didn't have to go to check-cashing outfits. They became mortgage-ready and we got five hundred people into homes. The functionally illiterate learned workplace literacy and carpentry math so they could read a ruler."

In March 1998, *Time* magazine featured the story "Miracle in New Orleans."

What could Tulane know about fixing a bureaucracy that was rotting away as much as the buildings in its care? A lot, it turns out. According to the Federal Government's rating system, Tulane has pulled off one of the most dramatic turnarounds in the history of public housing. Says Tulane President Eamon Kelly: "The university is the last institution you would pick to run public housing, until you look at the alternatives."

Wisely, Mason and Tulane first tackled nuts and bolts. They evicted criminals and drug users, reduced the backlog of work orders by 9,000 and improved response times for such things as plumbing repairs from months to days or hours. Just as important, they enlisted the support of citywide tenant groups who had once fought HANO bitterly.[22]

The Mason-Powell team tracked one hundred families and showed that positive change was possible. They came up with a plan to truly enhance the physical structure of all the public housing projects. For about $500 million, some of the buildings would be torn down, particularly the ones of lesser quality built as expansions of the projects in the 1960s. "Others were perfectly workable," Ron told me. "We had a great plan," he added, "to make the complex resident-owned and -operated." Mason and Powell showed how it could be done, and, most importantly, they demonstrated the limitations of Hope VI—a HUD program "charged with proposing a National Action Plan to eradicate severely distressed public housing."[23]

Specifically, Mason and Powell showed how to build into the HOPE VI program of 1992 (meant to replace public housing with economically integrated developments) a way to "structurally uplift tenants." According to Edward G. Goetz—the director of the Center for Urban and Regional Affairs at the University of Minnesota—HOPE VI was "a solution that privileges physical change over meeting the human service needs of public housing residents."[24] This was the opposite of what Ron was successfully doing. Goetz further notes:

> The HOPE VI program and its evolution into a demolition and redevelopment program . . . embodied the larger shift in public policy away from the objective of preserving public housing to one that directly financed large-scale removals in cities across the country. . . . Since 1994, HOPE VI has financed the demolition of more than 110,000 units of public housing in cities across the nation. Only 60,000 of the units have been or will be replaced in mixed-income projects subsidized by the program.[25]

"Residents knew if they moved out, they'd never move back in," said Larry. "Under our plan, 30 percent of the units would be for former public housing tenants." Instead, the federal funding for Ron Mason's program stopped altogether after 2000, with no real explanation: "Presidents, cabinet members, mayors come and go, but the system is intransigent." The "disperse and demolish" model for public housing, Ron explained, does not create the kind of interventions needed to make a dent in the fundamental problems identified with public housing—namely, poverty, crime, and lack of jobs. As Representative Baker's earlier quote demonstrates, Katrina was just the disaster needed to advance an otherwise untenable agenda. None of the protests offering thoughtful alternatives after Katrina had a prayer.

• • •

Initial legislative efforts to establish public housing programs in the United States failed in 1935 and again in 1936. It did not have many powerful advocates at the time. Even President Roosevelt was not a fan as yet. But eventually, as Goetz notes,

The press of economic conditions and the enormous potential for creating employment in the building trades through
a program of public housing changed the political prospects
of public housing. Roosevelt's New Deal was largely predi-
cated on the idea that public works could be used as a means
of generating jobs and reviving industrial output, and with
his other New Deal initiatives struggling in an increasingly
hostile Congress, Roosevelt put his full support behind public housing legislation in the U.S. Housing Act of 1937. Sen.
Robert F. Wagner (D-NY), the program's legislative sponsor
that year, sold it as the "next step in the country's economic
recovery," another New Deal public works program whose
primary benefit would be the employment that it generated.[26]

New Orleans was the first city to get public housing. By 1941,
the city had six projects, two of which—St. Thomas and Iberville—
were for white residents, four for black—C. J. Peete, B. W. Cooper, Lafitte, and St. Bernard. By the 1950s and '60s, public housing
design nationally had evolved into dehumanizing superblocks and
grim plazas—the tower-in-the-park model that became the face
of urban crime and poverty. When New Orleans's earlier projects
were expanded, they were shorter versions of the high-rise horrors.
Regardless of the era of construction or its quality, the destruction
of public housing has been an ongoing policy of the federal government all over the country since President Richard Nixon declared
an end to the funding of public housing in 1973. The implosion
in 1972 of Pruitt Igo in St. Louis presaged the eventual end of all
public housing. Budget cuts, disinvestment, and subsequent deterioration actually began in the 1960s, when the resident population
began to shift—at first almost imperceptibly—from white to black.
Diminished maintenance, decreased security, loss of social services,
and the closing of recreational amenities followed.

Once we understand that the real reasons for demolishing
public housing nationwide since the Nixon administration[27] were

(a) to eliminate public housing wherever possible and replace it with publicly funded developer projects known as "public-private partnerships" and (b) to disperse the poor so as to make them almost invisible, the official pronouncements after Katrina in New Orleans sound as hollow as they actually were. Architecture critic James Russell commented on the federal insistence on demolition: "This is an unnecessarily painful mess in which bureaucratic bull-headedness and ideology have trumped common sense."[28]

Those who argued on behalf of the demolition policy in New Orleans argued that dispersing the poor would diminish the crime associated with public housing. Predictably, this has proven untrue. Crime rates went up after the public housing was closed, even while many of the relocated inhabitants remained in distant places. In some cases this disruption has made things worse, because gangs defined by their residential location found themselves on each other's territory, prompting turf wars that wouldn't have occurred when individuals knew their place. "We saw this happen," Ron observed, "when we temporarily relocated some tenants from C. J. Peete to the St. Bernard Project in the 1990s."

"De-concentrating poverty" was another avowed reason for demolition that rings hollow. If you want to de-concentrate poverty—and address it—instead of dispersing it, the solutions offered were many, along the lines that Mason and Powell successfully instituted two decades ago. The reconfiguration of each project to *add* density with moderate and market-rate apartments would have answered the economic integration goal. Selective demolition would have allowed the reinstating of public streets, eliminated dangerous hidden spaces, connected each complex to its surrounding street grid, and introduced street-level uses.

No one romanticized the way things were; everyone wanted change. Alternatives to full-scale demolition included "selective demolition" and the addition of new, denser construction that would not only appeal to both moderate- and market-rate residents but also acknowledged the architectural, physical, and social value of what existed. A combination of renovation, demolition, and new building would achieve agreed-upon goals. Adding density and mixed-income units was clearly viable.[29] But the "demolish and rebuild" approach prevailed.

It is nothing short of a Utopian ideal to say that one can physically build poverty out and prosperity in. But is it also a good public-relations mantra? Bill Quigley, director of the Loyola University Law Center, said in an interview: "They always promise the poor will either be able to come back or will be provided better housing. In reality . . . they push all the poor people out and then allow, at most, about 10 percent to return."[30] Developers argued that if the percentage of poor residents was higher than 30 or 40 percent, the market-rate renters would stay away. History has proven otherwise.

Every gentrifying neighborhood in every city in the country started out more than 50 percent occupied by poor residents. Reasonably priced, quality housing opportunities drew middle-income residents back to long-deteriorated neighborhoods. That grassroots, back-to-the-city movement—starting in the 1970s and '80s—launched not only the regeneration of many cities but also, not surprisingly, the renewed interest by investors in downtown real estate. Just look at the neighborhoods formerly dominated by the poor and now considered chic or, at least, on an upward trajectory. In New Orleans, this surely applies to the Irish Channel, the Lower Garden District, Marigny, and Bywater, and to neighborhoods like St. Roch and Holy Cross that are moving in the same direction.

The national list is endless, from Georgetown in DC to the Upper West Side of Manhattan to Park Slope in Brooklyn to the Victorian Districts of San Francisco and Savannah and so on. Desirable housing options at reasonable prices are not a hard sell, regardless of who lives in the neighborhood. In actuality, this phenomenon has integrated—racially, economically, and ethnically—many neighborhoods, the kind that massive Urban Renewal, instead, disrupted or erased.[31]

The argument for de-densification of poverty is a leftover mantra from the Urban Renewal days of the 1950s and '60s that has been discredited everywhere, except when it comes to public housing. Cities across America are making every effort to *re-densify* their downtowns and residential neighborhoods. The lesson has long been learned that the thinning out of population promoted by Urban Renewal discouraged the kind of residential neighborhoods, public spaces, and retail uses that lead to safe, animated pedestrian-dominated streets. But can it really be argued that re-densification—or intensification, as it is sometimes called—is good for upscale neighborhoods but not for low-income enclaves?

The notion that the storms caused irreparable damage to public housing is not true. Shallow water penetrated one complex, and limited wind damage was evident elsewhere; but, as Ouroussoff notes, "[t]he problems facing these projects have more to do with misguided policy and the city's complex racial history than with bad design. The deterioration can be attributed to the government's decision decades ago to gut most of the public services that supported them."[32] This, too, is a national phenomenon. Many of the amenities and social services that have been reintroduced into the newly built projects existed when public housing was first built, primarily for white people in many cities.

Ouroussoff continues:

> Arguing that the housing was barely livable before the flooding unleashed by Hurricane Katrina, federal officials have cast their decision as good social policy. They have sought to lump the projects together with the much-vilified inner-city projects of the 1960s.
>
> But such thinking reflects a ruthless indifference to local realities. The projects in New Orleans have little to do with the sterile brick towers and alienating plazas that usually come to mind when we think of inner-city housing.

Some rank among the best early examples of public housing built in the United States, both in design and in quality of construction.

On the contrary, it is the government's tabula rasa approach that evokes the most brutal post-war urban renewal strategies. Neighborhood history is deemed irrelevant; the vague notion of a "fresh start" is invoked to justify erasing entire communities.

The demolished units, in fact, could be renovated "for less than $10,000" each but the new mixed-income units would instead cost "an average of $400,000" each, according to HANO's own insurance company.[33]

Quigley highlights the financial aspect of the story:

> The housing authority's own documents show that Lafitte could be repaired for $20 million, even completely overhauled for $85 million while the estimate for demolition and rebuilding many fewer units will cost over $100 million. St. Bernard could be repaired for $41 million, substantially modernized for $130 million while demolition and rebuilding less units will cost $197 million. BW Cooper could be substantially renovated for $135 million compared to $221 million to demolish and rebuild less units.[34]

One key question comes to mind: Where were all those so-called fiscal conservatives in Congress throughout all of this?

In an unsuccessful lawsuit brought against HUD secretary Alphonse Jackson et al. to stop demolition, lawyer and housing expert Robert R. Elliott submitted an affidavit in January 2007 attesting to the solidity of the buildings. As general counsel of HUD from 1974 to 1977, appointed by President Richard Nixon, Elliott oversaw the original implementation of the Community Block Grant Program and the Section 8 Housing Program, among others. In the context of his extensive experience since then in renovating multifamily housing, Elliott said:

> I examined housing units in all of the following four public housing projects: St. Bernard, Lafitte, B. W. Cooper and C. J. Peete. I found them to be very capable of renovation at far less cost than new construction. I also found them to be capable of being put back in service in a short period of time.
>
> The construction using concrete walls in the interior instead of "studs" and drywall means that there is far less renovation required to eliminate mold and create safe, decent and sanitary housing.
>
> It is also apparent that due to the strength of construction, the buildings of the four developments withstood the winds of Hurricane Katrina far better than "stick built" homes in the area. Such structures were often structurally wind damaged, and the interiors are much more difficult to reconstruct due to mold behind drywall and under wood floors.
>
> It is also apparent that HANO is allowing unnecessary damage to occur to the buildings by leaving them exposed to rain when at very low cost they could be secured pending renovation.[35]

At the insistence of the State Historic Preservation Office, each of the replacement developments retained and renovated a few of the original buildings on the site of each project, calling them Legacy Buildings. Some have apartments, others were converted to community centers. But to look closely at them is to see the emptiness of the rhetoric about the irreparable physical condition of these buildings.

Lafitte was the best of the "bricks." Even with the 1960s expansion, it was smaller than others and the antithesis of the density model of the 1960s. Lafitte had private entrances, balconies, and parquet floors, giving it a real garden-apartment feel. With

517 units and only three blocks wide, Jacques Morial pointed out, "Lafitte was well integrated into the surrounding community with no psychological boundaries. It had a couple of through streets and was close to employment and services." Lawrence Powell hit the nail on the head: "Anyone could see it was not true that most of the public housing was beyond repair. Lafitte was in perfect shape. It was designed well. They were hearty structures that could have been modified. The deals were made in Washington. The storm was the opportunity to give them away, and no political leaders stood up and said no to any of it."

One of the supposed reasons that the projects didn't work was that they were isolating; all activity occurred in the court-yards, hidden from the street. Petty and serious crimes could occur too far from public view. But the rebuilt Lafitte—now called Fau-bourg Lafitte—does just that. I took a tour of the project with an earnest young staff woman. "You know," she said, "New Orleans life is built around the interior courtyard and that is what was done here." Really? That is only true in the French Quarter with its luxury dwellings and delightful private courtyards—surely not the right model here. The rest of the city focuses on the front, the porch, the stoop, or just a plastic chair on the sidewalk. The front of Lafitte, with its assortment of pale-colored individual houses with balconies and modest front yards, faces Claiborne Avenue under the shadow of the I-10 but invites no daily life because the orientation is, once again, inward and away from the street. The newly built project looks like a stage set. A resident is never visible at the front. Instead, life is designed around the interior parking lots in the rear. So much for improving the model.

If the old buildings were so terrible and beyond repair, why are the Legacy buildings just a hair short of gorgeous? And they cost less per unit than the new ones.

Stand in front of the pedimented entryway of the single-story restored building on the edge of Lafitte. Its richly textured, skillfully laid brickwork and well-formed mortar joints exhibit a solid construction that can withstand an intense hurricane.[36] The building would be a standout in any upscale neighborhood. Next door is a similarly elegant restored two-story apartment house.

On another side of town, visit the two-bedroom, two-bathroom duplex of Doris Tennessee in one of five three-story, red brick Legacy buildings with thirty-seven apartments in River Garden—the HOPE VI replacement for the 1940 St. Thomas Project.[37] This simple three-story structure topped with slate roof is set around a small courtyard with two other similar buildings. Together, they represent a human-scale ensemble that set it apart from later big tower–style projects, the only units left of the original 120 buildings with 3,000 tenants. Whatever the flaws of these 1940s buildings, their construction quality exceeds that of many developments built privately since World War II as middle-income garden apartments. Doris's two-bedroom duplex apartment entrance is on the second floor, which seems to be the only complaint she can come up with—other than the fact that the doors to the street-level hallways are unlocked, thus providing the perfect shelter for shooting up and other drug transactions. "The drug problem is no different from the old project," Doris said when I visited.

The layout, Doris noted, is the same as in the new mock–New Orleans–style shotguns, creole cottages, and two-story galleried clapboard houses that fill the multibuilding complex. Doris is on a Section 8 voucher and doesn't qualify for the new buildings, but "when those high winds come, I'd rather be here," she added. Her spacious living room has a modest dining alcove and an elongated kitchen, with the wall separating from the living room open above counter height. The renovation of these units reportedly cost less than building the new ones, a spokesman for the developer, HRI, once conceded soon after Katrina.

• • •

Without Katrina, it is unclear how far the city could have gotten in eliminating public housing. Politically, the idea was untenable. Iberville, one of the best of the "bricks" and the last of the New Deal developments, sits on the corner of Canal and Basin Streets—the most valuable site of any of the projects. With 821 units on 23 acres, originally in seventy-four mostly three-story brick buildings featuring lacey wrought-iron railings and terra-cotta roofs, Iberville was a prime site for redevelopment. This project exemplifies that trend, starting in the 1990s when cities were regenerating and downtown real estate was ripening for private investment. Iberville abuts the downtown core and the French Quarter. The pressure was on. Vintage public housing developments in many cities were in the path of new development. They had to go.

Katrina only accelerated the value of the Iberville site. In 2004, Pres Kabacoff, one of the city's most active and politically well-connected developers, proposed to partially demolish the project as part of his vision for reinvigorating the city's tourism economy and the urban core. He wanted to revamp Canal Street with a music museum and big-box retail (he's still trying for the latter) and, in his words, create a kind of "Afro-Caribbean Paris" as the city center.[38] This proposal sent chills up the spine of many New Orleanians, especially since they know how frequently Kabacoff gets what he aims for. "[L]ocal politicians did not have the stomach for demolition of [Iberville's] 820 units and the massive dislocation that would come with it," notes historian Alecia P. Long. "Then Katrina came along."[39] Not surprisingly, Kabacoff got the $31 million federal grant after Katrina to rebuild Iberville under the Choice Neighborhood Initiative (CNI).[40] Kabacoff told Tyler Bridges of *The Lens* in 2013: "I don't think of myself as an opportunistic developer. I think of myself as on a mission."[41] What seems to escape him is that New Orleanians and tourists alike find the city appealing because it is itself unique and *not* a mock version of any other place.

Ironically, Kabacoff is responsible for some of the best preservation projects that have helped downtown retain its traditional feel. A New Orleans native, Kabacoff was born in 1945, graduated from LSU Law School, and then learned the development business from his father, Lester Kabacoff, who jump-started the revival of the Warehouse District by converting a cargo wharf into the riverside of the Hilton hotel. "My father knew tourism could be a big game, a distant second to oil and gas," Pres said in an interview at the house he built for himself and his wife, Sallie Ann Glassman, in the Bywater. Colorfully painted outside in a Caribbean palette, the house is adjacent to his successful ArtLofts, a tax-credit artist housing development.

The Warehouse District, now one of downtown's most desirable areas, is primarily residential. Both Pres and his father saw great potential in the slowly emptying warehouse buildings before the renewed interest in cities was on everyone's radar.[42] "Look at the building material, what there was to work with. Why wouldn't you want to live in a place like this?" he asked, referring to the loft buildings—but not to the "bricks."[43]

Pres Kabacoff became proficient at tapping into federal subsidies, such as the historic tax credits he is getting for saving sixteen of the original Iberville buildings while demolishing fifty-nine. That even sixteen of the original buildings are being saved and restored, thanks to those historic tax credits, is a major shift from earlier project demolitions and new construction. "There was a dispute within our own company over how many buildings to preserve," Pres said. In the end, he added, "we didn't want to have it just look like a cleaned-up public housing project. The key is to attract market-rate residents." Pres was speaking about a 40 percent low-income cutoff to attract market-rate tenants. The reality, however, is that nothing close to 40 percent of the former public housing tenants will be accommodated in any of the new developments. A one-for-one unit replacement is called for in the Iberville, but a good number of those units will be spread out within the larger three-hundred-block Treme neighborhood. There is no deadline for their construction.

According to sociologist Hilary Silver, "Since 1994, HOPE VI has demolished more than 500,000 public housing units."[44] National studies have found that an estimated 5–50 percent of displaced tenants return to the replacement developments.[45] Not surprisingly, neither HUD nor local housing authorities have made any real effort to track these former tenants. All manner of excuses, including privacy claims, have been offered. But one need only look at the zip codes of where the replacement Section 8 vouchers go; tenant names are unnecessary. Officially, no one seems to want to know the answer.

In New Orleans, several factors conspire to keep tenants from returning, particularly the strict selection criteria for admission. Ever since the onset of President Clinton's "One Strike and You're Out" policy, local authorities have been allowed to evict tenants if someone in the family is arrested for criminal activity. Given how easily African-Americans get arrested and convicted for both minor and major offenses regardless of guilt in New Orleans, this narrows the eligibility pool. Any family member can ruin it for an entire family.

Ten years after Katrina, most of the city's public housing projects are gone, especially those in or close to high-value downtown real estate. The privately owned, privately developed, primarily publicly funded replacements substantially reflect New Urbanist town-planning principles, with narrow pedestrian-friendly streets, neighborly front yards, and variations of quaint two- or three-story houses—some in pastel colors, some in faux historic styles. Several of the developments are as set off from their surrounding neighborhoods as they were before Katrina. All have economically mixed tenants. Social services of various kinds—learning centers, playgrounds, community centers—have returned, although maybe not as robustly as during the Work Projects Administration (WPA) period of Boy Scout troops, gardening clubs, adult education, and onsite healthcare that was budgeted out by the 1960s.

All the new developments present a good face to their neighborhood and to the city, and you can be sure that political and business leaders will tout their appeal to the outside world. It is much too early, however, to know if these structures will come through as hurricane-unscathed as the original red brick structures did. There is no evidence that entrenched poverty has been upbraided, and no effort has been made to determine how well the several thousand displaced families are faring with their vouchers or where they landed. The city's shamefully low-wage economy remains in place, and local families struggle to live a minimal life. Nor does evidence exist that dispersal has had an impact on crime rates. Without living-wage jobs that could compete with the illegal industries of the streets, it is unclear how much this can change.

For years, public housing detractors bemoaned the high cost of subsidizing housing for the poor—a policy considered by many to be an important component of a democratic society. The public housing subsidy is now drastically diminished. Developers and tax credit investors reap benefits from building new projects, and the largest housing subsidy of all—the mortgage interest deduction—survives for those fortunate enough to own a home.

The public housing story and the demise of Charity Hospital are the most blatant examples of the use of a "Katrina opportunity" to undermine the already overly challenged lives of New Orleans's low-income residents. Both instances limit the extent of the city's post-Katrina recovery.

Chapter 13

Women at the Forefront

When 150 New Orleans women, calling themselves Women of the Storm, breezed into multiple congressional offices to underscore the severity of the damage wrought by Hurricanes Katrina and Rita, they were upholding a long-held tradition. Women have been at the forefront of the battle for the regeneration of American cities for over a century. Observe any one of the many revived cities in America, explore the history of how the turnaround began, and you will likely find a major initiative started by a woman.[1] New Orleans is a star example.

In January 2006, the Women of the Storm spread out through the halls of Congress to voice the urgent need for funding to repair damaged homes, to rebuild the levees properly, and to restore the wetlands of the Gulf Coast. They delivered packets of detailed information to members of Congress, along with buttons, blue-tarp-colored umbrellas sporting their logo, and an invitation to visit the beleaguered city as guests of the group to see conditions for themselves.

"We put the whole thing together in twenty days," said Ann MacDonald Milling, one of the group's leaders and the originator of this idea. Ann is the classic uptown woman of high social standing. She was born in New Orleans but moved with her family to Monroe in northern Louisiana at the age of ten. She returned to attend Newcomb College, then the women's counterpart to Tulane University, and went to Yale for a master's in Modern European History. She had met New Orleans–born King Milling during her first year at Newcomb, and settling in New Orleans after they were married was never in doubt. Ann's activism started not long after their wedding.

Ann, a tall, slim, attractive woman with short, wavy blond hair, sits in the library of her elegant home just off St. Charles Avenue. She laughs at the memory of her early participation in the fight to stop the French Quarter Expressway. "There I was, eight months pregnant, wearing a red wool cape and handing out papers to lawyers, bankers, and anyone passing by. I guess that's when King realized I wasn't going to sit back and just be a quiet southern housewife."

The idea for the Washington visit came to Ann by Thanksgiving after the storms, when so few national leaders had come to see the devastation. "By year's end, only twenty-five congressmen and twelve mostly southern senators had come," she told me. "This gnawed at me." She posed the idea to a small group of friends and they were immediately onboard. "We wanted it to be more than a group of uptown swells," so they assembled a diverse group that included everyone from homemakers to lawyers. They worked fast. "We were living on adrenalin." They flew up to Washington, DC, for a one-day whirlwind. "Everything worked in our favor," Ann recalled. "It was a slow news day and all the press greeted us at the airport. It was daunting. I had never done this before. CNN had us on, so by the time we reached Congress, staff in many offices who keep a TV on knew about us."

By the spring of 2006, about 250 House members and 60 senators showed up to visit the city. "I'm told it was the largest congressional delegation to visit a site of any kind. We greeted them at the airport, left books on their pillows, and arranged tours and lectures," Ann said. "Everywhere we went, we told them how high the water was there. We repeated over and over that this was a man-made disaster. What really got them was the magnitude of the disaster and the fact that 1,700 people lost their lives."

How much impact Women of the Storm had on congressional action is hard to tell, but Congress was left with no doubt that the citizens of New Orleans meant business, that they were hard at work doing their part to rebuild their city, and that Congress itself had a responsibility to come up with its fair share of assistance. The group returned in September 2006 to underscore the "third plank of our agenda, the coastal wetlands," Ann added. "They knew we didn't come unless there was a serious issue to discuss." The experience, she said, was "an awakening. Once involved, people want accountability. We monitor how money is spent and make sure money under the RESTORE ACT doesn't get siphoned off in Baton Rouge for highways or other projects."[2]

"Why women?" Ann was asked. "Women protect their nest and our nest had been destroyed," she responded. Interestingly, now, almost ten years later, the New Orleans City Council is dominated by women elected since the storms. Why is this? As Ann put it: "Across America, women are finding their place. The glass ceiling has been shattered. We in the South just come later to the table."

Before the storms, eight levee boards across the state seemed to focus on everything but the efficacy of the flood protection system. Real estate development unrelated to flood protection and favorite projects of the politically chosen board members dominated the agenda. After the storms, when the state legislature resisted consolidating the eight levee boards and filling them with experts rather than political cronies, Ruthie Frierson and what became known as the "ladies in red" sprang into action. A real estate agent, former schoolteacher, and Newcomb College graduate, Ruthie gathered 120 women in her Walnut Street home on the edge of Audubon Park and set to work.

"We needed levee boards to focus on better flood protection only," she explained. "And to be filled with experts in hydrology, engineering, and other relevant areas—not to be political appointees. The governor needed to call a special session of the legislature to get this done." In three and a half weeks, the "ladies in red" secured 53,000 petition signatures. "This represented one-sixth of the five parishes covered," Ruthie told me. The group, dressed in their trademark red scarves and red blazers, attended every legislative committee hearing on the issue, argued the matter before editorial boards, and brought it to national attention through the media. Governor Blanco called a special session, and a constitutional amendment eventually consolidated the eight levee boards down to two—one on either side of the Mississippi.

In the late 1990s, former journalist Sharon Litwin organized a group of about a hundred women during a serious spike in crime. They went to the city and to Entergy, the energy company; identified crime hotspots throughout the city; and raised private funds for new, upgraded streetlights. They similarly organized neighborhood groups to work with city agencies, mobilized between six thousand and seven thousand households, handed out free garbage bags, and instructed citizens to clean the sidewalks and catch basins in front of their houses, leaving full bags on the sidewalk. City sanitation workers, homeless people, and prisoners picked up the bags. Sharon noted in an interview that "2,300 catch basins, which ease flooding during heavy rains, were cleaned out and probably none since. We did it the New Orleans way, with style, not screeching."

In earlier decades, when women of a certain social standing around the country were discouraged from entering the workplace, smart, talented women seeking an outlet for their energies often ended up battling massive Urban Renewal or highway-through-the-city construction programs. But their efforts were never just aimed at stopping community-killing programs; they labored hard to both rescue and rebuild their cities and often worked on behalf of the underprivileged.

Yet it was primarily from upper-class circles that women leaders emerged. The small but important efforts made by a diverse range of women are now the backbone of the city's post-Katrina civil society. Vanessa Guerlinger was an indispensible voice in the Lower Nine, fighting for the restoration of parks, a new school, and other projects. Carol Bebelle started years before Katrina but gained well-deserved attention after the storms as leader of the Ashe Cultural Arts Center to foster African-American arts and culture in the heart of a once-vibrant black community. Leah Chase, whose Dooky Chase's Restaurant probably hosted more power breakfasts than any other eatery in the city, served an often behind-the-scenes role in the city's racial politics. Hers was the first white-cloth restaurant open to African-Americans. Timolynn Sams, executive director of the Neighborhood Partnership Network, developed a citywide neighborhoods-based voice. Linda Usdin, a New Orleans native with a doctorate in public health from Tulane's School of Public Health and Tropical Medicine, rallied support from a group of foundations and with a local team launched LouisianaRebuilds.org right after Katrina, a twenty-four-hour call-in line and website for displaced residents. A local journalist, Deborah Cotton, edited the website. Linda subsequently succeeded in securing foundation funding in support of several nascent community groups, giving the participants an opportunity to grow new ideas. And Vaughn R. Fauria founded Newcorp to help small businesses survive by arranging for loans and assistance with business strategies.

Jeanne Nathan falls into a category all her own. A TV journalist, publicist, and political activist, she moved from her native New York to be a reporter for WDSU New Orleans in 1973. She recognized early on that the arts were an anchor for community revitalization in many places around the United States. With that knowledge, she and her husband, Bob Tannen, started the Contemporary Art Center (CAC) in 1975 in a vacant K & B Drugstore warehouse in the area considered skid row. Many people were skeptical, but "I knew it would help revive the Warehouse District and it did," she said in an interview. A tireless activist on behalf of the arts ever since, Jeanne pointed out that the arts are the second-biggest source of jobs in the state. Today, the CAC is the hub of a vibrant arts district.

This tradition of women leaders continues to inspire and inform activists in New Orleans. "Apathy and lack of involvement" were once common, Ruthie said, but the storms changed that. "We went from being enraged to finding hope through action."

· · ·

Sixty years before the Women of the Storm, Martha Robinson succeeded in directing congressional attention and concern to the potential fate of the French Quarter when a six-lane elevated expressway threatened to wipe out most of the Quarter. The city's social and political establishment—including the *Times-Picayune* and Congressman Hale Boggs and Senator Russell Long—were vigorously pushing its approval. Martha was undaunted, because she *was* a member of that establishment. A resident of Audubon Place, the city's most prestigious address, Martha was a New Orleans native, highly educated, fluent in French, assertive, and influential in many areas. She was the epitome of the *grande dame* and possessed a Rolodex that included every important political leader across the country. She was not afraid to use it.

Bill Borah, a key leader with her in the expressway fight, remembers Martha with great admiration. "She dazzled politicians everywhere and was a great spokesman for our fight," he said. "She helped make saving the French Quarter a national issue, making people realize it was a national treasure." She called, wrote, and met with key people in Congress; at one point, even senators from other states were making speeches on the floor of Congress about the need to save the Vieux Carré (French Quarter). In the process, she made historic preservation, not just the Quarter, a national issue.[3]

Bill told me that he learned a lot from Martha in their eventually successful defeat of the expressway: "She was from, and in, the establishment but a severe critic of it and wasted no time worrying about it. She took me under her wing and explained how New Orleans worked from the inside. She said the business community didn't understand the value of historic preservation and, in fact, they still don't. The French Quarter was only meaningful to them for tourism." No temporary defeat would discourage her. At the end of a raucous twelve-hour City Council hearing to reexamine the June 1966 expressway approval, Martha walked out, declaring: "We've just begun to fight."[4] Bill and his good friend Richard O. Baumbach, Jr., became on-the-ground, day-to-day leaders in the battle, which was fully financed by the Stern Family Fund. Bill occasionally argued with Martha over strategy. "She would look at me with those steely blue eyes," Bill recalled with a chuckle, "and say, 'Bill, your father wasn't even born here.' That was the end of it." Martha was probably the most formidable but certainly not the first of the women who labored hard to save the French Quarter early in the city's history. She capped a long line of Quarter defenders.

After the Louisiana Purchase in 1803, Americans started moving to New Orleans and settling on the other side of Canal Street.[5] The Quarter was no longer the most-desired residential district. Baroness Micaela Pontalba built two parallel luxurious apartment buildings in 1849 and 1851 on either side of Jackson Square. Micaela, born in New Orleans in 1795, planned the construction of the apartment buildings with shops on the ground floor, rightly seeing this as a source of new energy for the area.

Author Mary Gehman points out a fascinating advantage held by New Orleans women:

Because under French law a woman was sole owner of property which she inherited or brought with her from a former marriage, New Orleans women were free to sell, lease or rent their own property and to contract large building projects in their own names. They were also more apt to divorce or separate from their husbands than women elsewhere in America, since they had financial security. Women in Louisiana who owned property were granted the right to vote on tax issues as early as 1879, a full forty-one years before women were given the right to vote nationally.[6]

Under both French and Spanish law, women had unusual autonomy. With their own inherited money, they built a number of houses in the French Quarter "without the need for consent of or supervision by men."[7] Micaela solicited the proxy of property-owning women and made the difference for an election-day bond issue that provided "the first adequate sewerage and drainage system for the city."[8]

The character and life of the French Quarter early in the twentieth century were already changing as the successful French Creoles were moving up and out to the graceful mansions on Esplanade, the downriver border of the Quarter. Sicilian immigrants were moving in and taking their place. The buildings in the Quarter, already dilapidated, became more crowded and run-down. Adding more downward pressure on the district was the forced closure by the US War Department in 1917 of Storyville—the legendary red-light district at the edge of the Quarter.[9] With Storyville closed, buildings continued to deteriorate, particularly in the Quarter.

One of the first significant preservation communities evolved out of a women's book club, Le Petit Salon, an informal group that gathered after performances at Le Petit Theatre du Vieux Carré.[10] With Grace King as its first president and Dorothy Dix as vice president, the salon played a major role in the area's cultural revival and preservation.[11] "It took local women to see it as savable and restorable," noted author Fred Starr—a veritable walking encyclopedia of New Orleans history and culture.

Somewhat quietly, at first, women with independent resources began buying and fixing up Quarter properties for their own use. Grover Mouton, the director of the Tulane Regional Urban Design Center at the Tulane School of Architecture, underscores the historic and economic importance of the accomplishments of this generation of women. "Women were doing this during the Depression," he pointed out. "They created an economic base for the future of New Orleans at a very difficult time. No one else achieved as much again. This was a cornerstone moment in the history of this city." Two other women in particular, Elizabeth Werlein and Mary Morrison, also stand out as critical game-changers during this period.

Elizabeth Werlein was an outsider.[12] She was born into money in Bay City, Michigan, and studied in Europe. She came to New Orleans for a friend's wedding and met and married Uptown society figure Philip Werlein—a music publisher and the owner of a legendary music store. Elizabeth's effectiveness stemmed from a boldness unusual for women of the day; in fact, she was one of the first women to go up in a hot-air balloon, helping to identify potential airfields from the air. "It was a man's world," her granddaughter, Bitsy Werlein, said in conversation. "Women could hardly hire a lawyer."

With the close of World War I, the "new age" of modernism began, characterized by a rising disdain for the old and a growing infatuation with the new. "There were men planning to demolish buildings from Canal to Esplanade," said Bitsy, a longtime resident of the French Quarter. "They disliked what they considered the risqué lifestyle and saw the district as rubbish, only good for demolition."

Elizabeth was a staunch protectionist, relentlessly pestering owners to take care of and even restore their property. Her grandson Philip Carter noted in an interview that she went so far as to "report her best friend doing something wrong on the façade of her building." In the 1920s and '30s, new skyscrapers were the goal of many developers. As demolition activity heated up and collectors scavenged the historic ornamentation (not unlike what happened after Katrina), Elizabeth campaigned for regulations to prevent the loss of architectural details, as well as buildings. "She used to say that the French Quarter was built by individual artisans," Philip recalled; "that every door, every hinge and chimney, every archway, everything on every building was unique." She was especially intolerant of the removal of the ironwork unique to the Quarter, a legacy of its French creators.[13]

Elizabeth persistently campaigned for regulations to prevent more loss. She led successful lobbying of the state legislature in 1936 to pass a constitutional amendment authorizing the City Council to create the Vieux Carré Commission (VCC) and give it control over changes in the Quarter—an unheard-of concept at the time. Thus, the Vieux Carré Commission was established to regulate changes in the Quarter, including signs, exterior alterations, choice of materials—the *tout ensemble* of the district. The VCC's approach became a model for landmark preservation commissions around the country. Two years later, the preservationists established the Vieux Carré Property Owners Association (VCPOA)[14] as the civic watchdog of the VCC's review process, with Elizabeth as its first president. Philip recalled: "Grandma had a knack for convincing locals what is important. The mayor was like her designated agent. She walked into his office one day and the mayor remained seated. 'Mayor Maestri,' she told him, 'a gentleman rises when a lady comes into the room.'"[15]

Describing Elizabeth as "a one-woman force in the preservation movement in the 1920s until her death in 1946," Mayor Robert Maestri dubbed her the mayor of the French Quarter. According to author Scott S. Ellis, "Maestri ruled that no Quarter demolition permits would be issued without the approval of the VCC."[16] When the commission approved a building's demolition for a parking lot, Elizabeth and the VCPOA caused such a fuss that the commission reversed its decision and won a subsequent legal challenge. This case laid the foundation for the current framework of protectionist strategy. Elizabeth's greatest impacts were made "when she lined up support for the VCC's creation. This clubby sort of lobbying among fellow elites is still the usual New Orleans way."[17]

After Philip Werlein's death in 1917, Elizabeth moved from her Uptown home into the Quarter and "became the foremost clubwoman" of the city.[18] She would go on to head the Louisiana Women's Suffrage Party, the Louisiana League of Women Voters, and the Orleans Club Voters.[19] She died of cancer in 1946 at the age of fifty-nine, just when demolition pressures on the Quarter were becoming increasingly intense. Mary Morrison stepped in to fill the vacuum following Elizabeth's death.

Mary, another outsider, born in Canton, Mississippi, considered Elizabeth Werlein her mentor. She and her husband, Jacob, moved into the Quarter in 1917. Jacob wrote the pioneering textbook on preservation, *Historic Preservation Law*; he also headed up the legal committee for VCPORA, served as the president of the association, and spearheaded several landmark cases.

Mary was "a petite, feisty redhead," Betty Norris recalled during a conversation; she was known "to lead policemen around to get property owners to take rule-breaking signs down." She was also "very articulate," Betty said. "In an argument, Mary could cut you off at the knees. She had a golden tongue. She let you know how wrong you were. She had an amazing way with words, and by the time she finished, if you weren't on her side, you certainly understood what she meant."

Mary and these other formidable women rescued the French Quarter from its earliest perils, but some of the worst threats were still to come. By the 1950s, as the suburban exodus accelerated, New Orleans leaders thought the best way to compete with the suburbs was to tear down the old and build the new. The fight to preserve the French Quarter kept getting harder. By the 1960s, 40 percent of the Central Business District had been lost to "'speculative demolition."[20] The scale of tourism and convention business grew dramatically as the city built large new hotels in the Quarter, completed the Rivergate Convention Center, widened Poydras Street, and began construction of the Louisiana Superdome. Preservationists were challenged at every turn. They succeeded in getting a new hotel moratorium passed for the French Quarter in 1969. Quarter residents thought that this would cool off further deterioration of the residential character of the area, and existing hotel owners were happy to stave off new competition. Neither anticipated the swelling conversion of residential apartments to short-term visitor accommodations—a process that continues to seriously undermine the residential character of the Quarter even today. The city leadership exhibits no real interest in minimizing this erosion.

• • •

Throughout the middle to late twentieth century, as each threat to the fabric of New Orleans emerged, a new group of women rose to protect irreplaceable architecture and the cultural values embodied in threatened buildings. Effectively, however, these women were battling to save urbanism itself—all the interconnected and interdependent elements that make up the social, economic, and physical fabric of an enduring city. But it remained an uphill battle.

Historic preservation gained new momentum in New Orleans in the 1970s with the publication of a series of six books surveying important buildings and presenting local history.[21] Documentation can be a great catalyst: magnificent archival and actual photographs spotlight the city's architectural and social history. Two energetic friends, Mary Louise Christovich and Roulhac Toledano (both Newcomb College graduates), launched this series with photographer Betsy Swanson and, later, Sally Reeves. These women had certified uptown credentials and were outraged by the high-volume demolition of extraordinary antebellum homes. "We knew we had to alert the city to what was being lost," recalled Mary Lou in an interview in her magnificent sprawling Garden District house, "and this was the best way to show people how important this heritage was." Sally Reeves pointed out in conversation that "the books were of great importance when suburban migration was in full swing and the value of these historic buildings was not recognized."

The 1970s in New Orleans, as in New York and other old cities throughout the country, were the years of economic bust and serious urban population shrinkage. A group of women persuaded then–Mayor Moon Landrieu that the losses were seriously undermining the appeal of the city. Landrieu declared a moratorium on demolitions. No new historic district had been created since the Vieux Carré in 1936 through state legislation. But in 1975, the state passed a law revising the earlier limited French Quarter legislation to allow communities to designate additional historic districts and create landmarks commissions. The Lower Garden District was the first historic district designated—four years after the first of the six books, *The Lower Garden District,* was published. Creation of the city's Historic Districts Landmarks Commission followed, setting the stage for an eventual total of twenty districts around the city. Indeed, the importance of this book series cannot be overstated. It galvanized a new interest in buying, restoring, and occupying highly deteriorated historic gems.[22]

Duncan and Camille Strachan were among the first new buyers in 1971 of a Greek Revival house facing Coliseum Square in the Lower Garden District. The biggest problem in the neighborhood, Camille explained in conversation, was not vacancies but over-densification of existing dwellings. During the Depression, houses had been broken up into multiple apartments. "People were filling in front porches for kitchens and bathrooms, so the architectural integrity of the houses was compromised," she said. Along with other neighbors, Camille and Duncan formed the Coliseum

Square Association, promoting the neighborhood through events and house tours—a template that historic preservation groups had begun to use around the country.[23] "We used banana wagons for the tours in 1971," Camille recalled. "We had to teach people how to look at the houses, to get them to look up."

In the 1970s, progress was defined as "new"; thus a euphoria over "the new" caused much demolition, a low point for American cities. What always escapes notice, however, is how effective the historic preservation movement was in turning around cities as places to live in—instead of places to leave. New Orleans experienced the full force of this trend. People were still leaving when the preservation and return-to-cities movements took off nationally in the late 1970s and 1980s.[24] People didn't stop leaving cities. Rather, leaving and returning began to happen at the same time, as they do today. The widespread assumption that the city was no place to raise a family began to fade. A burgeoning preservation industry was born—with architects, contractors, construction workers, restoration specialists, craftsmen, old-house experts, tradespeople, lawyers, and accountants all providing critical assistance to shaken urban economies.

• • •

Like many preservation organizations around the country, the Coliseum Square Association was at the forefront of stopping a huge misguided transportation project—in this case, the location of the second Mississippi Bridge to the West Bank. "We really started the association to fight the proposed bridge at Felicity Street, but the fight also brought added attention to the incredible resources of the neighborhood," said Camille. The planned location and its long ramps would have wiped out most of this neighborhood. Instead, moving it parallel to the existing bridge adjacent to the Warehouse District, after prolonged civic resistance, minimized that impact. The neighborhood also won removal of the existing on-ramp that rose from Coliseum Square, transforming the park at the center into an elegant focal point.

The first location would have decimated the moneyed neighborhoods uptown, but it also would have totally divided the uptown and downtown of the city and plowed through a black neighborhood. Of course, sacrificing black neighborhoods, some quite prosperous, to build highways and Urban Renewal projects was a common strategy across the country at that time. Resistance rarely succeeded. The I-10 had already killed Claiborne Avenue, the central black commercial district that anchored Treme. This time a historic alliance between the white and black communities prevented a new misguided transportation project, the location of the bridge.

"One day," Camille recalled, "Oretha Castle Haley and Dorothy Mae Taylor [two key civil rights leaders] showed up on my doorstep. It was a happy meeting. They were concerned about the bridge impact on Central City. We all recognized how it would tear apart our neighborhoods. There was definitely a commonality of interests." It didn't seem unusual to her that this was a black/white alliance in the making. "In many ways," she added, "this was an integrated city. Neighborhoods were mixed. People knew each other better in those days. There had been generations of interaction."

Bill Borah also weighed in on the subject. "The African-American community had been through the I-10 Claiborne fight," he recalled, "so [in the early 1970s] they came to an Uptown meeting in the St. Charles Avenue home of a wealthy optometrist, called to oppose the bridge. This had never been done. It was an awkward moment when this group of African-Americans walked in. They were hesitant. Martha Robinson went right over to greet them, graciously introduced herself, made them feel at ease, and then took over the meeting and made the alliance happen. Bringing blacks into a home on St. Charles Avenue for meetings wasn't done."

A march was held, Bill recalled, from Magazine Street to a black church on a Sunday. "We all walked arm in arm. This, too, had never happened," he said, still marveling at the event. "I then spoke from the pulpit about the bridge. It was amazing." Bill went on to represent the group in a lawsuit to stop the bridge, working closely with Oretha. "She was key to making it all work," he added. "We worked well together backing each other up at City Council hearings." The bridge was built instead adjacent to the existing one downtown.

The most explosive era for New Orleans and probably for every community in the South was the time of school integration. In the 1950s and '60s, women in the African-American community were leaders in the Civil Rights Movement, which had some of its earliest stirrings in New Orleans. Throughout this period, some of the same women involved in historic preservation and battling expressways joined a host of other uptown women working on civil rights, voter registration, schools, and public facilities integration.

Dorothy May Taylor was born in 1928 in New Orleans and grew up to be a Head Start teacher. She became active in civil rights efforts, such as marches, sit-ins, picketing, voter registration, and school desegregation. In 1971, then–State Representative Ernest "Dutch" Morial resigned to become the first black juvenile judge. Taylor ran to fulfill that post, with Oretha Castle as her campaign manager. In 1971, she became the first black woman elected to the state legislature, where she gained a reputation for being fearless in the face of controversial issues. In 1984, she became the first black woman to head a state department, Urban and Community Affairs, gaining considerable statewide attention. By the time she was elected to the City Council in 1986, Taylor had twenty years of activism under her belt.

In the 1980s and into the '90s, City Councilwoman Taylor led the fight to desegregate the private clubs and Mardi Gras krewes around which New Orleans's very stratified social structure revolved. She introduced legislation in 1991 that would desegregate the clubs and krewes. If a club's krewe wanted to march in public, it would be required to desegregate. The uproar was tremendous, to which she replied during a Council session: "If you don't like to hear the word *discriminate*, then don't do it."[25] To this day, the name Dorothy May Taylor can provoke resentful sneers from those still longing for the exclusivity of some of the marching Mardi Gras krewes. But she was apparently as persuasive as she was articulate. "My head has been bloodied, but it is yet unbowed," she said of the 1991 ordinance, quoting from the poem *Invictus,* by the English poet William Ernest Henley, published in 1888. When strong attempts were made to weaken the ordinance, she told the Council: "We're being asked as lawmakers to be lawbreakers."[26] The attempts failed.

Oretha Castle Haley came from a line of activist women. Her paternal grandmother, Callie, sued to desegregate Charity Hospital and her mother, Virgie, supported the early organizing days of the Congress of Racial Equality (CORE) and the Freedom Rides by generously opening her Lower Ninth Ward home for "organizing central." "Anybody, black or white, involved in the civil rights struggle was welcome at 917 Conti," recalled Rudy Lombard,[27] then head of the CORE chapter. "The hospitality was huge." Both Oretha and her sister, Doris, were active in the struggles of the day. In 1959, they were among the organizers of "Don't Buy Where You Can't Work" campaigns targeting the stores on Canal and Dryades Streets.

State legislation was passed to bar picketing and sit-ins, acting like a red flag to the protesters. On September 17, 1960, four lunch-counter protesters—Oretha, Rudy, Cecil Gardner, and Sidney Goldfinch (the one white participant)—were arrested at McCrory's five-and-dime store. Chanting "Jail, no bail," they made history when a lawsuit was filed to protest their arrests as a violation of the Fourteenth Amendment. The case (*Rudolph Lombard et al., Petitioners, v. State of Louisiana*) went all the way to the Supreme Court, where Chief Justice Earl Warren, for the majority, wrote that the arrests were a violation of the Fourteenth Amendment and an attempt to "quash the sit-ins."[28]

"Nobody was more important to the movement than Oretha," Rudy told me in a telephone conversation from his home in Chicago. Oretha's younger son, Okyeame Haley, described the activity in the house as being like normal, everyday life. "Her talent was bringing diverse people together. If she made the call, they came," he recalled in an interview.

Betty Wisdom, serving on a variety of civic boards and working as a radio announcer,[29] helped organize and lead Save Our Schools (SOS), whereby white women transported white children whose parents wanted them to stay in integrated schools, defying mobs of angry protesters using foul language and throwing eggs and tomatoes.[30]

Rosa Freeman Keller, a Coca Cola heiress, worked vigorously for the desegregation of schools, public transit, and libraries.[31] She helped integrate the League of Women Voters, worked on SOS, served as president of the Urban League, financed the legal fight to integrate Tulane, and held interracial meetings in her Uptown home, something not done before. She and her husband, Charles, joined Edith and Edgar Stern in financing the development of Pontchartrain Park, the first suburban enclave for middle-class blacks within New Orleans's city limits.

Edith Stern—wife of Edgar, who financed the fight against the French Quarter Expressway—was another woman who worked for civil rights and voter registration. She followed the tradition set by her father, Julius Rosenwald of Sears & Roebuck fame, in funding all manner of educational and cultural opportunities for African-Americans, including heavily supporting Dillard University and other black educational institutions.[32]

I have a favorite story about Edith. Apparently, she heard there was an extraordinary singer in the choir of her cook's church. She went to hear and took Edgar. Enthralled, she whispered to Edgar: "We have to have a big dinner party in our home and invite her to sing and invite all our friends." Edgar replied: "You know that is not done here." "Well," she said, "our friends will just have to decide." The singer was Mahalia Jackson. No one, apparently, turned down the invitation to this elite party.

Throughout the twentieth century, New Orleans women did a lot that "wasn't done." They were, and continue to be, the main force moving this storied city forward. In the years since Katrina—as demonstrated by the stories in this book—women have indeed been at the forefront of the city's recovery, not only shaping public policy but demonstrating pathways to positive change.

"We're Still Here Ya Bastards"

Rebecca Solnit on the future: "Nothing is certain except that we can sometimes, with enough will and enough skill, shape and steer it."[1]

—Rebecca Solnit, author of *Storming the Gates of Paradise: Landscapes for Politics*

It is almost ten years since the levees failed and flooded the city. I am sitting in Café Dauphine in the heart of the Holy Cross neighborhood of the Lower Nine. This small, white-cloth restaurant in a onetime corner store is the perfect symbol of the Lower Nine's gradual comeback, particularly the more robust rebirth of the historic Holy Cross. Restored and reoccupied architectural gems are visible in all directions, but so, too, are empty deteriorated dwellings. The work that still needs to be done is apparent, but as I sit in this restaurant and watch a lunch crowd fill all twenty tables, the question is no longer "Will this get done?" but "When," "By whom," and "How." I think back to Josephine Butler, who said, "They may not come today, they may not come tomorrow, but they will come." And they have.

I am waiting to have lunch with Tanya Harris, the grand-daughter of Mrs. Butler. But first I am talking to Tia Moore-Henry who with her husband, Fred Henry Jr., and sister-in-law, Keisha Henry, opened this restaurant in June 2012 to instant success. The former storeowner was not coming back after the hurricanes, so the Henry trio bought the site with the idea that it was a nice place for a coffee shop. Like a classic Lower Nine family: grandma Henry lived across the street until she died. Other family members live either on the block or around the corner. Tia, petite and charmingly personable with a big smile, is from Lake Charles, about three hours north. That is where the Henry family went to escape Katrina. Fred, who had been an environmental health specialist for the school board, is also a skilled carpenter. After Katrina, he set about restoring family dwellings house by house. Only after four years did he have the time to design and build out the restaurant.

"That gave us time to think about this place," Tia recalled. "I thought the neighborhood would benefit more and draw from a wider audience, if we did a restaurant." And so they created "the first full-service, sit-down restaurant in this community ever." No one in this partnership trio "had any experience in the restaurant business." They were undaunted. "It took off from the beginning," Tia said, almost in disbelief. "Blessedly, everything just came together."

The modestly designed white-columned interior with simple moldings reflects Fred's polished craft. Tia's prediction was correct. The wider audience has come from both within and outside the neighborhood. Politicians, tourists, all sorts of people, she said. Most of the people from the neighborhood who could come back, she added, have returned. On this particular block, "almost the whole block was older people, many of whom couldn't come back" or have since died. But, she said, new young people are coming in—white, Hispanic, African-American.

To Tanya Harris, Café Dauphine is the next phase of the rebuilding she always knew would happen. "It signals a new era, actually an old era," she said, looking around with a big smile as she joined me for lunch. "We're coming back to where we started," she said of the Lower Nine. Tanya is not surprised at how things have evolved, nor that the area has changed, with diversity returning. "We're getting policemen, firemen, teachers. For the community to survive, you have to have diversity of income and race like we had. This is what we were prepared for. It's not what the experts expected. Their minds are fixed on run-of-the-mill expectations. New Orleans has its own unique character. It's like no other place and can't be measured by the same standards."

We laughed together and spoke fondly of Mrs. Butler. "She never hesitated, so I didn't hesitate," Tanya said. "Her prediction that others will come became my prediction." Sadly, Mrs. Butler now has Alzheimer's and lives with Tanya's sister, Tracy, who with her husband moved to Florida to follow a job after Katrina. Tracy still owns the house next to Tanya but rents it out. Mrs. Butler's house sits empty, filled with the problems that came with the discovery of defective Chinese dry wall that was used in the construction.[2]

Shawn Holahan remains in New Orleans but is currently living across town from her flooded Lakeview home in an uptown neighborhood within walking distance of Magazine Street. Her kids, all three now college graduates, are scattered. But they love to come home for Mardi Gras and other occasions, always bringing friends who are delighted to visit New Orleans. "I never thought I'd be back but I got the clarion call," Shawn told me. "I'm here but my kids are not. But my whole construct has changed. The advantage of Katrina was that it cleaned out my life closet and changed my perspective on things. It was a huge leveling event." She loves the vibrancy of her new neighborhood, "but I remain ready to leave, if any of my kids start having grandchildren I want to be near."

Living uptown is a world of difference from Lakeview. "Make-believe land is all around me," she said. "Uptown was always an isle of denial. It always felt separated from the rest of the city." Her neighborhood is above sea level, and during hurricane season she intends to stay unless there is no power. She never dealt with rebuilding the Lakeview house and sold it to a speculator instead. She has a positive view of the city, even with a few cautions. "I see it as a place of possibilities more than before but I also know I can get out. I worry the FEMA money is drying up and the wound is bigger than money allows to be repaired." She may be right. Learning from disaster is elusive.

Denise Thornton and her colleagues in Beacon of Hope shared their Katrina experiences with the post-disaster communities of Cedar Rapids, Iowa, after a flood; Minot, North Dakota, after a dam burst flooding the town; Staten Island, New York, after Hurricane Sandy; and LaPlace, Louisiana, after Hurricane Isaac. In each case, Beacon advised the local groups "doing the work" how to set up the tool lending library—a central information site, as they had done after Katrina. For each place, they showed how to create the local maps of who was back or not coming back, the condition of each dwelling, and other vital information. "We got more sophisticated about how to do this as we went along, adding infrastructure conditions like streets, streetlights, sewer problems," Denise said. "We knew this was important to do immediately after a disaster but, of course, we could never get funding to do it. For Lakeview, not long ago, we created an iPhone app to track blighted properties and determine if the people who got money to fix up their home actually did the work. Accountability is essential."

Denise found a post-disaster story similar to New Orleans in each of those other places. "Local groups did the work but middlemen got the money," she said. "I think FEMA tried to improve things but it can't figure out how to fund the ones doing the work, the ones actually gutting houses, making repairs. In New York, they handed out half a million dollars' worth of Home Depot credit cards—but what good is that if your house is not gutted? The ones who did the gutting didn't get funded." Of New Orleans, Denise said: "I don't think the city learned anything from how things really worked after Katrina or how to engage with the real people involved in recovery. That is never going to happen. People will still learn from each other and depend on each other in the future." Most frustrating, and perhaps most telling, Denise reported in the fall of 2014 that the city put out a request for proposals for a $250,000 contract to map the city, much like Beacon of Hope had done with volunteers after Katrina. This was exactly the kind of work that neither Beacon nor any other local group could get funding for after Katrina.

The solution to immediate post-disaster needs is not complicated, Denise said, and could be established ahead of time. "In at-risk communities, the Beacon-style organizations should be set up in advance of disasters. Map the community now, know where the elderly are and things like that. Update it periodically. Designate a place for food and water drop-off, where volunteers can be deployed and information learned. It could be a certified FEMA point to give money for gutting, or where United Way and others could donate, where tools could be borrowed, where a list could be kept of local contractors that are not fly-by-night out-of-towners." Sensible enough.

The essential thing is "disaster management," Denise said. It's a matter of supporting the locals who know the community and who are engaged in the aftermath of a disaster. That should be the singular lesson of this disaster. Understandably, Denise doesn't have much faith that this support will be provided. Government has a hard time putting faith and money behind locals; it is more suspicious of them than of the middlemen and well-connected big contractors who wind up with the lion's share of funding. Surely that is one of the unfortunate lessons of New Orleans's recovery.

• • •

It's surprising how many new people came to New Orleans after the storms to live. Tulane University geographer Richard Campanella explained that there were two waves of newcomers: professionals working on post-storm projects (planners, environmentalists, educators, social workers, civil rights activists, contractors, and criminal justice reformers), many of whom left after their projects finished or funding ran out; and skilled professionals who were drawn to New Orleans to live and work. The latter group included Teach For America people and others drawn to the charter schools, as well as film industry and new-media entrepreneurs. New entrepreneurs, especially web-based ones, started coming early.[3] *Forbes,* the *Wall Street Journal,* and other business publications hailed New Orleans as a great turnaround story for new businesses.[4] The chance for a more diversified economy seemed to improve each year.

Not surprisingly, many of the newcomers snapped up the recently rehabbed historic dwellings. Others bought fixer-uppers that they planned to rebuild themselves. Many of those formerly deteriorated houses could easily have made the demolition list—an observation that should be of particular interest to the many challenged cities across the country, such as Buffalo, Detroit, Baltimore, Philadelphia, Cleveland, and others that are drawing newcomers as part of the more than two-decades-long return-to-cities movement. The new, mostly young people who are being drawn to these challenged cities often seek great bargains in architecturally rich houses[5] in cities where they can make a difference and live inexpensively (i.e., not have to have a high-salary job that is difficult to come by). New Orleans has all that *plus* an appealingly rich and legendary culture, so it is no surprise that it is drawing new residents. In New Orleans, in contrast to many of the other challenged cities, citizen efforts successfully averted a more aggressive effort to demolish even more than has already been destroyed. Federally funded efforts continue to result in the demolition of empty or damaged homes here, despite the fact that the free market is solving this problem without any stimulus from government.

Now, ten years since the storms, no one seems to be worried that the city's population—378,715 as of 2013—will not fully recover to its pre-Katrina 452,170. But three lamentable circumstances remain. First, too many low-income, blue-collar New Orleanians have not come back owing to the demise of public housing, the considerable increase in rents, and the lack of living-wage jobs. Second, there is too much emphasis on boosting the tourist economy with more hotels and other low-wage businesses, instead of focusing on diversifying the economy. And, finally, many neighborhoods of great appeal to newcomers and first-time homebuyers have become "gentrified." The first two circumstances, which are thoroughly covered in this book, have clearly not been addressed by the top tiers of the city's civic and business pyramids. The third, gentrification, is a much more complex issue than is usually discussed and deserves serious attention. Gentrification is not solely a New Orleans phenomenon alone, nor is it a new one nationally; in fact, it is a phenomenon visible since the slow beginning of the return to cities. What's particularly interesting is that it is now occurring in a post-disaster city that a great many people thought would not recover.

The term *gentrification* initially gained currency when middle-class people began supplanting working-class residents in England in the late 1970s and '80s. In Canada, the process has been called "white painting"; in the United States, *gentrification* and *displacement* are used interchangeably.[6] By the 1980s, the phenomenon of newcomers moving into a neighborhood and old-timers moving out (some willingly, others not)—and of the newcomers' lifestyle dramatically changing the area's essential character—had become one of the most controversial aspects of urban revitalization.

Now, a decade after Katrina, gentrification is the biggest fear in some New Orleans neighborhoods.

The problem is that some newcomers object to long-standing neighborhood traditions, such as local music venues or street musicians. This becomes a cultural clash, and tensions inevitably rise. Conversely, some old-timers view new residents as a threat to their stability. But neither outcome is inevitable. The arrival of new residents does not have to have a negative impact on old residents or the culture. Without a constant flow of new blood and new businesses, any community will stagnate. Indeed, when the new arrivals inhabit and improve abandoned property, purchase property from a homeowner looking to move and cash in on the change, or bring new trade to local businesses, the impact is positive. At the same time, new political strength reinforces local demands for services from City Hall. Clearly, then, new residents are often an asset. Some would argue that they are a necessary ingredient of any revitalization effort. But when a neighborhood experiences inflated property values, major reassessments, and the increased tax bills that often follow—making it too expensive for residents of modest means to continue to own their property—the impact of gentrification becomes negative.

Solutions to this kind of dilemma are possible, *if* the political will to avert excessive displacement is present. For example, tax increases based on increased assessments can be imposed gradually, with a reasonable yearly maximum, such that the balance— if there is one—is deferred until the sale of the property. In this case, long-term residents would pay the increase if they cash in on the property value upswing, but are not penalized if instead they remain. Unfortunately, municipalities eager for increased revenue and insensitive to any human cost tend to resist such solutions. Politicians prefer to give tax breaks to affordable housing developers than provide a break directly to low- or middle-income homeowners.

Tax breaks for the increased value could also be offered to owners of rental properties willing to resist increasing rent beyond a modest amount. Cumulatively, such programs cost less than subsidies for developers—campaign contributors—of so-called affordable housing, but they don't offer the same political appeal. Of course, the assumption here is that official concern exists to cool the gentrification momentum. But that is not an automatic assumption. Government assistance of this nature is the hardest to come by.

The gentrification dilemma is not easy. There are no simple answers. Unqualified opposition to gentrification puts critics in the curious position of advocating for the "preservation" or protection of the status quo of the neighborhood that they profess to help. If a neighborhood is pockmarked by decay, that condition can only worsen in the absence of new investment by current or new owners. If all change is mislabeled as gentrification without distinctions, the real problem of gentrification is not addressed and its avoidance becomes improbable.

Consider, for instance, the Holy Cross neighborhood of the Lower Nine, which was gentrifying in an organic, gradual, and overall positive way since the storms. With the help of thousands of volunteers and dozens of foundations, this remarkable working-class community struggled to rebuild itself one restored house at a time. Confidence had grown and communal life was returning. A small grocery store opened in November 2014—a major boost for the community. It is owned by a local Army vet, Burnell Cotlon, who took four years to renovate a badly damaged building in the community—a community he believes in.[7] A CVS pharmacy had recently opened on Claiborne, and the new high school and fire station were up and running. It took a lot of aggressive protesting and organizing by community leaders to even get these facilities and two parks open. Holy Cross was leading the way for the whole beleaguered Lower Nine. But letting that kind of positive change and genuine community involvement run its course was not to be.

What unfolded in Holy Cross is a cautionary tale for the city's future, raising the question of whether once again hot-wired political connections and political horse trading will prevail over honest public process and substantive community input. Holy Cross is as much a small village as a city neighborhood—primarily a collection of shotgun houses and modest-scale cottages. It is a most inappropriate place for a sixty-foot-tall upscale condominium tower and complex with parking and retail on the ground floor—a virtual gated community. This is a project guaranteed to do nothing for Holy Cross but flood the streets with traffic and raise property values, rents, and taxes beyond the ability of many local residents to afford. But just that kind of project was approved by the City Council in May 2014, after a bitter fight, an ugly campaign waged by the developer (Perez Architects, APC), and a perverted public process that had the familiar feel of the old days of backroom dealing.[8]

The development site is the old Holy Cross school behind the natural levee at the Mississippi. After Katrina, the school moved to Gentilly and built a new facility, leaving fourteen grass-filled acres with an historic 1895 red brick administration building with clock tower empty and for sale. If the developer had proposed what was offered here—two towers (first at 135 feet, then 75 feet, lowered to 60), several hundred condo units, plus retail and the parking to match—in any upscale, politically potent neighborhood on the uptown side of the canal, community opposition would surely have prevailed. But this is the Lower Ninth Ward.

Another example is the Marigny, a neighborhood adjacent to the French Quarter, where in 2012 vigorous community opposition killed a proposed 75-foot tower—50 percent higher than the zoning allowed.[9] In the upscale Warehouse District, just at the edge of the Central Business District, residents defeated an out-of-town developer's request for a variance from the City Council to build a 75-foot hotel, 10 feet above the 65-foot limit.[10] A 65-foot tower in the dense Warehouse District in the shadow of downtown skyscrapers and a 60-foot height in the shotgun village of Holy Cross? How is only a 5-foot height difference justified between a somewhat remote village-like neighborhood and a downtown warehouse district adjacent to the central business district?

Nowhere during the long public process did anyone forewarn the Holy Cross neighborhood that the city's Master Plan could be totally distorted by the revised Comprehensive Zoning Ordinance (CZO) that would follow. Density and use were the focus of public debate, not height. Height does not automatically equate to density.[11] Residents assumed that the pre-Katrina height limit would remain unchanged because Holy Cross is an historic district. But the "revised" CZO redefined the "medium density" of the Master Plan as up to 60 feet.[12] That is a 50 percent increase and surely higher than the prevailing two-story standard. This is the kind of surprise that reinforces skepticism over any so-called planning process. As with many development projects of this type, there always seems to be a way to subvert the public will.

So many egregious offenses occurred here that there is cause to wonder whether the old pattern of "the New Orleans way" will selectively reemerge. When the proposal for the new condo development was first unveiled, community leaders voiced strong objections to the new local councilman, James Gray.[13] He challenged the community to come up with an alternative. It did. Seven Lower Nine community groups met for six months, working with urban designer Maurice Cox, head of the Tulane City Center.[14] The Center works with communities around the city on planning and design projects and is perfectly suited to help resolve this kind of conflict.[15] The community meetings attracted between thirty and seventy-five residents for each brainstorming session and produced three alternative plans for the site (all at the same density and with no tower), including the names of experienced developers willing to build them.[16] In the "new" New Orleans, such community engagement is supposed to mean something. It didn't in this case. The community's objections were loud, clear, reasonable—and ignored.

In contrast, the proposal's developer, Perez Architects, APC, created favorable petitions with more than four hundred signatures, of which only twenty-one have been verified as authentic by community groups who tracked every signature on the petitions. They allege the petitions "contained unauthorized signatures of residents, duplicate addresses, addresses to vacant or abandoned properties, and false residency claims."[17]

Evidently, logic and fairness are easily lost in development politics. On October 27, 2014, the Lower Ninth Ward Vision Coalition sent a request to the state attorney general, James D. Caldwell, for a "formal investigation into allegations of public fraud."

In the end, the developer dropped the height from 75 to 60 feet—but one should never call it a compromise when a developer drops from overwhelmingly too big to still too big and out of scale. And one should never call neighborhood resistance a form of NIMBY-ism (short for "not in my backyard") when, as in this case, a community complies faithfully with public process and offers a reasonable alternative, only to see the process subverted. None of these offenses swayed the City Council.[18] (One of the newest members, Jason Williams, bravely cast a "no" vote.)

Holy Cross dared to dream that the cynicism and corruption of the old, failed city had been washed away in the retreating floodwaters. Whether that is a dream deferred, and what it foreshadows for the next decade, remains to be seen.

• • •

In contrast to the inequities unfolding in the revised zoning process, a proposed property tax increase in 2014 that would have benefited the privately run, publicly funded Audubon Nature Institute was defeated, showing that some of the old ways of doing things might no longer survive.[19] The controversy also reveals the extensive powers of privately run public bodies, about which the public is rarely aware.

The Audubon Nature Institute is the privately run nonprofit management arm of the Audubon Commission, a public agency.

It oversees Audubon Park, the zoo, the aquarium, the butterfly garden and insectarium, Woldenberg Park on the waterfront, and other facilities that are key tourist attractions. Yet the Institute is not subject to any meaningful public oversight. The zoo and aquarium are among the select group of fourteen public authorities—like fire, police, public library, street and traffic control, economic development, and others—that automatically receive a designated portion of property taxes. The Institute's tax proposal was to replace the current designated tax with a new, larger fifty-year tax that would be tacked onto citywide property tax bills. Estimates indicated that it would bring the Institute $12 million annually.[20] The existing tax, which had a number of years left, was originally passed in the 1970s to cover desperately needed upgrades to the zoo. It was renewed in the 1980s to build the downtown aquarium. Both goals have long since been achieved.

Since the Institute is one component of an assortment of facilities and programs under the Audubon Commission, it is difficult to identify the various public and private funding sources on top of the earned income from its various entrance fee facilities. "Nobody can make heads or tails of their financial statements," Deborah Howell said in conversation. Deborah is an illustrator whose website has been a critic and a watchdog since 2001, with only a modest impact before this.[21] "You need a forensic accountant," she added. Ron Forman, head of the Institute since 1977 and a New Orleans mayoral candidate in 2006, had spearheaded the transformation of the zoo in the 1970s from a much-reviled "ghetto for animals" into a first-rate facility.[22] Forman said in response to press questions that the additional funds were necessary to upgrade existing facilities, although he never specified for which and for what, reported local activist Keith Hardie. Forman's salary was also a point of contention, fluctuating between $831,356 in 2009 and $693,065 in 2012.[23]

When the proposal received City Council approval to go on the ballot in December 2013, it initially drew little public attention.

Ten days before the March 15, 2014, vote, Deborah posted details of the proposal on her website. Jeff Thomas, a writer and computer consultant, also posted the proposal details in his weekly online newsletter, noting the "commercial nature" of the various operations with high-priced entry fees.[24] "On every tax bill we see money going to the zoo," he noted in a phone conversation. "Given all the other city needs, this was ridiculous. And it was being slipped in quietly in an off-year election with an expected low turnout." Jeff sounded the alarm in his newsletter and it went viral.

Keith Hardie, a lawyer and another Audubon Institute watchdog living near the park, also started e-mailing the New Orleans universe in a similar Paul Revere manner; he also established a Facebook page, "Say No to a Tax Hike." Traditional media, including talk-show radio, picked up the story. The issue became the talk of the city. Civic sentiment focused on the high-priced Institute offerings that also receive big public funding, whereas the free park and recreational sites of great importance to residents and visitors alike were at the mercy of the annual city budget.[25] And while there is great civic pride in the Institute's facilities, the issue of fairness was central to the debate. The tax proposal was resoundingly defeated, with the "no" vote totaling about 67 percent.[26] "The success," Deborah believes, "was because several unrelated media sources were doing the same thing. It had a snowball effect."

The conversation about the zoo reflects a larger debate over the inflated reliance on tourism in New Orleans, which promises to stay heated for years. Expanding tourism is having a direct impact on the city's livability.[27] Rents and home prices have mushroomed in recent years, as investors buy and use properties to house visitors. Prices at restaurants have risen, and access to them is harder. As Keith noted about the tax proposal defeat: "It was part of the reevaluation by citizens of how things were going since Katrina. People don't like spending money on fancy things appealing to the tourist when things ordinary citizens need go underfunded. Tourism already costs citizens a lot, and it benefits primarily people who profit big."

"The battle," as Deborah put it, "is to save New Orleans from its own attractiveness. We don't want to be like Venice [Italy], where only 30 percent of the city is occupied by local citizens." And where, one should note, the permanent population keeps diminishing and the tourist and second-home population keeps rising.[28]

The tourism bonanza may in fact be a mirage, at least for the local economy. Hosting the much-heralded Super Bowl in 2013, for example, netted the city only $500,000, Charles Maldonaldo reported in *The Lens*. Yet Mayor Landrieu has applied for the city to host the 2018 event. In a speech about how he would pay the city's big bills, Mayor Landrieu said: "Here's the truth: Most of the benefit went to others and to the state. Even though the Super Bowl is a multimillion dollar event, the city's general fund, your bank account, only netted $500,000, barely breaking even for the army of police, fire, EMS, sanitation, public works, permitting and other city employees who work . . . to make sure everything went off without a hitch."[29]

The highly touted idea that tourism supports the local economy is overblown in other ways, too. A look at where all those tourism tax revenues really go illustrates why New Orleans is effectively broke and the tourist-industry players are rich. The University of New Orleans Division of Business and Economic Research shows the breakdown, for example, of the $1 billion in hotel-room sales in 2012 on which there is a tax of 13 percent. Of the existing tax, only 1.5 cents on every dollar paid by hotel guests go to city government to help pay for police and fire protection, streets and infrastructure, and recreation programs for youth. The majority of the existing tax goes to state agencies.[30]

And, of course, most of those hotels are national chains, with profits heading right out of town. Even the clubs on Bourbon Street are reportedly mostly owned by out-of-staters, even though they occupy locally owned land.[31]

As the financial benefits from tourism accrue less and less to the locals and the costs remain substantially their burden, the future of New Orleans becomes a real question mark. Increasingly, it is the quasi-public agencies with extraordinary powers beyond local control that propose projects of enormous impact. The Convention and Visitors Bureau, for example, pursues a path that increases its own empire at public expense. A state agency, the Convention Center wants to allow construction of a private hotel, retail stores, and restaurants on public land adjacent to the Center.[32] Using its own bonds, and with state legislation, it can do this, despite strong public opposition. The Stadium and Exposition District has the same extensive powers. Much of what happens in the city affecting everyone flows from just these two entities, along with the private Convention and Visitors Bureau.

While all this unfolds in a high-impact but closed universe with minimal, if any, transparency, New Orleanians continue to struggle with many of the dilemmas presented in this book. Road Home early in 2014 sent out thousands of letters demanding repayment by homeowners of grants for reasons that stemmed, above all, from their administrative foul-ups.[33] No repayment appears to have been asked of underperforming contractors, including either one of the two who have been in charge of Road Home itself. FEMA keeps funding demolitions from its original flawed list created by nonprofessionals; this is particularly inappropriate in the many neighborhoods where the improved real estate market has been increasingly absorbing troubled properties. Many streetlights, broken streets, missing street signs, and neglected parks in nontourist neighborhoods remain in a post-Katrina state. The transit system is worse than ever:[34] as of September 2014, only 36 percent of pre-Katrina service had been restored whereas 86 percent of the population had returned. In 2004, the RTA had 301 buses operating; in 2012, only seventy-nine. The budget deficit is increasing, and operating expenses keep accelerating. The Federal Monitor of the police consent decree keeps pushing to reform the NOPD with great difficulty, and the fight over the future of the jail does not diminish.

Yet good news keeps coming as well. Chiquita International Brands is moving its shipping operations back from Gulfport, Mississippi, where it relocated in the 1970s.[35] The Port of New Orleans is a state agency, but hopefully, the jobs will be local and at a decent scale. For decades, the billions of bananas coming to this country through New Orleans were a defining industry. Chiquita is one of the world's largest shippers of fruit. Small companies and new entrepreneurs are coming to New Orleans as well. New local stores seem to be popping up all over the city, and new grocery stores keep opening closer to places that need them. Almost every neighborhood is experiencing positive improvements, thanks to both longtime homeowners and new residents.

Thus there is a mix of good news and bad news to report, but one significant issue looms over everything. It will not be resolved for years and promises to have a profound impact on the city and the region. After Katrina, the first celebrated reform was of the corrupt Levee Board System, which comprised multiple local boards that seemed more active in new real estate development than in floodwall maintenance. A constitutional amendment passed with 81 percent of the statewide vote to consolidate the levee boards into two Southeast Louisiana Flood Protection Authorities (SLFPA-E) and to appoint nonpolitical experts with scientific and technological expertise.[36] The vice president chosen was the highly respected John M. Barry. The SLFPA-E took its job so seriously that in July 2013 it filed a lawsuit against almost a hundred oil, gas, and pipeline companies for not honoring their responsibility—spelled out in their permits—to minimize damage, restore land that they destroy during drilling, or compensate the state in order to fund flood protection elsewhere.[37]

As Barry wrote in *Metropolis* magazine, regarding the delta wetlands south of New Orleans:

There is a slogan down here: "The levees protect the people, and the land protects the levees." The lost land once served

as a buffer, which protected metro New Orleans from hurricanes by cutting down storm surge; without that protection,
more devastating storm surges pound against the levee system. The increased—and increasing—storm surges require
the levee board to spend more money to protect lives and
property.[38]

When the lawsuit was filed, all hell broke loose and this critical post-Katrina reform sank under the weight of a state political system long serving the oil and gas industry instead of the
people. And even though members of the SLFPA-E board, unlike
other state boards, do not serve at the pleasure of the governor,
the entire state political apparatus swung into action to make sure
board members favoring the lawsuit were not reappointed. The
first three included Barry, but the remaining members still favored
the suit and prevailed over new members—so far. This lawsuit, or
a replacement, promises to go on for years.

In October 2014 two small energy companies settled out of
court, which will make it hard for Governor Jindal and others to
continue to call the lawsuit frivolous.[39] If the SLFPA-E membership eventually changes enough to withdraw its suit or if state legislative action succeeds in ending it, "this suit will end but others
will start with many of the same players," Barry said in conversation. "Almost certainly class action—maybe several—will be filed
by the same legal team."

As Barry put it in his *Metropolis* article: "What's at stake
in this lawsuit is the future of much of coastal Louisiana, including its port traffic (18 percent of all commercial shipping in the
United States passes through Louisiana) and energy infrastructure
(roughly 20 percent of the nation's oil refining capacity)."[40]

As this book has shown, the damage done to the city after
Hurricanes Katrina and Rita and then from the BP oil spill came
from above, whereas the real recovery came from below, through
a multitude of small, manageable investments and commitments

by individual residents and local businesses. While the survival and future of the Southeast Coast is dependent in good measure on this lawsuit, the future of New Orleans ultimately rests on the continued persistence and wisdom of its citizens.

• • •

It is fascinating to reread the news stories written after Katrina. All those planning, environmental, urban, and economic experts cautioned that the city would remain crippled for a long time and that nothing would get fixed without a well-thought-out plan. Caution was prescribed. They were wrong. The city *has* come back, certainly more quickly than any of them expected. Many residents returned (as soon as they were allowed) and started rebuilding, with caution and forethought different from what the experts had prescribed. And more often than not, they built smarter, with environmental adjustments that fit their requirements—not some citywide one-size-fits-all.

Remember, most of the solar installations are in the Lower Nine—and these were not even on the experts' list of how things should be done. Returnees came back not only with a determination and focus that the experts had underestimated but also with a new willingness to get engaged in a level of public process they had not experienced before. As Stephanie Grace observed:

> Katrina, and more specifically, the storm's aftermath, flipped a switch, and suddenly residents started taking matters into their own hands, lining up alongside one another and, in many cases, either facing down those old unresponsive elites or reversing the power dynamic and leading the way.
>
> Along the way, an interesting thing happened. Politicians realized that all that citizen-led progress made them look good, and they jumped on board. They also realized that the newly empowered community got things done, and

they learned to tap into its energy. The results have turned heads all the way to Washington.[41]

In the last ten years, considerably more wisdom and careful urban regeneration have been exhibited from the bottom up than from the top down. And certainly more humanity, justice, and fairness. It wasn't returning evacuees who approved the destruction of a self-organizing, market-based neighborhood in Lower Mid-City. It wasn't returning evacuees who approved the replacement of two functional and upgradable public hospitals by a two-hospital mega-project (with one of the two totally privatized before it even opened). It wasn't returning evacuees who prevented public housing residents from returning to their lightly damaged apartments or approved the elimination of so many of those units with the false promise of equitable replacement. It wasn't returning evacuees who signed away to a private contractor the city's transit system, which is more focused on serving tourists than residential neighborhoods. And it certainly wasn't local citizens who gave huge contracts to out-of-state, politically connected companies to do more expensively and less effectively what locals could do to advance recovery.

Indeed, it was citizen efforts that forced reform of the levee boards, forced a downsizing of the new jail, stopped the experts from shrinking recoverable neighborhoods, exposed corruption and lies in the government-sponsored blight cleanup and home rebuilding programs, jump-started a significant but small bayou restoration, enticed members of Congress to visit the city to witness firsthand the storms' destruction, forced the rethinking of how the city deals with water, and restored so many damaged homes and opened so many small businesses, leading to new growth that is visible all over the city.

As the stories in this book clearly show, when plans are big and geared toward private agendas, the results are at best mixed. Conversely, when plans are modest and meaningful to local residents and businesses, productive change—often big for its locale—is most beneficial to neighborhoods and the larger city alike. Those thousands of small or modest actions taken by New Orleans's residents—only a sampling of which have been presented in this book—added up to genuine repair and rebuilding that grow bigger and stronger each day.

Like the Live Oaks that symbolize the city, the civic branches grow long and stay strong because their roots are so deep and entwined with each other. The unique strengths of New Orleans have served the city well in the face of daunting disaster.

Acknowledgments

When I first took up part-time residence in New Orleans, many of my New York family and friends found it strange—if not nuts—that I could wrench myself for four or five months of each year from the city of my birth, which is so much a part of me and of which I am so much a part. Hopefully, after they read this book, they will understand.

Two editors made this book possible. First, Carl Bromley, who, after helping me through *The Battle for Gotham: New York in the Shadow of Robert Moses and Jane Jacobs,* encouraged me to adopt New Orleans and tell the story of its recovery after Katrina. Then, Daniel LoPreto took me through the editing process with great skill, helpful encouragement, welcomed enthusiasm, and a firm hand to make sure it was as good as it could be. To both of them I am forever grateful. I am also grateful for support from Joan Davidson and her program Furthermore grants in publishing.

The cover was inspired by a photograph by Sandra Morris. The photograph captured a real graffiti found on the side of a house right after Katrina.

This book could not have been written if not for the extraordinarily warm welcome I received from so many New Orleans residents. It was a badge of honor that some of them called me a "part-time local," and many of them became my good friends. They are an incredible and inspiring group, as diverse as the city itself and as passionate and caring as any city would be proud to have. To all who are listed here, I owe a debt of gratitude: Austin Allen, Charles Allen, Jay Altman, Jim Amoss, Justin Augustine, Michael Avery, Emilie Bahr, Mac Ball, Warrenetta Banks, Robin A. Barnes, John Barry, Carol Bebelle, John Berendt, Bob Berkibile, Jason Berry, Steven Bingler, Roy Blount, Bill Borah, Deborah Brown-Cassine, Bethany Ewald Bultman, Deirdre Johnson Burel, Beth Butler, Richard Cahn, Vivian Cahn, Richard Campanella, LaToya Cantrell, Sarah Carr, Philip Carter, Bernard L. Charbonnet Jr., Mary Louise Christovich, Ariella Cohen, Wayne Curtis, Mare Daley, Luisa Dantas, Tom Darden, Jim Dart, Jack Davis, Jarvis DeBerry, Karen De Salvo, Clancy Dubos, Lolis Edward Elie, Lolis Eric Elie, Dana Eness, Laura Flanders, Vaughn Fauria, Randy Fertel, Kristina Ford, Mindy Thompson Fullilove, Karen Gadbois, Beth Galante, Walter Gallas, Deborah Gans, Patty Gay, Meg Gibson, James Gill, Stephen A. Goldsmith, Stephanie Grace, Robert Green, Joan Griswald, Vanessa Guerlinger, Martin Gusman, Okeame Haley, David Hammer, Monique Harden, Keith Hardie, Tania Harris, Tracy Harris, Stacey Head, Michael Hecht, Norris Henderson, Ann Hess, Bill Hess, Susan Hess, Lance Hill, Shawn Holahan, Gen. Russel L. Honoré, George Hopkins, Jed Horne, Oliver Houck, Janet Howard, Deborah Howell, Mary Howell, Abbie Hurlbut, Michelle Ingram, Leslie Jacobs, Clifton James, Scott James, Michelle Jean-Pierre, Arthur Johnson, Sgt. John Johnson, Gilbert Julien, State Treasurer John Kennedy, Susan Kier, Darryl Kilbert, Michelle Kimball, Celia Kornfeld, Reed Kroloff, Michael Lanaux, Moon Landrieu, Caroline Leftwich, Nicholas Lemann, Sharon Litwin, Rudy Lombard, Meg Lousteau, Deborah Luster, Tony Mancini, Ray Manning, David Marcello, Bob Marshall, Louise Martin, Ron Mason, Richard McCarthy, Allison McCrary, Bill McDonough, Rod Miller, Ann Milling, R. King Milling, Michael Mizell-Nelson, Dr. James Moises, Mark Moreau, Gregory Morey, Jacques Morial, Neal Morris, Sandra Morris, Grover Mouton, Jeanne Nathan, Mary Nell, Bruce

Nolan, Brad Ott, Martha Owen, Martin Pedersen, Andre Perry, James Perry, Tom Piazza, Cathy Pierson, Allison Plyer, Lawrence Powell, William Quigley, Richard Rabinowitz, Wade Rathke, Dr. Anthony Recasner, Katy Reckdahl, Sally Reeves, Leonard Riggio, Sonya Robinson, Bobbi Rogers, Sandy Rosenthal, Mary Rowe, Gordon Russell, Donovan Rypkema, Kalamu Ya Salaam, Dr. Raynard Sanders, Michael Sartisky, Jeff Schwartz, Kenneth Schwartz, Rev. Gilbert Scie, Carey Shea, Harry Shearer, Ron Shiffman, Fred Starr, Walter Stern, Jack Stewart, Sandra Stokes, Camille Strahan, John Stubbs, Bob Tannen, John Taylor, Jeff Thomas, Oliver Thomas, Denise Thornton, Wally Thurman, Wayne Troyer, Linda Usdin, Sarah Usdin, Brad Vogel, David Waggonner, Reverend Dwight Webster, Bitsy Werlein, Thomas Willemeit, Jessica Williams, David Winkler-Schmidt, Karen Wimpelbeg, Peter M. Wolf, Darlene Wolnik, and Margie Zeidler.

Notes

EPIGRAPHS

1. Lawrence N. Powell, *The Accidental City: Improvising New Orleans* (Cambridge, MA: Harvard University Press, 2012), p. 163.

2. Joel Fletcher, *Ken and Thelma: The Story of a Confederacy of Dunces* (Gretna, LA: Pelican Publishing, 2005), p. 28.

PREFACE

1. August 29 is when Hurricane Katrina made landfall and is considered the hurricane's official date. Hurricane Rita hit a month later.

2. Roberta Brandes Gratz, *The Living City: How America's Cities Are Being Revitalized by Thinking Small in a Big Way* (New York: Simon & Schuster, 1989). See also Gratz, *Cities Back from the Edge: New Life for Downtown* (John Wiley & Sons, 1998), and Gratz, *The Battle for Gotham: New York in the Shadow of Robert Moses and Jane Jacobs* (New York: Nation Books, 2001).

3. I was a newspaper reporter at the old *New York Post* under Dorothy Schiff.

4. South Beach in Miami eventually surpassed the French Quarter in size.

5. Historic districts provide a good lesson in how scale can protect a diversity of uses, although in recent years the city leadership has let this balance erode in the mistaken assumption that favoring tourists over residents is economically advantageous.

6. Gratz, *Cities Back from the Edge,* p. 107.

7. Gratz, *The Battle for Gotham,* pp. 137, 273.

8. ACORN, together with planning programs at Pratt Institute, Cornell University, and the Louisiana State University (LSU) College of Art and

Design, organized a conference in Baton Rouge in November 2005 that brought Katrina evacuees together with community development experts and practitioners from around the country to relate their experience of working directly with communities. The meeting was webcast to thirty locations around the country where evacuees were located. Hundreds of New Orleanians in the Katrina diaspora participated. I attended as well.

9. See www.RobertaBrandesGratz.com.

10. Chris Rose, *1 Dead in Attic: After Katrina* (New York: Simon & Schuster, 2007).

11. Lawrence N. Powell, "New Orleans: An American Pompeii?," in *Satchmo Meets Amadeus,* ed. Reinhold Wagnleitner (Innsbruck, Austria: StudienVerlag, 2006).

12. Gathering places are the first things to return to recovering communities, as exemplified by the Main Squares of Prague and other former Iron Curtain cities after the Berlin Wall came down.

INTRODUCTION

1. City Park contains the world's biggest stand of Live Oaks (nearly 250 in number); see http://neworleanscitypark.com/live-oaks-of-city-park.

2. Quoted in Jennifer Farwell, "Sheltering Arms: Saving New Orleans' Historic Live Oaks," *Preservation in Print,* February 14, 2008.

3. Ibid.

4. Benyus made these remarks at a Bioneers Conference in San Francisco in 2008, as reported to me by Stephen A. Goldsmith, chairman of the Urban Ecology Program at the University of Utah and executive director of The Center for the Living City.

5. Tom Piazza, "Incontinental Drift," *Huffington Post,* August 31, 2010.

6. *The Big Uneasy* (2010), a film by Harry Shearer.

7. Ivor van Heerden and Mike Bryan, *The Storm: What Went Wrong and Why During Hurricane Katrina: The Inside Story from One Louisiana Scientist* (New York, Viking, 2006), p. 9.

8. van Heerden and Bryan, *The Storm;* Jed Horne, *Breach of Faith: Hurricane Katrina and the Near Death of a Great American City* (New York: Random House, 2006).

9. Nagin finally called for evacuation on the morning of Sunday, August 29, with Blanco at his side. See Gordon Russell, "Nagin Orders First-Ever Mandatory Evacuation of New Orleans," *NOLA.com* and *Times-Picayune,* August 13, 2010, http://www.nola.com/katrina/index.ssf/2005/08/nagin _orders_first-ever_mandatory_evacuation_of_new_orleans.html.

10. Many considered Governor Blanco's weeping inappropriate. I do not.

11. van Heerden and Bryan, *The Storm,* p. 149.

12. Horne, *Breach of Faith,* p. 147.

13. Mike Davis notes: "Most fatefully, [Homeland Security Secretary]

Chertoff inexplicably waited 24 hours after the city had been flooded to upgrade the disaster to an 'incident of national significance,' the legal precondition for moving federal response to high gear." See Davis, "Catastrophic Economics: The Predators of New Orleans," *Le Monde Diplomatique* (English edition), October 2, 2005.

14. van Heerden and Bryan, *The Storm*, p. 294.

15. Quoted in ibid., p. 294.

16. van Heerden and Bryan, *The Storm*, pp. 294–295.

17. Peter Dreier, "Katrina in Perspective: The Disaster Raises Key Questions About the Role of Government in American Society," *Dissent Magazine*, Summer 2005.

18. Horne, *Breach of Faith*, p. 84.

19. Ibid., pp. 65–66.

20. Under Road Home, a federally funded program administered by a private contractor chosen by the state, qualified homeowners were supposed to receive funds to rehabilitate their home. A cap was set at $150,000, although why a cap was set is hard to explain when people lost everything. The average payment per family was $40,000. For further information on Road Home, see www.RoadHomeProgram.org.

21. These tenants formed the bulk of the workforce. Unable to return, they were replaced by "undocumented Mexican laborers . . . living 10 to a room"; see van Heerden and Bryan, *The Storm*, p. 11.

22. Richard Campanella, *Bienville's Dilemma: A Historical Geography of New Orleans* (Lafayette: University of Louisiana Press, 2008), p. 153.

CHAPTER 1

1. *Nine Lives—A Musical Story of New Orleans*, Mystery Street Records and Threadhead Records. Reprinted with permission.

2. The Lower Ninth Ward is the entire area within New Orleans downriver of the Industrial Canal and farthest east before the next parish, St. Bernard. It is part of the larger Ninth Ward and was not differentiated from it until construction of the Industrial Canal in the 1920s, which effectively separated the Lower Nine from the rest of the city. Two bridges over the canal connect to Claiborne and St. Claude Avenues, which somewhat parallel the Mississippi River and divide the Lower Nine into three sections, St. Claude being the closest to the river.

3. Arsenic, lead, and assorted contaminants were spread throughout the city's soils.

4. "Lower Ninth Ward Neighborhood: Housing & Housing Costs," Greater New Orleans Community Data Center, July 31, 2006, http://www .datacenterresearch.org/pre-katrina/orleans/8/22/housing.html.

5. "State of the Ninth Ward," University of Illinois at Urbana-Champaign, Department of Urban and Regional Planning (Fall 2007).

6. Ivor van Heerden and Mike Bryan, *The Storm: What Went Wrong and Why During Hurricane Katrina: The Inside Story from One Louisiana Scientist* (New York, Viking, 2006), p. 96.

7. It must be noted that city voters rejected the Corps' proposals to build both a sophisticated removable barrier in the Rigolets, connecting Lake Pontchartrain to the Gulf of Mexico (which would have provided some protection from the lake), and another gate at the 17th Street Canal.

8. Richard Campanella, *Bienville's Dilemma: A Historical Geography of New Orleans* (Lafayette: University of Louisiana, 2008), p. 153. Campanella's book includes a thorough and extraordinarily useful timeline entitled "Historical Events of Geographic Significance in the New Orleans Area."

9. After Katrina, Holy Cross School did not reopen here. With its flood money, it built a new school in Gentilly.

10. In October 2014, the city allocated FEMA demolition funds for 608 of these houses, some of which could have been sold instead.

11. "Lower Ninth Ward Statistical Area," Data Center Research, March 28, 2014, http://www.datacenterresearch.org/data-resources/neighborhood -data/district-8/Lower-Ninth-Ward/.

12. In 2005, the New Orleans chapter of ACORN had nine thousand members, most of whom lived in the Lower Nine. Community organizer Wade Rathke founded ACORN in Little Rock, Arkansas, in 1970; opened a New Orleans office five years later; and moved himself, his family, and the headquarters there in 1978.

13. Richard Campanella in conversation with author.

14. Andrés Duany, "Restoring the Real New Orleans: How Do We Save the Crescent City? Re-create the Unique Building Culture That Spawned It," *Metropolis* magazine, February 2007.

15. Ibid.

16. There is some question as to whether Disraeli was the speaker, but attribution has been "common to him since 1895." See "Lies, Damned Lies and Statistics," Department of Mathematics at University of York, July 19, 2012, http://www.york.ac.uk/depts/maths/histstat/lies.htm.

17. Michael Eric Dyson, *Come Hell or High Water: Hurricane Katrina and the Color of Disaster* (New York: Basic Civitas, 2006), p. 7.

18. Campanella, *Bienville's Dilemma,* p. 169.

19. "American Mobility: Who Moves? Who Stays Put? Where's Home?," Pew Research Center, December 17, 2008, http://pewsocialtrends.org/files /2011/04/American-Mobility-Report-updated-12–29–08.pdf.

20. Bruce Eggler, "City Completed 25 Capital Projects in 2012 and Will Start 47 More in 2013, Mayor Landrieu Says," *NOLA.com* and *Times-Picayune,* January 2, 2013, http://www.nola.com/politics/index.ssf/2013/01 /city_completed_25_capital_proj.html.

CHAPTER 2

1. Quoted in Christopher Cooper, "Old-Line Families Escape Worst of Flood and Plot the Future," *Wall Street Journal,* September 8, 2005, http://online.wsj.com/articles/SB112614485840634882.

2. Quoted in Gary Rivlin, "A Mogul Who Would Rebuild New Orleans," *New York Times,* September 29, 2005.

3. Quoted in Lori Rodriguez and Zeke Minaya, "HUD Chief Doubts New Orleans Will Be as Black," *Houston Chronicle,* September 29, 2005.

4. Lawrence Powell, Marc and Constance Jacobson Lecture, Institute for the Humanities, University of Michigan, September 29, 2005.

5. Wade Rathke, *The Battle for the Ninth Ward: ACORN, Rebuilding New Orleans* (New Orleans: Social Policy Press, 2011), p. 44.

6. On September 5, 2005, after touring the Astrodome, Barbara Bush was a guest on the Public Radio show *Marketplace,* where she made those remarks. See http://www.snopes.com/Politics/quotes/barbara2.asp and "Former First Lady Barbara Bush Calls Evacuees Better Off," *New York Times,* September 7, 2005.

7. C. Ray Nagin, *Katrina's Secrets: Storms After the Storm* (New Orleans: CreateSpace, 2011), p. 291.

8. See "Bring New Orleans Back," n.d., www.bringneworleansback.org /Commission_Members/.

9. Frank Donze, "DA Candidates Raise Big Bucks for Primary," *Times-Picayune,* September 19, 2008.

10. Martha Carr and Jeffrey Meitrodt, "What Will New Orleans Look Like Five Years from Now?," *Times-Picayune,* December 25, 2005.

11. Mindy Fullilove, *Root Shock: How Tearing Up City Neighborhoods Hurts America and What We Can Do About It* (New York: One World/Ballantine, 2005).

12. Mindy Fullilove, *Urban Alchemy: Restoring Joy in America's Fractured Cities* (New York: New Village Press, 2013).

13. As Robert B. Olshansky and Laurie A. Johnson report in *Clear as Mud: Planning for the Rebuilding of New Orleans* (American Planning Association, 2010), ULI sent a team of fifty professionals mid-November for a week, issued a preliminary report a week later, and completed the final report on January 30, 2006.

14. Olshansky and Johnson, *Clear as Mud,* p. 45.

15. Richard Campanella in conversation with author.

16. The square block on which I live in the Bywater had two abandoned falling-down houses and two vacant houses needing work. One vacant house was quickly bought and fixed up. One falling-down house was restored in 2012, with many new elements inserted. A second vacant house was restored in 2013. As of this writing, one abandoned house continues to

deteriorate and a few others clearly need work.

17. Mark Waller, "Hurricane Katrina Eight Years Later, a Statistical Snapshot of the New Orleans Area," *NOLA.com* and *Times-Picayune,* http://www.nola.com/katrina/index.ssf/2013/08/hurricane_katrina_eight_years.html.

18. Kim Cob, "Group Seeks to Reclaim Homes in Lower Ninth Ward," *Houston Chronicle,* January 23, 2006, http://www.chron.com/news/hurricanes/article/Group-seeks-to-reclaim-homes-in-Lower-Ninth-Ward-1897004.php.

19. The same overwhelming instinct to rebuild in place despite buyout offers was subsequently demonstrated in New York and New Jersey after Sandy in 2012 and in Oklahoma after the tornadoes in 2013.

20. This statement by Oliver Thomas was confirmed and reiterated in a personal interview.

21. Quoted in Martha Carr and Jeffrey Meitrodt, "What Will New Orleans Look Like Five Years from Now?," *Times-Picayune,* December 25, 2005.

22. Louisiana city and state officials loathe eminent domain. It is rarely used.

23. Jed Horne, *Breach of Faith: Hurricane Katrina and the Near Death of a Great American City* (New York: Random House, 2006), p. 316. As Lawrence Powell noted in his lecture at the University of Michigan on September 29, 2005, "In New Orleans East a community of Vietnamese refugees not only re-formed amazingly fast after Katrina, but halted the expansion of an encroaching landfill."

24. "The New Orleans Index at Five," Greater New Orleans Community Data Center, n.d., http://www.coweninstitute.com/wp-content/uploads/2010/11/MeasuringProgress.pdf.

25. The continued existence of blighted properties, though diminishing in number, hasn't stopped the gentrification of the Bywater neighborhood in which I bought my house in 2007. In fact, the existence of those properties has provided the opportunity for new buyers.

26. Mike Davis, "Who Is Killing New Orleans?," *The Nation,* April 10, 2006.

27. FEMA's flood elevations, which set the height above the flood level that a house must be, came out in dribs and drabs during February 2009.

28. Horne, *Breach of Faith,* p. 250. Insurance companies used the same criterion in Hurricane Betsy.

29. David Hammer, "ICF's Oversight of Road Home Program Comes to an End," *NOLA.com* and *Times-Picayune,* December 28, 2009, http://www.nola.com/news/index.ssf/2009/06/icfs_oversight_of_road_home_pr.html.

30. For a detailed report on contract spending, see "Testimony of Steve Ellis, Vice President of Programs, Taxpayers for Common Sense Before Senate Democratic Policy Committee Oversight Hearing on Post-Katrina Reconstruction," May 19, 2006, http://www.taxpayer.net/user_uploads/file /TCS%20Senate%20DPC%20Katrina%20Contracting%20Testimony.pdf.

31. Jarvis DeBerry, "Road Home Has Callously Disregarded Louisianians—from Its Start Till Now," *Times-Picayune*, March 21, 2014.

32. Lawrence Powell, "Through the Eye of Katrina: The Past as Prologue," Keynote Address, the Second Howard Mahan Symposium, University of South Alabama, Mobile, AL, March 18, 2007, reprinted as "What Does American History Tells Us About Katrina, and Vice Versa?," *Journal of American History*, December 2007.

33. Michael Eric Dyson, *Come Hell or High Water: Hurricane Katrina and the Color of Disaster* (New York: Basic Civitas, 2006), pp. 49–50.

34. Gordon Russell and James Varney of the *Times-Picayune*, Eric Lipton and Ron Nixon of the *New York Times*, and Mike Davis of *The Nation*, to name just three. Jed Horne and Ivor van Heerdon give many examples in their books.

35. Horne, *Breach of Faith*, p. 93.

36. Dyson, *Come Hell or High Water*, p. 118.

37. Andrew Martin and Andrew Zajac, "Offer of Buses Fell Between the Cracks," *Chicago Tribune*, September 23, 2005, http://articles.chicago tribune.com/2005–09–23/news/0509230350_1_mayor-c-ray-nagin-bus -evacuation-buses.

38. Dyson, *Come Hell or High Water*, pp. 132–133. In addition, Lolita Baldor noted in the *Washington Post* (September 5, 2005) that KBR, a subsidiary of Halliburton, was highly criticized for its reconstruction work in Iraq.

39. William Quigley, *Storms Still Raging: Katrina, New Orleans and Social Justice* (Charleston, SC: BookSurge, 2008).

40. Dyson, *Come Hell or High Water*, citing "Troops Told 'Shoot to Kill' in New Orleans," *ABC News Online*, September 2, 2005, http://www.abc.net .au/news/2005–09–02/troops-told-shoot-to-kill-in-new-orleans/2094678.

41. Russell and Varney, "From Blue Tarps to Debris Removal." The authors also cite the Knight Ridder news service report "that neither the government nor the contractors have challenged."

42. Eric Lipton and Ron Nixon, "Many Contracts for Storm Work Raise Questions," *New York Times*, Sept. 26, 2005, http://www.nytimes.com /2005/09/26/national/nationalspecial/26spend.html?pagewanted=all&_r=0.

43. James Varney and Gordon Russell, "Blue Roof Costs Have Critics Seeing Red," *Times-Picayune*, February 19, 2006.

44. Nagin, *Katrina's Secrets*, p. 300.

45. Charles R. Babcock, "FEMA Contractor Lacks Building License," *Washington Post,* October 4, 2005.

46. Horne, *Breach of Faith,* p. 308.

47. Russell and Varney, "From Blue Tarps to Debris Removal."

48. van Heerden and Bryan, *The Storm,* p. 65.

49. Mike Davis, "Catastrophic Economics: The Predators of New Orleans," *Le Monde Diplomatique,* October 2, 2005.

50. Naomi Klein, *The Shock Doctrine: The Rise of Disaster Capitalism* (New York: Picador, 2008).

51. Ibid., p. 520, citing Rita J. King, *Big, Easy Money: Disaster Profiteering on the American Gulf Coast,* CorpWatch, August 15, 2006, http://www.corpwatch.org/article.php?id=14004. See also Dan Barry, "A City's Future, and a Dead Man's Past," *New York Times,* August 27, 2006.

CHAPTER 3

1. Rebecca Solnit, *A Paradise Built in Hell: The Extraordinary Communities That Arise in Disaster* (New York: Penguin, 2009), p. 305.

2. Previously known as the "Place d'Arms," where the militia mustered and trained, Jackson Square was named after General Andrew Jackson, who defeated the British in the Battle of New Orleans in 1815 at the end of the war. With paths radiating out from the Jackson statue at the midpoint and benches scattered around, the square, a stone's throw from the Mississippi River, is considered the city's center and a great gathering place.

3. Adam Nossiter, "New Orleans Schoolgirls Have a Message for the President," *New York Times,* January 13, 2006.

4. His first visit took place seventeen days after Katrina.

5. Nossiter, "New Orleans Schoolgirls Have a Message for the President."

6. Probably the most famous of these is the New York–New Jersey Port Authority originally formed to develop a rail connection between the states under the Hudson River, not to develop real estate like the World Trade Center. The rail connection was never built, but the Twin Tower World Trade Center was.

7. Barry is widely admired for his extraordinary book, *Rising Tide,* about the 1927 flood and creation of the Corps of Engineers.

8. Shawn Holahan, "Stop the Flooding," January 13, 2006, http://stopthe flooding.blogspot.com/.

9. Nossiter, "New Orleans Schoolgirls Have a Message for the President."

10. The screw pumps that drained the city, invented by A. Baldwin Wood, were installed in 1913.

11. New Orleans is predominantly a Catholic city.

12. In actuality, the state set the rules.

13. Moon Landrieu was the mayor of New Orleans from 1970 to 1978.

As a city councilman before that, he fought for desegregation. He was the first white mayor to bring African-Americans into his administration.

14. American Society for the Prevention of Cruelty to Animals.

15. The Hornets were renamed the New Orleans Pelicans in 2013.

16. The home page of the Beacon of Hope Resource Center can be found at www.beaconofhopenola.org.

17. Karl F. Seidman, *Coming Home to New Orleans: Neighborhood Rebuilding After Katrina* (Oxford University Press, 2013), p. 63, citing the 2000 US Census.

18. Seidman, *Coming Home to New Orleans*, p. 62.

19. "Living with History in New Orleans' Neighborhoods: Broadmoor," a publication of the Preservation Resource Center; available online at http://www.prcno.org/neighborhoods/brochures/Broadmoor.pdf.

20. Seidman, *Coming Home to New Orleans*, p. 79. In many homes in Broadmoor, the second floor is livable.

21. Lawrence Powell notes the "sense of fun and festival that defines the personality of the city. . . . We leap at the chance to throw a party, invent a new festival tradition, dance in the streets." See Powell, "New Orleans: An American Pompeii?," in *Satchmo Meets Amadeus,* ed. Reinhold Wagnleitner (Innsbruck, Austria: StudienVerlag, 2006), p. 145.

22. Roark eventually left to attend Yale Divinity School and is now an Episcopalian priest in Connecticut.

23. Seidman, *Coming Home to New Orleans*, p. 70.

24. Ibid., p. 85.

25. Students from Bard College still come every spring vacation to volunteer at the school, helping out with everything from one-on-one tutoring to physical work that needs to be done. The Bard Early College Program for local eleventh and twelfth graders offers two half-day college-level study days, thus completing one year of college.

26. NORA manages vacant land and property for the city.

CHAPTER 4

1. Walter Isaacson, *American Sketches: Great Leaders, Creative Thinkers, and Heroes of a Hurricane* (New York: Simon & Schuster, 2009), p. 66.

2. This is now the Greyhound bus station, where, as Randy Fertel points out, "Highway 61 begins on its way to the other Delta where blues was born and on to Chicago." See Fertel, *The Gorilla Man and the Empress of Steak: A New Orleans Family Memoir* (Jackson: University Press of Mississippi, 2011), p. 82.

3. The story of Savannah's escape from the era of demolition derbies and its rescue and regeneration by preservationists is told in my first book, *The Living City.*

4. Fertel, *The Gorilla Man and the Empress of Steak,* p. 103.

5. James Gill, *Lords of Misrule: Mardi Gras and the Politics of Race in New Orleans* (Jackson: University Press of Mississippi, 1997), p. 178.

6. Isaacson, *American Sketches,* p. 267.

7. Jane Jacobs, *The Death and Life of Great American Cities* (New York: Random House, 1961), p. 151.

8. Richard Rainey, "Mayor Mitch Landrieu Touts New Orleans Economy Under His Watch," *Times-Picayune,* December 12, 2013.

9. After Katrina, Vietnamese merchants snapped up many shuttered corner stores.

10. Jacobs, *Death and Life of Great American Cities,* p. 101.

11. The Planning Commission created an arts overlay for several streets that permits the sale of art, sales tax–free.

12. Dan Houston and Dana Eness, "Thinking Outside the Box: A Report on Independent Merchants and the New Orleans Economy," the Urban Conservancy in partnership with Civic Economics, September 2009, http://www.independentwestand.org/wp-content/uploads/ThinkingOutsidetheBox_1.pdf.

13. Houston and Eness, "Thinking Outside the Box," p. 8.

14. Streetcar suburbs geared to the transit-riding pedestrian are very different from the post–World War II suburbs totally oriented toward the car, even lacking sidewalks.

15. Europe invested in transit; the United States disinvested.

16. The sorry tale of how executives of the automobile, steel, utilities, and rubber tire companies and long-distance bus services conspired to put trolleys out of business is told in my *Cities Back from the Edge: New Life for Downtown,* pp. 106–107. A lawsuit proving the conspiracy—*United States v. National City Lines Inc. et al. 334 U.S. 573 (1948)*—was settled in 1948 with the culprits fined $1,000.

17. Veolia press release, March 15, 2010. The station was put on the National Register of Historic Places in 1973.

18. New Orleans was one of 50 "high-priority, innovative transportation projects" selected. See "New Orleans Regional Transit Authority and Veolia Transportation Receive U.S. DOT Grant of $45 million for Streetcar Expansion," *Business Wire,* March 15, 2010.

19. David Hammer, "Underground Surprises Sent Loyola Streetcar Costs Soaring," *Eyewitness News WWLTV,* April 9, 2014.

CHAPTER 5

1. Tom Piazza, *Why New Orleans Matters* (New York: HarperCollins, 2005), p. 32.

2. Karen Gadbois, "What Gets Squandered," *The Lens,* November 26, 2008, http://thelensnola.org/2008/11/26/what-gets-squandered/.

3. The perfect victory would have been no Dollar General store built.

4. Adam Nossiter, "Amid Ruined New Orleans Neighborhoods, a Gadfly Buzzes," *New York Times*, August 13, 2008.

5. NOAH was suspended when the FBI investigation began in 2008; see Michelle Krupa, "New Orleans Home Rehab Operation Suspended," *Times-Picayune*, August 1, 2008.

6. Antwan Harris, "Former Head of Nagin House-Gutting Program Gets 5 Years," *WWLTV.com*, October 17, 2014.

7. For further information on *The Lens*, see http://thelensnola.org /about-us/.

8. On St. Joseph's Night, the Indians emerge at an undesignated hour in search of their rival "gangs," dancing in the streets enacting an ancient ritual. Their ceremonial suits are elaborate creations of beadwork and feathers in resplendent color.

9. The New Orleans airport is Armstrong International Airport. In the middle of the terminal is a huge, larger-than-life statue of Armstrong blowing his horn.

10. Randy Fortel notes that "Lolis Edward Elie, a member of the most important civil rights firm in the city, Collins, Douglas and Elie, broke the race barrier at Ruth's Chris Steakhouse when he was brought to lunch by a conservative white politician who needed Elie's clout in the black community." See Fertel, *The Gorilla Man and the Empress of Steak* (Jackson: University Press of Mississippi, 2011), p. 152.

11. Rampart Street was named for the ramparts that once held back both the swamp and the Indians when it was the edge of town, sometimes called Back 'a Town.

12. Lolis Eric Elie, "So Much for Satchmo: How About Another Downtown Parking Lot?," *The Lens*, September 21, 2012.

13. Two multistory garages flank both sides of the lot.

14. Elie, "So Much for Satchmo."

15. Two obscure remnants of Storyville remain hidden in the Iberville Public Housing complex.

16. Randy Fertel, *The Gorilla Man and the Empress of Steak: A New Orleans Family Memoir* (Jackson: University Press of Mississippi, 2011), p. 36.

17. Jazz legend Sidney Bechet's childhood home, where he played music for the first time, was torn down as recently as October 2010. Like many musicians' houses, Bechet's was not in an upper-income neighborhood. It was occupied before Katrina but damaged, though not beyond repair, by the storm—a victim of the city's overzealous determination to remove blight. Blight is a designation too often attached to redeemable buildings.

18. Tom Sancton, *Song for My Father: A New Orleans Story in Black and White* (New York: Other Press, 2006), p. 150.

19. For a critical view of Lincoln Center as a project formula, see Gratz, *The Living City: How America's Cities Are Being Revitalized by Thinking Small in a Big Way* (New York: Simon & Schuster, 1989), p. 308.

20. Sancton, *Song for My Father,* p. 150. In contrast, the home in which Armstrong lived from 1943 until his death in 1971 is now a house museum in Queens, New York.

21. Elie, "So Much for Satchmo."

22. Quoted in Sancton, *Song for My Father,* p. 151.

23. Karen Gadbois, "A House Moved to Make Way for the Hospital Complex Finds New Life in Mid City," *The Lens,* September 18, 2013, http://thelensnola.org/2013/09/18/a-house-moved-to-make-way-for-the -hospital-complex-finds-new-life-in-mid-city/.

24. Karen Gadbois, "Blight Worsened by Housing Preservation Program, Hoffman Triangle Residents Say," *The Lens,* August 2, 2011, http://thelens nola.org/2011/08/02/medical-center-houses-blight-new-neighborhood/.

25. Charles Maldonado, "Mission Accomplished: Landrieu Administration Promises One Thing on Blight, Delivers Another," *The Lens,* April 22, 2014, http://thelensnola.org/2014/04/22/mission-accomplished-landrieu -administration-promises-one-thing-on-blight-delivers-another/.

26. Prices range from $5,000 to $175,000 for the mostly single-family homes. See Michelle Krupa, "Brisk Sales of Abandoned Properties at Recent New Orleans Redevelopment Authority Auction," *NOLA.com* and *Times-Picayune,* April 12, 2011, http://www.nola.com/politics/index.ssf /2011/04/brisk_sales_of_abandoned_prope.html.

27. In 1993, he was picked as Environmental Lawyer of the Year by the Environmental Law Society of Tulane Law School; in 1998, he was given the Distinguished Leadership Award for a Citizen Planner from the American Planning Association Louisiana Chapter.

28. No one built highways as well as Robert Moses in New York, and he was sought by other cities as a consultant to help plan similar highways for them. Like many early highway plans elsewhere, this one sat on the shelf until about 1957. That's when many other highway plans got activated; it's also when Bill and Richard got involved.

29. The Boston Club is one of the most prestigious, socially prominent clubs in New Orleans.

30. Joe M. Richardson, "Edgar B. Stern: A White New Orleans Philanthropist Builds a Black University," *Journal of Negro History,* Summer 1997.

31. Many historic preservation efforts around the country started with a fight to stop a proposed highway.

32. However, as one observer noted, "This older establishment lost political power to descendants of free people of color with the election of Dutch Morial in 1978."

33. At the very same time, Jane Jacobs was leading the fight in NYC against the Lower Manhattan Expressway.

34. Tom Piazza went on to say: "Nobody really knows the genesis of the Indians, although the oldest gang, the Creole Wild West, dates its founding to back in the late 1800s. Some say interest was stirred up by Buffalo Bill's traveling Wild West Show; others claim that a bond was forged between escaped slaves and local Indians who sheltered them and gave them sanctuary." See Piazza, *Why New Orleans Matters* (New York: HarperCollins, 2005), p. 45.

35. This information is provided in *Raised to the Trade* (2002), the New Orleans Museum of Modern Art exhibition catalogue.

36. "Tootie" was a 1987 NEA National Heritage Fellow. He was also the model for the lead character in *Treme*.

37. Fred Starr noted in conversation that there were also many "prolific architects and craftsmen of all races, especially German and Irish, as well as creoles of color."

CHAPTER 6

1. Katie Kelly, "Brad Pitt 'High' from New Orleans Rebuilding Project," *People,* December 1, 2008, http://www.people.com/people/article /0,,20243471,00.html.

2. Architectural juries are often created to select the winning design for a project.

3. For further information on GRAFT, see http://www.graftlab.com.

4. Michael Braungart and William McDonough, *Cradle to Cradle: Remaking the Way We Make Things* (New York: North Point Press, 2002). This book is no less than a manifesto calling for the transformation of industry from the Industrial Revolution model of "take, make, and waste" into an environmentally responsible system that reverses that cycle.

5. Brownfield mitigation is a process that removes poisons from the soil.

6. "Pitt's Star Power Fuels New Orleans Rebuilding," NPR's *All Things Considered,* December 3, 2007.

7. When former site residents and other Lower Nine residents were taken care of, the process was open to other low- and moderate-income applicants such as teachers, police, and city workers.

8. One architect reportedly said to another architect, "We're going to have to decide who we are designing for, us or them."

9. Gerald Clarke, "Rebuilding New Orleans: After Hurricane Katrina, Brad Pitt Breaks New Ground and Helps Rebuild the Lower Ninth Ward," *Architectural Digest,* January 2009, http://www.architecturaldigest.com /celebrity-homes/2009/brad-pitt-article.

10. Charles has since moved to New Orleans East.

11. And as Charles's grandmother told him: "Don't be ready to judge other people until you walk in their shoes."

12. Eileen Fleming, "Brad Pitt Talks with WWNO About Make It Right Project Goals," *WWNO* interview, March 12, 2012, http://wwno.org/post /brad-pitt-talks-wwno-about-make-it-right-project-goals.

13. In 2009, New Orleans artist Dawn DeDeaux created a piece for Prospect I featuring three front steps in a semi-translucent white material with an inside light so that it glowed in the dark.

14. *Times-Picayune* reporter David Hammer, who covered much of Road Home's troubled history, said that Road Home is "the largest disaster recovery program in U.S. history." The money goes to the state and is then contracted out to a private company. "The current contract is with HGI [Hammerman & Gainer International], from Lutcher, Louisiana," he explained. "The original contractor was ICF International, from Fairfax, Virginia. ICF was run out of the state on a rail in 2009. HGI has also had major questions because it used massive change orders to go from a minor player to the company in charge of the whole thing." In a June 2009 article, he went on to say that ICF "is generally reviled by Louisianians and essentially banned from new business with the state, but walks away $900 million richer and holding lucrative contracts with governments across the country"; see Hammer, "ICF's Oversight of Road Home Program Comes to an End," *Times-Picayune,* June 11, 2009.

15. One son works for a contractor in Kuwait and returns home periodically, another is a chef downtown, and a third works in maintenance for an off-track betting and casino company; one daughter is a nurse and the other is going to nursing school.

16. SUN is a tax-exempt nonprofit created to fight poverty through special programs with board members from Texas, Arkansas, and Louisiana—the three states it works in.

17. For further information on the Greater New Orleans Foundation, see www.GNOF.org.

18. With the critical help of Richard Moe, then president of the National Trust for Historic Preservation, the state received through the National Park Service almost $25 million for historic restoration grants for homeowners. Administered by then–Lieutenant Governor Mitch Landrieu, the program helped restore more than five hundred homes in New Orleans alone.

19. Millard Fuller, "How Did It All Begin?," in Fuller, *Simple Decent Place to Live: The Building Realization of Habitat for Humanity* (Nashville, TN: Word, 1995).

20. The Habitat financing model is unique. Because of a biblical prohibition against charging interest, Habitat houses are built with money raised and sold at no-profit and no-interest. A former Habitat employee explained

to me that the organization does not believe in mortgages so it holds the note on a house, as the debt is paid down over thirty years. See Jerome P. Baggett, *Habitat for Humanity: Building Private Homes, Building Public Religion* (Philadelphia: Temple University Press, 2011), p. 46.

21. These three buildings are still owned by the developer who wants to tear them down.

22. In January 2014, Mayor Landrieu announced that his goal of addressing ten thousand blighted properties had been reached. In June, *The Lens* published an article by staff writer Charles Maldonaldo indicating that a survey of three hundred properties on that list found that many were still blighted, or blighted again after demolition or cleanup, and that some houses still standing were marked as demolished. See Maldonado, "Mission Accomplished: Landrieu Administration Promises One Thing on Blight, Delivers Another," *The Lens,* April 22, 2014, http://thelensnola .org/2014/04/22/mission-accomplished-landrieu-administration-promises -one-thing-on-blight-delivers-another/.

CHAPTER 7

1. This body of water is officially known as the Bayou Bienvenue Wetland Triangle.

2. The pirogue is a flat-bottomed boat that is particularly efficient in marshes.

3. For further information on the Center for Sustainable Engagement and Development, see http://www.sustainthenine.org/about/mission-values.

4. After Katrina, Warrenetta lived in a FEMA trailer for two years before moving back into her home. She is a volunteer docent at the Global Green/ Holy Cross Project Visitor Center, where new builders, residents, and renovators go to learn about dual-flush toilets, tankless water heaters, energy-efficient appliances, solar panels, and compact fluorescent light bulbs.

5. Jacques's father, Ernest "Dutch" Morial, was New Orleans's first black mayor, serving from 1978 to 1986. His brother Marc was mayor from 1994 to 2002.

6. Developed after World War II, Pontchartrain Park was one of the first suburban-style subdivisions for middle-class blacks during the Jim Crow era. After the neighboring development, Gentilly Woods, was built, philanthropists Edgar and Edith Stern persuaded Mayor Chep Morrison to donate city land across the canal that the Sterns and Rosa and Charles Keller then had dredged and developed by the same builder of Gentilly Woods. For further information on Rosa Freeman Keller, see http://www.knowla.org /entry/846/.

7. An informative billboard stood for a while near the overlook, created by the Center for Sustainable Engagement and Development. One could

learn about everything that went wrong environmentally in New Orleans and along the nearby Gulf Coast (before the BP oil spill) from this informational display, which included photos, maps, and explanatory text: "The 1920s completion of the Industrial Canal—a five and a half mile waterway connecting the Mississippi to Lake Pontchartrain; the 1949 creation of the Gulf Intercoastal Waterway—a canal-like connection between the Gulf Coast and Florida and Texas; the 1964 completion of the Mississippi River Gulf Outlet (MR-GO)—a shortcut from the Gulf to the port; the increasing salinity of the water in the 1960s and '70s that killed all the cypress trees; the 1965 partial flooding of the Lower Nine during Hurricane Betsy; the 1973 construction of the East Bank Sewage Treatment Plant just east of the bayou; and the 2005 Hurricanes Katrina and Rita followed in 2008 by Gustav and Ivan."

8. In 2013, a Sierra Club study noted that since 2007, 10 percent of the city's solar permits went on homes in the Lower Nine. That's five times more per capita than in other parts of the city, providing a $45 monthly saving per house. See "Solar Power Flourishing in Lower Ninth Ward," New Orleans Public Radio, July 17, 2013, http://wwno.org/post/solar-power-flourishing-lower-ninth-ward.

9. Nutria are large beaverlike rodents that were imported for their fur at the beginning of the twentieth century. With few natural enemies, they turned Louisiana's wetlands into their dinner table, munching copiously on marsh grass and roots. Without roots to hold the marsh soils in place, the soils eroded and turned into open water.

10. Brady R. Couvillion et al., "Land Area Change in Coastal Louisiana from 1932 to 2010," US Geological Survey, June 1, 2011, http://pubs.usgs.gov/sim/3164/.

11. Randy Fertel, "The Mississippi River Delta Must Be Restored," New York Times, January 1, 2012, http://www.nytimes.com/2012/01/28/opinion/the-mississippi-river-delta-must-be-restored.html?_r=1&.

12. John Barry, Rising Tide: The Great Mississippi Flood of 1927 and How It Changed America (New York: Simon & Schuster, 1997), p. 16.

13. Bob Marshall, "Top State Official Rebuts Dire Warning, Insists Coast Can Be Saved," The Lens, February 27, 2013.

14. Melodi Smith and Jason Hanna, "Gulf of Mexico 'Dead Zone' Is the Size of Connecticut," CNN, August 5, 2014, http://www.cnn.com/2014/08/05/tech/gulf-of-mexico-dead-zone/.

15. George Friedman, "The Ghost City," New York Review of Books, October 6, 2005.

16. "What's at Stake," Coastal Protection and Restoration Authority, http://coastal.la.gov/whats-at-stake/.

17. "Coastal Louisiana," *Impact of Federal Programs on Wetlands Vol. II, US Department of the Interior,* http://www.doi.gov/pmb/oepc/wetlands2 /v2ch8.cfm.

18. Ibid.

19. "What's at Stake," Coastal Protection and Restoration Authority, http://coastal.la.gov/whats-at-stake/.

20. "Water Fowl Estimates in Louisiana's Coastal Zone," Louisiana Department of Wildlife & Fisheries, February 2014.

21. Katie Valentine, "Four Years After the Deepwater Horizon Oil Spill, the Gulf Is Still Suffering," *ThinkProgress,* April 20, 2014.

22. Randy Fertel, "Hearing the Bugle's Call: Hurricane Katrina, the BP Oil Spill, and the Effects of Trauma," *Environmental Disasters and Collective Trauma: A Journal of Archetype and Culture,* Winter 2012.

23. Richard Thompson, "4 Years After Spill Health Impact Questions Remain," *The Advocate,* May 17, 2014.

24. The Environmental Protection Agency disallowed the use of Corexit 9527 as unacceptably toxic. BP switched to Corexit 9500, apparently without the EPA's weighing in. Both forms are illegal in Great Britain.

25. Naomi Klein, "After the Spill," *The Nation,* January 2011.

26. Leslie Kaufman, "Gulf's Complexity and Resilience Seen in Studies of Oil Spill," *New York Times,* April 11, 2011.

27. Bruce Alpert, "Watchdog Group Reports Health Problems from Dispersant Use During BP Oil Spill," *NOLA.com* and *Times-Picayune,* April 19, 2013, http://www.nola.com/politics/index.ssf/2013/04/watchdog _group_reports_health.html.

28. Ibid.

29. Bob Marshall, "LSU Study: Damaged Minnow Shows BP Oil Seeping into Coastal Food Chain," *The Lens,* May 6, 2013.

30. Amy Wold, "Report: Oil Is Not Gone; Impacts on Wildlife Ongoing," *The Advocate,* April 9, 2014.

31. Sixty percent of that went to coastal projects, vetted and approved by the federally created Gulf Coast Ecosystem Restoration Council; 5 percent went to research, technology, and grants; and 35 percent was divided equally among the five states. Louisiana's share will be 30 percent for coastal parishes and 70 percent for the state, a tally that could range from $500 million to $1 billion. The state's fifty-year coastal restoration plan has a $50 billion price tag. See "The Restore Act," *Restore the Mississippi River Delta,* signed into law on July 6, 2012, http://www.mississippiriverdelta .org/our-work/overview/public-policy/clean-water-act-penalties/restore-act/.

32. In June 2014, Governor Jindal announced that $1 billion of BP recovery money will be put in the state's rainy-day fund, the Medicaid Trust for

the Elderly, and the Health Trust Fund, thereby balancing the budget instead of restoring the coast. See "Bobby Jindal Agrees to $1 Billion Earmark of BP Oil Spill Money," Associated Press, *NOLA.com* and *Times-Picayune,* June 14, 2014, http://www.nola.com/politics/index.ssf/2014/06/bobby_jindal _agrees_to_1_billi.html.

33. See "Louisiana Environmental Restoration," Southern Regional Water Program, n.d., http://srwqis.tamu.edu/louisiana/program-information /louisiana-target-themes/watershed-restoration/.

34. This reneges on the commitment to restore the land, a clause in every permit they get.

35. The Coalition to Restore Coastal Louisiana announced an interesting new program in 2014 to restore, maintain, and expand oyster reefs using recycled oyster shells collected from restaurants. One-third of the nation's oysters come from Louisiana.

36. The 1913 pumping system designed by A. Baldwin Wood is an engineering marvel. The pumps worked during Katrina but were overwhelmed when the levees broke and had to be shut down. The two oldest pumps from 1913 worked better than any of the newer ones, Nicolai Ouroussoff reported. See "How the City Sank," *New York Times,* October 9, 2005, http://www .nytimes.com/2005/10/09/arts/design/09ouro.html?pagewanted=all.

37. "The New Orleans Hurricane Protection System: What Went Wrong and Why?," American Society of Civil Engineers (ASCE) and Hurricane Katrina External Review Panel, 2007, http://www.asce.org/uploadedfiles /publications/asce_news/2009/04_april/erpreport.pdf.

38. Ironically, in 1915 the Dutch tried to lure A. Baldwin Wood to help them with their water management. Instead, he gave them his pump plans and his blessing and they built his system to drain the Zeider Zee, a project that has plagued them ever since. After that, they switched strategies—this time, building the drainage into the landscape. The new system is working brilliantly.

39. Erin Marie Daly, "Entergy Rises Out of Bankruptcy," *Law 360,* May 9, 2007, http://www.law360.com/articles/24337/entergy-rises -out-of-bankruptcy.

40. Shawn Kennedy, "Vitality Reborn, New Orleans Draws Developers," *New York Times,* September 25, 2012.

41. This quote is attributed to a spokesman for the mayor.

42. This is exactly what the Los Angeles Riverfront Revitalization Project is now doing along the first eleven of fifty-one miles of riverbed lined with cement by the Corps of Engineers in the 1930s after a flood. For further information, see "Los Angeles Riverfront Revitalization," 2015, http:// www.lariver.org/index.htm.

43. City of New Orleans, "Laffite Greenway Bicycle and Pedestrian Path," November 17, 2014, http://www.nola.gov/dpw/projects/lafitte-greenway/.

CHAPTER 8

1. Considerable resentment was apparent among the New Orleans design community toward the arrogance of so many outside architects who offered detailed solutions after little research and without really knowing anything about the place, the people, or the traditions. "Helicopter consulting" it could be called.

2. Cisterns were banned in New Orleans after a yellow fever epidemic in 1853.

3. As noted in conversation by Stephen A. Goldsmith (Chair, Urban Ecology Program, University of Utah, former Salt Lake City planning director and executive director of The Center for the Living City), this is an example outside of New Orleans that parallels the reviving of water resources that can help minimize flooding and improve landscapes.

4. New Orleans became one of the important national centers devoted to the exploration of outer space. The Michoud Assembly Facility, a sprawling industrial park, contains one of the largest production buildings in the country. The building was built for the space shuttle program, which in turn constructs Saturn One booster rockets for NASA's Apollo Program. The operation was then downsized when that program ended in 2010. Now, however, Michoud supports several major projects for the next generation of space vehicles. In partnership with the state and the University of New Orleans, it contains the National Center for Advanced Manufacturing. Two companies have teamed up to build a new "space plane" designed to shuttle passengers to and from the International Space Station.

5. White and free people of color came to New Orleans after fleeing the violence of the Haitian Revolution of 1804. Many brought slaves.

6. The biggest factors in the revival of The East—at least in terms of units of new housing post-storms—were the endless, pitifully dreary-looking apartment complexes along I-10 and elsewhere. They were incentivized by the Gulf Opportunity Zone ("Go-Zone") tax credits as well as by accelerated depreciation schedules and the like. Congress authorized these allocations immediately after Katrina and Rita.

7. A number of students assisted in the production of *Retrofitting the Rancher* (Spring 2006, New Jersey Institute of Technology): Chad Coronato, Astra Freet, Thomas Jardim, Hyung S. Kang, Andy Kim, Viren Patel, John Rago, Richard Rush, Patricia Sabater, and Matthew Schott. The instructor was Jim Dart.

8. In February 2011, Litwin inaugurated *NOLA Vie,* a weekly online feature magazine concentrating on cultural coverage, events, people, and neighborhoods. As a reader of it can attest, it is a delightful and useful supplement to regular press coverage.

9. See Roberta Brandes Gratz, "To Market, to Market," in Gratz, *Cities*

Back from the Edge: New Life for Downtown (John Wiley & Sons, 1998).

10. Ian McNulty, "Growing Momentum: Hollygrove Market Turns Three," *Gambit,* October 2011, http://www.bestofneworleans.com /blogofneworleans/archives/2011/10/18/growing-momentum-hollygrove -market-turns-three.

11. The Growers Pavilion was developed in collaboration with the Carrollton-Hollygrove Community Development Corporation and the New Orleans Food and Farm Network, a food justice organization that works with individuals, organizations, and growers to support sustainable growing practices and to make fresh food available wherever possible throughout the city.

12. This middle school had already become a charter school under the Recovery School District (see Chapter 11) but was open just a week before Katrina hit. It was one of the first schools to reopen after Katrina.

13. Recasner eventually left the school to run Agenda for Children; for more information, see http://www.agendaforchildren.org/about.html.

14. The Nation Institute is a nonprofit media organization affiliated with *The Nation* magazine; it supports investigative journalism, fellowships, and Nation Books (the publisher of this book).

15. In 1992, a schoolyard garden on Crenshaw Boulevard in Central Los Angeles led to the first student-managed and -operated natural food products company, Food from the Hood salad dressing. The proceeds fund college scholarships for the students. See Gratz, *Cities Back from the Edge,* p. 226.

16. Scott Cowen, formerly the much-celebrated head of Tulane (now retired), personally contributed half of the start-up money for this program.

CHAPTER 9

1. Mouton was commander of the Guard's Task Force Castle.

2. There are several first-rate private hospitals, but as a public hospital, Charity was totally depended upon by the majority low-income population.

3. Neglect and underfunding by the state and then LSU had taken their toll; building maintenance had been deferred.

4. Johnson's specialty is Prime Power Electrician, 205th Engineering Battalion.

5. He received a meritorious service award from the US Army for his work on Charity.

6. A version of this story first appeared in *The Nation* magazine in April 2011; see Roberta Brandes Gratz, "Why Was New Orleans's Charity Hospital Allowed to Die?," April 27, 2011, http://www.thenation.com/article/160241/why-was-new-orleanss-charity-hospital-allowed-to-die. In June, a response from LSU was published with my reply; see "Exchange," http:// www.thenation.com/article/161431/exchange.

7. Virgil McDill, "Hope for Big Charity," *Preservation in Print* (Preservation Resource Center of New Orleans, October 2008), p. 35.

8. One emergency-room doctor reported seeing architectural drawings posted on the wall of the hospital parking garage.

9. "Why Was New Orleans's Charity Hospital Allowed to Die?," *The Nation,* April 2011.

10. Jan Moller, "Charity Hospital Reimbursement Claims Inflated Through Error, Bias, FEMA Argues," *Times-Picayune,* November 3, 2009.

11. Ibid.

12. The Foundation for Historical Louisiana engaged Hillier. The study was released in August 2008; see http://fhl.org/uploads/files/ExecutiveSummary_Public.pdf.

13. "Medical Center of New Orleans: Charity Hospital Feasibility Study," Foundation for Historical Louisiana, August 20, 2009.

14. Lindy Boggs Hospital was eventually bought by another entity for easy conversion into a nursing home and small hospital.

15. Robert B. Olshansky and Laurie A. Johnson's *Clear as Mud: Planning for the Rebuilding of New Orleans* (American Planning Association, 2010) does a masterful job of describing the UNOP and other planning processes that unfolded after Katrina.

16. Additional city funds were made available to cover street and sewer work and the moving of utility lines—namely, a $7.5 million Urban Development Block Grant and $25 million in CDBG funds.

17. The initial VA site was on 6.2 acres, with the same number of beds.

18. This quote is taken from page 23 of the transcript of the public meeting.

19. At one point, consultant David Dixon told me, Blakely called to remind him that this "is not part of your charge."

20. A camelback is a shotgun house with a partial second floor at least halfway down the length of what would otherwise be a long, narrow, single-story shotgun. The camelback emerged as a way to avoid being counted as a two-story house by the tax assessor.

21. Julie Bloom, "Banksy Hits New Orleans," *New York Times,* August 28, 2008. The building and thus the mural were destroyed to make way for the hospital.

22. The city does not have precise records on what happened to all the houses, so it is unclear how many were saved, lost, or saved and then lost.

23. The new 1.7-million-square-foot Veterans Hospital reportedly has 120 acute-care beds, 20 psychiatric beds, 40 rehab beds, and 20 beds for hospice and palliative care. See Jessica Gonzales, "Hospitals Will Lean on Local, Outside Help for Staffing," *New Orleans City Business,* August 2013.

24. Adam Nossiter, "New Orleans Hospitals Plan Angers Preservationists," *New York Times,* November 26, 2011.

25. "Louisiana Post-Katrina Recovery Health Care," FEMA, July 24, 2014, https://www.fema.gov/louisiana-post-katrina-recovery-health-care.

26. "Advocating for Healthy People and Communities," Daughters of Charity Foundation of New Orleans, 2013, http://dcsno.org/foundation/inside.php?page=history.

27. Jed Horne, "Building Boom Changes New Orleans Cityscape," *The Advocate,* August 6, 2014.

28. Bill Lodge and Marsha Shuler, "Court Says State Owed Feds $239.5 Million," *The Advocate,* March 8, 2013.

29. This same process of collecting FEMA money for a public building and then turning it over or selling it to a private entity has happened with some of the city's public school buildings.

30. DeSalvo, New Orleans's health commissioner from 2012 to 2013, is now a senior official in the US Department of Health and Human Services.

31. "Adaptive Reuse Proposal Synopsis for Charity Hospital," *Save Charity Hospital,* August 28, 2014, http://savecharityhospital.com/content/adaptive-reuse-proposal-synopsis-charity-hospital.

32. Sheriff Marlin N. Gusman said in an interview that it is the city's responsibility to fund the mental health provisions to the tune of $4 million. That issue is yet to be resolved.

33. Sarah Carr, *Hope Against Hope* (New York: Bloomsbury Press, 2013).

34. Sarah Carr, "In New Orleans, a Case Study in How School, Health Care Decentralization Affect Neediest Children," *The Hechinger Report,* July 3, 2014, http://hechingerreport.org/content/new-orleans-case-study-school-health-care-decentralization-affect-neediest-children_16596/.

35. State Treasurer John Kennedy was the only public voice to question the needless costs.

36. Richard Moe, then president of the National Trust for Historic Preservation, met and fully briefed Donovan in November 2009.

CHAPTER 10

1. Quoted in Naomi Martin, "Federal Judge Rules Consent Decree Only Way to Fix 'Indelible Stain' of Orleans Parish," *NOLA.com* and *Times-Picayune,* June 6, 2013, http://www.nola.com/crime/index.ssf/2013/06/federal_judge_rules_consent_de.html.

2. For further information about this organization, see http://www.vote-nola.org.

3. James Ridgeway and Jean Casella, "America's 10 Worst Prisons: NOLA," *Mother Jones,* May 6, 2013, http://www.motherjones.com/politics/2013/05/10-worst-prisons-america-orleans-parish-opp.

4. The conditions in the jail are made worse by the fact that New Orleans youth, as well as mentally ill and homeless individuals, land there for little

or no cause. As noted in the previous chapter, many mentally disturbed people who would have been treated at Charity Hospital were now being sent to the jail. The crisis in mental health care in New Orleans, sparked by Charity's closure, deepened greatly when Governor Jindal slashed budgets and gutted mental health care statewide.

5. Susan Buchanan, "Size of Rebuild at Orleans Parish Prison Is Scrutinized," *Huffington Post,* December 1, 2013, http://www.huffingtonpost .com/susan-buchanan/size-of-rebuild-at-orlean_b_4369254.html.

6. *Jones v. Gusman,* Southern Poverty Law Center, 2012, http://www .splcenter.org/get-informed/case-docket/orleans-parish-prison-safety.

7. Quoted in James Ridgeway and Jean Casella, "America's 10 Worst Prisons," *Mother Jones,* October 5, 2013, http://www.motherjones.com /politics/2013/05/10-worst-prisons-america-orleans-parish-opp.

8. Quoted in Charles Maldonado, "Day 1: OPP Consent Decree Fairness Hearing," *Gambit,* April 1, 2013, http://www.bestof neworleans.com/blogofneworleans/archives/2013/04/01/day-1-opp-consent -decree-fairness-hearing.

9. As Robert McClendon reported in the *Times-Picayune,* the population in 2013 fell 11.9 percent to 2,473 prisoners, with a deficit of $3.8 million. See McClendon, "Orleans Parish Sheriff's Office Runs a Deficit as Jail Population Declines," *NOLA.com* and *Times-Picayune,* http://www.nola.com /politics/index.ssf/2014/07/orleans_parish_sheriffs_office_3.html.

10. Clancy Dubos, "Violent Jail, Violent City," *Gambit,* February 22, 2013, http://www.bestofneworleans.com/blogofneworleans/archives /2013/02/22/violent-jail-violent-city.

11. For further information about the New Orleans Innocence Project, see http://www.ip-no.org/.

12. According to Karl Dequine Harden, "Louisiana ranks in the highest in the nation in terms of the number of people per capita exonerated after serving time for crimes they did not commit." See Harden, "Panelists Describe La.'s Role as 'Ground Zero' for Prison Industrial Complex," *Louisiana Weekly,* November 16, 2014, http://www.louisianaweekly.com /panelists-describe-la-s-role-as-ground-zero-for-prison-industrial-complex/.

13. Dan Baum, "Deluged," *New Yorker,* January 9, 2006, http://www .newyorker.com/magazine/2006/01/09/deluged.

14. Leonard N. Moore, *Black Rage in New Orleans: Police Brutality and African American Activism from World War II to Hurricane Katrina* (Baton Rouge: Louisiana State University Press, 2010).

15. Ibid., p. 168.

16. Ibid., p. 202.

17. Paul Keegan, "The Thinnest Blue Line," *New York Times Magazine,* March 1996.

18. "Officer Len Davis, Two Others, Charged in Death of Kim Groves," *NOLA.com* and *Times-Picayune,* December 6, 1994, http://www.nola.com/crime/index.ssf/1994/12/officer_len_davis_two_others_c.html.

19. Ibid.

20. Moore, *Black Rage in New Orleans,* p. 225.

21. Ibid., p. 236.

22. Ibid., p. 244.

23. Sergio Hernandez, "NOPD Beating Death Trial Draws to a Close," *ProPublica,* April 11, 2011, http://www.propublica.org/article/nopd-beating-death-trial-draws-to-a-close.

24. The Louisiana Justice Institute, "Victim Impact Statement of Daughters and Family of Raymond Robair," September 15, 2011, http://louisianajusticeinstitute.blogspot.com/2011/09/victim-impact-statement-of-daughters.html.

25. Dan Abrams, "Inside Allegations That NOPD 'Looted' Cadillacs," *NBC News,* September 30, 2005, http://www.nbcnews.com/id/9542398/ns/msnbc-the_abrams_report/t/inside-allegations-nopd-looted-cadillacs/#.VGOfP4CwIzM.

26. Police Chief Ronal W. Serpas resigned in August 2014. He did not respond to requests for an interview.

27. In November 2014, the City Council approved a 5 percent pay increase.

28. Howard W. Mielke, Chris R. Gonzales, Eric Powell, Morton Jartun, and Paul W. Mielke Jr., "Nonlinear Association Between Soil Lead and Blood Lead of Children in Metropolitan New Orleans, Louisiana: 2000–2005," *Science of the Total Environment* 388, Nos. 1–3 (December 2007): 43–53.

CHAPTER 11

1. The quote is taken from Paul Tough, "A Teachable Moment," *New York Times Magazine,* August 17, 2008, http://www.nytimes.com/2008/08/17/magazine/17NewOrleans-t.html?pagewanted=all. See also Tough's *Whatever It Takes: Geoffrey Canada's Quest to Change Harlem and America* (Boston: Houghton Mifflin Harcourt, 2009).

2. They were in the wilds of Montana when Katrina hit.

3. In January 2014, the Louisiana Fourth Circuit Court of Appeals unanimously ruled that the seven thousand teachers and school employees were wrongfully terminated and will be paid two years' salary by the Orleans Parish School Board. It also noted that new job openings were filled primarily with younger, cheaper candidates and that the state "advertised for these positions nationally and contracted with Teach For America to hire inexperienced college graduates that did not have teacher certification." See Danielle Dreilinger, "7,000 New Orleans Teachers, Laid Off After Katrina,

Win Court Ruling," *NOLA.com* and *Times-Picayune,* January 16, 2014, http://www.nola.com/crime/index.ssf/2014/01/7000_new_orleans_teachers _laid.html. In October 2014, the state supreme court reversed this decision. The plaintiff's are attempting to go to the US Supreme Court. See Danielle Dreilinger, "New Orleans Laid-Off Teachers, After High Court Loss, to Appeal to the U.S. Supreme Court," *NOLA.com* and *Times-Picayune* October 31, 2014, http://www.nola.com/education/index.ssf/2014/10/new _orleans_laid-off_teachers.html.

4. Sarah Carr, *Hope Against Hope: Three Schools, One City, and the Struggle to Educate America's Children* (New York: Bloomsbury Press, 2013), p. 64.

5. Education reporter Jessica Williams explained to me: "Five or six are run by the Orleans Parish School Board directly. Fourteen are charter schools, with independent boards, that answer to the OPSB [Orleans Parish School Board]. The rest are charters under the RSD [Recovery School District] or BESE [the Louisiana Board of Elementary and Secondary Education] auspices."

6. The 80 percent of the schoolchildren who rode public transit to a school closer to home helped subsidize the city's transit system. Now, private bus companies are hired at great expense and the cost of transit is borne by families. Some charters reimburse for transportation, but even waiting for reimbursement can be a hardship.

7. The school population is now 45,000.

8. "Catholic schools form a different but parallel universe," explained Bruce Nolan, former religion editor for the *Times-Picayune.* "They were the refuge for middle-class families before Katrina. Now parochial education is under serious economic pressure. Tuition can be $5,000 or $9,000 for high school. With the continuing squeeze on the middle class, they are in competition with a system that may not be as good but is free."

9. Carr, *Hope Against Hope,* p. 19.

10. Stacey Teicher Khadaroo, "New Orleans Goes All In on Charter Schools. Is It Showing the Way?," *Christian Science Monitor,* March 1, 2014, http://www.csmonitor.com/USA/2014/0301/New-Orleans-goes -all-in-on-charter-schools.-Is-it-showing-the-way.

11. "The State of Public Education in New Orleans: 2013 Report," Cowen Institute, June 2013, http://www.coweninstitute.com/wp-content /uploads/2013/07/2013_SPENO_Final2.pdf.

12. Will Sentell, "Auditor Faults Charter School Oversight," *The Advocate,* May 24, 2013.

13. Andy Cunningham, "Audit: $7 Million in Recovery School District Property Missing," *WDSU-TV,* December 15, 2014.

14. Carr, *Hope Against Hope,* p. 66.

15. Ibid., p. 2.

16. Daniel J. Cardinali, "How to Get Kids to Class," *New York Times,* August 25, 2014, http://www.nytimes.com/2014/08/26/opinion/to-keep -poor-kids-in-school-provide-social-services.html.

17. Carr, *Hope Against Hope,* p. 64.

18. Leslie Jacobs is a highly successful entrepreneur who built a small family insurance agency into one of the largest in the South. She served on the OPSB and, at the time of Katrina, was on the BESE. Before Katrina, she was already a passionate champion of converting the public school system to a "business model" framework that could ensure "accountability." This "business model" concept has been the mantra of big-foundation supporters, among others.

19. Jessica Williams, "State Documents Detail Standardized Test Cheating, Irregularities at New Orleans Schools," *The Lens,* July 16, 2013, http://the lensnola.org/2013/07/16/state-documents-detail-standardized-test-cheating -irregularities-at-new-orleans-schools/.

20. Cindy Chang, "$1.8 Billion from FEMA for Hurricane Katrina School Rebuilding Is 'Worth the Wait,' Sen. Mary Landrieu Says," *NOLA .com* and *Times-Picayune,* August 26, 2010, http://www.nola.com/katrina /index.ssf/2010/08/18_billion_from_fema_for_hurri.html.

21. This funding has come through the state, which hired the contractors to rebuild or replace the buildings. Among other questionable practices, local black construction workers were repeatedly turned away from many of these construction sites, workers told me.

22. Carr, *Hope Against Hope,* p. 121.

23. Signs of the city's post-storm comeback have not missed this neighborhood. Every block has an increasing number of restored and upgraded homes, mostly modest shotguns. A significant number of below-standard unimproved houses remain as well. The improved dwellings increase in number the closer one gets to St. Claude Avenue, undergoing its own interesting upgrade. It is quite fitting that a source of hope for the continuation of the city's vibrant music tradition is located in the kind of community that the city's rich music tradition came out of.

24. The Unified New Orleans Plan process is described in detail in Robert B. Olshansky and Laurie A. Johnson, *Clear as Mud: Planning for the Rebuilding of New Orleans* (Chicago: Planners Press, 2010).

25. Michael Hecht, "Readying Workforce for the Boom: A Challenge That's Also a Huge Opportunity," *The Lens,* September 23, 2014, http:// thelensnola.org/2014/09/23/getting-workers-ready-to-join-in-the-boom-a -challenge-thats-also-a-huge-opportunity/.

CHAPTER 12

1. Edward G. Goetz, *New Deal Ruins: Race, Economic Justice, and Public Housing Policy* (Ithaca, NY: Cornell University Press, 2013), pp. 1–5.

2. Ibid., p. 89.

3. This point was made by architect and planner Robert Tannen in conversation.

4. They were transported by sea from Africa.

5. Pruitt Igo in St. Louis, taller than Fisher, was the era's worst example. Built in the 1950s, it was imploded in 1972, one of the first to be demolished. The 1950s and '60s high-density towers never worked. In the high-rise version, elevators remained broken, and corridors, stairwells, and balconies were never safe.

6. In the 1990s, New Urbanists started advocating a return to street grids with pedestrian-oriented sidewalks, neighborly front yards, and parking in the rear or on the street.

7. No one seems to know why the Mardi Gras Indians chose this holiday, but records indicate that this "meet and greet" has been happening since before World War I.

8. Some question this figure, claiming it is lower.

9. Katy Reckdahl, "The Long Road from C. J. Peete to Harmony Oaks," *Shelterforce,* Spring 2013, http://shelterforce.org/article/the_long _road_from_c.j._peete_to_harmony_oaks/.

10. Attempts were made to interview a HANO official, but e-mails went unanswered and no one answered the phone.

11. HANO never gave a population total and probably didn't know how many people lived in different apartments, but there were 5,100 units. Some estimates indicate slightly more than 3,000 of these were demolished, although that figure may not include unoccupied units.

12. Qualified low-income residents are given a voucher to apply toward the rent of an apartment they can find on the open market.

13. "Housing Choice in Crisis: An Audit Report on Discrimination against Housing Choice Voucher Holders in the Greater New Orleans Rental Housing Market," Greater New Orleans Fair Housing Action Center, September 2011, http://www.gnofairhousing.org/wp-content/uploads/2011/09 /HousingChoiceInCrisis2009.pdf.

14. Naomi Klein, *Shock Doctrine: The Rise of Disaster Capitalism* (New York: Picador, 2008).

15. Quoted in Charles Babington, "Some GOP Legislators Hit Jarring Notes in Addressing Katrina," *Washington Post,* September 10, 2005, http://www.washingtonpost.com/wp-dyn/content/article/2005/09/09/AR 2005090901930.html.

16. "5,100" is the most frequently cited number, although there are no definitive, verifiable numbers.

17. Nicolai Ouroussoff, "All Fall Down," *New York Times,* November 19, 2006, http://www.nytimes.com/2006/11/19/weekinreview/19ouroussoff .html?pagewanted=all.

18. James S. Russell, "U.S. to Destroy New Orleans Housing While Poor

Sleep in Tents," December 6, 2007, *Bloomberg.com*, http://www.bloomberg .com/apps/news?pid=email_en&refer=muse&sid=a4BOhsJzfYeU.

19. Ouroussoff, "All Fall Down."

20. Eventually they were allowed a quick in-and-out.

21. Congressional Republicans threatened to eliminate HUD altogether. See Stephen Barr, "Combatants Square Off over Survival of HUD," *Washington Post*, June 30, 1995.

22. S. C. Gwynne, "Miracle in New Orleans," *Time*, March 9, 1998, http://content.time.com/time/magazine/article/0,9171,987951,00.html.

23. "HOPE VI," *HUD.gov*, http://portal.hud.gov/hudportal/HUD?src= /program_offices/public_indian_housing/programs/ph/hope6.

24. Goetz, *New Deal Ruins*, p. 63.

25. Ibid., p. 69.

26. Ibid., p. 27.

27. Ibid., p. 49.

28. Russell, "U.S. to Destroy New Orleans Housing While Poor Sleep in Tents."

29. Many units in each public housing complex were already empty, so de-densification had already taken place with no positive impact, it should be noted.

30. Quoted in Annika Mengisen, "Inside the Iberville," *Nola Defender*, May 10, 2013, http://www.noladefender.com/content/in47side-ib1erville.

31. Robert Caro's famous chapter in *The Power Broker* on the building of the Cross Bronx Expressway illustrates the diversity naturally existing in the Bronx neighborhoods destroyed for the building of the highway. Many neighborhoods like that one were bulldozed for Urban Renewal and highway projects.

32. Nicolai Ouroussoff, "High Noon in New Orleans: The Bulldozers Are Ready," *New York Times*, December 19, 2007, http://www.nytimes .com/2007/12/19/arts/design/19hous.html?fta=y.

33. Lewis Wallace, "First Came Katrina, Then Came HUD," *In These Times*, January 18, 2008.

34. Bill Quigley, "A Tale of Two Sisters," *Counterpunch*, December 2006, http://www.counterpunch.org/2006/12/29/a-tale-of-two-sisters/.

35. Quoted in Benjamin T. Greenberg, "Declaration of Robert R. Elliott on New Orleans Public Housing," *Hungry Blues* (blog), January 25, 2007, http://hungryblues.net/2007/01/25/robert-elliott-nola-housing/.

36. This appears to have been meant for a community center, but as of the summer of 2014 it was still unoccupied.

37. According to the HANO website, St. Thomas had 120 buildings with 3,000 tenants.

38. Tyler Bridges, "Pres Kabacoff Outlines $1 Billion Vision to Redevelop New Orleans' Urban Core," *The Lens,* September 24, 2013, http://thelensnola .org/2013/09/24/pres-kabacoff-outlines-1-billion-vision-to-redevelop -new-orleans-urban-core/.

39. Alecia P. Long, "Poverty Is the New Prostitution: Race, Poverty, and Public Housing in Post-Katrina New Orleans," *Journal of American History* 94 (December 2007): 795–803.

40. Mengisen, "Inside the Iberville."

41. Bridges, "Pres Kabacoff Outlines $1 Billion Vision to Redevelop New Orleans' Urban Core."

42. In *Cities Back from the Edge* I reported on the slow but definitive return to cities, but experts dismissed the phenomenon as "too small, too inconsequential," ignoring the reality that this, in fact, is how all change evolves.

43. The late Tony Goldman, a New York preservation developer, was similarly prescient, making a real impact in the rebirth of South Beach in Miami, SoHo in New York, and downtown Philadelphia.

44. Hilary Silver, "Mixing Policies: Expectations and Achievements," *Cityscape: A Journal of Policy Development and Research,* No. 2 (2013), http://www.huduser.org/portal/periodicals/cityscpe/vol15num2/ch5.pdf.

45. Winton Pitcoff, "New Hope for Public Housing?," National Housing Institute, March-April 1999, http://www.nhi.org/online/issues/104/pitcoff .html.

CHAPTER 13

1. For several key examples from around the country, see Roberta-BrandesGratz.com.

2. "The RESTORE Act dedicates 80 percent of all administrative and civil penalties related to the Deepwater Horizon spill to a Gulf Coast Restoration Trust Fund and outlines a structure by which the funds can be utilized to restore and protect the natural resources, ecosystems, fisheries, marine and wildlife habitats, beaches, coastal wetlands, and economy of the Gulf Coast region." See "About the Gulf Coast Ecosystem Restoration Council," n.d., http://www.restorethegulf.gov/council/about -gulf-coast-ecosystem-restoration-council.

3. A decade later, in the mid-1970s, preservation would once again be thrust into the national spotlight—this time, by Jacqueline Kennedy Onassis, in her effort to save Grand Central Station.

4. Quoted in Richard O. Baumbach, Jr., and William E. Borah, *The Second Battle of New Orleans: A History of the Vieux Carré Riverfront-Expressway Controversy* (Tuscaloosa: University of Alabama Press, 1981), p. 100.

5. That's why the median on Canal Street was called the "neutral ground," serving to divide the French and American districts.

6. Mary Gehman, *Women and New Orleans: A History* (Marrero, LA: Margaret Media, Inc., 2009), p. ii.

7. Ibid., p. 25.

8. New Orleans suffragettes led the successful fight to vote on tax issues in 1879—nineteen years before women's suffrage succeeded. This proved significant when a suffrage leader, Kate Gordon, found "15,000 names [of property-owning women], two-thirds of whom were white and eligible to vote" (see Gehman, *Women and New Orleans,* p. 101).

9. The head of the Navy demanded this closure since the port was an important one for US ships supporting the war in Europe, declared in April 1917.

10. Le Petit Theatre du Vieux Carré is one of the nation's earliest small theaters. Some say it's the oldest community theater in continuous existence.

11. In 1925, the group bought the 1838 Greek Revival mansion, adjacent to the Petit Theatre, making it the salon's permanent home. "Architectural historians credit the group with initiating the restoration and rehabilitation of the French Quarter by purchasing one of its most valuable structures." See Mary Ann Wilson, "New Orleans Women's Book Clubs," in *Know Louisiana Encyclopedia of Louisiana,* ed. David Johnson, Louisiana Endowment for the Humanities, April 28, 2011, http://www.knowla.org/entry/665/.

12. For further information on Elizabeth Werlein, see http://architecture.tulane.edu/preservation-project/entity/300.

13. Elizabeth enlisted a photographer to document the distinctive wrought-iron work throughout the area and published a booklet, *Wrought-Iron Railings of the Vieux Carré,* the first of a number of publications that over the years effectively raised awareness and helped catalyze preservation efforts.

14. This name was later changed to Vieux Carré Property Owners, Residents and Associates (VCPORA).

15. Robert Maestri was the mayor of New Orleans from 1936 to 1946.

16. Scott S. Ellis, *Madame Vieux Carré: The French Quarter in the Twentieth Century* (Jackson: University Press of Mississippi, 2010), p. 44.

17. Ibid.

18. Indeed, she founded the Quartier Club to prove that respectable women could safely venture into the Quarter.

19. Ellis, *Madame Vieux Carré,* p. 43.

20. Mayor Dutch Morial, speaking about "how best to preserve our architectural heritage," assured the audience at the National Trust for Historic Preservation annual conference, held in New Orleans in October 1981, that

this kind of rampant demolition would not happen again. But Canal Place, which cleared several blocks downtown, was already in the works, helped by a generous federal grant. See Walter Gallas, "Neighborhood Preservation and Politics in New Orleans: Vieux Carré Property Owners, Residents and Associates, Inc. and City Government, 1938–1983," master's thesis in Urban and Regional Planning, Illinois State University, August 1996.

21. The six books are titled *The Lower Garden District* (1971), *The American Sector* (1973), *New Orleans Cemeteries* (1974), *The Creole Faubourgs* (1975), *The Esplanade Ridge* (1977), and *Faubourg Treme and the Bayou Road* (1980). No publisher wanted the project, but the Louisiana State Museum was persuaded to take it on. These volumes comprise an architectural inventory. Fred Starr called the series "an unparalleled monument to selfless devotion to research, civic commitment, volunteerism and sheer hard work."

22. The press played an important role as well. Articles by Jack Davis in *Figaro* spotlighted the demolition of grand houses, especially along St. Charles Avenue. Historic preservation was coming into focus on many levels at the same time.

23. An Upper West Side house tour of recently restored brownstones in the mid-1960s inspired my husband and me to buy one in 1968.

24. In New York, the Brownstown Revival Movement started in Brooklyn's Park Slope and on Manhattan's Upper West Side, marking the real beginning of the city's turnaround.

25. Quoted in James Gill, *Lords of Misrule: Mardi Gras and the Politics of Race in New Orleans* (Jackson: University Press of Mississippi, 1997), p. 23.

26. Ibid., pp. 245, 250.

27. Lombard died on December 13, 2014.

28. Shannon Frystak, "Oretha Castle Haley," *KnowLA: Encyclopedia of Louisiana,* February 25, 2014, http://www.knowla.org/entry/850/.

29. Betty quit the Orleans Parish School Board radio station because the board did not allow employees to advocate school integration.

30. Fred Starr told me that Betty was the niece of "John Minor Wisdom, a deep-dyed New Orleanian and Republican who, as a member of the Fifth Circuit Court of Appeals, was responsible for much of the most significant civil rights decisions."

31. Thus the library in Broadmoor is called the Rosa Freeman Keller Library.

32. Julius Rosenwald, a generous financial supporter of Booker T. Washington's Tuskegee Institute, funded several hundred one-room schoolhouses across the South for black children, known as the Rosenwald Schools.

CONCLUSION

1. Rebecca Solnit, *Storming the Gates of Paradise: Landscapes for Politics* (Berkeley: University of California Press, 2007), p. 11.

2. This additional disaster struck many New Orleans homes that were rebuilt. About 5,200 properties in Florida, Alabama, Mississippi, and Louisiana were affected. See Associated Press, "Judge Urged to Approve Chinese Drywall Settlements," *CityBusiness,* http://neworleanscitybusiness.com /blog/2012/11/13/judge-urged-to-approve-chinese-drywall-settlements/.

3. Jen DeGregorio, "These Two High-Flying Daredevils Could Have Located Their Technology Start-Up Anywhere, But They've Chosen to Invest in New Orleans," *Times-Picayune,* August 5, 2001.

4. See, for example, Adriana Lopez, "The One Thing Every Startup City Needs," *Forbes,* August 8, 2014, http://www.forbes.com/sites /adrianalopez/2014/08/14/the-one-thing-every-startup-city-needs/city -1406328593.

5. In their study of historic neighborhoods in shrinking cities, Donovan Rypkema and Cara Berton of "Place Economics" found that historic districts either "lost less or grew more when the larger city lost population." See Roberta Brandes Gratz, "In Shrinking Cities, Preserving Existing Buildings Can Stem the Loss, *Citiwire.net,* July 20, 2012, http://citiwire.net/columns /in-shrinking-cities-preserving-existing-buildings-can-stem-the-loss/.

6. For more on this history and the phenomenon of gentrification, see Chapter 3 of Gratz, *The Living City: How America's Cities Are Being Revitalized by Thinking Small in a Big Way* (New York: Simon & Schuster, 1989).

7. "Lower 9th Ward Man Opens Grocery in his Neighborhood," *WWLTV,* November 14, 2014, http://www.wwltv.com/videos/news/2014 /11/14/19051991/.

8. Richard Rainey, "Holy Cross, Lower 9th Ward Redevelopment Fight Goes to the City Council," *NOLA.com* and *Times-Picayune,* April 9, 2014, http://www.nola.com/politics/index.ssf/2014/04/holy_cross_lower_9th _ward_rede.html.

9. Bruce Eggler, "New Orleans City Council Rejects Controversial 75-Foot Apartment Building in Marigny," *NOLA.com* and *Times-Picayune,* September 6, 2012, http://www.nola.com/politics/index.ssf/2012/09 /new_orleans_city_council_rejec_1.html.

10. Richard Rainey, "Warehouse District Hotel Project Agrees to Height Limit; Passes Council," *Times-Picayune,* July 10, 2014.

11. A tall building can have fewer units per floor than a collection of shorter buildings.

12. A City Planning staff member revealed off the record that staff were not allowed to include neighborhood feedback in their report to the

commissioners—a highly unusual policy. In New York City, for example, staff must report community input. What's the point of that community process if it doesn't reach up to the commissioners?

13. Gray is a lawyer. The Louisiana Supreme Court disciplinary board recommended his disbarment for offenses not related to his council work. The preference of the local councilman usually prevails in a council vote.

14. Cox is the former mayor of Charlottesville, Virginia, and a professor at the University of Virginia.

15. For further information on the Tulane City Center, see http://www.tulanecitycenter.org.

16. Richard A. Webster, "Lower 9th Ward Residents Unveil Three Proposals for Redevelopment of Former Holy Cross School Site," *NOLA.com* and *Times-Picayune,* January 30, 2014, http://www.nola.com/politics/index.ssf/2014/01/lower_9th_ward_residents_unvei.html.

17. Nayita Wilson, "False Petition Claims Surface in Holy Cross Redevelopment Proposal," *The Louisiana Weekly,* April 15, 2014, http://www.louisianaweekly.com/false-petition-claims-surface-in-holy-cross-redevelopment-proposal/.

18. A few council members are reportedly thinking about running for mayor.

19. Richard Rainey, "Audubon Nature Institute Beats Drum for Support of a 50-Year Tax Plan," *NOLA.com* and *Times-Picayune,* March 10, 2014, http://www.nola.com/politics/index.ssf/2014/03/audubon_nature_institute_launc.html.

20. Ibid.

21. Deborah Howell's website can be found at saveaudubonpark.org.

22. Andrew Vanacort, "Proposed 50-Year Millage for Audubon Generating Controversy," *The Advocate,* March 11, 2014.

23. "Putting the 'Profit' in Non-Profit?," Save Audubon Park, 2010, http://www.saveaudubonpark.org/web/Index.asp?mode=full&id=1.

24. Andrew Vanacore, "Critics Want Self-Supporting Audubon Nature Institute," *The Advocate,* April 16, 2014.

25. Ibid.

26. Richard Rainey, "Audubon Nature Institute to Revamp Tax Proposal; Opponents Credit Social Media with Election Defeat," *NOLA.com* and *Times-Picayune,* March 17, 2014, http://www.nola.com/politics/index.ssf/2014/03/audubon_nature_institute_to_re.html.

27. "New Orleans' tourism industry is at a record high, according to new data from the 2013 New Orleans Area Visitor Profile study. The study shows that the city welcomed 9.28 million visitors in 2013, an increase of 3 percent, or about 272,000 people, from '12 (9.01 million). The 9.28 million visitors spent $6.47 billion, a 4.5 percent increase over '12 and the highest spending

in the city's history, according to the study." See Taylor Burley, "Destination New Orleans," *New Orleans Magazine,* June 2014, http://www.mynew orleans.com/New-Orleans-Magazine/June-2014/Destination-New-Orleans/.

28. John Hooper, "Population Decline Set to Turn Venice into Italy's Disneyland," *The Guardian,* August 26, 2006, http://www.theguardian.com /world/2006/aug/26/italy.travelnews.

29. Quoted in Charles Maldonaldo, "After Making Little on the 2013 Super Bowl, City Agreed to Similar Services for 2018 Bid," *The Lens,* July 31, 2014, http://thelensnola.org/2014/07/31/after-making-little-on-2013 -super-bowl-city-agreed-to-provide-similar-services-for-game-in-2018/.

30. University of New Orleans Division of Business and Economic Research, "UNO Metropolitan Report: Economic Indicators for the New Orleans Area," n.d., http://www.uno.edu/coba/DBER/MetroReport.aspx.

31. This was reported to me by a former club owner who wishes to remain anonymous.

32. Tyler Bridges, "Convention Center Seeks Approval to Finance Private Developments in Riverfront Overhaul," *The Lens,* April 18, 2013, http://thelensnola.org/2013/04/18/massive-riverfront-overhaul-would-use -convention-center-bonds-to-finance-private-developments/.

33. Andrew Vanacore, "'Road Home' Repayment Demands Rile Homeowners," *The Advocate,* February 27, 2014.

34. Kriston Capps, "New Orleans Transit Never Recovered After Katrina," CityLab, July 17, 2014, http://www.citylab.com/commute/2014/07 /new-orleans-transit-never-recovered-after-katrina/374570/.

35. Matt Gresham, "Chiquita Announces Company Will Return Its Shipping Operations to Port of New Orleans After Four-Decade Hiatus," n.d., http://portno.com/Chiquita_returns.

36. Russel Honoré, "Guest Commentary: Politics Threatens Levee Board Reforms," *The New Orleans Advocate,* April 18, 2013, http://thelensnola .org/2013/04/18/massive-riverfront-overhaul-would-use-convention-center -bonds-to-finance-private-developments/.

37. John Schwartz, "Louisiana Agency Sues Dozens of Energy Companies for Damage to Wetlands," *New York Times,* July 25, 2013, http://www .nytimes.com/2013/07/25/us/louisiana-agency-to-sue-energy-companies -for-wetland-damage.html?_r=0.

38. John M. Barry, "Why We're Suing the Oil Companies," *Metropolis,* January 2014, http://www.metropolismag.com/January-2014 /Why-Were-Suing-the-Oil-Companies/.

39. Mark Schleifstein, "Two Energy Companies Settle with East Bank Levee Authority for $50,000; Full Terms Not Disclosed," *NOLA.com* and

Times-Picayune, October 30, 2014, http://www.nola.com/environment/index.ssf/2014/10/two_energy_companies_settle_wi.html.

40. Barry, "Why We're Suing the Oil Companies."

41. Stephanie Grace, "Katrina Inspires New Orleans to Find Its Voice," *NOLA.com* and *Times-Picayune,* August 29, 2010, http://www.nola.com/katrina/index.ssf/2010/08/katrina_inspires_new_orleans_t.html. Grace is now with *The Advocate.*

Bibliography

Allured, Janet, and Judith F. Gentry. 2009. *Louisiana Women: Their Lives and Times*. University of Georgia Press.

American Guide Series. 1959. *Mississippi, a Guide to the Magnolia State*. Hastings House.

Antoine, Rebecca. 2009. *Voices Rising: Stories from the Katrina Narrative Project*. University of New Orleans Press.

Arena, John. 2012. *Driven from New Orleans: How Nonprofits Betray Public Housing and Promote Privatization*. University of Minnesota Press.

Armstrong, Louis. 1986. *Satchmo*. Da Capo Press.

Asbury, Herbert. 2003. *The French Quarter: An Informal History of the New Orleans Underworld*. Basic Books.

Ascoli, Peter M. 2006. *Julius Rosenwald: The Man Who Built Sears, Roebuck and Advanced the Cause of Black Education in the American South*. Indiana University Press.

Barclay, Lee. 2010. *New Orleans: What Can't Be Lost: 88 Stories and Traditions from the Sacred City*. University of Louisiana Press.

Barry, John M. 1998. *Rising Tide: The Great Mississippi Flood of 1927 and How It Changed America*. Simon & Schuster.

Baum, Dan. 2009. *Nine Lives: Death and Life in New Orleans*. Spiegel & Grau.

Baumbach, Jr., Richard O., and William E. Borah. 1980. *The Second Battle of New Orleans: A History of the Vieux Carré Riverfront Expressway Controversy*. University of Alabama Press.

Bergal, Jenni, Sara Shipley Hiles, and Frank Koughan. 2007. *City Adrift: New Orleans Before and After Katrina*. Louisiana State University Press.

Berry, Jason. 2011. *Earl Long in Purgatory*. University of Louisiana Press.

Berry, Jason, Jonathan Foose, and Tad Jones. 2009. *Up from the Cradle of Jazz: New Orleans Music Since World War II*. University of Louisiana Press.

Braungart, Michael, and William McDonough. 2002. *Cradle to Cradle: Remaking the Way We Make Things*. North Point Press.

Brinkley, Douglas. 2007. *The Great Deluge: Hurricane Katrina, New Orleans, and the Mississippi Gulf Coast*. Harper Perennial.

Brothers, Thomas. 2007. *Louis Armstrong's New Orleans*. W. W. Norton.

Bruno, R. 2011. *New Orleans Streets: A Walker's Guide to Neighborhood Architecture*. Pelican Publishing.

Cable, George. 2000. *The Creoles of Louisiana*. Pelican Publishing.

Campanella, Richard. 2014. *Bourbon Street: A History*. Louisiana State University Press.

___. 2008. *Bienville's Dilemma: A Historical Geography of New Orleans*. Center for Louisiana Studies, University of Louisiana Press.

___. 2006. *Geographies of New Orleans: Urban Fabrics Before the Storm*. Center for Louisiana Studies, University of Louisiana Press.

___. 2002. *Time and Place in New Orleans: Past Geographies in the Present Day*. Pelican Publishing.

Campanella, Richard, and Marina Campanella. 1999. *New Orleans Then and Now*. Pelican Publishing.

Carter, Hodding. 2009. *The Past as Prelude: New Orleans 1718–1968*. Firebird Press.

CNN. 2005. *Hurricane Katrina: CNN Reports: State of Emergency*. Andrews McMeel Publishing.

Colten, Craig E. 2004. *An Unnatural Metropolis: Wresting New Orleans from Nature*. Louisiana State University Press.

Crutcher, Michael E. 2010. *Treme: Race and Place in a New Orleans Neighborhood*. University of Georgia Press.

Cummins, Light Townsend, Judith Kelleher Schafer, Edward F. Haas, Michael L. Kurtz, and Bennet H. Wall. 2008. *Louisiana: A History*. Harlan Davidson.

Dyson, Michael Eric. 2006. *Come Hell or High Water: Hurricane Katrina and the Color of Disaster*. Basic Civitas Books.

Eckstein, Barbara. 2005. *Sustaining New Orleans: Literature, Local Memory, and the Fate of a City*. Routledge.

Editors of *Time* Magazine. 2005. *Time: Hurricane Katrina: The Storm That Changed America*. Time.

Eggers, Dave. 2009. *Zeitoun*. McSweeney's.

Elie, Lolis Eric. 2013. *Treme: Stories and Recipes from the Heart of New Orleans*. Chronicle Books.

Ellis, Scott S. 2009. *Madame Vieux Carré: The French Quarter in the Twentieth Century*. University Press of Mississippi.

Evans, Eli N. 1993. *The Lonely Days Were Sundays: Reflections of a Jewish Southerner*. University Press of Mississippi.

___. 1989. *Judah P. Benjamin: The Jewish Confederate*. Free Press.

Evans, Freddi Williams. 2011. *Congo Square: African Roots in New Orleans*. University of Louisiana Press.

Evans, Walker, and James Agee. 2001. *Let Us Now Praise Famous Men: The American Classic, in Words and Photographs, of Three Tenant Families in the Deep South*. Mariner Books.

Federal Writers' Project and Works Progress Administration. 1938. *New Orleans City Guide*. Houghton Mifflin Company.

Fertel, Randy. 2011. *The Gorilla Man and the Empress of Steak: A New Orleans Family Memoir*. University Press of Mississippi.

Flaherty, Jordan. 2010. *Floodlines: Community and Resistance from Katrina to the Jena Six*. Haymarket Books.

Flucker, Turry, and Phoenix Savage. 2010. *African Americans of New Orleans*. Arcadia Publishing.

Ford, Kristina. 2010. *The Trouble with City Planning: What New Orleans Can Teach Us*. Yale University Press.

Forman, Sally. 2009. *How They Did It: Profiles of New Orleans Entrepreneurs*. Idea Village Press.

Forum for Urban Design. 2005. *New Orleans Rebuilds*. Forum for Urban Design.

Fullilove, Mindy Thompson, M.D. 2004. *Root Shock: How Tearing Up City Neighborhoods Hurts America and What We Can Do About It*. Ballantine Books.

Garvey, Joan, Mary Lou Widmer, Kathy Spiess, and Karen Chappetta. 2012. *Beautiful Crescent: A History of New Orleans*. Pelican Publishing.

Gehman, Mary. 2009. *The Free People of Color of New Orleans: An Introduction*. Margaret Media, Inc.

___. 2005. *Women and New Orleans: A History*. Margaret Media, Inc.

Germany, Kent B. 2007. *New Orleans After the Promises: Poverty, Citizenship, and the Search for the Great Society*. University of Georgia Press.

Gisleson, Anne, Tristan Thompson, and Catherine Burke. 2010. *How to Rebuild a City: Field Guide from a Work in Progress*. Press Street.

Gruber, J. Richard, Jim Rapier, and Mary Beth Romig. 2010. *Missing New Orleans*. Ogden Museum of Southern Art.

Grunwald, Michael. 2006. *The Swamp: The Everglades, Florida, and the Politics of Paradise*. Simon & Schuster.

Haas, Edward. 1986. *Delesseps S. Morrison and the Image of Reform: New Orleans Politics 1946–1961.* Louisiana State University Press.

Hankins, John Ethan, and Steven Maklansky, eds. 2002. *Raised to the Trade: Creole Building Arts of New Orleans.* New Orleans Museum of Art.

Hirsch, Arnold R., and Joseph Logsdon. 1992. *Creole New Orleans: Race and Americanization.* Louisiana State University Press.

Holland, Robert A. 2008. *The Mississippi River in Maps & Views: From Lake Itasca to the Gulf of Mexico.* Rizzoli.

Home Decor Press. 2010. *How They Did It.* Home Decor Press.

Honoré, Lt. General Russel L., and Trent Angers. 2012. *Leadership in the New Normal.* Acadian House Publishing.

Horne, Jed. 2008. *Breach of Faith: Hurricane Katrina and the Near Death of a Great American City.* Random House Trade Paperbacks.

Houck, Oliver A. 2010. *Down on the Batture.* University Press of Mississippi.

Institute for Media Analysis. 1992. *The Stern Fund: The Story of a Progressive Family Foundation.* Institute for Media Analysis.

Isaacson, Walter. 2009. *American Sketches: Great Leaders, Creative Thinkers, and Heroes of a Hurricane.* Simon & Schuster.

Kelman, Ari. 2003. *A River and Its City: The Nature of Landscape in New Orleans.* University of California Press.

Kemp, John R. 1997. *New Orleans: An Illustrated History.* American Historical Press.

Klein, Gerda Weissmann. 1984. *A Passion for Sharing: The Life of Edith Rosenwald Stern.* Rossel Books.

Klein, Naomi. 2008. *The Shock Doctrine: The Rise of Disaster Capitalism.* Picador.

Laborde, Peggy Scott, and John Magil. 2006. *Canal Street: New Orleans' Great Wide Way.* Pelican Publishing.

Lachoff, Irwin, and Catherine C. Kahn. 2005. *The Jewish Community of New Orleans.* Arcadia.

Larson, Susan. 1999. *The Booklover's Guide to New Orleans.* Louisiana State University Press.

Ledner, Albert C., et al. 1974. *A Guide to New Orleans Architecture.* American Institute of Architects.

Lehner, Peter, and Bob Deans. 2009. *In Deep Water: The Anatomy of a Disaster, the Fate of the Gulf, and How to End Our Oil Addiction.* OR Books.

Lemann, Nicholas. 1992. *The Promised Land: The Great Black Migration and How It Changed America.* Vintage.

Levine, Bruce. 2013. *The Fall of the House of Dixie: The Civil War and the Social Revolution That Transformed the South.* Random House.

Lewis, Peirce F. 2003. *New Orleans: The Making of an Urban Landscape.* University of Virginia Press.

Long, Judy. 2000. *Literary New Orleans.* Hill Street Press.

Maklansky, Steven. 2006. *Katrina Exposed: A Photographic Reckoning.* New Orleans Museum of Art.

McDonough, William, and Michael Braungart. 2013. *The Upcycle: Beyond Sustainability—Designing for Abundance.* North Point Press.

McKinney, Louise. 2006. *New Orleans: A Cultural History.* Oxford University Press.

Miller, John. 2004. *New Orleans Stories: Great Writers on the City.* Chronicle Books.

Moore, Leonard N. 2010. *Black Rage in New Orleans: Police Brutality and African American Activism from World War II to Hurricane Katrina.* Louisiana State University Press.

Norman, Benjamin M., and Matthew J. Schott. 1976. *Norman's New Orleans and Environs.* Louisiana State University Press.

Oliver, Nola Nance. 1941. *The Gulf Coast of Mississippi.* Hastings House.

Olshansky, Robert B., and Laurie A. Johnson. 2010. *Clear as Mud: Planning for the Rebuilding of New Orleans.* American Planning Association/Planners Press.

Percy, Walker. 1999. *Love in the Ruins.* Picador.

___. 1998. *The Moviegoer.* Vintage.

Piazza, Tom. 2011. *Devil Sent the Rain: Music and Writing in Desperate America.* Harper Perennial.

___. 2008. *City of Refuge: A Novel.* Harper.

___. 2005a. *Understanding Jazz: Ways to Listen.* Random House.

___. 2005b. *Why New Orleans Matters.* Harper.

Pitt, Brad, with a contribution by Kristin Feireiss. 2009. *Architecture in Times of Need: Make It Right—Rebuilding New Orleans' Lower Ninth Ward.* Prestel.

Powell, Lawrence N. 2012. *The Accidental City: Improvising New Orleans.* Harvard University Press.

Quigley, William P. 2008. *Storms Still Raging: Katrina, New Orleans and Social Justice.* BookSurge Publishing.

Rasmussen, Daniel. 2011. *American Uprising: The Untold Story of America's Largest Slave Revolt.* Harper.

Rathke, Wade. 2011. *The Battle for the Ninth Ward: ACORN, Rebuilding New Orleans, and the Lessons of Disaster.* Social Policy.

Reed, Betsy. 2006. *Unnatural Disaster: The Nation on Hurricane Katrina.* Nation Books.

Reed, Julia. 2008. *The House on First Street: My New Orleans Story.* Ecco.

Rose, Al. 1978. *Storyville, New Orleans: Being an Authentic, Illustrated Account of the Notorious Red-Light District.* University of Alabama Press.

Rose, Chris. 2010. *Dave Anderson: One Block.* Aperture.

___. 2007. *1 Dead in Attic: After Katrina.* Simon & Schuster.

Rosenberg, Daniel. 1988. *New Orleans Dockworkers: Race, Labor, and Unionism, 1892–1923.* State University of New York Press.

Sancton, Tom. 2010. *Song for my Fathers.* Other Press.

Seidman, Karl F. 2013. *Coming Home to New Orleans: Neighborhood Rebuilding After Katrina.* Oxford University Press.

Solnit, Rebecca. 2010. *A Paradise Built in Hell: The Extraordinary Communities That Arise in Disaster.* Penguin Books.

___. 2008. *Storming the Gates of Paradise: Landscapes for Politics.* University of California Press.

Solnit, Rebecca, and Rebecca Snedeker. 2013. *Unfathomable City: A New Orleans Atlas.* University of California Press.

Squires, Gregory, and Chester Hartman. 2006. *There Is No Such Thing as a Natural Disaster: Race, Class, and Katrina.* Routledge.

Starr, Frederick. 2014. *Une Belle Maison: The Lombard Plantation House in New Orleans's Bywater.* University of Mississippi Press.

___. 2005. *Southern Comfort: The Garden District of New Orleans.* Princeton Architectural Press.

___. 2001. *Inventing New Orleans: Writings of Lafcadio Hearn.* University Press of Mississippi.

___. 1985. *New Orleans Unmasqued: Being a Wagwit's Sketches of a Singular American City.* Dedeaux Publishing.

Sublette, Ned. 2009a. *The World That Made New Orleans: From Spanish Silver to Congo Square.* Lawrence Hill Books.

___. 2009b. *The Year Before the Flood: A Story of New Orleans.* Chicago Review Press.

Sullivan, Lester. 2003. *New Orleans Then and Now.* Thunder Bay Press.

Survivors, Volunteers, and Others. 2006. *The Post-Katrina Portraits.* Available online at http://www.postkatrinaportraits.org/.

Tagore, Rabindranath, and Herbert F. Vetter. 2004. *The Heart of God: Prayers of Rabindranath Tagore.* Tuttle Publishing.

Tidwell, Mike. 2006. *The Ravaging Tide: Strange Weather, Future Katrinas, and the Coming Death of America's Coastal Cities.* Free Press.

___. 2004. *Bayou Farewell: The Rich Life and Tragic Death of Louisiana's Cajun Coast.* Vintage.

Times-Picayune. 2006. *Katrina: The Ruin and Recovery of New Orleans.* Spotlight Press.

Toledano, Roulhac, Mary Louise Christovich, and Robin Derbes. 2003. *New Orleans Architecture: Faubourg Tremé and the Bayou Road*. Pelican Publishing.

Toledano, Roulhac, Sally Evans, and Mary Louise Christovich. 1996. *New Orleans Architecture, Volume IV: The Creole Faubourgs*. Pelican Publishing.

Tyler, Pamela. 2009. *Silk Stockings and Ballot Boxes: Women and Politics in New Orleans, 1920–1963*. University of Georgia Press.

van Heerden, Ivor, and Mike Bryan. 2007. *The Storm: What Went Wrong and Why During Hurricane Katrina: The Inside Story from One Louisiana Scientist*. Penguin.

Walker, Rob. 2005. *Letters from New Orleans*. Garrett County Press, LLC.

Widmer, Mary Lou. 2008. *New Orleans in the Sixties*. Pelican Publishing.

___. 2007. *New Orleans in the Forties*. Pelican Publishing.

___. 2004. *New Orleans in the Fifties*. Pelican Publishing.

Wolf, Peter M. 2013. *My New Orleans, Gone Away*. Delphinium.

Index

Roberta Brandes Gratz is an acclaimed urbanist who has published four previous books on the subject, including most recently *The Battle for Gotham: New York in the Shadow of Robert Moses and Jane Jacobs*. Her writing has also appeared in the *Nation*, the *New York Times Magazine*, and the *Wall Street Journal*. She previously served on New York City's Landmark Preservation Commission and NYC's Sustainability Advisory Board. With Jane Jacobs, she founded The Center for the Living City, to build on Jacobs's work. She splits her time between New York and New Orleans.

The Nation Institute

NATION
BOOKS

Founded in 2000, **Nation Books** has become a leading voice in American independent publishing. The inspiration for the imprint came from the *Nation* magazine, the oldest independent and continuously published weekly magazine of politics and culture in the United States.

The imprint's mission is to produce authoritative books that break new ground and shed light on current social and political issues. We publish established authors who are leaders in their area of expertise, and endeavor to cultivate a new generation of emerging and talented writers. With each of our books we aim to positively affect cultural and political discourse.

Nation Books is a project of The Nation Institute, a nonprofit media center dedicated to strengthening the independent press and advancing social justice and civil rights. The Nation Institute is home to a dynamic range of programs: the award-winning Investigative Fund, which supports ground-breaking investigative journalism; the widely read and syndicated website TomDispatch; the Victor S. Navasky Internship Program in conjunction with the *Nation* magazine; and Journalism Fellowships that support up to 25 high-profile reporters every year.

For more information on Nation Books, The Nation Institute, and the *Nation* magazine, please visit:

www.nationbooks.org

www.nationinstitute.org

www.thenation.com

www.facebook.com/nationbooks.ny

Twitter: @nationbooks